Pottery Ethnoarchaeology in the Central Maya Highlands

Foundations of Archaeological Inquiry

Pottery Ethnoarchaeology in the Central Maya Highlands

Michael Deal

THE UNIVERSITY OF UTAH PRESS
SALT LAKE CITY

Foundations of Archaeological Inquiry
James M. Skibo, editor

∞ Printed on acid-free paper

Library of Congress Cataloging-in-Publication Data

Deal, Michael, 1952–
    Pottery ethnoarchaeology in the Central Maya Highlands / Michael
Deal.
      p.   cm. — (Foundations of archaeological inquiry)
    Includes bibliographical references and index.
    ISBN 0-87480-560-0 (hardcover : alk. paper). — ISBN 0-87480-561-9
(pbk. : alk. paper)
    1. Tzeltal pottery.   2. Maya pottery.   3. Ethnoarchaeology—
Mexico—Chiapas.   4. Mayas—Mexico—Chiapas—Antiquities.
I. Title.   II. Series.
F1221.T8D43   1998
338.4'7738'097275—dc21   98-12945

To Jane,
for putting up with me and this book
for a very long time

Contents

Figures

Tables

Preface

The following case study is based on eth-noarchaeological fieldwork undertaken in 1978 and 1979 as part of my doctoral research at Simon Fraser University (Deal 1983). Several subsequent journal articles and chapters in edited volumes have drawn upon the same information base. The present volume follows the general format of the 1983 thesis but large portions of the text have been rewritten, expanded, and updated to 1997. The major change is the inclusion of a new chapter on the social and economic context of Tzeltal pottery making. Additional information is also provided on the interactions of potters and consumers within and between Tzeltal communities (See also Hayden 1988a).

The information presented here was collected by the author and other members of the Coxoh Ethnoarchaeological Project. This project was the brainchild of Brian Hayden (1988b). It was designed to coordinate with an existing program of the New World Archaeological Foundation (NWAF) known as the Coxoh Archaeological-Ethnohistorical Project. The latter focused on archaeological and historical research concerning an extinct Maya speaking group known as the Coxoh, who were inhabiting the Upper Grijalva River drainage basin of Chiapas at the time of the Spanish conquest. The Spanish forced the Coxoh to congregate in seven small communities (i.e., Coneta, Coapa, Cuxu, Excuintenango, Aquespala, Comitan and Zapaluta). Comitan and Zapaluta (now known as Trinitaria) slowly changed from Indian to Ladino populations, while the other five were occupied by the Coxoh until the early 19th century (Lee 1979a). Coneta and Coapa have been mapped and excavated by archaeologists from the NWAF and yielded considerable evidence on Coxoh settlement patterning, material culture variability, diet, and degree of acculturation (Lee 1977, 1979a, 1979b, 1980; Lee and Bryant 1988; Lee and Markman 1977a, b).

The Coxoh Ethnoarchaeological Project extended the archaeological and ethnohistorical groundwork into the ethnographic present and sought to establish material culture links between the extinct Coxoh and modern Maya groups bordering the recorded Coxoh territory (see Hayden and Cannon 1984a; Hayden 1988a). The modern Maya groups targeted were the Tzeltal and Tojolabal of Chiapas and the Chuj of Guatemala. In particular, ongoing linguistic research by Lyle Campbell (1978) favored a close link between Tzeltal and Coxoh. Between 1977 and 1979, members of the Coxoh Project conducted ethnoarchaeological fieldwork in over 150 households in six Maya communities. This consisted of extensive investigations in the Tzeltal communities of Chanal and Aguacatenango and the Chuj community of San Mateo Ixtatan, and shorter visits to the Tojolabal communities of Bajucu and San Miguel and the Tzeltal community of

Cancuc. Further, regional surveys were undertaken in Chiapas (M. Blake and S. Blake 1979) and Western Guatemala (Shaughnessy and Luciw 1979) to identify communities suitable for future research.

Information collected at each Maya household concentrated on family social structure, craft activities, settlement characteristics, economic background, and the variability in household material culture. The information was established as a database for the interpretation of Coxoh Maya archaeological remains, using the *direct historic approach* (Baerreis 1961). This approach assumes a direct historical continuity between the past and present and is "generally considered to provide the highest probability of being correct because the conditions of time, space, and cultural affinity of the groups who produced the two sets of compared data are most analogous" (Stiles 1977:95). Technically, despite the close cultural affinity of the two groups, the modern Tzeltal do not occupy the same territory as the extinct Coxoh, and therefore the use of our data for the interpretation of Coxoh remains might be more appropriately termed *synthetic cultural description* (see Baerreis 1961). Although our ethnoarchaeological research has proved useful for the interpretation of extinct Coxoh culture, it may be better suited for future archaeological research in the Central Highlands area of Chiapas. There are indications that the Central Highlands have been inhabited by Tzeltal and Tzotzil speaking peoples since Classic times (Campbell 1978, 1988; Culbert 1965:82). Consequently, the present study does not concentrate on problems of Coxoh archaeology, but presents general models of pottery production, use and discard, which are believed to be relevant to a much broader geographical segment of the Maya region.

The work of the Coxoh Project continued a trend toward more extensive use of ethnographic analogy in reconstructing Maya prehistoric socioeconomic conditions and cultural practices (e.g., Becquelin 1973; Gifford J.C. 1978; Green 1972; Howry 1978; Majewski 1974; Miles 1957a; Price 1974; Vogt

1964). Much of the ethnoarchaeological work has been and continues to be done by archaeologists frustrated with the lack of detail in existing ethnographies concerning settlement characteristics and material culture (Dillon 1984:2; Schiffer 1978:229). This is certainly true of the literature concerning the Tzeltal and Tzotzil Maya. However, there is a small body of useful comparative literature on pottery making for the Central Highlands, and especially dealing with the major Tzeltal potting center of Amatenango (Bryant and Brody 1986; Collier 1975; Culbert 1959, 1965; Heyman 1960; Hunt 1962; J. Nash 1959, 1970; M. Nash 1959, 1961, 1966, 1967; Rey 1976) and the Tzotzil center of Chamula (Howry 1970, 1978; Pozas 1977; Rus 1969). Published information on the formerly important Tzeltal production center of Tenango (Blom and LaFarge 1927; Redfield and Rojas 1939; Rey 1976) and the Tojolabal center of Yocnajab (Basauri 1931; Howry 1978; Montagu 1958) is less comprehensive (see also Daltabuit and Alvarez 1977).

The ethnographic literature also includes an extensive geographical and economic census of the Central Highlands, which was conducted by the University of Chicago's Man-In-Nature Project (McQuown 1959). Edward Calnek's 1962 dissertation (Calnek 1988), which resulted from this project, is an invaluable ethnohistoric source for the area. Most of the archaeological literature concerning the Chiapan Highlands appears in the series *Papers of the New World Archaeological Foundation*. One important exception is the Becquelin and Baudez report (1979) on the excavations at Tonina. The standard source of information on archaeological pottery of the Central Highlands is Culbert's 1965 study, while Becquelin and Baudez (1979) describe the prehistoric pottery of the Ocosingo Valley and Lee (1979b) provides information on Colonial Coxoh pottery.

Any study of this size cannot be completed without the assistance and encouragement of many agencies and individuals. To begin with, the Coxoh Ethnoarchaeological Project received financial support from the Canadian Social Sciences and Humanities Research Council, the Canada Council and the Brigham Young University, New World Archaeological Foundation. In addition, the author received a Doctoral Fellowship from the Social Sciences and Research Council of Canada and two graduate scholarships from Simon Fraser University. Jane Deal and Peter Deal helped immensely with the typing and editing of the final manuscript.

I wish to acknowledge the assistance of several Mexican officials, who supplied the Coxoh Project with letters of introduction to Maya communities, including Alfonso Villa Rojas and Felix Baez-Jorge (Directors, INI), Jamie Litvak-King and Carlos Navarrete (UNAM), Francisco Polo Sifuentes and Luis Lujan Munoz (Directors, INAH), Jose Castaneda M. (Director, INI), and Marta Turok (INI, San Cristóbal de las Casas). Further, I would like to acknowledge the many Maya administrative officials who supported our work, including Manuel Ensin Gomez (*Presidente Municipal,* Chanal), Timoteo Gomex (*Regidor Primero,* Chanal), Francisco Vasquez Hernandez (*Agente Municipal,* Aguacatenango) and Jose Perez Hernandez (*Regidor Primero,* Aguacatenango).

An immense debt of gratitude is owed to those individuals who worked as interpreters in the Maya communities, including Gilberto Gomez Hernandez (Chavin) and Juan Gomez Lopez (Chavin) in Chanal, and Augustin Hernandez Espinosa *(Comiseriado Ejidal)*, Carmen Hernandez Jiron *(Policia)*, Juan Agular Hernandez, Aucensio Juroz Aguilar *(Juez Secundo)*, Francisco Vasquez Hernandez *(Agente Municipal)*, Feliz Juarez Perez *(Suplente)*, and Civilio Hernandez Vasquez *(Juez Primero)* in Aguacatenango. Special thanks is also extended to those many individuals who received us in their homes and tolerated our unusual interests.

Thomas Lee Jr., John Clark and Douglas Bryant of the New World Archaeological Foundation provided the author with information on pottery production in Yocnajab and Amatenango. I am grateful to Nicholas David, Philip Hobler and Richard Boyer for their valuable comments on the 1983 thesis. I am also indebted to those colleagues who reviewed various incarnations of this manuscript, namely, Bill Longacre, Jim Skibo, Carol Kramer and two anonymous Mesoamericanists.

Besides the author, the members of the Coxoh Ethnoarchaeological Project included Brian Hayden (Director), and at various stages, Mike and Susan Blake, Russell Brulotte, Aubrey Cannon, Margot Chapman, Jane Deal, Huguette Hayden, Gayel Horsfall, Paula Luciw, Olivier DeMontmollin, Ben and Peggy Nelson, Roxane Shaughnessey, Geof and Joanna Spurling and Cathy Starr. Brian Hayden was my graduate supervisor and it was he who encouraged me to undertake this study. My debt to Brian can never be fully repaid.

Introduction

...a paraphrase from the canons of curbstone philosophy—the methods of studying pottery get better all the time, but the pottery stays about the same. (Burgh 1959:40)

RESEARCH BACKGROUND AND GOALS

In the fall of 1976, as the Coxoh Ethnoarchaeological Project was being fleshed out from a grant application to a logistical reality, ethnoarchaeology was only beginning to get serious recognition as a field of research (Stiles 1977). Hayden's (1979) trial project in the Guatemala Highlands would serve as a basic blueprint for later fieldwork, but individual team members were responsible for developing questionnaires and observational strategies for answering questions related to their particular areas of research. The available literature contained very few pottery (ceramic) ethnoarchaeology studies. The principal sources for inspiration were fieldwork reports by Longacre among the Kalinga (1964, 1974), David among the Fulani (David and Hennig 1972), and Arnold among the Yucatecan Maya (1971, 1975). Matson's (1965) edited volume *Ceramics and Man* included classic papers by Balfet on the organization of pottery production and by Matson on ceramic ecology. Behavioral archaeology was on everyone's mind (Schiffer 1972, 1976), and formation studies offered a new and exciting direction for ethnoarchaeological inquiries.

The 1970s also saw a perceptible shift in emphasis in Mesoamerican archaeology from elite to residential excavations. Researchers had long recognized that a better understanding of individual households was necessary before reliable inferences could be made about larger, more abstract social units (clans, lineages, etc.) and before a clearer understanding of the economic basis of Maya civilization could be attained (e.g., Kidder 1934; Ricketson and Ricketson 1937; A. L. Smith 1929; Wauchope 1934). However, few attempts at rigorous survey and excavation of domestic units were undertaken until the 1950s when work began at Mayapan (Pollock et al. 1962), and when settlement pattern studies began in areas such as the Belize Valley (Willey et al. 1965). In recent years there has been a proliferation of residential (or household) studies (e.g., Santley and Hirth 1993; Wilk and Ashmore 1988), and Sheets (1992:19–25) has even adopted this body of research as a theoretical framework for interpreting the prehistoric village site of Cerén, El Salvador.

From the inception of the Coxoh Ethnoarchaeological Project the major goal was to provide a body of ethnographic data that was more extensive, of better quality, and more relevant to making archaeological inferences than was presently available for Mesoamerican archaeologists. In terms of pottery, a literature survey indicated that there was relatively good information concerning pottery production in Maya villages specializing in potting, while little attention had been paid to non-specialist pottery production. With the new emphasis on household archaeology, more information was needed concerning the variability of pottery use from household to household, as well as the secondary use (reuse) of pottery and pottery discard behavior. The latter two types of behavior are particularly important for understanding the processes responsible for the formation of archaeological pottery assemblages at the household level.

Another important goal of this study was to identify and evaluate the factors which contribute to variability in household pottery assemblages and the spatial patterning of pottery within household compounds. This topic has wide-ranging implications for many pottery-related archaeological studies. For example, at the most basic level, an agriculturally-based subsistence economy requires special tools and facilities for food processing, storage, and domestic and ritual consumption. Pottery satisfies many of these needs, therefore pottery variability and patterning are of interest to those researching the technological needs of agricultural peoples (e.g., "agro-ceramic" studies; Lowe 1971) and the role of technology in cultural-environmental adaptation. The latter can be viewed as one of the most important goals of processual archaeological research.

At the household level of analysis, individual household pottery requirements can be thought of as varying according to socio-economic conditions within the household. Therefore, pottery variability and patterning should reflect these conditions. The recognition of household socioeconomic conditions is, of course, important for anyone studying intracommunity socioeconomic or political organization. The distribution of fine quality, decorated pottery versus plainware pottery has often been used by archaeologists as an indicator of relative household wealth or economic status, and in reconstructing community organization (e.g., Michels 1979), yet there appears to be little concern for testing the strength of such associations. Another goal of this study was to examine the relationship between the modern household's pottery assemblage and its social and eco-

nomic position within the community (see Chapter 6).

The intensity of pottery production itself is a source of pottery variability and spatial patterning. It can strongly affect the frequency, diversity, and spatial arrangements of pottery within potting households. Such information can be important to the study of the development of craft specialization at both household and community levels. Furthermore, consistencies in the spatial organization of domestic production itself can be used to develop models with which to search for and evaluate the elusive hard evidence of prehistoric production areas (Deal 1994b).

Functional variation between formal pottery types, and the spatial distributions of pottery-related activities and features contribute further variability and patterning at the household level. Knowledge of how this variability and patterning is created in an ethnographic context, in terms of household functional requirements, potting activities, and use and reuse strategies, is important for making inferences of pottery-related behavior and vessel function represented in archaeological assemblages. Additional variability and patterning result from disposal and abandonment behavior prior to archaeological recovery, therefore these factors are also of interest to those investigating household pottery assemblages.

THEORETICAL BACKGROUND

The archaeological record is viewed here as the physical evidence of the human past. A portion of this record, excavated, or read as text (Hodder 1991), becomes the data that is interpreted through the use of general principles and models. This procedure, known as middle-range theory (MRT), is defined by Dark (1995:40, 205) as the "logic linking material data and its interpretation." For processualists like Binford (1977), the "goal of middle-range theory is not to explain human behavior but to infer it from material remains recovered from archaeological contexts" (Trigger 1995: 450). Binford (1983) presents ethnoarchaeology as the major focus for middle-range research. Ethnoarchaeology draws upon both archaeological and ethnographic techniques to build models of behavior–material culture interactions and identify principles that condition these interactions. Ethnoarchaeology is also an "indispensable part of behavioral inference" in behavioral archaeology archaeology (Walker et al. 1995:8) and it is even important to post-processual interpretations in their implicit use of processualist middle-range principles (David 1992:333;Tschauner 1996).

As indicated above, the spatial focus of this study is the household. The household unit, or household compound, is recognized as the locus of most activities associated with family domestic, economic, and private ritual life. In this context, pottery is the primary artifact class associated with pottery production, as well as numerous ritual and domestic activities such as food preparation, alcohol production, and domestic ritual. Pottery refuse patterning within archaeological household compounds is the principal evidence for the reconstruction of such activities. Households cannot be considered in complete isolation, since family ties generally extend to the neighborhood (barrio) and village. For both the archaeologist and ethnographer, a village may be envisioned as a self-contained, year-round settlement (Chang 1972:16), which in plan and appearance expresses the attitudes and values of its inhabitants (Fraser 1968:8). Further, a farming village normally features a subsistence base of crop and animal husbandry, supplemented by the utilization of a variety of resource outlets, such as mines or fishing stations. Ethnoarchaeologists have sought solutions to a wide range of uniquely archaeological problems related to village life (Kramer 1982:1; see also Watson 1979) through simplifying complex ethnographic situations (i.e., model building), or attempting replicative experiments within modern villages. While the study communities are true farming villages, the term "community" is often used here as a more general term to facilitate comparisons among villages, smaller hamlets, and larger commercial towns.

Pottery (or Ceramic) ethnoarchaeology has recently emerged as a major subfield of village-related studies in ethnoarchaeology (Longacre and Skibo 1994). Early pottery-related ethnographic studies conducted under the rubric of "ethnoarchaeology" focused on the manufacture, distribution, use and life expectancy of pottery vessels and ceramic change (Kramer 1985). While these have continued to be important areas of study, other recent research has dealt with the relationships between agriculture and production (Graves 1994), craft learning frameworks (Hayden and Cannon 1984b), the nature of standardization (Rice 1996b:179ff.), the identification of archaeological production areas (P. J. Arnold 1991b), gender issues (London 1987), and demographic estimates (Tani 1994). Studies concerning the use and life-expectancy of pottery vessels, along with other aspects of a vessel's life history (i.e., use-wear, reuse, and recycling) and disposal, are now subsumed under the study of cultural formation processes. These studies are particularly important for modelling ceramic assemblage formation (Shott 1996). Further, ethnoarchaeological studies have served to point out weaknesses in current analytical techniques, such as refitting (Sullivan 1989) and compositional analysis (D. E. Arnold et al. 1991) and have spawned whole new approaches to the study of pottery (e.g., van der Leeuw 1991). In general, pottery ethnoarchaeological studies are following recent trends in ethnoarchaeological research involving model building, formation processes and the evaluation and refinement of existing archaeological recovery techniques (Deal 1994a).

The present study began with a basic tenet of the cultural materialist paradigm: that techno-economic and demographic factors constitute the major determinants of sociocultural (and artifactual) variability and spatial patterning (Harris 1980; Schiffer 1983a). Culture is viewed here as systemic, dynamic, adaptive, and participatory (Binford 1962, 1964, 1965). Artifact variability and patterning are believed to result from behavioral, operational processes, especially in terms of production, use, reuse, and deposition. This general conceptual framework is readily applied to the variability created by the need to produce pottery. Pottery production creates pottery variability through the diversity of its products (i.e., variations in vessel form and paste) and creates patterning through the byproducts of pottery making activities (e.g., the residues of forming and firing practices), the storage of drying or finished products, and specialized pottery types and potting tools. While not given priority here, Maya social realities are also considered to have important effects upon pottery variability and patterning, and especially in terms of the household developmental cycle and spatial patterning of ritual behavior (e.g., Deal 1988b).

The finished products generally function within the technological or sociological subsystems and are constrained by them. For example, an incense burner functions in ritual contexts, while watercarrying jars function within a technological (resource-exploiting) context. Further, the internal arrangements of structures and associated features and pottery vessels are affected by often implicit traditional social rules (e.g., relating to male versus female space). Pottery variability, in terms of vessel frequency and type diversity, is largely conditioned by household use and reuse requirements, which are related to household socioeconomic conditions. The spatial patterning of pottery is directly affected by the association of differential use and reuse, and storage activities within and around structures and other features, such as sweatbaths and patios.

Vessel degradation affects vessel frequency and type diversity in terms of rates of breakage and replacement. These factors are also constrained by economic and practical considerations. In addition, household disposal and abandonment behavior further alter the variability and patterning of pottery. Thus, monitoring the changes in pottery variability and spatial patterning from production to disposal within the ongoing cultural system is seen as a precondition to understanding and interpreting the archaeological record.

FIELDWORK IN THE MAYA HIGHLANDS

Fieldwork began in the spring of 1977 with great optimism. Reality set in as we tried to establish ourselves in a Maya village. Two attempts were made to establish a base in a Tojolabal village. After just two days of interviews in one village, rumours spread that we were missionaries posing as anthropologists and a general meeting was called. The Tojolabales had recently expelled a missionizing evangelist and were suspicious of any strangers. Our interpreter returned from the meeting in a very agitated state and informed us that if we did not leave by the following morning we risked beheading by machete! A second attempt was made in another village, but when the same rumors began to circulate the decision was made to abandon the area. In retrospect, this was a good move. Working in the Tzeltal area was a completely different experience. Both Chanal and Aguacatenango had had experiences with anthropologists and most people were very cooperative. An ironic situation occurred when one Chanal household changed their mind about being interviewed. Our amused interpreter told us that they thought we were going to cut off their heads with machetes!

Surveys were conducted in the Tojolabal, Tzeltal, and Chuj Maya regions in order to identify villages retaining traditional values and material culture (Blake and Blake 1979; Hayden et al. 1977; Shaughnessy and Luciw 1979). We believed that such communities would be most similar to those represented by the archaeological record. Once a community was selected, and permission was obtained to work there, it was necessary to find households willing to be included in our study. Unfortunately, the possibility of acquiring a random sample of households within a "closed corporate" Maya community was remote (see Vogt 1962:649; Wolf 1957). As the example above illustrates, even after we were established in a village, many householders were still highly suspicious due to past experiences with strangers or for purely superstitious reasons (e.g., those involving curing or sorcery).

In both Chanal and Aguacatenango local men were hired as interpreters for the project. The use of interpreters was necessary, since most of our informants were illiterate and spoke only Tzeltal. In Chanal, one of the interpreters was the Secretary of the community's municipal council and the other was a high school student on summer leave. In Aguacatenango, seven council members acted as interpreters on a rotating basis. Our procedure was to ask interpreters to approach people who might be willing to be interviewed. Once some degree of cooperation was established, attempts were made to interview households with as varied social and economic backgrounds as possible. These included households in each neighborhood that represented a wide range of occupations (e.g., potters, weavers, carpenters, butchers, curers, merchants) and both upper and lower echelons of the community civil and religious hierarchies. Variations in sodality organization and family composition were also sought. Surveyed households covered the complete range of community wealth and social status. The number of interviewed households in Chanal represented approximately 10 percent of the community (or 53 of 560 households), while the Aguacatenango sample represents approximately 18 percent of that community (50 of 280 households).

Initial interviews in each community were conducted at the households of our interpreters. This was done in order to prepare them for our interview which included four questionnaires (filled out by one of the investigators) concerning family census information, land use, economic information, and pottery use and manufacturing (see Deal 1983). Any further observations deemed pertinent to the questionnaires, such as personal stories related, were noted, and inquiries were made concerning the use of specific items of material culture and their locations of use and uselives. Besides the interviews, our procedures included mapping of structures and the compound layout, making a complete inventory of household material culture, and photographing interesting features, structures, and pottery.

All other interviews were arranged by the interpreters, one or two days in advance. The interpreters would explain to prospective household heads exactly what was involved in an interview (kinds of questions, inventory taking, length of visit, etc.), why we wanted to interview them (i.e., that we wanted to learn about the way they live today so that we could better understand contemporary communities and the remains left by their ancestors), and that we would be reimbursing them for the loss of a day's work. Informants were also told that they did not have to answer anything that they did not want to answer, and that they could stop the interview at any time. Further, they were promised that the information we collected would only be used for our own research and would not be given to the Mexican government.

Interviews were conducted by two teams consisting of three investigators and one interpreter. During an interviewing session (which lasted from four to eight hours depending upon the size of the household and its material inventory, as well as the enthusiasm of the person being interviewed), one person asked questions from the questionnaires through the interpreter. Generally only the household head answered social and economic questions, although attempts were always made to ask females about pottery production and use. The distribution of potting and non-potting households is indicated in Figures 1.1 and 1.2. One other person drafted scale maps of each structure and the entire compound, adding the location of as many items of material culture as possible. A third person made a list of the items (numbers of chairs, pots of each type, etc.) in each structure and around the compound. Separate permission was requested for entrance to each structure. The first person to finish his or her task would take photographs, again, asking permission for each item photographed. Before leaving a household, a Polaroid photograph was taken of the entire family and given to them. The picture taking generated much enthusiasm and often led to invitations to visit other households.

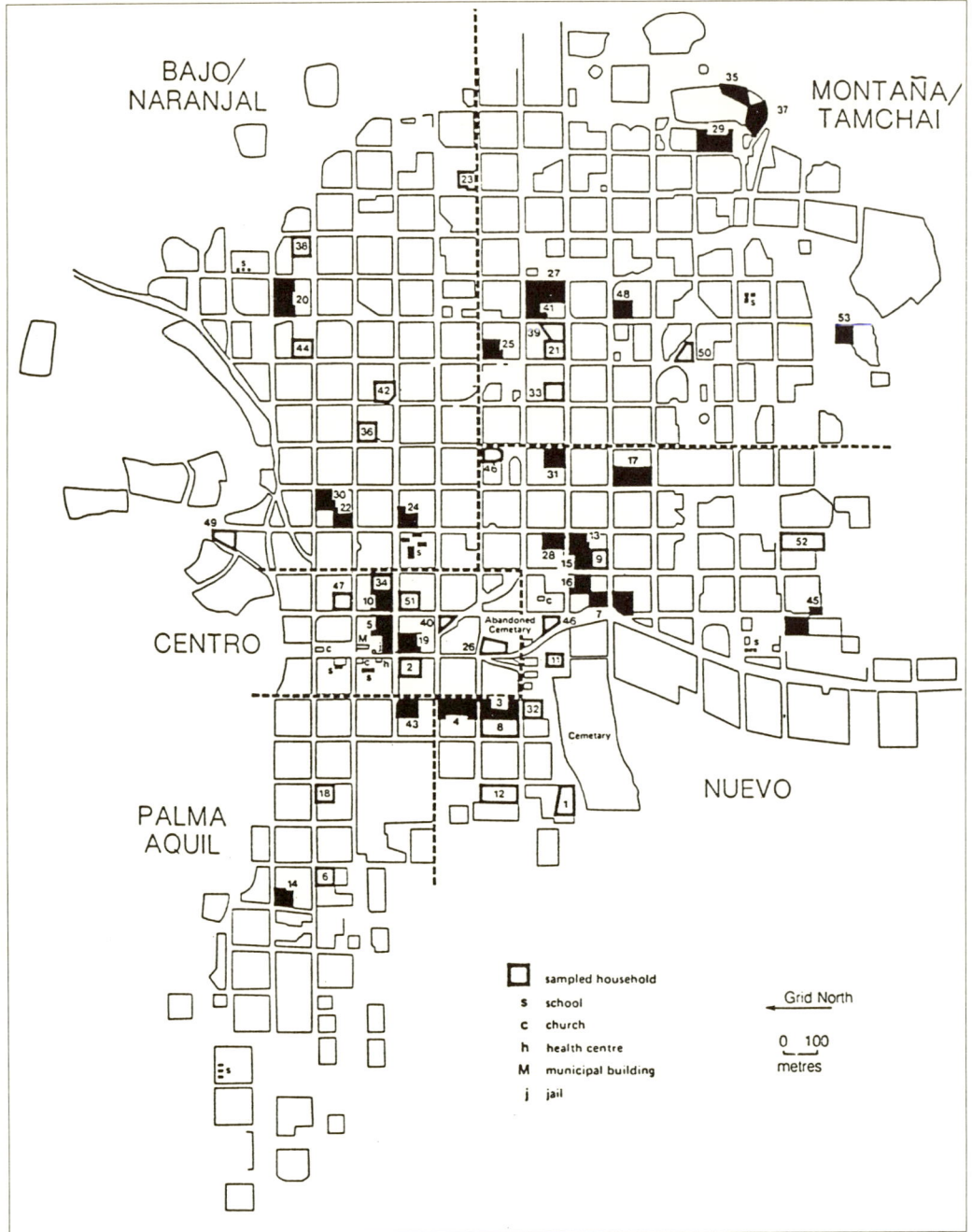

Fig. 1.1. Map of Chanal, 1977, indicating barrio divisions and surveyed households. Potting households are black.

Besides the household interviews, individual project members devoted as much time as possible to a number of specialized studies concerning pottery making, the local exchange or goods and services, glass-tool production, *mano* and *metate* production, the ethnobotany of local herbs, *milpa* working practices, work group organization, and community *cargo* organization. Clay and temper samples were collected from potters if

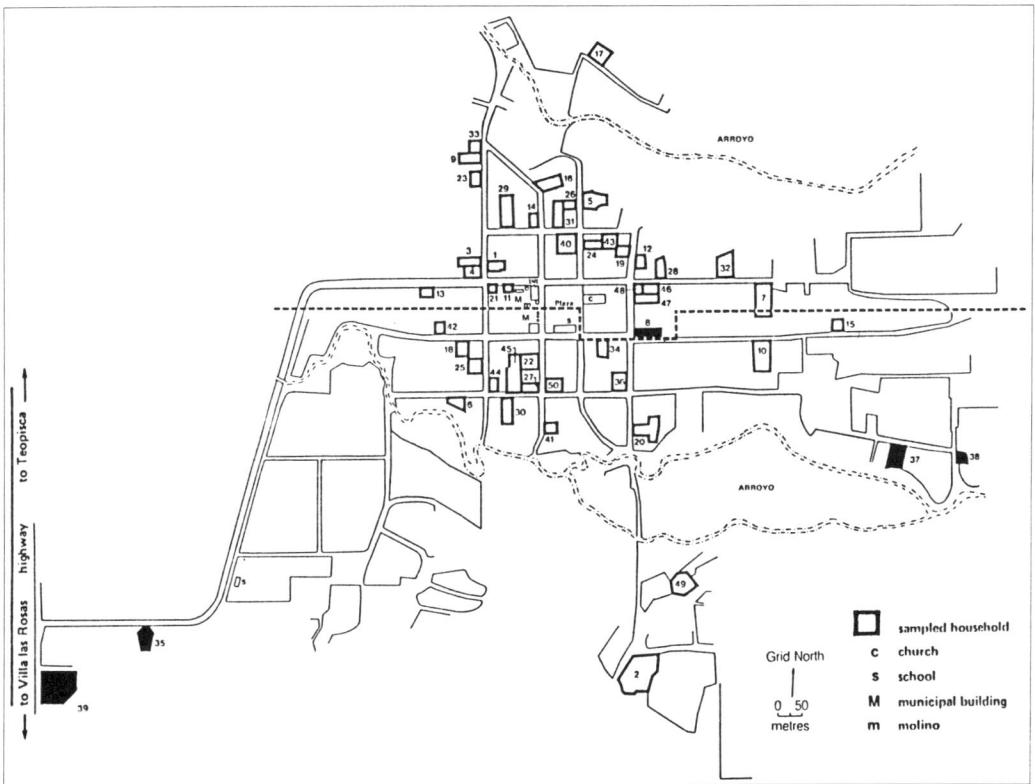

Fig. 1.2. Map of Aguacatenango, 1979, indicating barrio divisions and surveyed households. Potting households are black.

these materials were on hand. A few archaeological features (sweatbaths, storage pits, and house or kitchen floors) were excavated at abandoned housesites within the villages, and two Aguacatenango abandoned housesites were surface collected (Brulotte 1979). Further, several field trips were made to local archaeological sites, including the Coxoh sites of Coneta and Coapa, local and regional markets and shops (Figure 1.3) and the specialized pottery making communities of Amatenango, San Pedro, San Ramon, Yolakitak and Yocnajab. Finally, library research concerning the Tzeltal was conducted at the Na-balom Museum Library in San Cristóbal de las Casas, and at the Instituto Nacional Indigenista (INI) archives.

All pertinent data collected through interviews and material culture inventories were coded for statistical manipulation using the MIDAS statistical package (Fox and Guire 1976) on the MTS (Michigan Terminal System) facilities at Simon Fraser University. Coded data on over 7,000 individual pottery vessels included locational information (within compound and barrio), emic type, community of origin, distance to potter's household, specific potter, current vessel use and condition, and morphological attributes (i.e., height, maximum width, rim diameter, basal diameter, number of handles, presence of spout). Besides various descriptive statistics, the present study utilized certain nonparametric statistical tests that had previously been adopted by Brian Hayden and Aubrey Cannon (1984b) for studying other traditional forms of Tzeltal material culture.

PRESENTATION AND ORGANIZATION
The general framework for the following study consists of three descriptive models that outline pottery production, use and reuse, and disposal at the household level.

Fig. 1.3. Jane Deal and Geof Spurling recording measurements on new Tojolabal vessels in a Comitan pottery shop, 1977.

archaeological pottery remains in order to recover socioeconomic information.

Chapter 2 introduces the study communities and outlines the social and economic background of pottery production in the Central Maya Highlands. Chapter 3 presents the model of domestic pottery production which focuses on how pottery making is learned, the environmental constraints on production intensity and specific production activities. Domestic production in the study communities is contrasted with regional specialist production. The use of ethnographic information as an aid for identifying prehistoric potting households is also addressed.

Chapter 4 considers the household in terms of the consumption of pottery and related items such as gourd containers and industrial replacements for pottery. Consumption is related to various social and economic characteristics of households within the study communities. Chapter 5 considers the household as a unit of pottery disposal. Disposal is described in terms of stages of household development from initial establishment to abandonment and concomitant changes in the household pottery inventory. Chapter 6 deals with the treatment of archaeological pottery remains for the interpretation of prehistoric household socioeconomic conditions. Various techniques for converting sherds to whole vessel counts are reviewed. A simple diversity measure is presented as a useful tool for exploring modern (and by analogy prehistoric) household and village socioeconomic conditions. The final chapter reviews the archaeological implications of the three household models and makes some suggestions for future pottery ethnoarchaeological research.

The discussion surrounding each model explores the variation in behavior associated with these activities and allows predictions concerning the nature of the relationships between these activities and their archaeological manifestations (i.e., pottery assemblages) Statistical analyses are used to identify configurations of household pottery inventories which are related to different social and economic activities and social contexts, such as family size, wealth, and status. Further, various methods are considered for treating

2

Social and Economic Context

Continuity with the past was what confronted me the deeper I penetrated the Maya pattern of life. Continuity with a subtle inflection.
(J. E. S. Thompson 1963:127)

SETTING

The Tzeltal are one of nine Maya linguistic groups in the Mexican State of Chiapas, and along with the Tzotzil and Chol, constitute the nearly one half million Maya of the Central Highlands (Figure 2.1). During 1977 and 1979, members of the Coxoh Ethnoarchaeological Project surveyed 103 households in two of the more traditional Tzeltal communities in the southern Chiapas Highlands, namely, Chanal and Aguacatenango. These communities were also included in the University of Chicago, Man-in-Nature Project, which is an invaluable source of ethnohistorical, ethnographical, and ecological information on the Tzeltal Highlands (McQuown 1959).

Chanal is situated on a mountain slope about 2250 m above sea level, in an area characterized by pine forest and karst topography (Figure 2.2). The community originated as a *colonia* of Oxchuc and began to appear on official lists of Tzeltal communities by 1854 (Trens 1942:516). One source suggests that it was founded early in the 18th century (Lopez 1977; Hayden and Cannon 1984a:6). According to local folklore, the name "Chanal" (meaning literally "the serpent"; Robles 1966:24; Slocum and Gerdel 1976:131) was selected when a group of elders, meeting at the site to choose a name, found a multicolored snake in a spring (Esponda J. and Guiteras Holmes 1986:221, note 1). The original location of Chanal was

part of a large farm *(hacienda)* that was worked on a sharecropping basis by a group of Oxchuc families. Eventually, they were able to purchase approximately 42,000 ha when the owner moved away (Calnek 1959). The community remained a *paraje*-vacant town until the 1930s, when an influential *Presidente* of the *Comite de Educación* persuaded people in the *parajes* to move into town (Calnek 1959). Today the community is linked to other areas by an extensive system of trails and by a three-hour drive over a very rough road to the Pan American Highway. The first *tiendas* and *cantinas* opened in Chanal shortly after the road was constructed in the 1950s.

Aguacatenango is located in the fertile bottom land of the Amatenango Valley, about 2000 m above mean sea level (Figure 2.2). The community can be reached via paved highway and is less than one hour's drive from the regional markets of San Cristóbal de las Casas, Comitan, and Pinola (Villa Las Rojas). According to local folklore, the original inhabitants came from a place called Bahuitz, close to Oxchuc, and were guided to the present site by a group of elders (Verbitsky 1959a:1). The Tzeltal name for the community is Tze'te' (J. Nash 1959:11). The name "Aguacatenango" is a Nahuatl place-name that was probably applied to the community due to strong Central Mexican influence in the Chiapas Highlands in the Postclassic period (Calnek 1988:12). The

9

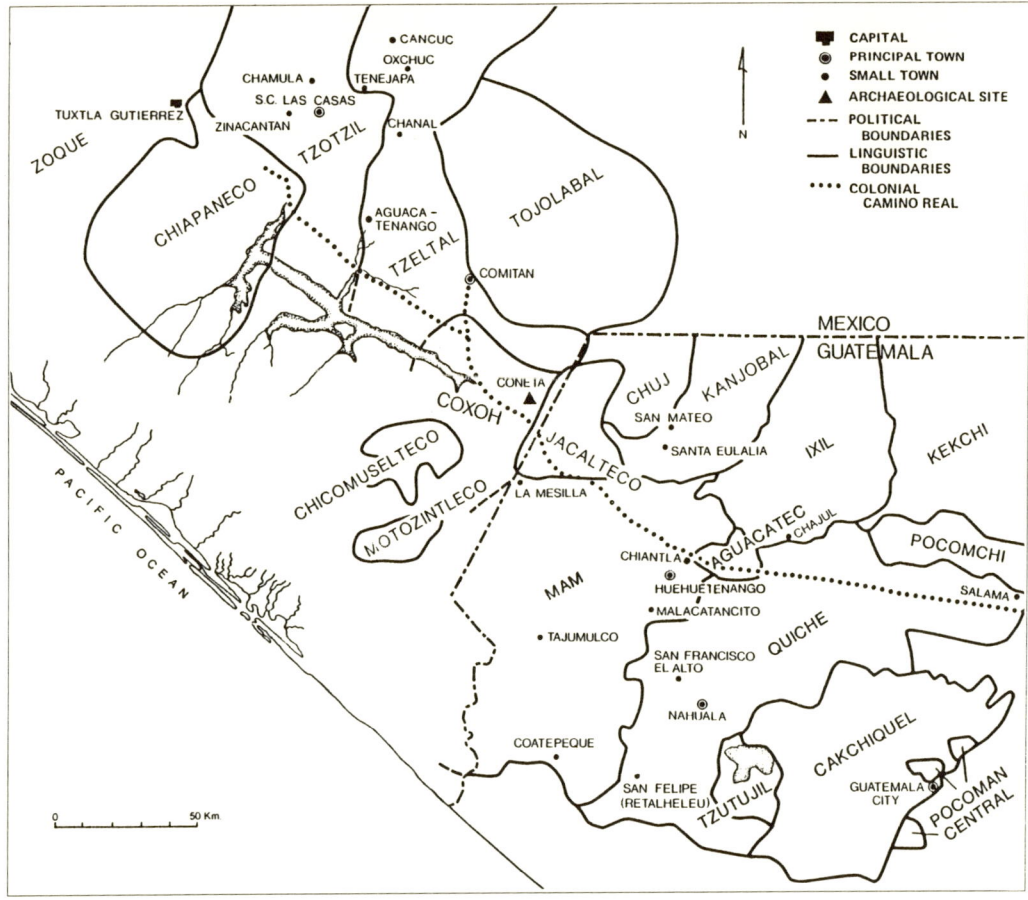

Fig. 2.1. Map of Chiapas, Mexico, indicating major linguistic areas (including the extinct *Coxoh*) and major communities.

community first appears in a regional census in 1611, with a population of 720 (Verbitsky 1959:1, after Culebro 1932:124). However, the presence of prehistoric ceramic sherds in wattle-and-daub walls and the widespread reuse of archaeological *metates* attests to a precolonial origin for the community. In one household, a Classic period bowl was being used as a dog feeding dish. Agricultural terraces in the hills around the community are also believed to date to precolonial times. During the colonial period, Aguacatenango was known as the Pueblo of Aguacatenango and was formed by the two politically separate communities *(parcialidades)* of Aguacatenango and Quetzaltepeque (Hunt and Nash 1967:263). These two communities ex-

ist today within Aguacatenango as corporate neighborhoods (barrios).

Chanal, for several reasons, must be considered the more traditional of the two communities. These reasons include (1) the high degree of Tzeltal monolingualism, (2) the retention of Maya month names in relation to agricultural practices, (3) the retention of traditional dress by the women, and (4) the use of offertory pits in the construction of houses and municipal buildings. The relative strength of the Chanal *cargo* system also suggests a closer link to traditional values. An apparent decline in traditional values in Aguacatenango might be directly linked to that community's recent involvement in the Ladino economy and a concomitant adop-

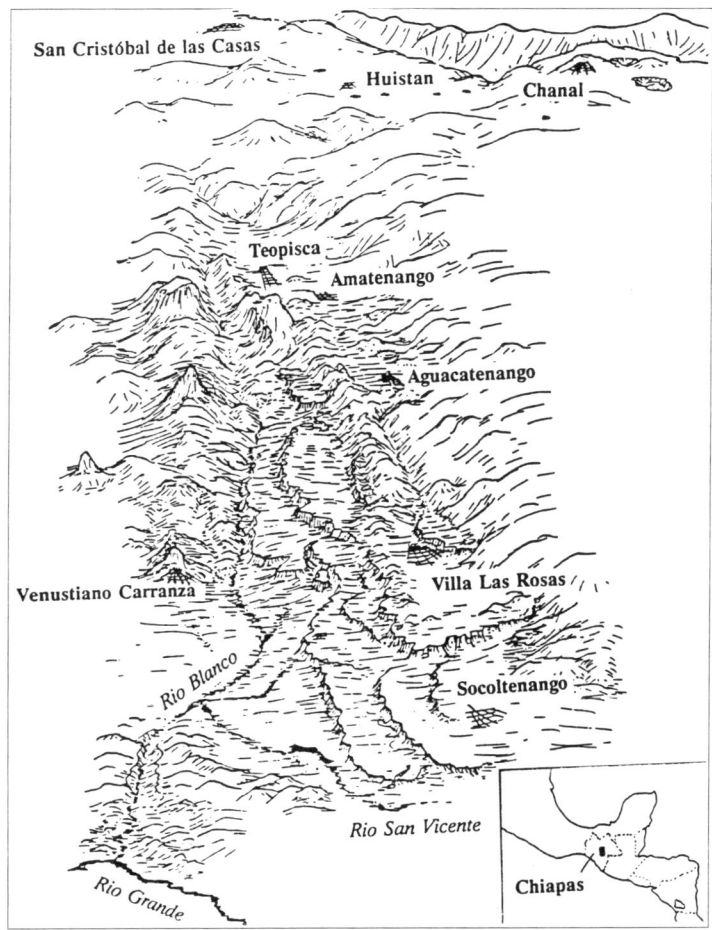

Fig. 2.2. Physiographic map of a portion of southern Chiapas, including locations of study communities (adapted from Wagner 1959).

tion of Ladino standards. This is evidenced by their tendency to pay in cash for services (Hayden and Cannon 1984a:338). In one way, at least, Aguacatenango is more traditional. It retains the dual-barrio system, with its important social and economic ramifications.

SETTLEMENT SYSTEM

In 1938 Chanal became a free *municipio* with a *Presidente Municipal*. According to a 1980 census by the State of Chiapas, the entire *municipio* had a population of 5019 people, 2624 males and 2395 females, 45 percent of which were monolingual (Esponda J. and Guiteras Holmes 1986: 222–223). The *mu-*

nicipio was reported to be 2956 km² in size, with a population distributed among ten *parajes* and *colonias*, including Chanalito, Naranjal, La Mendoza, Sachibalte, Saquilchen, Siberia, Natilton, Onija, Tzajalnich, and Frontera Mexiquito. There were also town halls *(cabildos)* at several small ranchos within the *municipio,* each associated with sacred sites where guardian spirits are believed to live. Each of these was administered by two *jefes,* or *cabildos de milpa,* who collected money for the fireworks, candles, and incense used in agricultural rites at these sites (Calnek 1959:12). Similar rites have been associated with *parajes* of Tenejapa and Oxchuc, where officials, accompanied by musi-

Fig. 2.3. Chanal from ridge below cemetery. Note *Presidencia* at upper right.

Fig. 2.4. Chanal *Presidencia*, 1977.

cians, visit several sites within their *paraje* at crucial times during the agricultural cycle (Hunt and Nash 1967: 257).

In 1977, Chanal itself had a permanent native population of about 3900, living in approximately 560 households. The local school teacher was the only Ladino allowed to live in the community. During the 1940s, the town was laid out in its present grid pattern of 100 m² blocks divided into four 50 m² houselots *(sitios)* and a municipal head office *(Presidencia municipal)* was constructed (Figure 2.3–2.4). At the time of our visit the community center consisted of the *Presidencia,* local PRI (Partido Revolutionario Institutional) offices, jail, health center, church, school, and basketball court. Formerly, high-

land and lowland farmers formed two loosely arranged corporate neighborhoods (the dual-barrio system) that regulated their own land use and marriage arrangements, and claimed equal representation in the community government (Calnek 1959:6–7; Esponda J. and Guiteras Holmes 1986:223). In 1977, there were four barrios, namely Palm Akil, Tamchay (Montana), Naranjal (Bajo) and Nuevo. Barrio affiliation was mainly associated with school administration and public work group organization, such as committees for street cleaning before important festivals.

In 1979, Aguacatenango had a permanent population of about 1900 people living in approximately 280 households. The community center was organized in a similar fashion to that of Chanal, and included a town hall *(cabildo),* INI (Instituto Nacional Indigenista) office, church, and a school around a central plaza (Figure 2.5). The dual-barrio system was still in operation, and the community was divided by an imaginary line crossing the central plaza. Hunt and Nash (1967:262) consider this system to be of native origin, while the multiple-barrio system is more characteristic of an acculturated community. Hunt (1962:203) described the neighborhoods within the two barrios as localized *patrilines,* since men rarely lived outside their natal barrio, while women circulated within

Fig. 2.5. Aguacatenango, viewed from highway, 1979.

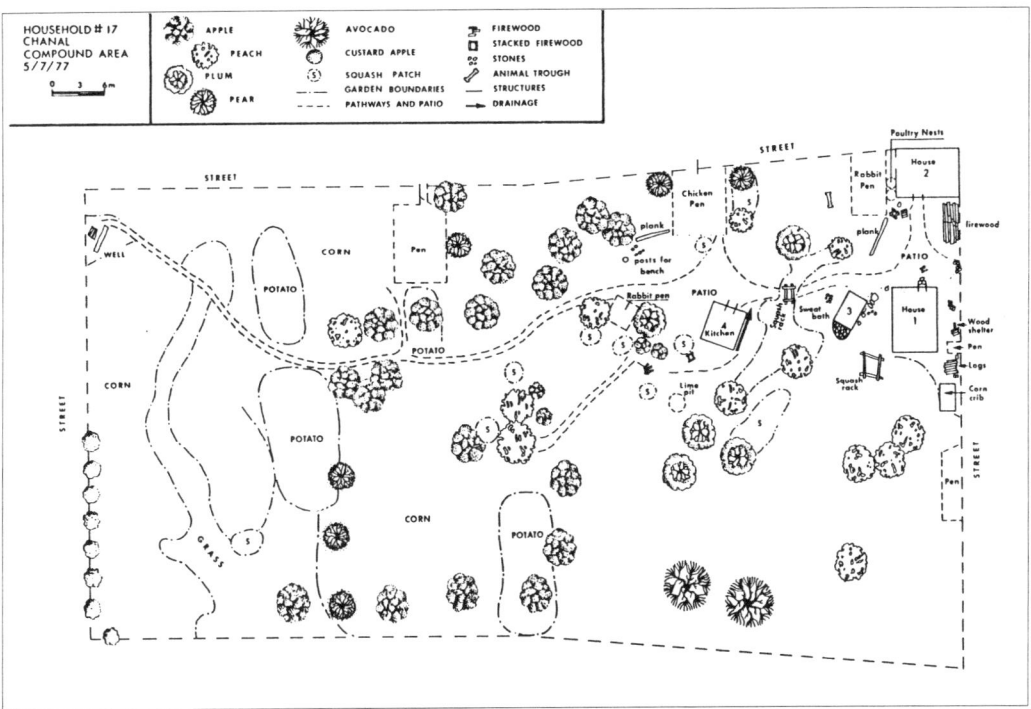

Fig. 2.6. Chanal Household 17, illustrating typical arrangement of household features and gardens.

and between barrios due to marriage arrangements. Each barrio also controlled its own resources (e.g., only barrio members could collect palm or berries within its own boundaries; Hunt and Nash 1967:265).

Household land plots averaged just over 1000 m² in Aguacatenango, but generally, were more than 3000 m² in Chanal. High wooden fences were used to separate individual household compounds. The basic house-

Fig. 2.7. Chanal cemetery, with individual structures erected in family plots.

hold consisted of a house, kitchen, and sweatbath arranged around a patio work area, but household features could also include a house altar, storage structure(s), corn bin, garden, terraces, orchard, well, and animal pens (Figure 2.6). In Chanal, the remainder of the compound, except for pathways, was cultivated with corn, while in Aguacatenango gardens were generally small mixed vegetable and flower patches. There is some evidence indicating the survival of precolonial practices of astronomical alignments involving house structures, altars, doorways and patios (for discussion see Deal 1987:182–185). In Chanal most house altars (64%) faced east or north (i.e., positions suggesting sunrise and zenith), while in Aguacatenango there was a definite preference for a western orientation of altars (i.e., 59%; Deal 1987:Table 2.1; also see Gossen 1979: 128–129; Howry 1976:214). The notion of ritual opposition is also important, with the altar being the focal point of male space and the hearth being the focal point of female

space (also see Gossen 1979:122, 125; Vogt 1969:83).

Most Chanal houses were built from hand hewn or sawn planks, or split poles, with wooden shingle roofing, while Aguacatenango houses were generally built with wattle-and-daub walls and thatched roofs. Separate kitchens were usually less elaborate than the main house. At the community level, most variations in household building materials and practices, as well as the presence or absence of a sweatbath, appear to be a function of local resources and environment, while house floor shape and roof style seem to reflect cultural affiliation (S. Blake 1988:37; Blake and Blake 1988). In Chanal, the more expensive wall material, sawn plank, was used primarily by high income and high status households, while split pole and wattle-and-daub walls characterized households of lower wealth and status (M. Blake 1988). Further, the number of structures in a compound seemed to be an important indicator of household economic level, but not social ranking, while there was a tendency for households of both higher social and economic ranking to be situated closer to the community center (M. Blake 1988). Families also had their own burial plots in the Chanal cemetery, and burial structures and secondary reburials were generally associated with higher status individuals (Figure 2.7).

ECONOMY

Both communities relied heavily on corn and bean agriculture, although not everyone grew beans (see Tables 2.1, 2.2). While the soil within Chanal is suitable for large garden plots, much of the area around the community was marginal for agriculture. Therefore, corn fields *(milpas)* are generally located 8 km or more from the community, and men spend much of the week away from their homes. Fields were cleared using the slash and burn technique *(rozar)*, with the aid of axes and machetes, and an iron-tipped digging stick was used in planting (see Palerm 1967 for general discussion). An important distinction is made between those who farm highland *(jamaltic)* and lowland *(alantic)* milpas, which vary according to soil quality, climate, and length of growing season (Calnek 1959:2). The growing season for corn and beans was scheduled around seasonal rains, and frost at higher altitudes (above 1600 m). The amount of rain and the timing of the rainy season have important implications for yearly crop yields. In Aguacatenango, farmers planted three different types of fields, thereby staggering planting and harvesting times. Corn matured more quickly in the lowland *(Tierra caliente)* fields, but highland *(Tierra fria)* corn was hardier (Hunt 1962:80). Some fields, closer to the community, were plowed and irrigated as a safeguard to a rain shortage. Fruit trees, timber, firewood, and wild game were also important to highland subsistence, while lowland farmers could also grow coffee, sugarcane, oranges, and bananas (Esponda J. and Guiteras Holmes 1986:227).

Chanal household garden plots and orchards also produced potatoes, chilies, cabbage, avocados, peaches and apples. Aguacatenango farmers cultivated avocados, custard apples *(anona)*, *guayabas*, *chayotes*, peaches, apples, and oranges (also see Hunt 1962:78, Figure 6). Some people in both communities raised chickens, pigs, and horses, while some Chanal farmers also raised sheep, goats, and occasionally cattle. In Aguacatenango, truck farming became popular in the 1970s.

While farming was the primary occupation among Tzeltal men, both communities had several part-time specialists, including merchants (store owners), butchers, carpenters, masons, corn alcohol *(trago)* distillers, and musicians. Chanal also had a professionally trained male nurse and Aguacatenango had at least one full-time midwife. Traditional curers were also encountered in Chanal, Aguacatenango, and Cancuc.

Cash was in short supply in Chanal. Most foodstuffs, and also pottery, were obtained through exchanges for designated quantities of other foodstuffs, such as eggs, beans, chilies, or oranges. Eggs were often used for purchasing goods not available in the community. Besides work on the lowland coffee plantations and as hired labor on local *fincas*, money could be earned through the sale of lumber, firewood *(ocote)*, and crafts. According to Calnek (1959:3), Chanaleños sold eggs, potatoes, chickens, pigs and horses in San Cristóbal de las Casas and potatoes in Comitan, and returned with salt, *panela* (partly-refined sugar), granular sugar, clothing, medicine, and fireworks for the church. Chilies and onions were also obtained through trade in nearby San Pedro, a *colonia* of Huistan.

Besides pottery making, a number of other crafts were practiced in Chanal and Aguacatenango. For both communities, this included basket making, sewing, leather working, and the production of *maguey* fibre cordage and net bags. Aguacatenango men once specialized in hat making, but factory-made hats became available after the construction of the Pan American Highway, and there was also greater access to farmland after the agrarian

Fig. 2.8. Aguacatenango woman wearing blouse with traditional community design.

Fig. 2.9. Chanal weaver using traditional back-strap loom.

reforms of the 1930s (Verbitsky 1959a:2). Today the men make candles and brooms, and the women make blouses (Figure 2.8). Several Chanal women make woollen blankets using back-strap looms (Figure 2.9). A few individuals in each community made tools and ritual items from bone, horn and glass. Some of these tool forms, such as corn huskers *(tapiscadores)* and rattle handles, have been recovered from colonial and pre-colonial archaeological sites, and are therefore of special interest to archaeologists (Hayden and Cannon 1984a:83–106). Some weavers also used large bone needles for

sewing together sections of blankets. Traditional lithic technology persisted in the form of glass working (Deal and Hayden 1987; Hayden and Deal 1989; Hayden and Nelson 1981). Twenty-four glass workers were identified in the two communities and 43 cases of glass used for domestic functions (i.e., craft activity, tool production and maintenance) and 26 cases for ritual functions (i.e., blood-letting tools) were recorded.

COMMUNITY POLITICAL AND RELIGIOUS ORGANIZATION

At the community level, it would be difficult to discuss either politics or religion without including the other. The sociopolitical structure of 20th century indigenous communities in the Central Highlands has been dominated by civil-religious hierarchies, known as the *cargo* system (for a discussion see Albores 1978:67–100; Breton 1973:61; Cancian 1967; Wasserstrom 1983). The traditional *cargo* system has three elements, namely civil and religious ladders of authority and the sponsorship of festivals, which Earle (1990:115) refers to as the *fiesta* system. An individual accrues prestige (and rank) while ascending and/or crossing between these ladders. Implicit in this system is the use of religion to legitimize political authority, which is a practice that appears to date to precolonial times (Earle 1990:120).

Chance and Taylor (1985) believe that the modern *cargo* system began in the 16th century as a civil hierarchy imposed on local communities by the Spanish (i.e., the municipal town council, or *cabildo* system), which may have included some lower offices derived from prehispanic positions. During the 17th and 18th centuries, and possibly earlier, religious sodalities, known as *cofradias*, were introduced to look after the affairs of the local saints (see Earle 1990). Four *cofradias* are reported for 18th-century Aguacatenango (Wasserstrom 1983:88). Finally, the modern *cargo* system developed in the late 19th and early 20th centuries as the *cofradia* system was being undermined by Church and State, and the responsibility for local saints was placed in the hands of household spon-

TABLE 2.1.
The Agricultural Cycle in Chanal (Adapted from McQuown 1959, Figure 10).

Chanal	Highland *(Jamaltic)*	Lowland *(Alantic)*
January	harvest corn	harvest corn
February		harvest corn
March	slash and burn, plant corn, squashes, beans, and potatoes	harvest corn
April	plant (as above)	slash and burn, plant corn in last week of month
May	plant (as above)	plant corn
June	harvest potatoes	
July	weed, harvest potatoes	plant beans
August	weed, harvest potatoes, corn ears at *elote* stage	weed, plant beans, corn at *jilote* stage
September	mature ears of corn *(macizo)*	ears of corn in *elote* stage
October	mature ears of corn, clear new land	clear new land
November	clear new land	clear new land
December	clear new land, harvest beans, squash, and corn	clear new land, harvest beans

sors (Rus and Wasserstrom 1980; Chance 1990:29). At the same time, precolonial status differences between indigenous nobles and commoners were no longer being recognized (Chance 1990:20; also see Calnek 1988:33–43 concerning the precolonial class system in Chiapas). Chance (1990:27–30) sees these major structural changes as indigenous responses to external attempts to gain control of indigenous politics, and he believes that extant *cargo* systems are themselves being transformed into predominantly religious hierarchies that are set apart from civil authority. He feels that this is also implicit in DeWalt's typology of civil-religious hierarchies (DeWalt 1975). The *fiesta* system, in particular, is closely linked to community and ethnic identity (Earle 1990:116). At the community level, there are many possible factors affecting the breakdown of civil-religious hierarchics, including ladinoization, relative

prosperity, population pressures, occupational specialization, and closer incorporation into the national cash economy (Cancian 1967:293–296; DeWalt 1975).

Each Tzeltal community has its own distinct version of the *cargo* system. Rus and Wasserstrom (1980) suggest that differential development was related to a community's economic position within the region. The traditional view of the *cargo* system has been that individuals were willing to spend their wealth, which itself is incompatible with traditional lifeways, on public festivals in order to gain prestige and social standing. Cancian (1965) has argued that in the Tzotzil community of Zinacantan, the *cargo* system served the opposite purpose, namely, to legitimize the acquisition of status and wealth (see Rus and Wasserstrom 1980:467). Similarly, Hayden and Cannon (1984a:154; also see Hayden and Gargett 1990) cite several cases from

TABLE 2.2.
The Agricultural Cycle for Aguacatenango (Adapted from McQuown 1959, Figure 10).

Aguacatenango	Irrigated (Riego)	Highland (Tierra Fria)	Lowland (Tierra Caliente)
January	irrigate, plow, plant corn	harvest corn	harvest beans
February	plow, plant corn	harvest corn	
March	second irrigation, first weeding		
April	irrigation and weeding	last week, plant corn and beans	last week, plant corn
May	second weeding, plant beans	plant corn and beans	plant corn and beans, weeding
June	weeding, plant beans	weeding	weeding in early weeks
July	corn in *jilote* and *elote* stages		
August	corn matures, harvest		plant beans
September	harvest		
October		mature corn	mature corn, harvest
November		harvest beans	
December	plow		

the Coxoh Project where high ranking *cargeros* increased their wealth while in office.

Cancian (1967:285–287) includes *mayordomos, regidores, alcaldes,* and *principales* among the more common positions (also see Adams 1988 for a recent comparison of Highland Maya *cargo* systems). The *mayordomo* is a religious position associated with the care of local saints and sponsorship of fiestas. The *regidor* is a civil position involved with tax collection, work group organization, and dispute settlement. The *alcalde* is the highest civil position in most communities. *Principales* are retired civil leaders who are regarded as community elders, and who retain considerable political power within their communities, and especially in selecting people for *cargo* positions. These men may also be exempt from taxes and work groups (Cancian 1967:284). In Chanal, *principales*

have held the real power for some time in important decision-making matters, such as resolution of disputes and loans (Calnek 1959).

Chanal, in the late 1970s, had a very traditional civil-religious hierarchy which had changed relatively little since first recorded in 1935 (Esponda J. and Guiteras Holmes 1986:227). Each hierarchy consisted of a "ladder" of public offices (*cargos*) which tended to be mutually exclusive, and both the civil and religious heads were powerful men (Figure 2.10). Selection of candidates for *cargo* positions was supervised by the *principales,* but higher offices required previous service at lower levels (see Table 2.3 for a summary of the positions as they existed in 1977). The civil hierarchy was mainly responsible for the administration of community affairs, including police protection and the settling of local disputes. The religious hierarchy was re-

TABLE 2.3.
Summary of *Cargo* Positions in Chanal (1977) and Aguacatenango (1979).

Chanal Civil Hierarchy	Chanal Religious Hierarchy
Presidente Municipal	*Presidente de Iglesia*
Sindico Municipal	*Gobernador*
Juez Grande, Agente Municipal, Regidor (Primero)	*Alferez* (large festivals)
Presidente de Mejores Materiales	*Regromal*
Delegado Juez Chico, Comandante	*Alferez* (small festivals)
Comiseriado Ejidal/Vigilancia, Tesorero	*Mayor*
Presidente de Comite de Escuela, Regidor Chica	*Mayordomo (Junta de Iglesia)*
Policia, Jefe de Militador, Presidente de 16 de Sept., Comite de Escuela	

Aguacatenango Civil Hierarchy	Aguacatenango Religious Hierarchy
Juez (primero)	*Alcalde Rezador*
Juez (secundo)	*Principales*
Agente	*Maestro de Coro, Maxtol*
Suplente (Rejumala)	*Presidente de Comite de Iglesia*
Comiseriado Ejedal, Regidor (Primero), Sindico	*Comite de Iglesia (Pixcal)*
Policia (Comisión)	

sponsible for guardianship of local saints, administration of the church, and for the perpetuation of important public religious festivals (i.e., through the *fiesta* system). The community did not have regular visits by a Catholic priest. The office of *Alferez Primero,* which is a prerequisite to the higher religious postings in Chanal, involved a considerable outlay of money to provide food and drink, and equipment (including pottery) for certain festivals. The latter included two large festivals, namely Virgen Candelaria and San Pedro Marteles, as well as the smaller festivals of San Juan Bautista, San Antonia, Virgen Seradora and Virgen Guadelupe (Figure 2.11). Relatively wealthy household heads were prime candidates for *alferez,* and eventually, higher *cargo* positions.

In Aguacatenango, in the late 1970s, the *cargo* system existed in a less elaborate form, with the civil hierarchy dominating (Figures 2.12, 2.13). Unlike Chanal, many wealthier individuals had the option of not participating in public office, and therefore, household wealth differences tended to be more pronounced. This breakdown was probably related to events in nearby Amatenango where there was a shift from *principale* guardianship, linked to ancestor veneration, to a younger civil hierarchy with external, more nationally-oriented, political connections (Chance 1990:37, after Nash 1970).

19

Fig. 2.10. Chanal *Presidente de Iglesia* (left) and *Presidente Municipal* (right) officiating at San Juan Bautista fiesta, 1977.

TZELTAL HOUSEHOLD ORGANIZATION

The household was the basic organizational unit in both communities. It was also the spatial focus of the socialization of Tzeltal children, most socioeconomic activities, and the deposition of refuse. The typical household consisted of a nuclear family or a small extended family, and the average family size for those included in our survey for both communities was seven. In Chanal, polygyny was quite common (also see Calnek 1959:13; Redfield and Villa Rojas 1939:115). In 1977, several interviewed men had one wife in Chanal and another at a rancho near their *milpa*. One man had four wives and another was married to two sisters. Similar cases were recorded in the 1950s, as well as instances of bride exchange and two brothers married to two sisters (Calnek 1959:14). In plural marriages the first wife generally retained the higher social status (see Esponda J. and Guiteras Holmes 1986:231–234 for a further discussion of marriage arrangements, bride service, and polygamy in Chanal).

The household head was generally the eldest male and interhousehold affiliation was based on his ancestry. Female household

Fig. 2.11. San Juan Bautista fiesta day, Chanal, 1977: flute and drum corp followed by *alferez*.

Fig. 2.12. Aguacatenango *cargeros*, 1979, including the five high ranking officials and *policia* officer on far right.

Fig. 2.13. Religious *cargero* ringing bell in Aguacatenango church, 1979.

heads appear to be uncommon today, but a 1778 census reported several communities, including Aguacatenango, with female heads for more than one-quarter of the households (Wasserstrom 1983:97). Men of the same Tzeltal surname (i.e., denoting common ancestry) form lineages, and one man acts as lineage head (see also Esponda J. and Guiteras Holmes 1986:228ff). In Chanal, lineages were also grouped according to Spanish surnames into "clans," but clan organization is now defunct. The lineage head might be responsible for organizing cooperative work groups among lineage members and hosting lineage ritual gatherings. Hayden and Cannon (1984b:336, Table 1) have demonstrated that both kin and nonkin relationships were important in the organization of labor (e.g., house building) and economic (e.g., *milpa*) work groups in Chanal and Aguacatenango. Hunt (1962) reported that during the 1950s women did not form work groups in Aguacatenango. In 1979, a large female work group was organized to fish the shallow lake between the community and the highway (Figure 2.14). Women walked across the lake in a line, and in unison, periodically scooping up small fish in baskets.

Both communities followed a bilateral kinship system that was characterized by the merging of siblings with collateral relatives (Romney 1967:225–227, 230–231; also see Esponda J. and Guiteras Holmes 1986:235). Ritual kinship relationships were also established in which godparents were selected for a newborn child. A boy had a godfather *(padrino)* and a girl had a godmother *(madrina)*. The godparent and his or her spouse became the *compadre* and *comadre* to the child's parents. It was the potential godparent who initiated the relationship, which was followed by ritualized negotiations, involving gifts of food and liquor (Calnek 1959:14). Parents and godparents would conduct regular visits and provide mutual help in planting *milpas*.

Fig. 2.14. Aguacatenango female work group fishing in lake beside community.

Among the Highland Maya there was a clear distinction between public and private religion. Public religion was associated with the religious hierarchy, the church, intercommunity pilgrimages (i.e., *romerías;* see Adams 1988:183–192) and the *fiesta* system, while private rituals (e.g., baptisms, weddings, funerals, family saint celebrations, agricultural rites) were more closely tied to rituals conducted at household altars (Deal 1988a). The persistence of precolonial agricultural rites has often been linked to the persistence of traditional farming practices (Thompson 1954:26), and various offerings (e.g., incense, candles, flowers, and foods) were made to natural deities (i.e., often identified with Catholic saints) and ancestral spirits prior to planting, harvesting, and dehusking of corn in the *milpa.*

Ancestor or lineage cults of the Central Highlands are also believed to date to precolonial times (Calnek 1988:48; Vogt 1964). Ancestor spirits are believed to inhabit certain sacred places (e.g., caves in mountains, wells, archaeological sites), and special pilgrimages are made to these sites to petition for favors in agriculture and curing (e.g., Blom and LaFarge 1927:254; Gossen 1979; Holland 1964; Lee 1972). In particular, caves have played an important role in Tzeltal religious beliefs and folklore (Calnek 1988:49; Miles 1965:285; J. Nash 1959:58; J.E.S. Thompson 1970:316; Verbitsky 1959a:2). Ancestral spirits were assigned to important caves surrounding Chanal, and human bones from a

local cave were recorded on one household altar (Deal 1987:175; also see Blom 1954). Some Chanal *cargeros* kept wooden idols, representing ancestors, on their altars and petitioned them with offerings of spiritual foods (Hayden 1987:179). According to Mark Gumbiner (Calnek 1959:17, note 11), the entire community would go to a cave called Muculchan on the day of Santa Cruz (May 5th) to petition for rain.

There is a traditionally-held belief among the Maya of the Central Highlands that each man has an alter ego in animal form, called a *nahual* (see Calnek 1988:52–57). This spirit is imprisoned in the mountains by his departed ancestors, but is released if he commits a sin. The household altar also serves as a point of contact between the man, his animal spirit and his ancestors, where offerings must be made to atone for the sin. The *nahual* is also a source of medical power that is used by the curer *(curandero)* for good and by witches *(brujos)* for evil. Prolonged illness is often attributed to witchcraft and accusations of witchcraft are common in some Tzeltal communities (M. Nash 1960). Verbitsky (1959a:2) reports of a particularly powerful *nahual* believed to live in one of the caves in the hills surrounding Aguacatenango. According to Calnek (1959:15–16), the community of La Palizada, near Amatenango, was actually founded by individuals who where driven out of Chanal under suspicion of witchcraft.

3

Household as Production Unit

Metal or enamel containers do not have souls as do gourds and handmade pottery. (J. Nash 1970:53)

The basic unit of pottery production among the Tzeltal, and throughout Mesoamerica in general, is the household. Therefore, the first potential source of pottery variability and patterning at the household level is pottery manufacture itself (see Figure 3.1). Variability and patterning within a potting household are strongly affected by the level of pottery production, which is geared to household economic needs (both consumption and exchange). The level of production is also constrained by certain factors related to production, namely, the level of specialized knowledge and skill of the potter, the diversity and quantity of available pottery-making resources, and the efficiency of production. In the present chapter, three levels of household production are recognized, and each is characterized in terms of differential household economic needs. Potential pottery variability and patterning are addressed in terms of the effects of production-related constraints upon the potting household. It has been suggested that pottery variability at this level can yield inferences concerning residence behavior, corporate group strength, and other aspects of community social structure (e.g., Deetz 1968; Longacre 1964; Michels 1979). The level of pottery production in Chanal and Aguacatenango will be addressed in relation to the development of pottery making specialization in the Central Highlands of Chiapas. The final section of the chapter deals with the archaeological visibility of domestic potting households.

ECONOMIC NEEDS AND LEVEL OF PRODUCTION

The intensity of production in Tzeltal potting households, and therefore the level of specialization, was determined by the economic needs of the residents. Balfet (1965) has recognized three levels of pottery production among the Maghreb of North Africa, namely, domestic, elementary specialization, and artisan specialization (also see Peacock 1981; Santley et al. 1989). These three categories were also applicable to Tzeltal potters. Among the Tzeltal, domestic scale pottery production was characterized by a low frequency of pottery making events, the production of small quantities of a few vessel forms, and local consumption of the finished products. At this level of pottery production, the goal of the potter was to complete the household inventory, replacing vessels broken during the previous year, and adding vessels if the household had grown in size. Producer and user were synonymous in domestic production.

Specialist pottery manufacture presents a more complex situation, since the potter is also influenced by social and economic forces outside of her own household. Pottery specialization is often equated with the relative intensity of production, regardless of level of

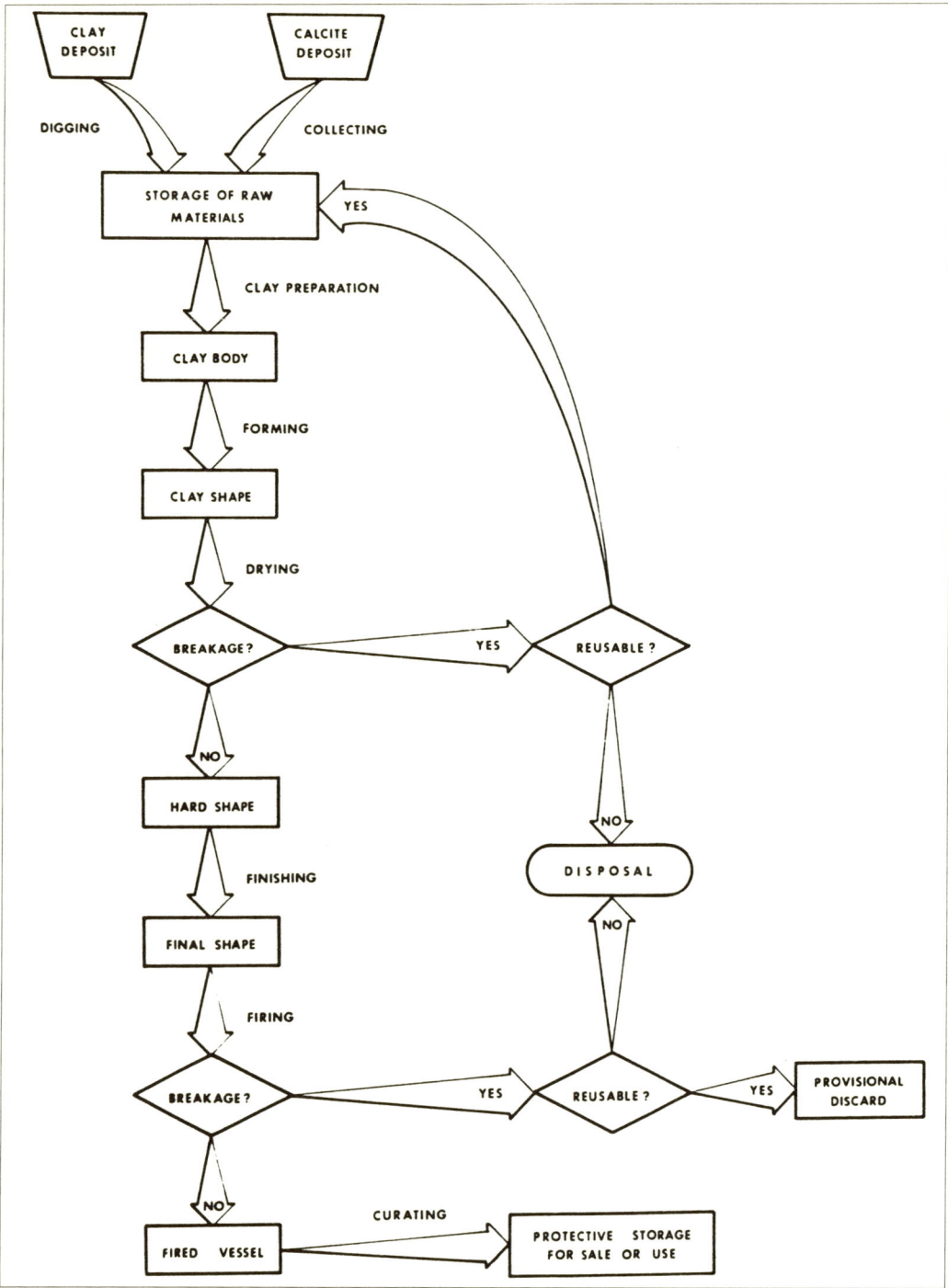

Fig. 3.1. Tzeltal pottery production model, indicating manufacturing activities, progressive material state of vessel and decision-making related to breakage during production. (Based on observations on Chanal potters).

sociopolitical complexity (Rice 1996b:179), and it is closely tied to the notion of standardization (see discussion under microtraditions). Tzeltal elementary specialists were generally women who were forced to contribute to the household economy by producing beyond the requirements of the immediate family. They might sell or barter surplus vessels to other members of the community, or possibly in the regional market in San Cristóbal de las Casas, or they might make specialized vessel forms on commission for local religious festivals (i.e., low-level sponsorship). Among elementary specialists pottery making events occurred more frequently (i.e., seasonally, or in a few cases, on a year-round basis), and larger quantities of vessels were produced. However, they still produced a limited number of forms.

The artisan specialists were even more dependent upon non-subsistence sources for their livelihood. They often had inadequate farmland and were forced to sell crafts or work as field laborers. These households, including households #3 and #4 in Chanal, generally produced pottery on a year-round basis. Production, including the collection of raw materials, vessel manufacture, and selling of the final products, was carefully scheduled. Most transactions were on a cash basis. Middlemen played an important role at this level, by purchasing from the potter and reselling vessels in local or regional markets, and occasionally by peddling in more remote communities (also see Nicklin 1971:13). The specialist produced a large variety of vessel forms, exhibiting more uniform shapes, size ranges, and decorations.

In Costin's recent typology for the organization of specialist production, both groups of Tzeltal specialists would fall within the category of individual specialization (see Costin 1991; Costin and Hagstrum 1995:620–621). Both groups are generally independent of sponsorship, and work in small, kin-based operations that are dispersed within many communities. The main difference is that artisan specialists practice full-time production. By contrast, Amatenango is an example of community specialization, with "household-

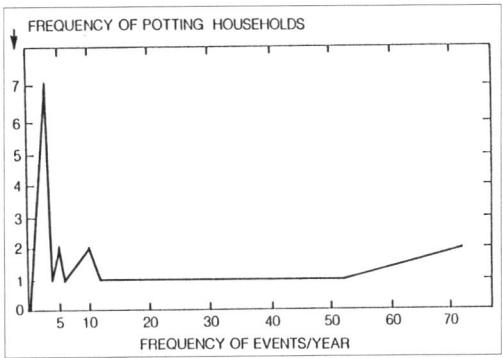

Fig. 3.2. Frequency of pottery making events per year for 25 Chanal potting households.

based production units, aggregated within a single community, producing for unrestricted regional consumption" (Costin and Hagstrum 1995:621). From an archaeological perspective, the Tzeltal region today would appear as scattered villages and homesteads with dispersed household production sites, along with a few specialist villages with nucleated production (see Costin 1991:27).

While most previous ethnoarchaeological pottery studies in Mesoamerica focused on full-time pottery-making specialists (e.g., D. E. Arnold 1971; Foster 1960; Reina and Hill 1978; R. H. Thompson 1974), the vast majority of pottery in Tzeltal Maya communities, such as Chanal, was produced on a domestic or elementary specialist level of production (see Table 3.1; Figure 3.2). The same might be said of Aguacatenango potters, except that in the last decade a few artisan specialists moved to the community from nearby Amatenango. However, the Amatenango potters had not yet trained any local potters.

Considering the low scale of production, it was not surprising that most Chanal and Aguacatenango potters belonged to the lower and middle economic ranks (see Chapter 4). For the 28 potting households in Chanal, 11 (39%) had low economic ranking, 16 (57%) had middle ranking, and only one (4%) of the households belonged to the upper economic ranking. Similarly, four of the five potting households in Aguacatenango were of low economic ranking while

TABLE 3.1.
Summary Data on Household (HH) Pottery Production in Chanal.*

HH #	Potters	Season	Events/ Year	Vessels/ Event	Range/ Year	Potter's Estimate	Combined/ Year
3	1	All Year	52–72	5–6	260–432	108	108–432
4	1	All Year	52–72	5–12	260–864	291–540	260–864
5	1	Mar	7+	?	?	14	14
6[1]	1	Jan–May	52–100	5	260–500	53	53–500
7	2	Mar	3	8–9	24–27	38–65	24–65
10	1	Jan–Mar	12	4–5	48–60	22	22–60
13	2	Dec–Mar	2–3	3–4	6–12	9–10	6–12
14	3	Jan–Mar	3	7	21	29	21–29
15	3	Dec–Mar	4–5	12–15	48–75	?	48–75
16	1	Feb–Mar	4	2–3	8–12	13–19	8–19
17	3	Dec	1	6–9	6–9	8–9	6–9
19	1	Dec–Mar	3	2–3	6–9	2–3	2–9
20	1	Jan–Mar	3	8–9	24–27	16	16–27
22	1	Jan–Feb	1	2	2	2	2
24	1	Jan–Mar	6	3–4	18–24	21	18–24
25	2	Apr	5–6	8	40–48	24–37	24–38
27	1	Dec	2	10–15	20–30	34–35	20–35
28	1	Mar	2–3	?	?	46–49	46–49
29	1	Jan–Feb	10	3	30–50	65–70	30–70
30	1	Jan–Apr	3	3–5	9–15	7–14	7–15
31	2	Dec–Apr	4–5	7–13	28–65	10+	28–65
35	1	Dec	3	2	4	5–9	4–9
37	2	Dec	2	6–8	12–16	7–8	7–16
41	1	Dec	1–2	2	2–4	5	2–5
42[2]	1	Jan–Mar	?	?	?	41	41
43	1	Apr	2–3	4–5	8–15	42	8–42
45	2	Dec–Apr	10+	4–6	40–60	325–335	40–335
48	2	Dec–Jan	2	20	40	65	40–65
53	1	Nov–Jul	3	2–3	6–9	36–37	6–37

*Range/year refers to the number of vessels produced per year, based on the potter's estimate of the number of pottery-making events per year and the number of vessels produced per event. Combined/year refers to the number of vessels produced per year, taking into account the potter's estimate of the number produced during the previous year (1976).

[1] Potter is semi-retired due to arthritis and now works only once a week.

[2] Polygamous household, in which household pottery is made by the second wife who lives in a small hamlet outside Chanal.

the fifth was of middle ranking. For wealthier households there was no economic pressure on the women of the household to learn pottery making. In many poorer households women did not make pottery simply because they did not know any potters who would teach them.

LEARNING ENVIRONMENT

In addition to economic need, the environment in which a potter learns the specialized skills and knowledge of pottery production plays an important role in determining her productive capacity as a potter (also see Spier 1976). As mentioned above, women who do not know a practicing potter are less likely to become potters, even though it would be economically advantageous for the household. Most of the potter's repertoire (i.e., the functional and stylistic diversity she can produce), as well as the amount of pottery she can consistently produce, are established during learning experiences early in her life. The following discussion outlines three important aspects of the learning environment, namely, social interactions associated with training, the relationship between teacher and pupil (teaching models), and the age at which the craft was learned. Pottery variability which results from different learning environments is discussed under the heading of microtraditions.

LEARNING INTERACTIONS

In Chanal, verbal exchange and visiting were the most common mechanisms associated with the spread of pottery making knowledge. Informal work groups, usually organized along lineage lines, were formed to collect raw materials and to share tools and facilities (e.g., temper grinding equipment or firing location). Although several women often worked together while modelling and firing pottery, there was no division of labor comparable to the "assembly-line" kind of production practiced in Amatenango (Hunt 1962:80). Even within work groups, each woman prepared her own clay, ground her own temper, and modelled and fired her own pottery. However, such groups do result in an information exchange between the participants, and this tends to lead to a low level of standardization in techniques and undoubtedly contributes to the formation of distinctive community styles (or vessel forms). These groups also function to reinforce kinship ties and neighborhood relations. The archaeological indicators of such activity would be similar to those caused by work exchange groups, which according to Hayden (1978:Table II), are characterized by a high level of homogeneity in work related tools and behavior (see Table 3.2). The intensity of work group interactions and consequent homogeneity in material patterning is related to

the frequency of pottery making events, the number of potters involved, and their ages.

Teaching of pottery making techniques is another reason for interaction that results in information exchange. Tzeltal girls received little formal training in pottery making. A pupil learned primarily through watching and experimenting on her own rather than through structured lessons. This was also true among Chuj potters interviewed in San Mateo Ixtatan in 1979 (see Hayden and Cannon 1984b), and appears to be a general rule even in large pottery-making centers like Amatenango and Chamula, and elsewhere (e.g., Longacre 1981:60; Stanislawski and Stanislawski 1978; Weigand 1969:31–32).

The scheduling of informal lessons depended upon the frequency of pottery-making events. Pupils would visit the teacher's home for periodic lessons, and on a less structured schedule if the teacher and pupil lived in the same household. It might be assumed that this form of learning would result in a high level of stylistic homogeneity between the work of teacher and pupil, but this does not seem to be the case in Chanal. New potters developed their own style over time, often resulting in very little resemblance between their work and that of their teacher(s). Additional influence existed in the form of imported vessels, which potters freely copied if they believed the imported ware to be an improvement on their own style.

Several Chanal potters, such as Tomasa Lopez Gomez (Household 7), claimed that they learned to make pottery primarily by watching their neighbors work, rather than from any specific teacher. This kind of informal learning, along with the copying of imported wares, results in an indirect flow of information on pottery making. Copying styles of pottery salvaged from abandoned housesites or archaeological sites are further examples of this form of learning (also see Stanislawski 1977). It is difficult to assess the effect that this kind of interaction has on the archaeological record. It may have very little effect (i.e., being a product of contemporary economic/market conditions), or it may be

TABLE 3.2.
Pottery-Making Learning Interactions.

Reason for Interaction	Predominant Mechanism	Archaeological Indicator
Teaching	Visiting	High Level of Stylistic Similarity
Economizing on Resources or Information Exchange	Communal Work Groups	High Level of Stylistic and Tool Form Similarity
Accidental Encounters or Indirect Information Exchange	Visual Observations and Verbal Encounters	High Stylistic Similarity or Imitation
Family Alliances or Migration	Personnel Exchange	Intrusion of Extracommunity Styles and Forms

the primary mechanism by which a generalized community style is developed and maintained. There is a recognizable "Chanal style" although there is a great deal of variation among the styles of individual potters within the community (see discussion under microtraditions).

A young girl's acquaintance with pottery making techniques often began with helping at minor tasks such as gathering raw materials and grinding temper. Tzeltal girls would begin by making miniature copies of the vessels made by their teachers. In one Chanal potter's household even some young boys made toy pots in play. The crude miniature vessels found at many archaeological sites have often been identified, and probably correctly, as the work of children or a potter's apprentice.

Potters began experimenting with pottery making over a wide range of ages. The range for Chanal, Aguacatenango, and San Mateo Ixtatan was 6 to 78 years, with a median age of 18 years (see Table 3.3). Hayden and Cannon (1984b:350) investigated the relationship between the intensity of production of the mother and age at which potting was learned in 18 households from Chanal, as well as Yolakitak, a hamlet of San Mateo Ixtatan. The amount of pottery produced per year in each household was plotted against the ages at which girls in the households had learned how to make pottery. Since the rela-

tionship appeared to be curvilinear, values for the number of vessels produced by potters in the girls' households were converted to logarithmic values. The resulting graph (Figure 3.3) illustrates a strong and significant negative correlation ($r = -.8586$) between the two variables. This shows that the intensity of production directly influenced the age at which a girl began learning the craft. Not surprisingly, the more intensely pottery was produced in the household of orientation, the earlier girls began to make pottery.

Pottery-making techniques and styles can also be affected by intercommunity personnel exchanges. Occasionally, a Chanaleño man will marry a woman from an outlying *paraje* or from outside the *municipio*. On even rarer occasions, a new family will move into the community. If new arrivals happen to be potters, then new techniques and styles might be introduced. The few Amatenango potters that moved to Aguacatenango, were spreading Amatenango forms and styles in that community. Such events must have also occurred in Precolumbian times (e.g., see Whallon 1968).

LEARNING MODELS
In households where pottery was produced primarily for domestic use, and the frequency of production was low, girls tended to learn pottery making later in life (often after mar-

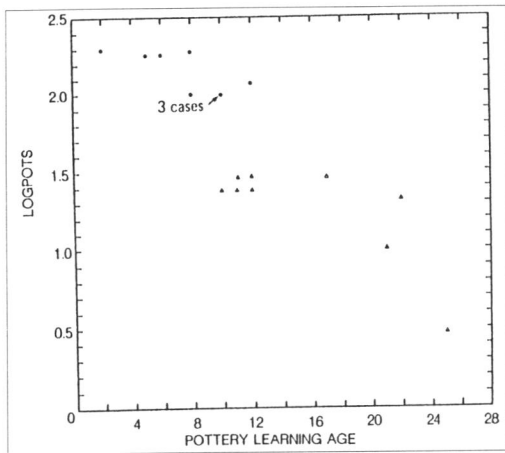

Fig. 3.3. Graphic relationship between the age at which individuals learned to make pottery as a function of the log of the frequency with which pottery was made in the household where the potters grew up.

riage), and they frequently learned their craft through non-kin relationships. In Chanal, three teaching models were most common, including, mother/daughter, spouse's mother/daughter-in-law, and non-kin teacher/pupil relationships (Table 3.4). Teaching networks can be relatively complex. In Chanal, Guadalupe Hernandez Gomez (Household 4), learned her craft after marriage from her husband's sisters and mother, then she in turn passed this knowledge on to her own daughter and her brother's wife's mother (another non-kin relationship). For Aguacatenango and San Mateo Ixtatan, mother/daughter and non-kin, and especially neighbor/neighbor, teaching relationships were the most common.

Similar learning patterns have been recorded among the Huichol of northern Mexico and the Hopi of the American Southwest. Among the Huichol, where each household made pottery for its own domestic use, girls generally learned how to make pottery only after they were married. They might follow recollected models from their mothers and grandmothers and older sisters, but usually took their final models from the family of their spouses (Weigand 1969:32). Hopi girls, who often grew up in households of el-

ementary or artisan specialists, learned from watching relatives or friends (Stanislawski 1977:400). If the older relatives of a household made pottery a girl might begin experimenting between five and 15 years of age. If her mother had small children to tend, then she might learn from her aunts or grandmother. If a girl's relatives did not make pottery, they might learn after marriage from potters in their husband's family or from their neighbors.

Hendry (1992:100) collected detailed information of pottery-making learning behavior in the specialist community of Atzompa, Oaxaca, during the 1950s. As in the Central Maya Highlands, pottery making was learned early and primarily from relatives (including in-laws). Learning was achieved informally through watching and imitating an expert. However, since pottery was being made in almost every household, observations were not restricted to one's own mother. Hendry (1992:111) notes that the primary motive for learning pottery making was financial. They made pottery to help support the family.

In Maya communities where pottery making was an economic specialty, such as Amatenango, Chamula, and the Chuj community of Yolakitak, since almost all women made pottery on a frequent basis, girls were more likely to learn pottery making at a young age and within their family of orientation, and especially from their mother or sisters (e.g., Howry 1976:150). Early in this century some Chamula men began to make large ritual cooking jars. This trade was originally learned from their mothers but later began to be passed on through father/son and brother/brother relationships. Among potters interviewed in Yolakitak, 24 (80%) said that they learned (or were learning) from their mothers while only six (20%) had learned (or were learning) though their spouse's family. Similarly, in Amatenango, girls began making pottery at about age 11 under their mother's tutelage and were experienced potters by the time they married, between the ages of 14 and 17 (J. Nash 1970:55). Two generations ago, however, girls were generally married at age

TABLE 3.3.
Approximate Ages at Which Pottery Making Was Learned in Four Maya Communities.

Community:	Chanal	Aguacatenango	San Mateo Ixtatan	Yolakitak	Total
Age Learned					
6	2	—	—	—	2
7	—	—	—	1	1
8	—	—	2	3	5
9	—	—	—	2	2
10	4	3	—	8	15
11	1	1	—	1	3
12	1	—	1	4	6
13	—	3	—	2	5
14	—	—	—	—	0
15	2	—	—	4	6
16	—	—	—	—	0
Unmarried	*10 (42%)*	*7 (58%)*	*3 (60%)*	*25 (93%)*	*45*
17	—	—	—	—	0
18	3	—	—	—	3
19	—	—	1	—	1
20	5	1	—	1	7
21	1	—	—	—	1
22	3	—	—	—	3
23	—	—	—	—	0
24	—	—	—	—	0
25	1	—	—	1	2
26	—	—	—	—	0
27	—	2	—	—	2
33	—	1	—	—	1
34	—	1	—	—	1
60	—	—	1	—	1
78	1	—	—	—	1
Married	*14 (58%)*	*5 (42%)*	*2 (40%)*	*2 (7%)*	*23*
Total	24	12	5	27	68
Median Age	18	13	12	10	13
Mean	18.7	18.4	21.4	11.8	16.0
s.d.	13.8	9.4	22.0	3.9	11.3

11 or 12, and a girl was more likely to learn pottery making from her mother-in-law.

Hayden and Cannon (1984a) viewed Maya craft-learning frameworks as a kin-extensive mode of craft learning based on the relative economic independence of the nuclear household. Craft learning tended to be dispersed between nuclear families and other households from both parents' sides of the kin network, as well as some unrelated individuals. Less than 30 percent of overall recorded craft learning for Chanal, Aguacatenango, San Mateo Ixtatan, and Yolakitak took place outside the family of orientation (see Table 3.5). However, when compared to other craft activities, pottery making proved to be the most variable in terms of kinds of teaching relationships and rated relatively low in terms of the strength of the family of orientation as a teaching unit.

TABLE 3.4.
Pottery-Making Teaching Patterns for Two Tzeltal Maya (Chanal and Aguacatenango) and
Two Chuj Maya (San Mateo Ixtatan and Yolakitak) Communities (Combined Teachers and
Pupils of Interviewed Potters).

Community:	Chanal	Aguacatenango	San Mateo Ixtatan	Yolakitak	Total
Family of Orientation					
Mother	34	6	10	24	74
Sister	0	1	0	0	1
Brother's Daughter	0	1	0	0	1
Son's Daughter	0	1	0	0	1
Subtotal (61%)	34	9	10	24	77
Mother's Kin					
Mother's Mother	0	0	1	0	1
Mother's Sister	0	1	0	0	1
Subtotal (1.6%)	0	1	1	0	2
Father's Kin					
Father's Mother	3	0	0	0	3
Father's Sister	1	2	0	0	3
Subtotal (4.8%)	4	2	0	0	6
Husband's Kin					
Husband's Mother	11	0	0	5	16
Husband's Sister	2	0	3	1	6
Subtotal (17.5%)	13	0	3	6	22
Spouses of Other Kin					
Son's Wife	1	0	0	0	1
Daughter's Sister-in-Law	1	0	0	0	1
Brother's Wife	1	0	1	0	2
Husband's Brother's Wife	1	0	0	0	1
Father's Brother's Wife	1	0	0	0	1
Father's Brother's Son's Wife	1	0	0	0	1
Subtotal (5.6%)	6	0	1	0	7
Non-kin (9.5%)	6	3	3	0	12
Total (100%)	63	15	18	30	

Statistical tests by Hayden and Cannon (1984b) suggested that lineage strength among Tzeltal and Chuj Maya strongly influenced whether a craft was learned from the immediate family, extended family, or nonkin. Nuclear family-centered craft learning in the three Maya communities tended to occur in households on either end of the economic scale, with poorer households having minimal or no cooperative relationships with other households, and richer households having the greatest degree of economic independence.

MICROTRADITIONS

Variability in the potter's learning environment is manifested in the formal functional, formal stylistic, and decorative stylistic diversity of her pottery. Such diversity is reflected in archaeological assemblages as pottery traditions. Bray and Trump (1970:236) define a pottery tradition as a sequence of "pottery

TABLE 3.5.
Teaching Patterns for Most Common Crafts (>10 cases) in Four Maya Communities.

Status of Teacher:	Family of Orientation	Father's Kin	Mother's Kin	Spouse's Kin	Other Spouses[1]	Other[2]
Craft (n):	%	%	%	%	%	%
Hatmaking (16)	93.8	—	—	6.2	—	—
Sewing (158)	82.3	0.6	—	2.5	1.3	13.3
Broommaking (20)	85.0	—	—	—	5.0	10.0
Glassworking (54)	77.8	1.8	—	—	3.7	16.7
Boneworking (26)	73.1	3.9	—	3.9	—	19.2
Weaving (58)	72.4	1.7	6.9	5.2	—	13.8
Fiberworking (80)	70.0	3.8	—	2.5	1.2	21.3
Construction (54)	64.8	3.7	3.7	3.7	—	24.1
Woodworking (13)	61.5	7.7	—	7.7	—	23.1
Furniture making (10)	60.0	—	—	—	—	40.0
Basketry (24)	45.8	—	—	12.5	8.3	33.3
Pottery making[3] (124)	56.5	4.8	5.6	19.4	7.3	6.4
All 12 Crafts (637)	70.8	2.5	2.0	6.6	2.7	15.4

[1] Includes self-taught craftspeople and non-kin teachers.
[2] Includes previous spouses, now living separately, and co-wives.
[3] Includes intended pupils of interviewed potters, and also those they are presently teaching.

styles which develop out of each other and form a continuum in time." At the regional level, the internal variations of a tradition are patterned around technological, formal, or stylistic aspects (Rands 1964). At the community level, pottery "microtraditions" can exist in the work of the individual potters, the potting lineage, and the potting work group, as well as the overall community style (see DeBoer 1984). The ethnographic study of pottery-making learning behavior provides insights into how microtraditions are established and perpetuated, how variations (innovations) occur, how socioeconomic, demographic, and spatial constraints affect their development, how much variability exists within and between all of these units, and how distinctive they will be archaeologically. For example, Hosler (1996) describes an Andean pottery-making community where newly established microtraditions (i.e., Hosler's "technological microstyles") can be identified at barrio, workshop, and intra-workshop levels, which reflect strong gender and class distinctions. Of particular interest

in this study is how competing intracommunity microtraditions can potentially create pottery variability at the household level.

Among Tzeltal potters, a microtradition might involve the transmission of information on both time-proven techniques and recent innovations. As at the level of regional pottery traditions, internal variations of a microtradition are patterned according to technological, formal, and stylistic aspects. Technological information concerns:

(1) the location and accessibility of various resources (i.e., clays, tempers, pigments, and fuels) and their relative quality;
(2) formulas for paste ingredients that specify which clays and tempers to use and in what amounts;
(3) instructions on production techniques, including the degree of grinding of clays and tempers, use of various potting tools, forming and finishing procedures, and kiln construction;
(4) scheduling of when to collect materials, prepare pastes, form, dry and fire vessels,

as well as lengths of time for aging clays, drying and firing;

(5) measures to insure production efficiency, such as the use of wasters to prevent fire marks on vessels, and the reuse of leftover materials and fuels.

Formal information concerns basic body shapes, addition of appendages, and remodelling (e.g., perforating, adding effigies), and details of proportion, including thickness of wall, base, and rim, location of handles, relative size, neck height, rim diameter, and curvatures. Lastly, stylistic information concerns surface treatments, such as burnishing or slipping, decoration, such as painting or embossing, and design complexity and specific motifs.

Variations, which are often subtle, in all these aspects could occur at the level of individual potter, lineage, work group, or community. However, technological quality seemed to be stressed over stylistic design. For example, potters who claimed to be able to identify the pottery of other potters put a strong emphasis on technological and formal indicators, that is, those closely related to function. Among the Tzeltal and Chuj, these included body shape, wall thickness, fineness of ground temper, shape of handle section, neck height, ratio of mouth diameter to maximum diameter, degree of polishing, size of punched holes, basal form, and also a variety of rim characteristics and variations in the forms of appendages (also see Hayden 1984). Similarly, Kalinga potters stressed formal criteria in recognizing the work of other potters (Longacre 1981:62). Further, innovation among the Tzeltal, as among the Tzotzil potters of Chamula (Howry 1978:248), tended to involve functional (rather than aesthetic) changes to vessel form.

Certain factors related to the learning environment are seen to affect variability (randomization) in microtradition patterning in nonspecialist communities. These factors include innovation, frequency of production, and the adequacy of potting materials. Stark and Longacre (1993) report innovation among the Kalinga in the form of genera-

Fig. 3.4. Single-handled cooking jar *(chikpin)* from Aguacatenango, modelled after an imported vessel form.

tional shifts in vessel forms and decorations. For the potters of Chanal innovation seems to be more on the level of the individual. Chanal potters began innovating early in their careers. Obviously, when a pupil was learning to make pottery she would try to duplicate the work of her teacher. However, in Chanal, potters seldom stayed strictly with the formal variants they were taught. Even within the bounds of material availability, the potter's personal skill, and her cultural traditions, a plethora of combinations of technique, form, and style was possible, and most potters were continually innovating and copying from other potters. Since decoration was generally absent, this was restricted mainly to vessel shape and changes in rim and handle form. For example, in one Chanal household, two daughters had copied their mother's vessels in terms of body shape, but each of the three potters made radically different rim forms (Table 3.6). Another Chanal potter invented a unique form of flat (everted) rim for her cooking pots, which, she claimed, allowed her to carry the vessels without spilling the contents. One Aguacatenango potter made a unique body form for her cooking pots that she copied from an imported jar form (Figure 3.4).

TABLE 3.6.
Vessel Body Shapes Made by Chanal Potters.

Body Shape*	Number of potters	SPH	ELV	ELH	OVA	OVB	CYL	HYP	FRS
1. *Poket*	26	2	6	1	15	6	—	1	1
2. *Chalten*	14	2	—	6	3	3	—	—	1
4. *Sets'*	14	3	4	1	2	—	2	—	3
7. *Oxom*	84	14	64	—	30	29	8	1	—
8. *Chikbin*	37	4	28	1	1	5	2	—	—
13. *Neochab*	9	1	3	—	3	—	—	—	3
14. *Chikpom*	12	9	1	—	2	4	—	—	—
18. *Chixnajab'il*	11	2	6	1	1	1	1	—	—

*Body shapes are derived from photographs: SPH=spherical; ELV=elliptical (vertical axis); ELH=elliptical (horizontal axis); OVA=ovaloid (widest diameter above center); OVB=ovaloid (widest diameter below center); CYL=cylinder; HYP=segmented hyperboloid; FRS=frustrum.

New sources of inspiration came more often from pottery acquired in the nearby hamlets of San Pedro and San Fernando, rather than from Amatenango pottery. For example, most Chanal potters made wide-mouth jars (*oxom*) and single-handle jars with a vertically elliptical body shape (*chikbin*). This form was also common in the hamlets of San Pedro, San Fernando, San Antonio, and Siberia. In contrast, the spherical and ovaloid body shapes, with widest diameter above the center, that are made in Amatenango were much less common in Chanal (see Table 3.6). The wide-mouth jar was the one type that all Chanal potters made, and it was most commonly imported from within the peripheral distribution zones. Amatenango cooking vessels were sold only locally, while most of the specialized vessel forms that Chanal imported from Amatenango were not made by Chanal potters. The major exceptions were the small and large hemispherical bowls *(poket)* which seemed to be direct copies of the imported Amatenango bowls.

One Chanal potter produced her own variant of the distinctive spiked Tojolabal censer, which is characterized by three or four straps meeting above the bowl and crowned by a bird effigy or cluster of spikes (Figure 3.5; see Deal 1982). The Chanal variant had three rows of spikes on each strap and a bird effigy, while the pedestal bowl was typical of Chanal censers. No other variants of the Tojolabal spiked censer were observed in Tzeltal communities.

According to the "standardization hypothesis," production intensity is reflected in increased product uniformity (Kvamme et al. 1996:116). Standardization is an aspect of pottery variability that is generally linked to full-time pottery specialization (e.g., D. Arnold and Nieves 1992; P. Arnold 1991b; Blackman et al. 1993; Costin 1991; Costin and Hagstrum 1995; Hagstrum 1985; Kvamme et al. 1996; Longacre et al. 1988; Sinopoli 1988). Costin and Hagstrum (1995:622) make a distinction between intentional and mechanical attributes of product standardization as a useful device for interpreting archaeological assemblages. Intentional attributes reflect the technical, morphological, and stylistic choices made by the potter, while mechanical attributes are introduced unintentionally due to the potter's training, skill, and experience.

In a recent review, Rice (1996b:179) stressed the distinction between standardization as a process and standardization as the outcome of that process (i.e., a characteristic

Fig. 3.5. Chanal variant of Tojolabal incense burner form.

of the pottery itself). She urged archaeologists to be careful not to confuse efforts to study the process with efforts to study the products. She suggests that the term "uniformity" would be more appropriate for the qualitative state of the products (Rice 1996b:179). Further, she suggests that ethnoarchaeogists do not study standardization as process due to the synchronic nature of their research. Instead, they focus on pottery uniformity, which can be used as time-series data for a particular group or region (Rice 1996b:180). This latter approach is used here, as ethnographic and ethnohistoric information is used to speculate on the nature of Tzeltal pottery specialization.

Some recent ethnoarchaeological studies indicate that the relationship between specialist production and standardization (uniformity) is not as clear as once believed. D. E. Arnold (1993:238–239) questions the value of paste uniformity as an indicator of specialization in the Quinua area of Peru. D. E. Arnold and Nieves (1992:94) found that product variation, which is believed to decrease as the process of standardization increases, was affected by the manufacturing technique used, market demands, and idio-

syncratic notions of the potter concerning vessel shape and dimensions. Longacre and others (1988) compared two Philippine potting groups and found that the full-time potters of Paradijon produced a much more uniform product than domestic Kilinga potters. However, London (1991) reports considerable variability in the work of craft specialists in Paradijon through the selection of clays, choices of manufacturing techniques, and the role of nonspecialists in assisting with finishing and decoration to meet production deadlines. Further, P. J. Arnold (1991b) found that part-time potters could achieve a product uniformity on par with that of full-time specialists in modern southern Veracruz communities. According to P. J. Arnold (1991b:364), they achieved this uniformity through measurements based on hand spans, the use of wooden stick measures, and normative ideas of vessel dimension. For nonspecialist communities like Chanal, it is probably the infrequency of production that prevents most potters from acquiring the skills needed to produce highly standardized vessels forms.

The less frequently a potter makes pottery, the more she must rely upon her memory to repeat the production sequence. Much of the innovation in form and style at the domestic level may be unintentional and unrepeatable. One example was witnessed, in Chanal, of pottery made over a period of several years by a single potter, in which there was very little similarity between vessels made a year or more apart. A similar "age effect" has been recognized as a source of design element variability in potting over time among both the Kalinga (M. Graves, cited in Longacre 1981:63) and the Hopi (Stanislawski 1978: 220–221). By contrast, among the strictly organized pottery-making households of Amatenango, where production was a year-round occupation, formal and decorative standardization caused an increase in microtradition patterning among household work groups. Furthermore, Amatenango potters were producing for a larger, regional market, in which the consumers had certain expectations about the quality and appearance of the product (e.g., form, weight, size, location of handles) which were beyond the capabilities of most Chanal potters. For nonspecialist potters, producing for their own household or neighbors, such expectations were less rigid. For the neighbor, convenience and the ability to barter for pottery were more important.

Reina and Hill (1978:231–251) related regional market expectations among Guatemalan Indian consumers to the concept of *costumbre* (literally "custom"), which stressed emulation and conformity of personal values at the community level. In other words, potters believed that they had to conform to *costumbre* to be competitive in the regional market. Such conscious conservatism in pottery production might contribute to the longevity of certain vessel forms recurring in the archaeological record, but it is more likely that the reason lies in the fact that generalized vessel forms have been successfully adaptive over time in relation to a stable agricultural subsistence strategy (see D. E. Arnold 1984b:16). In and around Chanal, as well as San Mateo Ixtatan, the mountainous terrain has excluded all but the traditional agricultural techniques (e.g., Wagner and Hotchkiss 1959).

One of the conclusions of D. E. Arnold's study of Pokom Maya pottery (1978a:58) was that pottery variability between communities can be related to differences in pottery-making resources between the communities. An example of this situation occurred in the Chanal area. Nine Chanal potters were asked why they did not make the narrow-mouthed jars *(kib)* which everyone bought from Amatenango. Six of them said that they had tried, but that the form was too difficult to make. One woman even believed that there was a god in the Amatenango church that told the potters how to make these vessels. The other women (and one of the former), however, gave logical environmental reasons for not making this vessel form. They admitted that the local clay was not fine and smooth enough, and that they do not have the fine sand temper used by Amatenango potters. Narrow-mouthed jars made with Chanal clay were said to collapse at the shoulders. A Tojolabal potter, interviewed in San Miguel, also claimed not to make this vessel form because she did not have the right kind of clay.

The archaeological importance of microtradition patterning was brought to a head during the 1960s. Studies of the spatial patterning of stylistic attributes in pottery assemblages from sites in the American Great Plains (Deetz 1965, 1968), New York State (Whallon 1968), and the American Southwest (Leone 1968; Longacre 1964) assumed that household or intracommunity microtraditions were sensitive to rules of residence (matrilocality) and descent (matrilineality). However, ethnoarchaeological studies among the Hopi and Tewa (Stanislawski 1977, 1978; Stanislawski and Stanislawski 1978) and the Kalinga (M. Graves, cited in Longacre 1981) suggests that the situation is more complex. The Stanislawskis pointed out that pottery teaching models tended to crosscut lineage, language, and residence barriers, while Graves found other factors beside learning frameworks contributing to design variability, such as seasonality of production and idiosyncratic tastes of the potter over time.

The relatively low level of production per household, and the loose nature of pottery-making instruction in a community like Chanal undoubtedly results in a residential mixing of microtradition information. Under these conditions, and given complex learning networks, it would be meaningless to try to make reliable inferences concerning residence behavior on the basis of stylistic (formal and decorative) variation within the community. It may be more reliable in communities like Chanal, and especially in specialist communities like Amatenango, to look for pottery patterning in terms of work group or neighborhood microtraditions (also see Longacre 1981:63; Stanislawski 1978:221). However, as the Hayden and Cannon (1984b) study indicated, the presence of pottery making itself may be related to household lineage strength, economic level, or various other factors. Further, a recent study by Ralph and Arnold (1988) among Yucatecan Maya potters identifies kinship ties as more important than socioeconomic status in determining the willingness to innovate.

ENVIRONMENTAL CONSTRAINTS ON THE LEVEL OF PRODUCTION

Another production-related factor that constrains the level of production within a potting household is the physical environment of the area in which the community is located. Maya pottery making is a resource-exploiting technology and therefore much of the behavior involved in the production of pottery is related to various environmental conditions. These conditions are particularly important in terms of the procuring of resources, the seasonality of pottery production, and the scheduling of pottery-making activities (D. E. Arnold 1975, 1985). A potter's understanding of the quality of materials available and the strategies for coping with climatic variations can exert considerable influence upon the diversity and quality of her product, as well as the volume of vessels she can produce.

From an archaeological perspective, the environmental constraints on pottery production are reflected primarily in the paste composition of pottery vessels, in terms of the material content and quality of the clay, the availability (or choice) of temper, clays, and slips, and the degree of firing. On the other hand, environmental constraints such as climate, which contribute to the quality and form of the finished product, are not easily determined from the archaeological record. D. E. Arnold (1978a:41) has also stressed the importance of outlining pottery-environmental relationships, so as not to obscure any possible environmental variables when determining how social and ideological conditions of manufacture articulate with pottery (techno-economic) data. For example, how do strategies related to procurement of raw materials affect the identification of potting households?

PROCUREMENT OF RAW MATERIALS

Resource procurement behavior in Chanal and Aguacatenango included the gathering of clay *(lum)*, the collecting of temper, in the form of calcite cobbles *(bax)* or fine-grained

Fig. 3.6. Clay source for potter in Chanal Household 35, located in Barrio Montaña.

sand *(hi')*, the collecting of firewood *(si'* or *zi')* for fueling the open kiln, and the storage of these raw materials before production. Clay, temper (calcite and/or sand), and firewood represented the minimum material requirements of the Tzeltal potter.

As a rule, clay was gathered from the nearest known source as it was needed. Aguacatenango potters all used the same clay source, which was located near a well beside the Pan American Highway (approximately 200 m from the entrance to the community). In Chanal, potters exploited several different clay deposits, a few of which were located within the community (Figure 3.6), while all others were located in the nearby hills. Only two Chanal potters used more than one source, both of whom used a particular red clay for making perforated jars *(chixnajab'il)* used as colanders. Chanal pottery-making resources were all found within community boundaries, and clay deposits were used communally and across barrio boundaries. One clay pit in an abandoned lot in barrio Nuevo was particularly popular. No potter interviewed travelled more than five km from her home to collect clay, and the mean distance of the potters' estimates was 1.04 km (see Table 3.7). This figure is consistent with Arnold's (1976:95) statement that the primary resources for pottery production generally occurred within five km of a pottery-making community.

In contrast, potters of Amatenango tended

TABLE 3.7.
Distance to Clay Source for Chanal and Aguacatenango Potters.

Chanal Household #	Barrio	Location of Source	Distance (km)*
3	Nuevo	(1) River	5.0
3	Nuevo	(2) Barrio Tamchai	1.0
4	Nuevo	Barrio Nuevo	3.0
6	Palm Aquil	Not specified	2.0
7	Nuevo	Barrio Nuevo	0.3
9	Nuevo	Barrio Nuevo	0.6
10	Centro	Not specified	3.0
13	Nuevo	Barrio Nuevo	1.0
14	Palma Aquil	Barrio Palma Aquil	1.0
15	Nuevo	Barrio Nuevo	0.2
16	Nuevo	Barrio Nuevo	0.2
17	Nuevo	Barrio Nuevo (?)	0.6
19	Centro	Not specified	0.7
20	Bajo	Barrio Bajo	0.3
24	Bajo	Barrio Tamchai	2.0
25	Tamchai	Barrio Nuevo	0.8
27	Tamchai	Edge of community	0.7
28	Nuevo	Barrio Nuevo (?)	0.5
29	Tamchai	Southeast edge of Barrio Tamchai	0.2
30	Bajo	Not specified	2.5
31	Nuevo	Barrio Nuevo (?)	0.5
35	Tamchai	Southeast edge of Barrio Tamchai	0.2
37	Tamchai	Barrio Nuevo	0.2
41	Tamchai	(1) Black clay from river	0.2
41	Tamchai	(2) Red clay from Barrio Tamchai	1.0
43	Palma Aquil	Near Palma Aquil cross	0.8
45	Nuevo	Barrio Nuevo	0.5
48	Tamchai	Barrio Nuevo	0.7
53	Tamchai	Barrio Nuevo	0.6
n=29			*mean*=1.04
			s.d.=1.11

Aguacatenango Household #	Barrio	Location of Source	Distance (km)*
35	First	Near highway	0.2
37	First	Near highway	2.0
38	First	Near highway	2.0
39	First	Near highway	0.2
n=4			*mean*=1.10
			s.d.=1.04

*Since Chanal is sectioned into blocks of roughly 50 m², distances to clay sources were recorded by blocks for most households and converted to kilometers. Distances for four Chanal households (#14, #24, #29, #41) and three Aguacatenango households (#37, #38, #39) were estimated from the community maps and informant information. (?)=probable source.

Fig. 3.7. Amatenango potter working on porch.

to use more than one clay source. During the 1979 season, the author, Russell Burlotte, and D. Donne Bryant (New World Archaeological Foundation) accompanied a family of Amatenango potters on an expedition to gather clay (also see Bryant and Brody 1986). The clay source was located upon the banks of a small stream on the outskirts of barrio Bochibal, which was about one km north of the community center. According to our informants, this was the only good source of the white (sakilum) and black (ekalum) clays, while the yellow clay (cannalum) at the source was too granular for body paste. The white clay was used for most vessel forms while the yellow clay was usually reserved for wide-mouth (cooking) jars. For better quality yellow clay they travelled to a source in barrio Madragal. According to June Nash (1985:335) the area where clay was collected is now inhabited, and the new residents collect and process it and truck it to the village center to sell to potters.

In Chanal, raw clay was mined with an improvised digging stick and wrapped in corn husks or palm leaves and transported in a maguey fibre bag (red). The Amatenango potters used a spatula-like metal blade with a wooden handle for mining clay. Hard clumps of clay were loosened using this tool, and these were beaten into subhemispherical shaped parcels (about 30–40 cm in diameter and weighing about 12 kg) to facilitate transport by tumpline (Figure 3.7). A stream

cobble was selected at random to serve as a beating tool. A parcel could be formed in about five minutes. One parcel was made for each person. The parcels were wrapped in cloth shirts and aprons and attached to a tumpline. The women then helped each other to lift and strap the bundles onto their backs. According to our informants, one clay parcel was needed to make one large narrow-mouthed jar (cantaro) or four large tripod vases (macetas).

Temper is an additive that affects the working properties of the clay paste (D. E. Arnold 1971:39). Chanal and Aguacatenango potters added a nonplastic crystalline calcite (bax) temper to their clay body. Calcite cobbles were collected in the hills around Chanal and in the warmer areas below the community. Informant estimates on the distance to calcite sources ranged between two and eight km (with a mean of 4.9 km). Aguacatenango potters also had a ready source of calcite in the hills around the community (see Table 3.8). One potter however, claimed to use a source at a distance requiring one-half day for a round trip.

Amatenango potters, and also the two Amatenango potters living in Aguacatenango, used a fine-grained dolomite sand temper for vessels not intended for use on the hearth (Heyman 1960). This sand was gathered locally in both communities. The Aguacatenango potters collected sand from an outcrop about 400 m from the main highway. The potters of Amatenango used three different sand tempers that they identified by color (black, white, and yellow). The potters of the northern Tzeltal community of Tenango also used ground sandy limestone (hi') as a temper (Redfield and Rojas 1939:111) and the Tzotzil Maya of Chamula added sand and ground chert (pedernal) to their potting clay (Pozas 1977:287).

The other essential resource was the fuel for the potting fires. Potters in Chanal gathered local oak, pine bark, and pine kindling for this purpose. One Aguacatenango potter claimed to use local cypress wood as a fuel. Amatenango, on the other hand, was defor-

TABLE 3.8.
Distance to Calcite Sources for Chanal and Aguacatenango Potters.

Chanal Household #	Barrio	Location of Source	Distance (km)*
4	Nuevo	River	5.0
6	Palma Aquil	River	5.0
10	Centro	Not specified	8.0
14	Palma Aquil	River	5.0
20	Bajo	Not specified	4.0
28	Nuevo	Mountain	?
30	Bajo	Lowlands	5.0
48	Tamchai	Not specified	2.0
n=8 (mean based on 7)			*mean=4.86*
Aguacatenango Household #	**Barrio**	**Location of Source**	**Distance (km)***
35	First	Mountain	3.75 (1/2 legua)
37	First	Mountain	2.0
38	First	Mountain	1/2 day return
39	First	Mountain	0.3
n=4 (mean based on 3)			*mean=2.02*

*Distances for three Chanal households (#4, #6, #14) were estimated from community maps and informant information.

ested within several kilometers radius due to its pottery-making activities (Howry 1973), and Amatenangeros travelled several kilometers to the southeast of the community with small carts to obtain firewood (Figure 3.8). Oak is the preferred fuel, but pine is more frequently used due the diminishing supply of oak (Bryant and Brody 1986:77).

Energy was also expended in obtaining certain pottery-making tools. Quartzite pebbles seemed to be used universally among Tzeltal, and also Tzotzil and Tojolabal, potters, for burnishing pottery. Most Chanal potters, and native Aguacatenango potters, acquired these smoothing stones (*alisadores*) locally. Smoothing stones made from other materials were only found in three of the surveyed households. One Chanal woman used an avocado pit, while one other used a cue ball that her husband had picked up at a pool hall in coastal Chiapas, and in Aguacatenango, one potter used two dried clay balls to produce a burnished effect. Most active potters tended to save particularly good

stones while occasional potters tended to throw them away (or misplace them) after one use. The curation of smoothing stones was very prominent among Amatenango potters, and also among the Amatenango potters living in Aguacatenango. Amatenango potters seemed to go great distances to acquire good smoothing stones, including places such as El Puerto (8 km) and Venustiana Carranza (60 km). According to Bryant and Brody (1986:83), Tenam Puente, located about 50 km southeast of Amatenango, was another important source for quartz smoothing stones. They also indicate that quartz smoothing stones are very common in Late Classic house mounds at Tenam Puente, and suggest that the people of that site may have traded these stones throughout the Central Plateau in prehistoric times.

Smoothing stones were chosen with great care and different parts of a stone served different functions, and were even given different names (Figure 3.9). According to one informant, only the ends of the stones were

Fig. 3.8. Amatenangeros returning with cartloads of firewood for pottery making (Photograph by D. Donne Bryant).

Fig. 3.10. Small travertine boulder being used by Aguacatenango potter for mixing pigments.

Fig. 3.9. Pebble smoothing stones with working edges appearing as lighter gray in photograph, Aquacatenango Household 35.

used for smoothing while the sides of flat stones might be used to form the inside of a vessel rim. John Clark (New World Archaeological Foundation) attempted to purchase a smoothing stone from a family of Amatenango potters, and after failing on one attempt, persuaded the grandmother to sell him a stone from a collection that had belonged to her mother (Clark personal communication, 1979). She produced a small bowl full of stones and sold him a damaged one for 10 pesos ($.50). These stones were all highly polished from use and the one purchased had visible striations and a highly lustrous shine on one end (also see Hodges 1964:31). Clark suggested that the great

value and high degree of curation of these stones may be attributed to the highly commercial atmosphere of the community.

Some potters also visited archaeological sites to find *manos* and *metates* for grinding up calcite. These were often passed on from mother to daughter. In fact, both Amatenango potters living in Aguacatenango had received *manos* and *metates* in this way. One Aguacatenango potter also used a small travertine boulder *metate* for grinding pigments (Figure 3.10). This was found to the south of Aguacatenango, near the hamlet of El Puerto.

SEASONALITY

Seasonal changes of weather and climate have a pronounced affect on the frequency of pottery-making activities, and especially in terms of drying newly formed vessels and firing (see also Papousek 1974; Rice 1987: 315). Drying is an extremely important and very delicate step in pottery production. Water occurs in the capillary spaces between clay particles and is also chemically bound to the crystal structure of the clay (D. E. Arnold 1976:96; Shepard 1976:72, 81). If vessels dry too rapidly, a dangerous situation develops where the unevenness of drying or excessive shrinkage may cause cracking, and if the vessel is not sufficiently dry, water trapped in the vessel can cause damage during firing due to excessive shrinkage or the formation of steam (D. E. Arnold 1976:97; Shepard 1976:72, 81). Similarly, O'Neale (1976:56) suggests that the length of the drying period may be inversely related to the proportion of vessels broken during firing.

In Tzeltal communities, clay was often allowed to sit in reused pottery vessels which caused it to absorb more water and thus increase its plasticity before modelling. Subsequent removal of water from the clay body caused the loss of plasticity and resulted in a durable vessel form. By air drying the vessels before firing most of this water was removed, and any remaining water could be removed in a pre-firing process. Instead of pre-firing, Chanal potters would allow a longer drying period. The Baers' (1950:39) reported a similar situation among the Lacandon Maya of Petha.

Climatic dampness has several adverse effects on pottery production. According to D. E. Arnold (1976:97), it increases the drying time necessary between manufacture and firing and thus increases the susceptibility of the pottery to breakage. It weakens the vessel walls after partial drying, causing malformation, cracking, or breaking, and reduces the firing temperature by dampening fuel. Further, dampness may cause breakage, blackening and irregular heating.

The rainy season in Chanal, Aguacatenango, and Amatenango was from June to September. Even potters who worked year-round produced less pottery during this period of relative high humidity. Chanal potters claimed that rainy weather, especially in July and August, often caused the pottery to fall apart. Potters who worked year-round moved potting activities indoors on rainy days and sometimes even fired their pottery in the kitchen hearth. During the rainy season, drying pottery was generally stored in the kitchen rafters over the hearth.

The reduction in potting activity in Chanal during the rainy season is illustrated in Figure 3.11, which records the number of potters

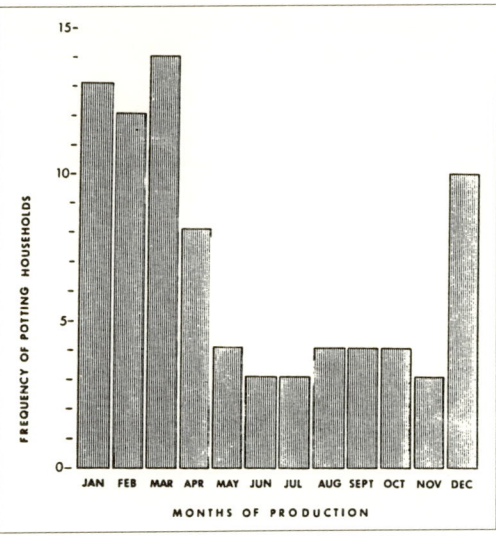

Fig. 3.11. Seasonal flux of pottery making in Chanal.

who worked during each month of the year in 1976. Only three Chanal pottery-making households worked year-round while most others worked only during the winter months of December to March. Even in the Chuj potting community of Yolakitak, all potters produced pottery intensively only during the dry months (March to April) and only occasionally during the rest of the year. June Nash suggested that the main deterrent to pottery production in Amatenango during the rainy season was the lack of a closed kiln (1970:57). However, the rainy season also benefitted pottery making in Amatenango, in that clay could be more easily gathered when it was damp (J. Nash 1970:48). This explains why huge stockpiles of clay parcels were observed in the porches of Amatenango households during the summer of 1977. Even during the dry, sunny months of January and February, high winds complicated drying, and therefore caused a reduction in output in Amatenango (M. Nash 1961:118).

SCHEDULING

Prolonged bad weather might throw off the scheduling of potters who work year-round. This could be overcome by overproducing on sunny days during the rainy season or by working inside on rainy days and firing several times on the first sunny day. Seasonal variations in climate also caused scheduling conflicts with various social and subsistence activities. The latter include the size and local importance of certain festivals, relative success of other economic activities, and the number of other commitments of the potter.

Non-potting Tzeltal households tended to restock their pottery inventories during the week of an important festival. Major pottery-making communities such as Amatenango reached peak production capacity just before and during the larger festivals of local importance (see M. Nash 1961:187–188). This did not affect the production of most Chanal potters unless they were commissioned to make vessels for a *cargo* official for a particular festival.

Other economic activities also affected the scheduling of pottery production. In a year when *milpa* production was down pottery making could provide an important income supplement for a household. Pottery making was always an important income supplement in Amatenango, and especially in years of crop failure (Hunt 1962:81). In Aguacatenango, where there were few potters, crop failure was more likely to result in a higher migration rate for work on coastal plantations (Hunt 1962:81). Most Aguacatenango women made blouses for sale to tourists in San Cristóbal de las Casas. One woman said that she only made pottery when she was not busy making blouses.

The number of small children a potter had also limited her production volume. This would be especially significant in communities such as Chanal and Aguacatenango where potters tended to work separately, and child care would take precedence over pottery making. However, even the well-organized production of Amatenango potters was considerably restricted by the presence of small children (M. Nash 1961).

Summary of Environmental Constraints

Several environmental factors affected the time and location of pottery production, and also paste composition, forms, and quality of the vessels produced. The ability of the individual potter to deal with these constraints upon pottery production had a tremendous influence upon the variability of her product (i.e., diversity and volume). Varying outlays of time were necessary for the procurement of clay, tempers, and fuels. In Chanal and Aguacatenango, resources were gathered from the nearest available source as they were needed. This was seldom outside a five km radius of the community. Such procurement strategies, after Bishop and others (1982:317), might be characterized as either nondiscriminating, with little preference for variants of available resources, or discriminating, with concentration on resources with specific qualities. Communities that specialized in pottery making, such as Amatenango, tended to exploit a larger variety of potting materials and were willing to travel further to procure them (i.e., a specializing procurement strategy; Bishop et al. 1982:317). Similarly, DeBoer (1984) found that among the Shipibo-Conibo potters, Zipf's principle of least effort did not account for all procurement behavior when distance to resources was considered. However, as with the Shipibo-Conibo, the procurement behavior of Amatenango potters might also, to some extent, depend on social factors such as trade connections and kin distributions. This was particularly true of the more exotic materials, such as pigments and smoothing stones.

Certain activities such as drying and firing of pottery were very susceptible to seasonal fluctuations of weather and climate. These fluctuations also affected scheduling of pottery-making activities in that they might conflict with cultural activities, such as festivals, agricultural tasks, and child care. Although no major factors were identified which significantly affected the interpretation of pottery variability within communities, on an intercommunity level, these factors were obviously important in accounting for technological variability associated with different levels of household production, and especially in terms of paste composition.

Fig. 3.12. Calcite *(bax)* grinding equipment, cobble *mano* and reused *metate.*

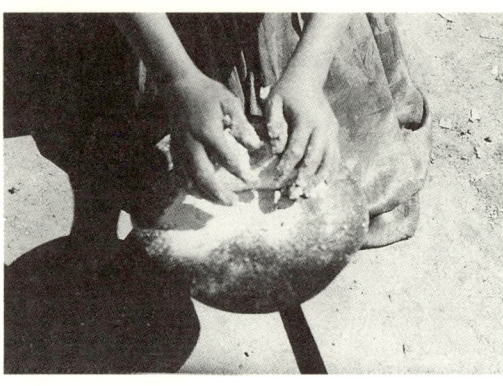

Fig. 3.14. Chanal potter adding ground calcite to raw clay.

Fig. 3.13. Amatenango potter grinding calcite (Photograph by D. Donne Bryant).

PRODUCTION ACTIVITIES

An additional constraint on the level of production attained by an individual potter, although admittedly less important than those already discussed, was her expertise, or efficiency. Actual production activities of temper preparation, modelling (or forming), drying,

finishing, and firing of vessels were relatively consistent for all potting households in Chanal and Aguacatenango and were not drastically different from activities of the larger pottery-making centers. However, differences occurred at both the qualitative and quantitative levels. For example, potters who sold their vessels had to produce a better quality of vessel, quickly and efficiently, and a wide variety of functional types to be competitive. They also required a larger, and often more specialized, tool kit (see Tables 3.9 and 3.10). This seems to be generally true of any specialist versus domestic producer. The median number of tools used by Chanal potters was four. Only two of the 15 (13%) potters who produced exclusively for domestic use used more than four tool forms, while eight of the 13 (62%) potters who produced for sale used more than four tool forms. Variations in pottery-making activities in Chanal and Aguacatenango are discussed below, with special emphasis on pottery-making tool diversity, degree of cooperation among potters, and their efficiency at producing a durable product.

The first two procedures involved in pottery production, digging of clay and gathering of calcite cobbles, were discussed in the section on procurement of resources. Behavior involved with the preparation of the plastic clay body consisted of converting the calcite cobbles into fine grains or powder, and

Fig. 3.15. Chanal potter working clay disk into bowl-like base of single-handle jar *(chikpin).*

Fig. 3.17. Chanal potter adding final coil to single-handle jar *(chikpin).*

Fig. 3.16. Chanal potter making third coil in cooking vessel construction.

Fig. 3.18. Chanal potter adding handle to single-handle jar *(chikpin).*

the clay of vessels not destined for use in hearths.

PREPARATION OF CLAY BODY

mixing the ground calcite with raw, aged clay (i.e., clay that had been allowed to sit and absorb moisture). The two Amatenango potters living in Aguacatenango followed the Amatenango practice of adding sand temper to

The grinding of calcite temper was generally done with a damaged or broken *mano* and *metate,* or a sandstone boulder *metate* like the one recorded at the Coxoh site of Coneta (Hayden 1976). In Chanal these were often shared by one or more related households. Calcite grinding generally took place

TABLE 3.9.
Pottery-Making Tool Classification (Adapted from Scheufler 1968).

Working Process	Task Requirements	Tools and Equipment
Clay Mining		
Digging	to dig clay	digging stick (metal blade or improvised)
Maintenance of clay	to prevent clay from drying to quickly	corn husk, palm leaf, rag, or plastic wrap
Transport of clay	to carry clay and/or calcite	woven maquey-fiber bag *(red)*; tumpline
Storage of clay and temper	to temporary storage materials	reused pottery vessel, wooden box, tin can, or gourd
Treatment of Clay		
Reduction of calcite	to break up cobbles	hammerstone
Grinding	to grind temper and/or pigments to fine powder	reused *mano* and *metate*; flat limestone boulder
Mixing clay and temper	to prevent dispersal of materials while kneading	three-legged stool *(matsul mate)*; wooden square *(cha'tay)*
Construction of Vessel		
Forming (Modelling)	to support vessel while forming	three-legged stool, wooden square, precursory wheel
Temporary clay storage	to store clay for retrieval while modelling	wooden square, stone cobble, three-legged stool
Moistening of fingers and clay	to store water for moistening	reused pottery vessel, bucket
Drying and Finishing		
Drying	to store newly made vessels	kitchen rafters
Perforating	to make holes in vessel wall	pointed stick, nail, knitting needle
Fettling	to remove excess clay	knife, reused machete, roof tile fragment
Smoothing and Consolidating	to rub dried vessel	river cobble *(alisador)*, avocado seed, hard clay ball
Decorating		
Incising	to carve details	knife
Painting and Slipping	to mix paint or slip	bowl
	to apply paint or slip	cane brush with frayed end or feather tip
	to guide design application	decorated potsherd
Firing		
Pre-firing	to support vessels	planks
Preparing kiln (open fire)	to prepare firing area	open space *(horno)*
	to fuel kiln	oak bark, cypress, resinous pine
	to form kiln	pyramid of kindling and stone props
Firing	to support vessels and fuel	stone cobbles
	to protect vessels from fuel	potsherd wasters
	to adjust fuel	long pole
Dismantling kiln	to remove vessels	long pole

TABLE 3.10.
Distribution of Various Pottery-Making Tool Forms in Chanal and Aguacatenango.

Working Process and Tool	Chanal Households (n=31)	Aguacatenango Households (n=5)	Total
Temper Preparation			
Hammerstone	2	1	3
Mano	18	5	23
Metate	21	4	25
Modelling			
Three-legged Stool*	2	—	2
Wooden Square	31	4	35
Stone Clay Support	1	1	2
Water Container*	3	1	4
Finishing			
Knife (for fettling)	12	4	16
Rag*	2	—	2
Smoothing	29	4	33
Perforator	2	1	3
Scraper (for fettling)	—	1	1
Slip Mixing Container	—	1	1
Paint Brush	1	2	3

*Low frequency is due to inadequate recording of the use of this item in pottery making.

on the potter's household patio or on the patio of another household where the potter worked (see Table 3.11). Most of the debris from this activity would eventually be swept to the edge of the patio (see Chapter 5). However, archaeologists might expect small portions of the calcite powder and scattered crystals to be incorporated into the hard patio floor, especially if sweeping was not done immediately and the same location was used each time (Deal 1988a). This activity was generally done a day or two before each pottery-making event, while some potters preferred to prepare a large batch to last for several events. Some potters also kept a cobble hammerstone on hand for reducing the calcite cobbles before grinding (Figures 3.12, 3.13) or used their calcite grinding *mano* as a hammerstone.

The mixing of raw clay and temper to form a clay body was done by kneading just before forming (Figure 3.14). This operation was often done on a small three-legged stool *(matsul mate)* or on a small square wooden plank *(cha'tay)*, where it was left in storage during the forming process. One potter kept a flat cobble on her patio that served as a clay storage stand while she was modelling. An Aguacatenango potter used her calcite grinding *metate* for this purpose.

Clay mixing, like calcite grinding, generally took place on the household patio (or patio of another household). Besides the stand for clay, a container of water was kept nearby for dampening the clay and moistening the potter's fingers.

FORMING OF CLAY SHAPE

In 1977, project members were fortunate to be able to observe and photograph two Chanal potters at work. One woman, Catarina Gomez Moreno, was an occasional domestic potter, while the other woman, Juana Lopez Gomez, would be considered an elementary specialist. Juana produced the best quality pottery of all the Chanal potters interviewed and was the only Chanal potter to experiment with painting her pottery.

The time required to model a small wide-mouth jar *(olla)*, from clay preparation (excluding the grinding of calcite temper) to clay shape, was between 20 and 30 minutes for both potters. A three-legged stool served as a stand on which raw clay and temper were kneaded together. When the right consistency was attained, the clay was set aside and just enough tempered clay was removed to form a flat disc-shaped base. This disc was then worked into a shallow, roughly smoothed bowl, using the palm of the hand, thumb, and forefinger (Figure 3.15). Following this, successive coils, approximately two cm in diameter, with a length approximately the circumference of the vessel at the level where it was to be added, were rolled between the palms and added to the base. The first coil was attached to the rim of the shallow base and the walls were smoothed. The second coil, which was much thinner, was added to the interior around the base and was smoothed into the base and lower body of the vessel (Figure 3.16). Additional coils of the larger size were added until the desired height was reached (Figure 3.17). These coils were only roughly smoothed, and mostly on the interior of the vessel. The last coil added was smoothed and extended into a flaring rim. The body coils were then smoothed together, and the belly was extruded by smoothing with the fingers. Lastly, the rim was worked into its final form, and the vessel was ready for drying.

In her demonstration, Juana continued to model her small jar into a pitcher. This was accomplished by adding a handle and making the mouth of the vessel more elliptical (Figure 3.18). To add the handle, a section of the rim was squeezed to raise it above the rest of the rim. Another coil was rolled and attached to this raised section and smoothed into it. A slight crook was made in the coil raising it above the rim. The bottom foot of the handle was attached to the shoulder and smoothed into place. Final touches consisted of smoothing the rim and body with frequent wetting of the fingers. It is important to note that a potter will sometimes use the leftover kneaded clay from a forming event to quickly model a small all-purpose bowl *(sets')* rather than curating the clay for another occasion or mixing it with some untempered clay. It is significant that almost all of the examples of this bowl form found in Chanal were recorded in the households of potters. Other households also needed all-purpose bowls but generally used industrially made bowls.

DRYING TO PRODUCE HARD SHAPE

Newly formed vessels were dried before firing to reduce plasticity through dehydration, and thereby created a "hard shape." The critical effects of drying on production success have been discussed. Special care was taken to insure that vessels would dry properly. For example, Chamula potters wedged sticks into the mouths of drying vessels to prevent twisted lips (Rus 1969:3). In Chanal and Aguacatenango vessels were dried outside in the shade on sunny, windless days. Otherwise they were dried indoors in the shade, in the rafters, or by the fire at night. The length of time that vessels were allowed to dry varied from a few days to as long as two months in one Chanal household. Breakage due to cracking or accidental disturbance was very likely to occur during this process. If a vessel was damaged while drying it could be ground up and its clay mixed with more prepared clay to form new vessels.

Vessels that had been partially dried to "leather hardness" received functional and decorative finishing before they were fired. In Chanal this included polishing, perforating and fettling. Fettling techniques, employed to tidy up newly made vessels (see Hodges 1964:31), included the removal of excess clay from the inside of a colander after the perforations had been made. Small metal nails, pointed sticks, bone awls, or knitting needles were used for making perforations. Basal trimming was another fettling technique by which excess clay around the base of the vessel was removed after forming. A reused machete or knife usually served this function. Polishing (or smoothing) was both a functional and decorative technique. Rubbing the surface of a hard vessel body with a quartzite pebble reduced porosity by compacting the surface of the clay, while at the

TABLE 3.11.
Location of Pottery-Making Activities in Households of Two Tzeltal and
Two Chuj Maya Communities.

Tzeltal:	Chanal: (n=29)			Aguacatenango: (n=5)		
Activity:	Temper Grinding	Modelling	Firing	Temper Grinding	Modelling	Firing
Location:						
Main House	2	2	1	1	3	—
Kitchen	1	2	8	—	—	—
Patio of Self	20	24	6	1	1	—
Patio of Kin	2	1	—	—	—	—
Circum-patio	3	—	10	2	—	1
Garden	—	—	1	—	—	1
Pathway	1	—	—	—	—	—
Abandoned Site	—	—	1	—	—	—
Outside Sitio	—	—	2	—	—	—

Chuj:	San Mateo Ixtatan: (n=9)			Yolakitak: (n=13)		
Activity:	Temper Grinding	Modelling	Firing	Temper Grinding	Modelling	Firing
Location:						
Structure*	2	2	7	11	12	6
Patio	3	7	1	1	—	4
Circum-patio	—	—	—	—	—	2

*Main structure and kitchen are generally combined in both Chuj communities.

same time, each stroke of the tool imparted a small, smooth, decorative facet on the vessel. Amatenango potters did their compacting before the vessel was slipped and painted. The use of smoothing stones is a widespread practice in Mesoamerica. Krotser (1980:130) notes that potters of Tenochtitlán, were forced to use large round seeds to polish pots because suitable stones were not available.

Only one Chanal potter had experimented with painting. She used oil paints and followed designs in her son's art book from school to decorate small wide-mouth jars. The two Amatenango potters living in Aquacatenango followed the Amatenango prac-

tice of painting certain vessel forms. Painting was done with a brush, fashioned from a piece of cane *(carrizo)*, frayed at one end, or fitted with a feather tip. One potter had a special *metate*, made from a travertine boulder, for grinding her pigments. Black, red, yellow, and white pigments were purchased from other communities. In 1979, a palm-sized portion cost about five pesos ($.25).

FIRING

The final production process is the firing of finished vessels. According to Colton (1939: 63), there are three fundamental principles involved in this process: (1) fuel must be

Fig. 3.19. Chilil potter firing single large vessel.

supplied that will attain temperatures between 500 and 1000 degrees centigrade; (2) heat radiation must be minimized, and (3) the burning fuel must be kept from touching the objects being fired.

Unfortunately, we did not get measurements for firing temperatures for Chanal and Aguacatenango. However, they must have been less than the larger pottery fires of Amatenango, which have been measured at 900 degrees centigrade (Heyman 1960). Heat radiation was minimized by building a pyramid of fuel around the vessels to be fired and using stones to hold the fuel and vessels in place. Colton called this arrangement a "tem-porary kiln" (1939:64), in which the ashes held their form during the firing process and prevented heat radiation. A similar arrangement was used by the Maghreb potters of North Africa (Balfet 1965:167). Pottery sherd "wasters" were placed between the fuel and the pottery to prevent the burning fuel from touching the vessels being fired. Despite this precaution each vessel received some exterior fireclouding (or "firemarks"). D. Donne Bryant observed an Amatenango potter actually break up an unused *comal* to get a suitably sized waster (personal communication, 1979).

Chanal potters and potters in peripheral communities generally fired in small batches of around five or six vessels, or two to four medium or large vessels (Figure 3.19). Very large wide-mouth jars *(oxom)* or unrestricted plates *(samets)* were likely to be fired separately. A special open kiln for *samets* was observed in the Huistan *paraje* of San Pedro. A single vessel was supported on three stones or broken vessels (firedogs), and a pyramid of kindling was built around the vessel. The fire was set using kindling and bark placed under the vessel between the supports. Similarly, in Chamula, Howry (1978:247) reported considerable variation in the openness of the kiln and fuel size between male and female potters, and especially *samet* makers.

Fig. 3.20. Amatenango potters dismantling open potting hearth (Photograph by D. Donne Bryant).

Fig. 3.21. Kitchen pottery firing, San Mateo Ixtatan, Guatemala. Three vessels are being fired beneath the wood while three others are being prefired outside.

In Amatenango, potters generally fired much larger batches of vessels (several dozen) and often had two or more fires going at once, or had vessels in different stages of firing (Figure 3.20). The probable reason for these large bonfires was fuel conservation, since wood had to be carted in from several kilometers to the southeast of the community (also see Hodges 1964:36; Nicklin 1979:448). All Amatenango pottery was given a preliminary prefiring to complete dehydration, which began with the drying process (Figure 3.21). During prefiring, vessels were placed on a rectangle of boards, or in a circle on the ground, and a small fire was set in the middle. Each vessel was turned several times to ensure that all areas were heated. One final firing, of approximately six dozen vessels, in the streets of Amatenango was timed at just under one half hour (see Foster 1967:114, Figure 8). The fires were tended constantly, with long poles being used to adjust the position of the burning firewood.

AN ETHNOARCHAEOLOGICAL CLASSIFICATION OF TZELTAL POTTERY

According to Lewis Binford (1968:271), " . . . if archaeologists and ethnologists are to

work with common problems, their observations must be geared toward gathering data on the same variables, despite the obvious differences in their fields of observations." It follows from this line of reasoning that if ethnologists (or ethnoarchaeologists) and archaeologists wish to compare data sets based on observations of the same variables, then (1) similar methods of measuring and analyzing these variables should be used whenever possible (see Chapter 6), and (2) a common classification system should be used when dealing with the same problems (also see Read 1982:57; Thompson 1991:341). In order to establish accord between this ethnographic pottery study and current Maya archaeological studies, Tzeltal pottery is classified here using the general structure and terminology of the *type-variety approach* of pottery analysis. This approach has been well established among Mayanists since the early 1960s (for discussion see E. W. Gifford 1976; Matheny 1970; Sabloff and Smith 1970; Sinopoli 1991:51–53; Willey et al. 1967). However, the present study differs somewhat from the standard type-variety approach in that it addresses production and socioeconomic questions and therefore uses formal-functional types rather than the customary stylistic types. The latter have been used primarily to address problems of culture history and regional pottery exchange. This study does address some problems concerning stylistic variation, although these are dealt with under the concept of ware.

THE TYPE CONCEPT

According to Hayden (1984:80) typology refers to systems of categorization which aim at revealing information (e.g., evolutionary, functional, technological, social) about the nature of human behavior in relation to artifacts. The ultimate aim of any typology is to *classify objects in order to solve anthropological problems* (Hayden 1984:80; also see Brown 1982; Hill and Evans 1972; Taylor 1948:127). Similarly, Rice (1996a:153) has suggested that "types are merely analytical tools in service to a research design" and that styles may someday be perceived in the same

TABLE 3.12.
Summary of Tzeltal Formal/Functional Types and Their Relative Frequencies Based on
Household Inventory Counts.

VESSEL TYPES:	TZELTAL (SPANISH)	CHANAL	AGUACATENANGO
Domestic Types:	*Ten Types:*	*n = 2506 (74.94%)*	*n = 3426 (80.31%)*
1. Small Hemispherical Bowl	*poket* (apastli)	209 (6.25%)	440 (10.31%)
2. Small Restricted Bowl	*sets'* (vasija)	16 (0.48%)	57 (1.34%)
3. Small Elliptical Bowl	*chalten* (sarten)	38 (1.14%)	88 (2.06%)
4. Small Frustrum Bowl	*sets'* (cazuela)	44 (1.31%)	8 (0.09%)
5. Unrestricted Plate	*samet* (comal)	223 (6.67%)	115 (2.06%)
6. Frustrum Solid	*makil sti'* (tapa)	5 (0.15%)	1 (0.02%)
7. Small Wide-Mouth Jar	*oxom* or *pin* (olla)	1438 (43.01%)	526 (12.33%)
8. Single-Handle Jar	*chikbin* (jarro)	187 (5.59%)	1706 (39.99%)
9. Large Perforated Jar	*chixnajab'il* (pichacha)	3 (0.09%)	96 (2.25%)
10. Narrow-Mouth Jar	*kib* (cantaro)	343 (10.26%)	389 (9.12%)
Ritual Types:	*Nine Types:*	*n = 743 (22.22%)*	*n = 771 (18.08%)*
11. Large Hemispherical Bowl	*poket grande* (apastli)	49 (1.46%)	110 (2.58%)
12. Small Unrestricted Bowl	*borcelana* (cajete)	291 (8.70%)	406 (9.52%)
13. Single-Handle Bowl	*neochab*	9 (0.27%)	0 (0.00%)
14. Pedestal-Base Bowl	*chik'pom* (incensario)	108 (3.23%)	58 (1.36%)
15. Pedestal Cylinder	*somjebal cantela* (candelero)	21 (0.63%)	3 (0.07%)
16. Large Wide-Mouth Jar	*oxom grande* (olla)	200 (5.98%)	81 (1.90%)
17. Large Composite Jar	*tenosha* (tinaja)	14 (0.42%)	64 (1.50%)
18. Small Perforated Jar	*chixnajab'il chica* (pichacha)	41 (1.23%)	37 (0.87%)
19. Pedestal Jar	*yahuil nichim* (florero)	10 (0.30%)	12 (0.28%)

Craft-Making Types:	One Type:	n = 62 (1.85%)	n =3 (0.07%)
20. Spindle Whorl	*pe'tet* (malacate)	62 (1.85%)	3 (0.07%)
Tourist Types:	*Nine Types:*	n =30 (0.90%)	n =61 (1.42%)
21. Tripod Bowls	(molcajete)	1 (0.03%)	1 (0.02%)
22. Effigy Vessel	(alcancia)	4 (0.12%)	5 (0.12%)
23. Figurine	(animalito, estatuilla)	5 (0.15%)	10 (0.23%)
24. Small Composite Jar	*tenosha chica* (tinaja)	10 (0.30%)	10 (0.23%)
25. Flaring-Mouth Dish	(cenicero)	0 (0.00%)	1 (0.02%)
26. Single-Handle Cup	(vasso)	6 (0.18%)	15 (0.35%)
27. Wide-Mouth Vase	(maceta)	4 (0.12%)	16 (0.38%)
28. Loop-Handle Bowl	*mochelum* (canasta)	0 (0.00%)	2 (0.05%)
29. Incurving-Rim Bowl	*poket* (batea)	0 (0.00%)	1 (0.02%)
Obsolete Types:	*Two Types:*	n =3 (0.09%)	n =5 (0.12%)
30. Cylindrical Jar	*balal oxom* (tecomate)	3 (0.09%)	0 (0.00%)
31. Pedestal Vase	*chinpin* (jarra)	0 (0.00%)	5 (0.12%)
Totals:	*Thirty-one Types*	*3344(100.00%)*	*4266 (100.00%)*

way. The stated problem orientation of the present study deals with pottery variability and spatial patterning at the household level of analysis. This variability and patterning is believed to be strongly affected by variations in vessel functional requirements of the household. These functional requirements are in turn largely dependent upon the socioeconomic and demographic needs of the household. Potters tend to gear their production to these respective needs and to manufacture a range of functional classes of vessels to meet these needs. Therefore, in order to deal with the problem of pottery variation and patterning at the household level, it is important to use a typology that is sensitive to vessel function. Similarly, Lischka (1975:227) suggests that functionally relevant typologies are more useful than stylistic typologies for examining associations between pottery vessels and activity areas.

While working in the field it was found that emic (or indigenous) types had consistent dual formal-functional meanings. Similar conclusions were reached by Culbert (1959) during his study of the Tzeltal potters of Amatenango, by Howry (1978:252) during his study of the Tzotzil potters of Chamula, and by R. Thompson (1958:29) in his study of Yucatecan pottery making. The Tzeltal of Sivacá (Becquelin and Baudez 1979:302) also name their vessel forms according to function, but further distinguish three classes of cooking vessel (i.e., cooking with water, cooking with oil, and grilling). Vessel form and function are also important factors for many of the problems with which archaeologists deal and which are central to the concerns of this study. For this reason, it was decided to use the local emic typology as a working basis for the present classification since it would be useful for dealing with household requirements and would be preferable to a purely archaeological typology

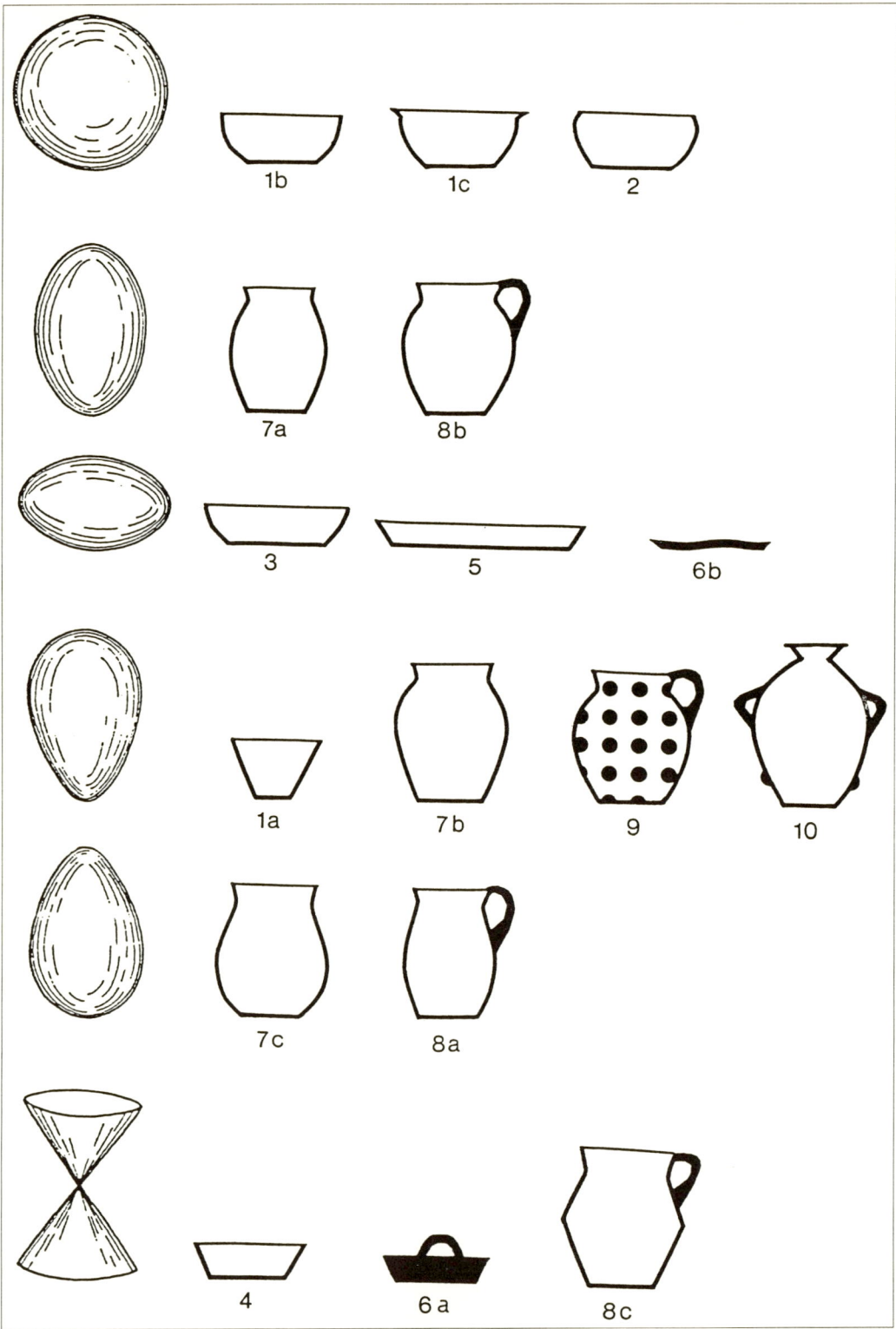

Fig. 3.22. Line drawings of Chanal and Aguacatenango domestic vessel forms, with type number and letter representing morphological variants. See Appendix B.

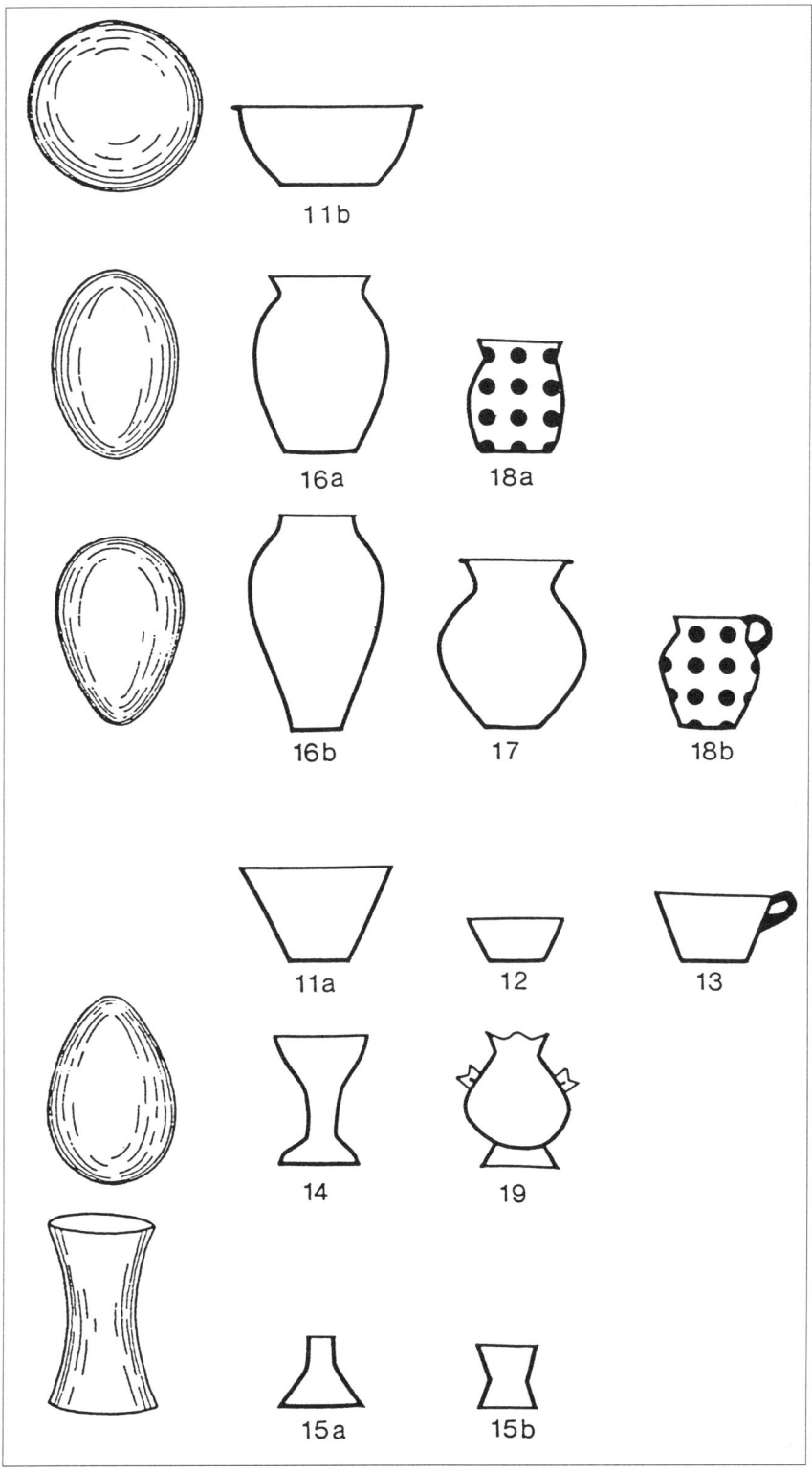

Fig. 3.23. Line drawings of Chanal and Aguacatenango ritual vessel forms, with type number and letter representing morphological variants. See Appendix B.

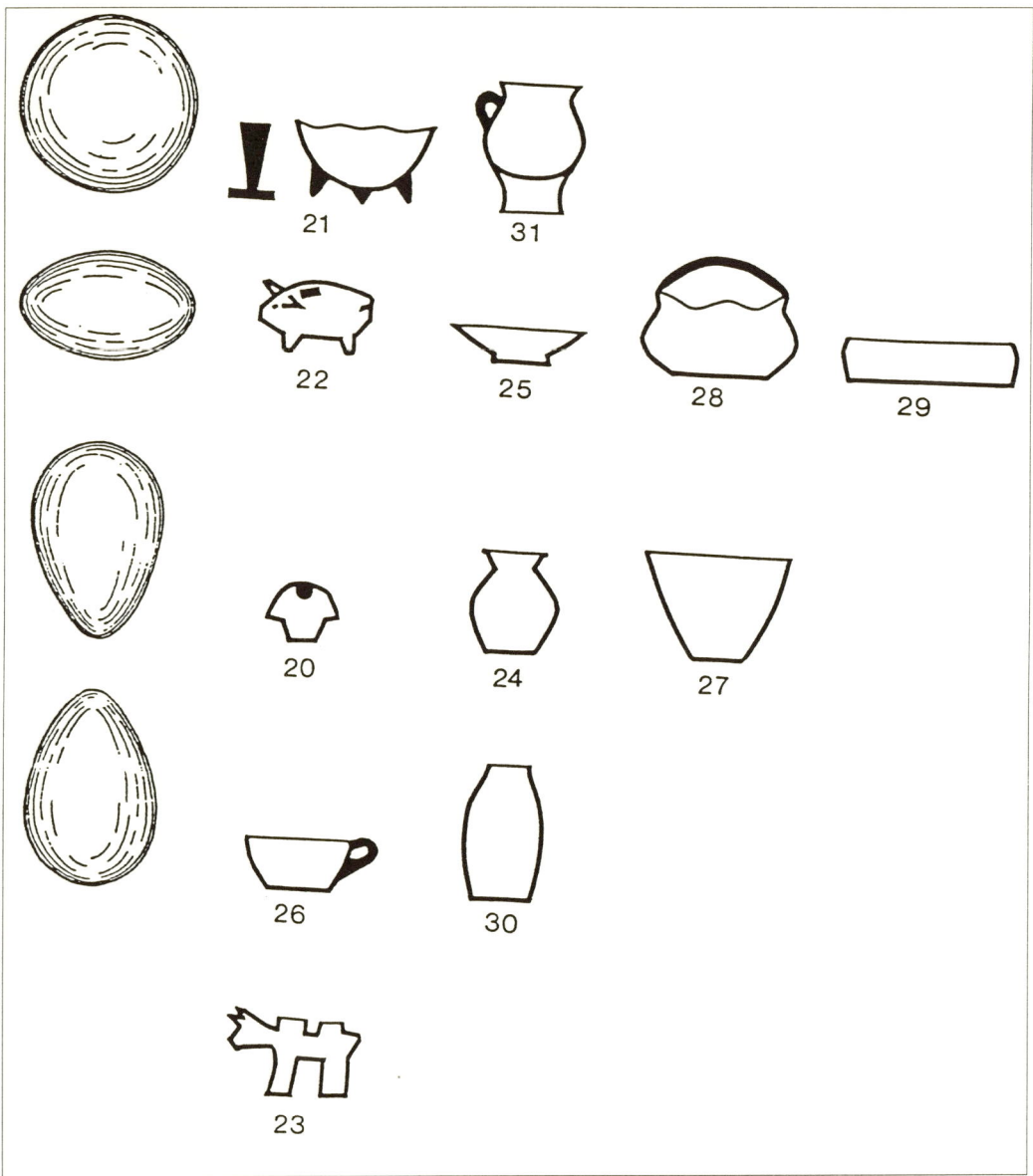

Fig. 3.24. Line drawings of Chanal and Aguacatenango miscellaneous vessel forms, with type number. See Appendix B.

(depending upon the degree of elaboration desired of the types). In order to facilitate comparison between modern and Precolumbian vessels, etic descriptive names (emphasizing formal attributes) were also given to the emic types. The formal typology is presented in Appendix B, but summarized here in Table 3.12 (see Figures 3.22–3.25).

Although formal-functional pottery type

ascriptions seemed to be universal among the Tzeltal, some variation in the emic typology did occur between different informants, between producer and user, and between communities. Specifically, these included:

(1) Producers and users sometimes had varying expectations about how a given vessel should look and the behavior associated with it (i.e., how it is to be used). Emic termi-

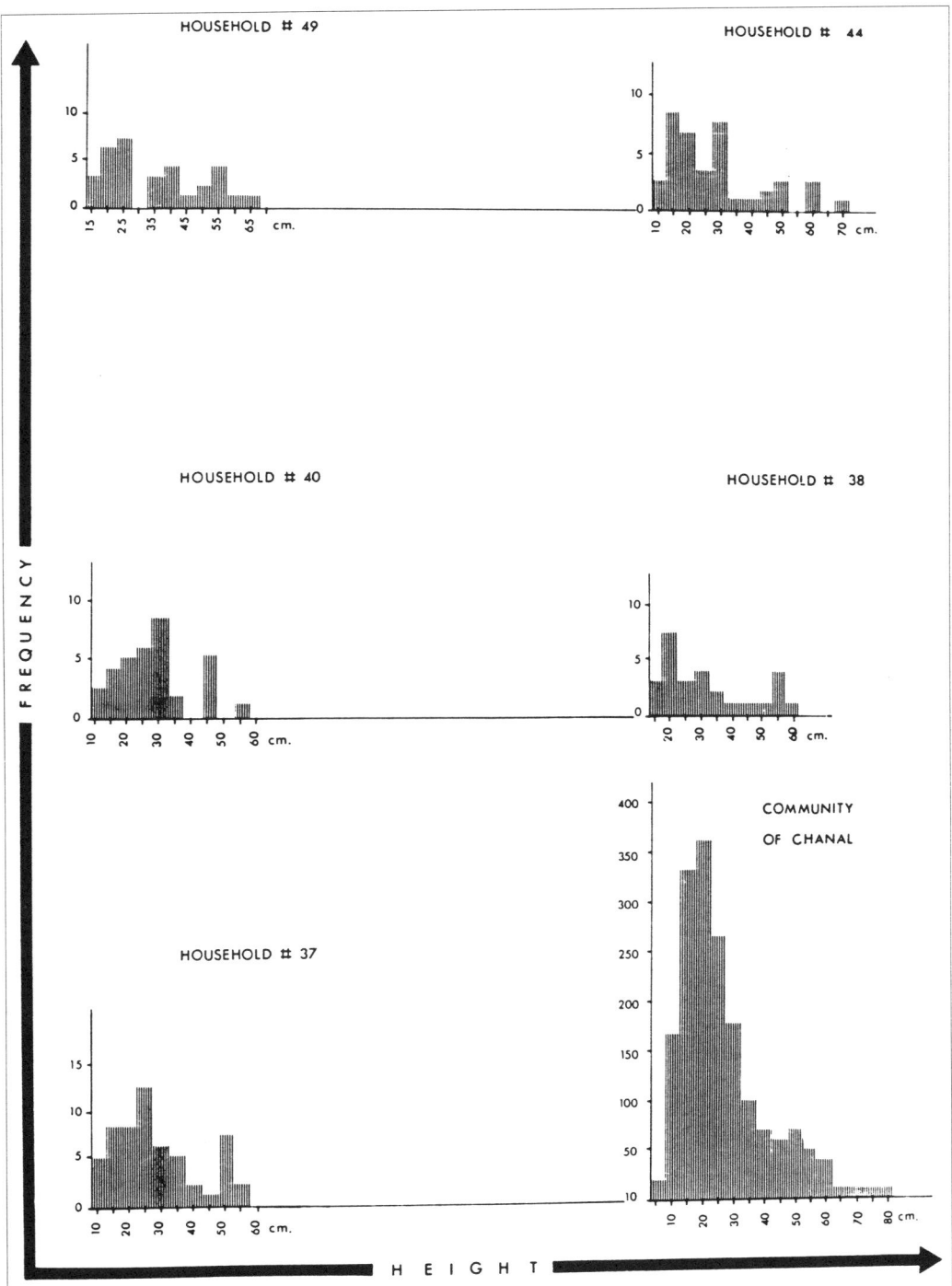

Fig. 3.25. Histograms of wide-mouth jar *(oxom)* height for five Chanal households and for the entire community.

nology for general domestic vessel forms, and especially bowl forms, was quite flexible, while major formal types such as narrow-mouth jars were highly standardized. For example, Culbert (1959:5) sampled several hundred narrow-mouth (watercarrying) jars without noting a single deviant from the pattern of rolled rim, flat base, three body handles and a height/orifice diameter ratio between 2.5 and 3.5 cm.

The views of producer and user were more likely to differ concerning primary vessel function than concerning description of vessel form. For example, a large jar form produced in Amatenango, was said by the producer to be a water storage vessel (Culbert 1965), but said by the Chanal users to be a beer brewing vessel. In Chanal and Aguacatenango this same jar form was used both to store and carry water, and none of the large jars intended by the producer for storage were actually observed being used for storage.

(2) Variation in formal attributes sometimes resulted in the lumping together or splitting up of certain emic types by different informants. For example, wide-mouth jars and single-handle (occasionally spouted) jars might be given the same emic type-name (*oxom* in Chanal and *pin* in Aguacatenango) because they fulfilled similar functions and could be used interchangeably. It was more common, however, to separate the latter type of jar into the emic category of *chikbin* (or *chikpin*) which was a vessel used for the heating of water for coffee. This single-handle jar was completely interchangeable with handleless forms in Aguacatenango, while in Chanal, where it occurred less frequently, it served almost exclusively as a heating pitcher. Aguacatenango informants generally lumped the two forms under the same name, while Chanal informants almost always used two separate names. These forms would likely be viewed as separate classes in archaeological, etic typologies.

(3) Vessel proportions (size, neck width, etc.) were important criteria for emic type ascriptions (Culbert 1959; Howry 1978:246; also see Longacre et al. 1988:106–107). For example, a *poket* could be a large or small bowl, an *oxom* (or *pin*) could be a large or small wide-mouth jar, and a *chixnajab'il* (or *chichina*) could be a large or small perforated jar. However, the small *poket* and *oxom*, and large *chixnajab'il* served domestic functions while the larger sizes served ritual functions. Howry (1978:249) noted a similar dichotomy in Chamula. These functional differences occurring between smaller and larger sizes of certain vessel forms were not always clearly reflected in the emic terminology. The Spanish terms for small or large (*chica* or *grande*), rather than the Tzeltal terms, were often appended to the type name to emphasize such functional differences (e.g., *oxom* and *oxom grande*).

Certain formal-functional categories might be difficult to isolate archaeologically, unless there is a clear bimodal distribution in sizes. Comparisons of modern Chanal wide-mouth jars (see Figure 1.5) indicated that such a distribution often existed at the household level, while a "blending affect" took place when the size (represented by vessel height) of wide-mouth jars was compared over the entire sample. It is not unreasonable to assume that definite size and volume ranges within distinctive formal types, such as the wide-mouth jar and perforated jar, generally represent more than one primary function. In fact, this assumption is often made in the archaeological literature (e.g., Matson 1965; Whallon 1969), especially for the identification of storage vessels (e.g., Bawden 1982: 169; Sheets 1979). A similar situation occurs in Buhera, Zimbabwe, where Lindahl and Matenga (1995) derive formal-functional types at modern abandoned homesteads from vessel height (estimated from rim diameters) and sherd thickness in comparison with measurements taken from modern vessels.

The latter point brings up the problem of how archaeologists can recognize functionally relevant types in archaeological assemblages. Mayanists have traditionally focused on decorative stylistic attributes (surface treatment and design elements rather than formal attributes) when classifying their pottery (e.g., Brockington 1967; J. C. Gifford 1976; Sanders 1961; R. E. Smith 1971). While detailed stylistic typologies may be useful for developing chronologies and for studying interactions on the intersite and interregional levels, stylistic variation over time in the Maya area has little functional relevance (Shepard 1964a). In regions, such as the Central Highlands of Chiapas, where there is little stylistic variation, paste and temper can serve as the dominant variables in type classification (Culbert 1965:49). However, except at a general level, paste composition is not always a useful indicator of vessel function (Bishop et al. 1982:313). Although vessel form tends to be closely related to decorative stylistic variation (e.g., DeBoer 1983:19; Friedrich 1970; Plog 1980a; Watson 1977:388), formal attributes are more likely to reflect vessel function (Lischka 1978). For example, there is a close relationship between morphological characteristics and the function of specific Tzeltal vessel forms (see Tzeltal pottery classification in Appendix B.)

Clearly, more experimentation with archaeological assemblages is called for, in order to establish functionally relevant types (for a general discussion of functional studies see Orton et al. 1993, or Rice 1996a: 138–143). The traditional methods of determining vessel function are archaeological context (e.g., Grebinger 1971; Salmon 1981) and comparisons with ethnographic and ethnohistoric sources (Deal 1982; Feldman 1982; Folan et al. 1979; Hendrickson and MacDonald 1983; Joesink-Mandeville 1976). Some Classic Period Maya vessels even had "name tags" indicating vessel form, size or function (Houston et al. 1989). Many recent studies have focused on formal attributes (e.g., Braun 1980; Ericson and DeAtley 1976; Lischka 1978; Morris 1974a:59; Nelson 1985; M. F. Smith 1985). Other methods that can provide functional inferences include studies of vessel use-wear (e.g., Bray 1982; Chernela 1969; Griffiths 1978; Hendrickson 1992; Schiffer 1989), absorbed and adhering residues (e.g., Charters et al. 1995; Hally 1983a; Heron and Evershed 1992; Skibo

1992; Skibo and Deal 1995), and material and design analysis (e.g., D. E. Arnold 1971; Bishop 1980; Braun 1982, 1983; Ericson et al. 1972; Hammond 1971; Matson 1969; Rands et al. 1975; Rands and Bishop 1980; Rice 1977; Rye 1976, 1981; Shepard 1964a, b; Steponaitis 1983; Woods 1985). For example, Skibo (1992) and M. Koybayashi (1994) have used ethnoarchaeological data on vessel use-alteration (i.e., use-wear, residue analysis and carbon deposition) in the identification of vessel function. Assuming that the use of information derived from all these methods can facilitate the establishment of reliable functional "boundary conditions" for specific formal types, these types should be useful for interpreting household pottery-related activities and socioeconomic and demographic conditions.

What is being suggested here is not that Mayanists dispense with highly refined, decorative stylistic typologies, but that such typologies are more suitable for intercommunity studies, while formal typologies, developed according to functionally related attributes, are more useful for intracommunity (interhousehold) comparisons. It is unlikely that a single typology could adequately reconcile functional and stylistic attributes (Brown 1982:180). Both approaches, or either one independently, can be used on a single assemblage.

THE WARE CONCEPT

As stated above, pottery formal and functional variation is dealt with here within the concept of the "type." Variation attributable to decorative style will be dealt with within the concept of "ware" (see Rice 1987: 286–287). In terms of the pottery used by the Tzeltal, this is manifested primarily in surface treatment variation (i.e., slipped, unslipped, and glazed), although painted designs occur on some slipped and glazed vessel forms.

The concept of ware, based on both stylistic attributes and paste composition, has often been misused in Maya pottery studies (Rice 1976; Sabloff and Smith 1970). The present study incorporates the interpretation of this concept introduced by Rice (1976; also see Ball 1977:662), in which the attribute classes of paste composition and surface treatment are treated independently. Paste ware (Rice 1976:539) primarily reflects the "availability and diversity of ceramic resources within a particular area," whereas wares based on surface treatment are primarily determined by cultural factors (i.e., they reflect stylistic variation). J. C. Gifford (1976:17) has also stressed that surface treatment can be considered almost purely cultural inspiration. Following Rice's interpretation, paste ware becomes an analytic unit which crosscuts the classificatory units of stylistic type and stylistic ware (based on surface treatment). Further, paste wares can often be used to relate paste composition to functional types, and especially for differentiating vessels which are to be used on the hearth from those which are not. Even stylistic wares can sometimes help in identifying vessel function, and especially for differentiating ritual from domestic vessels.

It is obvious from ethnographic studies that analysts must be careful when lumping vessels with similar surface treatments and basic form within the same ware category and ignoring paste composition. For example, Howry (1978:253–254) identifies the water-carrying jars at Amatenango, Chamula, Tenango, and Yocnajab as a single ware based primarily on slip (and secondarily on form). However, this classification tends to mask both the inherent stylistic traditions and resource differences between the four communities. In reality, the slips (and design elements) of these jars are easily distinguishable, and in the present classification they would represent four separate stylistic wares, as well as four separate paste wares. Within Amatenango, paste wares and stylistic wares should be identical, since all potters are believed to use the same clay sources (Bryant and Brody 1987). However, most Chanal potters (or potting families) use different clay sources, and therefore paste and stylistic wares are less likely to overlap.

In the present study, only gross stylistic variations were used to distinguish between local and imported wares. Potters born in Chanal and Aguacatenango did not decorate their vessels and the decorations on imported vessels had no meaning in themselves beyond the distinction between decorated and non-decorated. Decorated vessels were associated with imported, fine quality wares which were often purchased for ritual use. By contrast, someone studying pottery making within Amatenango would probably have further divided Amatenango slipped into red-slipped and white-slipped, or by decorative elements in order to characterize lineage microtraditions.

In terms of the above discussion, pottery produced by the Tzeltal Maya is distinguished here as slipped wares or unslipped wares and is further differentiated by community of manufacture (i.e., Amatenango slipped or Amatenango unslipped). Glazed wares were imported from the ladino centers of San Cristóbal de las Casas (barrio San Ramon) and Chiapa de Corzo. In an archaeological sense, the unslipped wares of Chanal and the small surrounding communities might be indistinguishable on formal grounds (either stylistic, or functionally relevant formal attributes), but should be distinguishable though material analysis and have thus been dealt with as separate wares.

THE CONCEPTS OF SPHERE, COMPLEX, AND SUBCOMPLEX

The concepts of sphere, complex, and subcomplex provide a useful framework for the discussion of the regional distribution of pottery, in terms of intercommunity exchange and the development of craft specialization, as well as for comparisons between major pottery production centers. A ceramic complex is "the sum total of associated ceramics which has a convenient and easily distinguished geographical and temporal meaning" (Culbert 1967:92). Further, when two or more complexes share a majority of their common types they are considered a "ceramic sphere" (Culbert 1967:99). The contemporary Highlands of Chiapas is recognized as a ceramic sphere made up of five complexes, each representing a major

TABLE 3.13.

Chanal and Aguacatenango Pottery Classification According to the Type-Variety Approach.

Sphere: Chiapas Highlands; Complex: Amatenango; Chanal Inventory:

Type Diversity/Subcomplex:	Domestic	Ritual	Trade	Rare
Chanal unslipped	8	6	—	5
Siberia unslipped	1	1	—	—
Natilton unslipped	—	1	—	—
Onija unslipped	1	—	—	—
Frontera Tzajalnich unslipped	1	—	—	—
San Fernando unslipped	4	1	—	—
San Pedro unslipped	5	3	—	—
Yolo unslipped	1	1	—	—
San Antonio unslipped	—	1	—	—
Floresta unslipped	—	1	—	—
San Augustine unslipped	—	1	—	—
Yocnajab unslipped	—	1	—	—
Amatenango unslipped	1	—	—	—
Amatenango slipped	2	3	3	1
San Ramon glazed	4	—	1	—
Chiapa de Corzo glazed	—	1	—	—
Mexican glazed	—	—	1	—
Total:	28	21	5	6

Sphere: Chiapas Highlands; Complex: Amatenango; Aguacatenango Inventory

Type Diversity/Subcomplex:	Domestic	Ritual	Trade	Rare
Napite unslipped	1	—	—	—
Aguacatenango unslipped	5	3	—	—
Amatenango unslipped	6	2	—	—
Marcos Becerra unslipped	1	—	—	—
Pinola unslipped	2	—	—	—
Palizada unslipped	1	—	—	—
Tzajala unslipped	1	1	—	—
San Jose unslipped	1	1	—	—
Yocnajab unslipped	4	1	—	—
Amatenango slipped*	2	5	9	1
San Ramon glazed	5	—	1	—
Chiapa de Corzo glazed	—	1	—	—
Mexican glazed	1	—	2	—
Total:	30	14	12	1

*Includes Amatenango potters living in Aguacatenango.

TABLE 3.14.
Frequency and Percentage of Pottery Contributed to Chanal and Aguacatenango by
Each Supply Zone.

Supply Zone:	Total	Percentage	Ritual	Percentage	Domestic	Percentage
Chanal						
Intercommunity	1609	48.06	246	7.35	1363	40.71
Peripheral	255	7.62	43	1.28	212	6.33
Unknown Source	621	18.55	105	3.14	516	15.41
Intrasphere	862	25.75	407	12.16	455	13.59
Intersphere	1	0.03	—	—	1	0.03
Total	3348	100.00	801	23.93	2547	76.07
Aguacatenango						
Intercommunity	180	4.22	14	0.33	166	3.69
Peripheral	3499	82.00	367	8.60	3132	73.40
Unknown Source	62	1.45	2	0.05	60	1.41
Intrasphere	518	12.14	402	9.42	116	2.72
Intersphere	8	0.19	—	—	8	0.19
Total	427	100.00	785	81.61	3482	81.61

pottery-making center and the geographical area in which they dominate production of certain vessel forms (Howry 1978:253). These complexes include the Tzeltal communities of Amatenango (southern Tzeltal area) and Tenango (northern Tzeltal area), the Tzotzil community of Chamula, the Zoque community of Ixtapa and the Tojolabal community of Yocnajab. Vessels produced by these five communities are distinguishable from those of adjoining regions on both formal and decorative stylistic grounds. Both Chanal and Aguacatenango belong in the Amatenango Chiapas Highlands Complex. Except for the occasional Yocnajab vessel, no vessels made within the other complexes of the Chiapas Highlands Sphere were recorded in either community.

A complex can be further divided into "subcomplexes" which represent significant cultural categories (Culbert 1967:93) such as religious versus domestic, mortuary, or class distinctions. Four basic subcomplexes which crosscut Tzeltal communities, and which are useful for the study of pottery variability at the household level, focus on domestic, watercarrying, ritual and trade (tourist market) behavior. For Tzeltal informants, differences in tempering material (kind and amount) and vessel form seem to be the major criteria for distinguishing between such subcomplexes. Except for minor variations between communities, all communities within the Chiapas Highlands Sphere share a similar range of vessel forms for domestic and ritual functions. Virtually all tourist trade items found in Chanal and Aguacatenango originate in Amatenango or the Ladino kilns of San Ramon. Further, Amatenango potters have a virtual monopoly on watercarrying jars used in both Chanal and Aguacatenango. At the household level, these subcomplexes are manifested in household activity sets.

A summary of the classification of Chanal and Aguacatenango pottery according to the type-variety scheme is presented in Table 3.13. The Chiapas Highlands Sphere is seen as a geographically distinct, pottery production and exchange network, which is dominated by five pottery-making communities. The geographical area in which each of these communities dominate exchange is considered a pottery complex. Chanal and Aguacatenango are situated within the Amatenango Complex. The variation in Chanal and Aguacatenango functional requirements is mani-

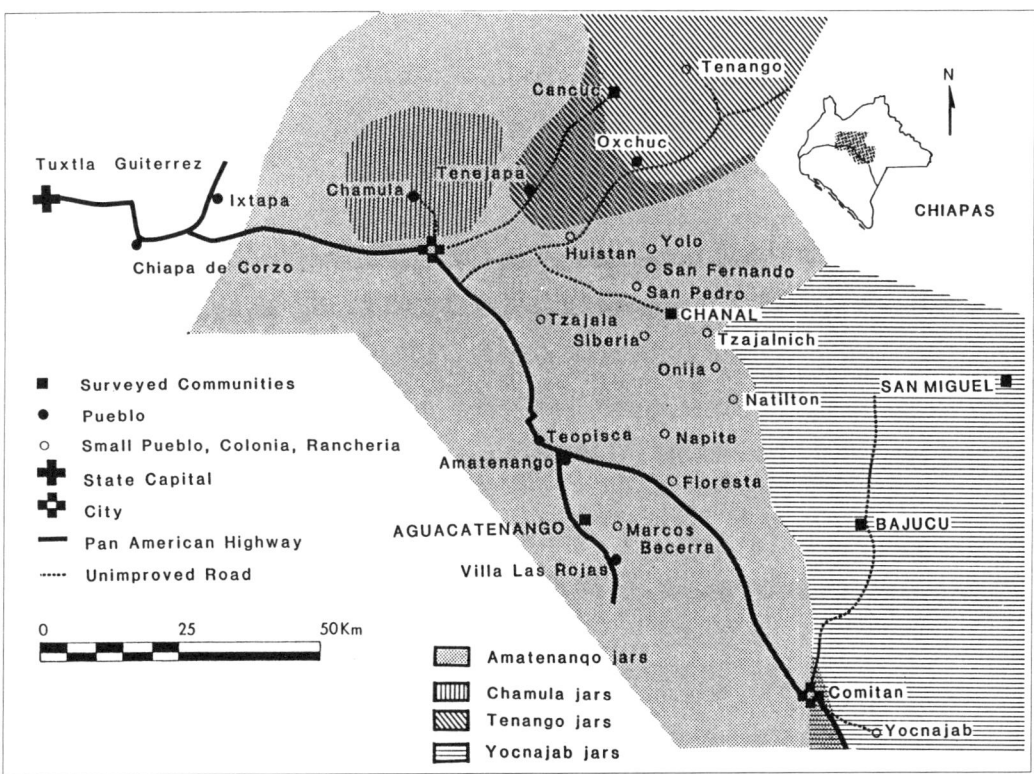

Fig. 3.26. Map of the Chiapas Highlands, indicating major potting communities that provide pottery to Chanal and Aguacatenango, and the overlapping distribution zones of the narrow-mouth jar *(kib)* forms made in Amatenango, Chamula, Tenango and Yocnajab. The city in the center is San Cristóbal de las Casas.

fested in formal-functional types within broad regional functional categories (sub-complexes). Decorative stylistic variation (in the form of surface treatment) is manifested in the wares produced by individual communities within the complex. The dynamic nature of pottery distribution within the Chiapas Highlands Sphere is discussed further in the next section.

DOMESTIC PRODUCTION VERSUS VILLAGE SPECIALIZATION

In order to consider why Chanal and Aguacatenango were not self-sufficient or exploitative (i.e., in terms of trade) in pottery production, we must take into account both ethnographic and ethnohistoric factors that contribute to a change from domestic production to village specialization. Accordingly, the following discussion reviews the

present situation of these two communities within the regional exchange network and considers available ethnohistoric information to speculate on how the current situation developed (Figure 3.26).

The communities that supplied both Chanal and Aguacatenango with pottery could be viewed as four distinct geographical distribution zones; intracommunity, peripheral, intrasphere, and intersphere. In Chanal, the intracommunity distribution zone satisfied at least 50 percent of the total pottery consumption needs of the community (see Tables 3.14–3.15). In contrast, Aguacatenango potters produced less than 5 percent of the pottery consumed by the community, while more than 80 percent was made in Amatenango.

The second geographical zone, defined as the peripheral distribution zone included sev-

Fig. 3.27. Pottery shop in Indian market, San Cristóbal de las Casas.

eral small production centers in *parajes, ranchos,* and *colonias* within about a 10 to 15 km radius of the two communities. Middlemen or the potters themselves or a member of the potter's immediate family made regular trips into Chanal and Aguacatenango to peddle pottery wares from door to door. The third geographical zone included communities that supplied the regional market in San Cristóbal de las Casas, and were located within a 15 to 100 km radius of the two communities. Howry (1976:259) considered San Cristóbal de las Casas a major "bulking" point for the pottery-making centers of the region, and especially Amatenango and Chamula (Figure 3.27). The lead-glazed wares of the Ladino potters of Chiapa de Corzo and San Ramon, a barrio of San Cristóbal de las Casas, were also prominent. The small glazed, wheel-made bowls of Chiapa de Corzo were purchased and resold by Chanal merchants. The only wares not produced within a 100 km radius of the two communities were a handful of small factory produced cups from Central Mexico. These were included in the inter-

sphere distribution zone. They were also made available to the Tzeltal through the pottery shops of San Cristóbal de las Casas.

Amatenango would be included in the intrasphere distribution zone for Chanal, but it must be considered part of the peripheral zone for Aguacatenango due to the proximity of the two communities. Occasionally, Amatenango pottery found its way directly to Chanal via middlemen who made semi-regular visits by truck, by Chanal merchants who stocked a few narrow-mouth jars *(kib),* and by Chanaleño pilgrims who visited Amatenango during its two major festivals. In contrast, many Amatenango potters peddled their wares door-to-door in Aguacatenango.

It seemed surprising that Chanal, with more than 150 active potters and abundant resources for pottery making, exported almost no pottery and imported more than 40 percent of the vessels consumed by the community (i.e., based on inventory counts; see Table 3.14). The 19 percent of vessels of undetermined origin were certainly produced within the peripheral distribution zone and at least some of these were likely made in Chanal itself. Still, 26 percent of the vessels recorded in Chanal came from the intra-sphere distribution zone. The Aguacate-nango situation was equally perplexing, be-cause less than 5 percent of the vessels consumed by the community was made lo-cally despite the fact that Aguacatenangeros shared many of the same resources as Amate-nango. Some clay deposits exploited by Ama-tenango potters were actually located on Aguacatenango lands but were not exploited by Aguacatenangeros (Hunt 1962:82). In ad-dition, M. Nash (1966:73) pointed out that any village within the approximately 3100 square km region around Amatenango had access to virtually the same resources but none of them have developed pottery making as a specialization.

Most of the basic differences between Chanal and Amatenango pottery production were manifested in the organization and in-tensity of production (see Table 3.16). Al-most every Amatenango household produced pottery. Pottery making was a community specialty (see Costin 1991:8) and the potter's productive skills and knowledge were not ex-ported (M. Nash 1966:73). In sociological terms, Amatenango possessed the strong "closed corporateness" that Reina and Hill (1978:199) saw as characteristic of Guatemala Highland pottery production centers and as one factor in the maintenance of the traditional practices and accouter-ments of Maya culture.

All Amatenango girls were taught to make pottery and lived within an atmosphere of constant pottery production. The women of the household gathered raw materials, con-structed, decorated, and fired the pottery in an assembly-line fashion. The men gathered firewood, helped with the final stages of firing, and often marketed the final product. Pottery making in Chanal was a more loosely organized affair. Potters generally worked alone and the men did not participate. Chanal potters produced only the less elabo-rate plainwares, while Amatenango potters produced plainwares, and also a variety of slipped and decorated wares. Amatenango

had a virtual monopoly in the southern Tzeltal area on one essential vessel form, the narrow-mouth jar, used for water carrying (the *kib*).

The community of Amatenango was es-tablished in the early Colonial period (J. Nash 1970:2), and it has been a major pottery production center since at least the last century. Even before the building of the Pan American Highway in 1955, Amate-nango pottery was peddled by horseback to small communities within an 80 km radius (J. Nash 1970:91). Ethnohistoric documen-tation of Tzeltal and Tzotzil pottery making is conspicuously lacking (Calnek 1988:18), but Culbert (1965:46, 72) believes that Ama-tenango pottery production may represent a pottery tradition known as Huistan Hard, which began in the Postclassic and probably was still in production at the time of con-quest. Further, Culbert (1965:46–47) states that specialization probably existed in the Central Highlands during each period from the Classic to the present.

Amatenango and Aguacatenango had a very close producer-consumer relationship. Aguacatenango households used more than 75 percent Amatenango vessels, while serv-ing as suppliers of tempering material for some Amatenango potters. The latter group took cobbles of calcite in exchange for pot-tery. In Amatenango, pottery production served as an important safeguard against crop failure, while in Aguacatenango a crop failure meant a higher migration rate of men to the lowland *fincas* for wage labor (Hunt 1962:81).

Chanal was a *paraje*-vacant town until about 1930 (see Chapter 2), and people who moved into the community at that time re-tained close kinship ties with the small sur-rounding communities. This situation proba-bly accounted, at least in part, for the dependence upon these communities for at least 15 percent of the pottery consumed in Chanal, and also the close formal similarities between Chanal pottery and pottery pro-duced in the surrounding communities. Re-cent ethnoarchaeological studies suggest that pottery consumption in general is closely

TABLE 3.15.
Pottery Distribution Zones for Chanal and Aguacatenango, Indicating Type Diversity Provided by Each Source.

Type Number:*	1	2	3	4	5	6	7	8	9	10	11	12	13	14	15	16
Supply Zones:																
Chanal																
*Intercommunity: Peripheral***	x	—	x	x	x	x	x	x	x	x	—	—	x	x	x	x
Siberia	—	—	—	—	—	—	x	—	—	—	—	—	—	—	—	x
Natilton	—	—	—	—	—	—	x	—	—	—	—	—	—	—	—	—
Onija	—	—	—	—	—	—	x	—	—	—	—	—	—	—	—	—
Frontera Tzajanish	—	—	—	—	—	—	x	—	—	—	—	—	—	—	—	—
San Fernando	x	—	—	—	x	—	x	x	—	—	—	—	—	—	—	x
San Pedro	x	—	x	—	x	—	x	x	—	x	—	—	—	x	—	x
Yola	—	—	—	—	—	—	x	—	—	—	—	—	—	—	—	x
San Antonio	—	—	—	—	—	—	—	—	—	—	—	—	—	—	—	x
Intrasphere																
Floresta	—	—	—	—	—	—	x	—	—	—	—	—	—	—	—	—
San Augustina	—	—	—	—	—	—	—	—	—	—	—	—	—	—	—	x
San Ramon	—	—	x	—	—	—	x	x	—	—	—	—	—	—	—	—
Yocnajab	—	—	—	—	—	—	x	x	—	—	—	—	—	—	—	—
Amatenango	x	x	—	—	—	—	—	—	—	x	x	x	—	—	x	—
Chiapa De Corzo	—	—	—	—	—	—	—	—	—	—	—	x	—	—	—	—
Intersphere																
Central Mexico	—	—	—	—	—	—	—	—	—	—	—	—	—	—	—	—

Type Number:	1	2	3	4	5	6	7	8	9	10	11	12	13	14	15	16
Supply Zones:																
Aguacatenango*+																
Intercommunity Peripheral	—	—	x	—	x	x	x	x	—	—	—	—	x	—	—	x
Marcos Becerra	—	—	—	—	—	—	x	—	—	—	—	—	—	—	—	—
Pinola	—	—	—	—	—	—	x	x	—	—	—	—	—	—	—	—
Amatenango	x	x	x	x	x	—	x	x	x	x	x	—	x	x	—	x
Palizada	—	—	—	—	—	—	x	—	—	—	—	—	—	—	—	—
Napite	—	—	—	—	—	—	x	—	—	—	—	—	—	—	—	—
Tzajala	—	—	—	—	—	—	x	—	—	—	—	—	—	x	—	—
San Jose	—	—	—	—	—	—	—	x	—	—	—	—	—	—	—	x
Intrasphere																
San Ramon	—	—	x	—	x	x	x	x	—	—	—	—	—	—	—	—
Yocnajab	x	—	—	—	x	—	x	x	—	—	—	—	—	x	—	—
Chiapa De Corzo	—	—	—	—	—	—	—	—	—	—	—	x	—	—	—	—
Intersphere																
Central Mexico	—	—	—	—	—	—	—	—	—	—	—	—	—	—	—	—

Type Number:*	17	18	19	20	21	22	23	24	25	26	27	28	29	30	31
Supply Zone:															
Chanal															
Intercommunity: *Peripheral***	—	x	—	x	—	—	x	—	—	x	x	—	—	x	—
Siberia	—	—	—	—	—	—	—	—	—	—	—	—	—	—	—
Natilton	—	—	—	—	—	—	—	—	—	—	—	—	—	—	—
Onija	—	—	—	—	—	—	—	—	—	—	—	—	—	—	—
Frontera Tzajanish	—	—	—	—	—	—	—	—	—	—	—	—	—	—	—
San Fernando	—	—	—	—	—	—	—	—	—	—	—	—	—	—	—
San Pedro	—	—	—	—	—	—	—	—	—	—	—	—	—	—	—
Yola	—	—	—	—	—	—	—	—	—	—	—	—	—	—	—
San Antonio	—	—	—	—	—	—	—	—	—	—	—	—	—	—	—
Intra-sphere															
Floresta	—	—	—	—	—	—	—	—	—	—	—	—	—	—	—
San Augustina	—	—	—	—	—	—	—	—	—	—	—	—	—	—	—
San Ramon	—	—	—	x	—	—	—	—	—	x	—	—	—	—	—
Yocnajab	—	—	—	—	—	—	—	—	—	—	—	—	—	—	—
Amatenango	—	—	x	—	—	x	x	x	—	—	—	—	—	—	—
Chiapa De Corzo	—	—	—	—	—	—	—	—	—	—	—	—	—	—	—
Intersphere															
Central Mexico	—	—	—	—	—	—	—	—	—	x	—	—	—	—	—

Type Number:	17	18	19	20	21	22	23	24	25	26	27	28	29	30	31
Supply Zones:															
Aguacatenango*+															
Intercommunity *Peripheral*	—	x	—	—	—	—	—	—	—	—	—	—	—	—	—
Marcos Becerra	—	—	—	—	—	—	—	—	—	—	—	—	—	—	—
Pinola	—	—	—	—	—	—	—	—	—	—	—	—	—	—	—
Amatenango	x	x	x	—	—	x	x	x	x	x	x	x	x	—	x
Palizada	—	—	—	—	—	—	—	—	—	—	—	—	—	—	—
Napite	—	—	—	—	—	—	—	—	—	—	—	—	—	—	—
Tzajala	—	—	—	—	—	—	—	—	—	—	—	—	—	—	—
San Jose	—	—	—	—	—	—	—	—	—	—	—	—	—	—	—
Intrasphere															
San Ramon	—	—	—	x	—	—	—	—	—	x	—	—	—	—	—
Yocnajab	—	—	—	—	—	—	—	—	—	—	—	—	—	—	—
Chiapa De Corzo	—	—	—	—	—	—	—	—	—	—	—	—	—	—	—
Intersphere															
Central Mexico	—	—	—	—	—	—	—	—	—	x	—	—	—	—	—

*Type number corresponds with type numbers in classification (Appendix B).

**In order of relative distance from Chanal and Aguacatenango.

*+Not including forms made by resident Amatenango potters.

TABLE 3.16.
Comparison of Pottery Making in Chanal and Amatenango.

Community:	Chanal	Amatenango
State of Production:	household (domestic)	village specialization
Economy:		
Time commitment	occasional/part-time	part-time/full-time
Investments	time only	cash for pigments and travel
Number of Potters	1–3 friends and/or relatives	extended family/guild
Organization	potters work separately	assembly line
Locality	sedentary	sedentary
Division of labor	generally none	considerable
Time involved making		
one vessel	<20 min.	>30 min.
Seasonality	dry season (Dec.–Mar.)	year-round
Market	home use or intracommunity	local/regional
Procurement of		
Raw materials:		
Clay	local (<1 km)	local (<1 km)
Calcite temper	distant (2–8 km)	local
Sand temper	not used	local
Water	local	local
Fuel	local	distant (>5 km)
Pigments	Not used	distant (purchased)
Smoothing stones	local	distant (8–60 km)
Technology:		
Manufacturing technology	hand/small tools	hand/small tools
Wheel (no moving parts)	not used	guild only
Kiln	open fire	open fire*
Clays	black and red	black, white, yellow
Temper(s)	calcite	calcite and three types of sand
Fuel	pine kindling and oak bark	pine kindling, oak bark, cypress
Range of function type		
produced	narrow	wide
Range of wares	unslipped only	red and white slipped/ unslipped

*The one potters' guild in Amatenango has a closed kiln built for them by I.N.A.H. but it was not in use during the present study.

linked to social ties between communities (e.g., Kramer and Douglas 1992; Longacre and Stark 1992; M. T. Stark 1992).

D. E. Arnold (1975:192; 1978b; 1985: Chapter 7) believes that pottery-making specialization can begin as an adaptation to poor agricultural land in areas where ceramic resources also occurred. Elsewhere he states that ... *people would not choose to become craft specialists if the subsistence base was adequate* (D. E. Arnold 1980:147). A case can easily be made for this situation in the Central Highlands of Chiapas. For example, Collier (1975:76) has linked the dependence on household industry and wage labor in Amatenango and Chamula to lack of ade-

Fig. 3.28. Tenango style narrow-mouth jar *(kib)* at community well, Cancuc, 1979.

quate farmland. Deteriorating agricultural land combined with the availability of good clay and temper have also been linked to the recent emergence of male potters and the subsequent increase in pottery specialization in Chamula (Howry 1973:10; Rus 1969:68). Similar relationships between problems in agriculture and the emergence of pottery production in Amatenango suggest that agricultural-based events in the past may have led to and perpetuated pottery specialization. Blom and LaFarge (1927:382) give a similar explanation for the growth of pottery making as a specialization in Tenango (Figure 3.28).

In Chanal, another limiting factor to the development of pottery specialization was population density. There was a much smaller market in the Chanal area that could be exploited by potters. Even in the more densely populated area around Amatenango there was probably not a large enough market to support more than one community specializing in pottery production. If regional pottery exchange was as competitive in the past as it is today, then it is not surprising that one community came to dominate an area despite the wide availability of resources.

Culbert (1965:47, 67) has suggested that the manufacture of San Gregorio coarse vessels, during the Early Postclassic (Yash phase), might parallel the situation recorded in the Chanal area, in which several communities had potters who made a few plainware vessels for local use while finer vessels were imported from larger centers. During the Yash phase, as in Chanal and the surrounding communities, certain basic vessel forms were similar, but paste, color, and finish had different ranges at each site, suggesting local production in communities sharing the same basic pottery-making tradition. Similarly, studies at Palenque (Rands 1967; 1988:181) and Tikal (Fry 1979; Fry and Cox 1974) indicate that domestic vessel forms, and especially wide-mouth jar forms, were characterized by highly localized distribution. Even potting centers like Amatenango could only find a local market for most of its domestic pottery, while specialized forms were widely distributed.

The above discussion provides one possible scenario for the rise of specialization in Amatenango and the present role of Chanal and Aguacatenango as consumers. According to this scenario, during the Colonial period the community of Amatenango was established on the flat bottomland of a major highland valley, known today as the Amatenango Valley. Among the settlers were a few potters who shared potting information linked to a tradition that began in the Late Classic or early Postclassic in the Huistan Valley. Due to a combination of widely available resources for pottery production and an undependable, overused, or inadequate agricultural base, pottery making flourished and a community style developed. Amatenango pottery eventually came to dominate the limited valley market, and today it continues to expand its market due to improved roads and methods of transport. Aguacatenangeros concentrated on agriculture and took advantage of their proximity to Amatenango by exchanging food surpluses and calcite for pottery.

Chanal was established more recently due to land shortages in Oxchuc. The community remained small and dispersed until the 1930s. While potting resources were plentiful, they were of relatively poor quality for making complex vessel forms, and the specialized knowledge of production of trade wares was lacking. Further, specialized vessel forms could be acquired through well-established trade routes over which Amatenango and Tenango pottery was peddled. With the expansion and consolidation of the community in the 1930s, more potters probably settled in the community, and potting knowledge spread through kin and nonkin relationships, and the available resources were utilized for vessels requiring little skill or high quality clays. While this scenario is purely speculative, it is consistent with currently available ethnographic, ethnohistoric, and archaeological sources.

ARCHAEOLOGICAL VISIBILITY OF THE POTTING HOUSEHOLD

It is important to archaeologists to be able to identify production locations before they can address issues related to the socioeconomic conditions of pottery production. Recent Mesoamerican studies have considered this problem and identified several potential criteria for recognizing production locations (P. J. Arnold 1991b; Curet 1993; Deal 1988b, 1994b; B. Stark 1985). These include abandoned raw materials, tools and facilities, and their spatial organization within households, the trace residues and microdebitage of production, and pottery inventory statistics. One recent study uses stylistic information (including painted images and glyphs) and paste characteristics to identify possible production locations for Classic Period polychrome vessels (Reents-Budet et al. 1994). Together these criteria embody the archaeological visibility, or . . . *actual amount of physical remains, however clearly or ambiguously they might be perceived* (Deetz 1977:94), of pottery production. In the Maya area the situation is complicated since no clear evidence of Precolumbian kilns has been identified. Rice (1996:175) notes a possible kiln at a Maya site in Honduras (after Schortman and Urban 1992), and

Bryant and Brody (1986:82) claim that Maya Plumbate and Peten Gloss pottery were probably kiln fired. Precolumbian kilns have been identified at several sites outside the Maya area, in Nayarit (Bordez 1964), Oaxaca (Balkansky et al. 1997; Swezey 1973; Winter and Payne 1976), Central Mexico (Healan 1979) and Veracruz (P. J. Arnold et al. 1993; Santley et al. 1989). However, open firing was undoubtedly the typical method of firing among the Prehispanic Maya, and it is still more common than European-style kiln firing among the modern Maya.

Much of the previous research has focused on the visibility of artisan workshops rather than domestic potting areas. However, pottery-making tools have been used occasionally for recognizing domestic potting households in the Maya area. In a single domestic structure at the Late Classic site of Yerba Buena, Chiapas, Bryant (1988:76, Figure 32) has postulated the presence of a potter from the occurrence of a ball of calcite-tempered clay, raw calcite fragments, iron oxide pigment and two distinctively worn smoothing stones. One or more of these items have been recovered from Late Classic and Postclassic house mounds at Los Encuentros, Ojo de Agua, and Guajilar in the Upper Grijalva Basin (Bryant and Brody 1986:83; Bryant and Clark 1979). Another example, was recorded at the Cerén site, El Salvador. The western portion of the roofed porch (Area Two) of household one at Cerén has been interpreted as a pottery manufacturing location based on the presence of a lump of red oxide pigment (hematite), a hand-formed ball of fine clay, and an andesite flake smoothing tool (Sheets 1979:40–41, 1992:44). At Tikal, Becker (1973:399) postulated the presence of potting households based on high vessel frequencies and type diversity relative to other households and house groups. These inferences are consistent with the finding of the present study (see Chapter 6). In Chanal, of 49 potting and nonpotting households in which locally made pottery could be adequately identified, potting households averaged 36.8 local vessels (s.d. 25.2), while nonpotting households averaged 26.2 local

TABLE 3.17.
Chanal Pottery Manufacturing Activities and the Relative Visibility of
Their Archaeological Residues.

Systemic Context	Archaeological Context	Strength of Visibility
Procurement of raw materials	Raw materials (clay, calcite, sand, fuels)	Away from Household
Storage of raw materials	Reused vessel storage Container/contents	Mid-High
	Raw materials	Mid-High
Temper preparation	Calcite powder	Low
	Reused *mano/metate*	Mid-High
	Hammerstone	Mid
Preparation of clay body	Prepared clay	Low-Mid
	Calcite powder debris	Low
	Sand debris	Low
Forming	Surplus clay debris	Low
Drying	Sherds from damaged vessels	Low-Mid
Finishing	Fettling debris (from base, perforations, etc.)	Low
	Slip or paint spillage	Low
	Discarded/lost smoothing stone	Mid-High
Firing	Charcoal/ash deposit	Mid
	Stone vessel props	Mid
	Wasters	Mid
Storage for use or sale	Large body sherds and incomplete vessels (wasters)	Mid-High

vessels (s.d. 19.2). Further, potting households averaged 7.1 locally made formal-functional types (s.d. 3.), compared to 5.2 (s.d. 2.9) for nonpotting households.

The remainder of this discussion focuses on a general model of domestic pottery production for Chanal and Aguacatenango (Table 3.17). The model shows tools and byproducts with potential archaeological visibility for each step of the production sequence, and includes estimates of the relative strength of visibility of each artifact and feature, based on their durability and frequency of occurrence. The sequence begins with the procurement of raw materials for pottery making. This entails the removal of clays, tempering materials, and wood fuel from their natural context and placing them into an ethnological (systemic) context. These materials are gathered in varying quantities depending upon the season of the year, distance to and topography of the resource area, the number of people collecting and the relative amount of pottery a potter makes, or intends to make during the season. Of these materials, tempered and untempered clay, ground and unground calcite temper, sand temper, and mineral pigments have a high potential for archaeological visibility (Table 3.18), and especially if mircodebitage analysis is used (Fladmark 1982). Bryant and Brody (1986:83) trace the use of calcite temper from Late Classic through the Colonial period, while volcanic ash was used as a temper in earlier pottery.

In Chanal, both households that had ceased production and households that were just beginning to make pottery had clay or

Fig. 3.29. Calcite storage in broken vessels.

pottery manufacturing. In the 32 active potting households, 77 partially broken pottery vessels were recorded being reused to store raw materials for pottery making, including 47 storing clay, 28 storing calcite temper, and two storing sand. Among the four inactive households, six pottery vessels were being used to store clay and three to store calcite.

In total, 107 containers were being used for the storage of raw materials in Chanal and Aguacatenango potting households. This included 86 pottery vessels and 21 storage containers that were industrially manufactured, locally made wooden containers, or gourd bowls. For the active potting households, clay was being stored in two tin cans, one bucket, and one wooden box, and calcite was stored in five tin cans, three buckets, one wooden box, two gourd bowls, and three plastic bags. One small plastic tub was used to store pigments. In one inactive household, a bucket was being used for calcite storage, and in another, 10 calcite cobbles were being stored in a wooden washing basin *(batea)*. If the industrially made containers were not available, then it is likely that even more pottery containers would have been in use for raw materials storage. The distribution of these containers varied considerably with areas in and around the main living structure and sweatbath being the most common (see Table 3.19). The use of pottery vessels for raw material storage has important implications for the recognition of potting households at archaeological sites. The pottery container, as well as its contents, are potentially visible in archaeological situations, and because the containers are generally partially incomplete or in poor repair, they are likely to be left upon site abandonment. Even if the container is discarded, some clay or other material is likely to adhere to the vessel walls.

Certain pottery-making tools have high potential archaeological visibility, including smoothing stones, hammerstones, specialized *manos,* and *metates* (Table 3.19). The smoothing stone is exclusively a modelling and burnishing tool, while *manos, metates,* and hammerstones are used for the crushing and grinding of calcite cobbles into fine

calcite on hand. Of the 36 potting households recorded in Chanal and Aguacatenango, 28 (78%) had supplies of tempered and/or untempered clay on hand, while 25 (69%) had supplies of ground and/or unground calcite temper. By contrast, no nonpotting household in Chanal had either temper or clay on hand. In Aguacatenango, three interviewed potters used a variety of sand tempers and two potters used mineral pigments. In each case these were stored within the compound. Only five Chanal potting households (16%) did not have raw materials on hand.

The fact that such a high proportion of households stored raw materials for potting was very significant, since these raw materials are of little value and would likely be left in situ during housesite abandonment. Moreover, small amounts of all these materials would be likely to occur in household refuse areas, patios, and unused spaces within structures. Calcite cobbles were often loosely stored inside structures, while ground calcite, and sometime cobbles, as well as sand and clay were generally stored in reused damaged pottery vessels (Figure 3.29). Bryant and Brody (1986:77) report a similar practice for Amatenango. Temper was often spilled in

TABLE 3.18.
Frequencies of Archaeologically Visible Pottery-Making Materials in Chanal and Aguacatenango Households (x=Present but Frequency or State not Specified).*

Household #	SS	CM	CT	CH	CL	CA	SA	PI	PC	PT	OC	OT
Chanal												
3	X	2	1	—	X	t	—	—	1	—	—	1
4	1	1	1	—	X	c	—	—	2	1	—	1
5**	X	—	—	—	—	—	—	—	—	—	—	—
6*+	X	—	—	—	—	c	—	—	—	—	—	1
7	X	1	1	—	X	—	—	—	—	—	—	1
9*+	1	—	—	—	X	X	—	—	3	1	—	—
10	X	1	1	—	X	t	—	—	1	2	—	1
13	X	1	1	—	X	—	—	—	—	—	1	—
14	1	1	1	—	X	c	—	—	5	1	—	—
15	1	—	1	—	X	t	—	—	1	—	2	2
16	1	—	—	—	X	t	—	—	—	2	—	1
17	1	1	—	—	X	t	—	—	8	3	—	5
19	—	—	—	—	—	—	—	—	—	—	—	—
20	X	1	3	1	X	c/t	—	—	6	3	1	—
22	X	1	1	1	X	c/t	—	—	—	—	—	1
23*+	—	—	—	—	X	t	—	—	2	2	—	1
24	X	—	1	—	X	—	—	—	1	—	—	—
25	1	2	2	—	X	t	—	—	8	4	—	—
27	X	2	2	—	—	—	—	—	—	—	—	—
28	1	1	1	—	X	—	—	—	1	—	—	—
29	X	—	—	—	X	—	—	—	1	—	—	—
30	X	3	2	—	—	—	—	—	—	—	—	—
31	X	—	1	—	—	X	—	—	—	—	—	1
35	1	1	1	—	X	t	—	—	1	2	—	—
37	X	—	1	—	X	X	—	—	1	3	—	—
39*+	—	—	—	—	X	—	—	—	1	—	—	—
41	X	1	1	—	—	t	—	—	—	1	—	—
43	X	2	1	—	X	t	—	—	2	2	—	—
45	1	1	1	—	X	t	—	—	2	—	—	—
48	X	—	—	—	—	—	—	—	—	—	—	—
53	X	1	1	—	X	c/t	—	—	—	1	—	—
Aguacatenango												
8	1	1	—	—	X	—	X	—	1	1	—	—
35	2	4	5	—	X	c/t	X	X	3	3	—	1
37	X	1	1	—	X	X	—	—	1	—	—	—
38	1	2	2	2	X	X	—	—	—	—	—	—
39	6	2	3	—	X	t	X	X	1	1	—	1
Frequency	39	34	37	4	28	24	3	2	53	33	4	17

*Pottery-making tools: SS=smoothing stone, CM=calcite *mano*, CT=calcite *metate*, CH=calcite hammerstone; raw materials: CL=clay, CA=calcite (t=ground, c=cobble), SA=sand, PI=pigments; storage containers: PC=clay in pottery vessel, PT=temper in pottery vessel, OC=clay in other container, OT=temper in other container.

**Potter uses *mano* and *metate* stored in mother's compound.

*+Potter was not actively potting when survey was conducted.

TABLE 3.19.
Storage Locations of Pottery-Making Tools and Materials in Chanal and Aguacatenango.

Location:	Inside House	Inside Kitchen	Inside Storehouse	On/around Patio	On/ bordering Patio
Tool Storage					
Smoothing stone	8	4	—	—	2
Mano	6	3	—	2	5
Metate	6	2	—	1	9
Hammerstone	—	—	—	—	2
Subtotal	20	9	0	3	18
Raw Materials					
Clay/sherds	5	1	—	7	3
Calcite	8	3	2	3	3
Sand	2	—	—	—	1
Pigments	1	—	—	—	1
Subtotal	16	4	2	10	8
Total	36	13	2	13	26

Location:	Outside Walls of House	Outside Walls of Kitchen	Outside Walls of Storehouse	Around Corn Bin	Compound (away from structures)
Tool Storage					
Smoothing stones	—	—	—	—	—
Mano	5	4	—	—	2
Metate	5	3	—	—	3
Hammerstone	1	—	—	—	—
Subtotal	11	7	0	0	5
Raw Materials					
Clay/sherds	6	3	3	2	2
Calcite	4	1	3	3	—
Sand	—	—	—	—	—
Pigments	—	—	—	—	—
Subtotal	10	4	6	5	2
Total	21	11	6	5	7

temper. One Chanal potter used a river cobble as a *mano,* while two others used river cobbles as hammerstones. *Metates* often served as supports for the surplus clay while modeling or as a modelling stand. The fact that the *manos* and *metates* used by potters for grinding temper were generally well worn, recycled, incomplete, or badly damaged suggests that they too might be left at a site upon abandonment. Their use by potters is evidenced by fine grains of ground calcite incorporated into the grinding surface of these tools (Figure 3.30; see Deal 1988b). In addition, in Chanal, there was a definite tendency for potting households to have two or more *manos.* This reflects the addition of reused *manos* for pottery making to the household inventory. Of 22 Chanal nonpotting households with *metates* and 28 potting households with *metates,* the nonpotting

Fig. 3.30. Heavily pitted calcite grinding metate, Chanal Household 30. Note that the working surface appears white due to a residue of fine calcite powder.

households averaged 1.4 (s.d. 0.7) *metates* per household, while the potting households averaged 2.1 (s.d. 0.8) *metates* per household.

In Chanal, only potting households and households with former potters possessed smoothing stones. However, only 14 (42%) of the potting households that claimed to use smoothing stones actually had them on hand or could find them. Most people had lost or misplaced them. This loose curational behavior suggests that a given potter might contribute several smoothing stones to the archaeological record. On the other hand, they were so small and occurred so infrequently that they could easily be missed in an archaeological excavation. When recovered, they are a good indicator of a potting household. Smoothing stones have even been found in the grave of a Mimbres potter in the American Southwest (Shafer 1985).

If abandoned at a site, these potentially visible tool forms might be discarded or left at their location of storage rather than at their location of use, although these locations were sometimes very close together. Activities involving the use of these items generally took place on the household patio, which was swept after each event. Smoothing stones were almost always stored inside the main house or kitchen, while the larger temper-preparation tools were found in several dif-

ferent locations inside or around the outside walls of the main house or kitchen, or more often along the edge of the patio. The *metates* were the largest tools and those most likely to be used and stored in a single location (The use and storage locations were generally the same.) In Amatenango, smoothing stones were kept in small bowls in the porch, while grinding stones were stored in the porch or along the outside wall of a structure (Bryant and Brody 1986:77).

Pottery firing equipment, such as hearth, stone props, and wasters, are also potentially visible remnants of pottery-making activity (Figure 3.31). The interviewed potters generally had one or two specific locations for firing pottery that they used repeatedly. The potters of Amatenango prefer firing locations that are sheltered from the wind (Bryant and Brody 1986:77; also see Reina and Hill 1978: 40). Of course, the more often a location was used the more likely it would be visible in the archaeological record. Traces of firing activity would include some fire-reddening of the soil, possibly charcoal and ash deposits, thermally fractured rock used for propping vessels, and potsherd wasters. Wasters are often sought out in archaeological situations, despite problems with identification, which are based upon the degree of distortion due to overfiring (e.g., Bordez 1964; Rye 1981:111). Finsten (1995:57) makes a useful distinction between usuable and unusable wasters and considers only the unusable wasters as evidence of production locations, along with clay lumps and mold fragments. Usuable wasters are deemed unreliable for this purpose since they may have been removed from the production area for potential reuse. In domestic contexts, many potters are not concerned with discolorations on vessel walls since their pottery is made for home use rather than for sale, and therefore, they do not use wasters. The discovery of a firing hearth also depends upon the area of the site excavated. Excavations limited to house mounds would probably miss potting hearths since they were often located away from structures and patio (Deal 1994).

Additional materials with generally low

Fig. 3.31. Stored materials from dismantled Amatenango street firing, including charred wood, wasters, and stone cobble vessel props.

potential archaeological visibility include the byproducts of pottery–making activities. Examples of this would include the debris from calcite grinding, ground calcite and sand from preparation of clay body, surplus clay from modelling and finishing activities (Figure 3.32), spillage of slip or pigment during decorating, and sherds and partially complete vessels discarded or set aside after breakage during drying and firing. Other than the breakage of vessels, these materials might occur in relatively small amounts, yet in situations where an activity is repeated many times a year in one location, such as calcite grinding, a gradual deposit may leave a permanent record of the activity. In this situation, a descriptive model of the pottery-making behavior of living potters presents a useful interpretative tool.

Assuming similar production methods, our Tzeltal Maya data concerning pottery production shows that it should be possible to identify potting households in Precolumbian Maya sites. Certain pottery-making equipment, raw materials, and firing equipment seem to have relatively high potential for deposition, recovery, and recognition in archaeological contexts. If micro-debitage analysis is used, byproducts of temper grinding should also be visible (Deal 1988b). Some non-potting Aguacatenango households had calcite on hand to trade for pottery in Amatenango. However, it seems reasonable to assume that the occurrence of two or more of the common pottery-making artifacts and/or features in association would be sound indicators of pottery production in a given household. Further, spatial models of contemporary pottery production might also improve our ability to predict the locations of prehistoric potting facilities and activity areas (Deal 1994b).

SUMMARY

The present chapter has dealt with the pottery variability and spatial patterning peculiar to Tzeltal pottery-making households. Pottery variability within potting households concerns not only vessel frequency and type diversity, but also microtradition variation in terms of technical, formal, and stylistic differences in the product manufactured. The spatial distribution of pottery in potting households versus nonpotting households

Fig. 3.32. Excess clay being trimmed from the bases of newly made cooking jars *(oxom)* before firing, Chanal Household 14.

Three levels of pottery production were recognized in the Tzeltal area, including domestic manufacture, elementary specialization, and artisan specialization. The latter two forms of specialization are variants of individual specialization in Costin's (1991) typology for the organization of specialist production. The rise of community specialization in Amatenango seems to be related to the economic needs of that community (i.e., supplemental to agriculture), along with the availability of pottery-making resources and the development and maintenance of the specialized knowledge for exploiting these resources.

If archaeologists wish to base inferences of post-marital residence behavior on pottery stylistic variation, or if they wish to study intracommunity craft specialization, then they must be able to recognize archaeological potting households. Information on Chanal pottery making indicates that potting households can be recognized most reliably through the identification of discarded pottery-making tools and the residues of pottery production. The former includes smoothing stones, hammerstones, *manos* and *metates* used in pottery paste preparation and forming activities, and stone props and wasters used in firing activities. The latter includes deposits of clay, temper, and pigments, often in reused vessels. Traces of these materials may also be left at production areas or on pottery-making tools. Remnants of firing hearths may also survive. In addition, relatively high vessel frequency or type diversity counts may be useful as supporting evidence in households where clear identification of potting activity cannot be made on pottery-making tools or production byproducts alone.

primarily concerns the storage of vessels between stages of manufacture and between manufacture and sale, as well as the storage of raw materials in reused vessels. Not surprisingly, all of this variability and patterning seems to intensify as the level of production increases.

4

Household as Consumption Unit

As with all artifacts, ceramics are part of a living totality, and they must be understood in their functional and symbolic role. (Deetz 1977:50)

The present chapter concerns the provisioning, use and reuse of pottery, and the archaeological implications of these activities. Provisioning is presented as a form of social interaction that affects the amounts of local versus nonlocal pottery in a Tzeltal household inventory. A descriptive model is developed that highlights variability in pottery use and reuse (Figure 4.1). According to the model, pottery use and reuse are two distinctive cycles of activity. During the use cycle, a given pottery vessel is used for its specific primary function, then, if necessary, cleaned, dried, and curated in a protected storage location. While in storage, it might itself become a temporary storage container. The cycle of use and curation events is completed when the pottery vessel is broken. If the vessel is not immediately repaired, thus renewing the cycle, or immediately disposed of outside the compound, it is placed in a temporary storage location (see Chapter 5). Many of these stored vessels, or vessel fragments, are eventually selected for reuse. Reuse is an economic strategy that reduces the provisioning needs of a household (Deal and Hagstrum 1995; Stanislawski 1969). During the reuse cycle, a vessel or item is used for a secondary or, if broken again, tertiary function generally unrelated to its original function. At any time, during either cycle, a vessel might be deemed useless and discarded (see Figure 4.2). The closing section of this chapter provides a review of the Precolumbian pottery sequence for the Central Highlands that examines the potential for making comparisons at the activity set level between modern and Precolumbian pottery assemblages.

POTTERY PROVISIONING AND SOCIAL INTERACTION

Archaeologists are often concerned with tracing the sources of a household's pottery (see Chapter 6). This topic can be addressed in a contemporary setting with a discussion of pottery provisioning, which involves certain pottery-related interactions. The major provisioning mechanisms are gift-giving, borrowing, and exchange (see Table 4.1). Gift-giving is often associated with the provisioning of newly established households, especially after marriage. In fact, a Chanaleño mother has a social obligation to provide a recently married daughter with enough pottery to setup housekeeping. This is a kind of informal *lateral cycling* (Schiffer 1987:29). The Kalinga practice of potters' giving vessels as gifts when visiting relatives in other communities (Stark and Longacre 1993:6) does not appear to be a common practice among the Tzeltal. Pottery gift-giving may not be archaeologically visible since it might occur only once over the occupation span of the housesite, and most of the vessels would be broken within a year (see Chapter 5).

TABLE 4.1.

Provisioning Related Social Interactions and Archaeological Indicators.

Predominant Mechanism	Reasons for Interaction	Archaeological Indicator
Gift-giving or Borrowing	Altruism or Social Obligation	Effect is Negligible or at a Constant Low Level
Intracommunity Exchange (Commodity for Commodity or Cash)	Provisioning (Potter's Family or Middleman)	Existence of Local Wares in Household Inventories
Intercommunity Exchange (Commodity for Commodity or Cash)	Provisioning (Local Market or Middleman)	Existence of Imported Wares and/or Industrial Goods in Household Inventories

TABLE 4.2.

Tzeltal Food Preparation and Serving Vessel Activity Set.

(1) Bowl, small hemispherical *(poket)*: used for serving cooked vegetables or corn gruel.

(2) Bowl, small restricted *(sets')*: used for serving cooked vegetables or corn gruel, or ladle.

(3) Bowl, small elliptical *(chalten)*: used for frying vegetables and, occasionally, meat or fish.

(4) Bowl, small frustrum *(sets')*: used for serving cooked vegetables, frying vegetables.

(5) Plate, large unrestricted *(samet)*: used for roasting tortillas.

(6) Solid, frustrum *(makil sti')*: used for potlid.

(7) Jar, small, wide-mouthed *(oxom)*: used for boiling vegetables.

(8) Jar, single-handle *(chikbin)*: used for making coffee, boiling vegetables, making home remedies.

(9) Jar, perforated *(chixnajab'il grande)*: used for washing lime-soaked corn

Borrowing may represent a constant low level of influence on a household's pottery inventory and the eventual archaeological assemblage. Among the Tzeltal, most of this activity took place just prior to major religious festivals, but also during preparations for weddings, baptisms, birthdays, deaths, house building, harvests, *cargo* duties, and even for general use when supply was short. In Aguacatenango, 35 household heads claimed to borrow pottery one to four times per year and 33 households claimed to lend pottery one to six times per year. Several informants said that they would lend to anyone in the community, however, most borrowing and loaning seemed to take place between immediate neighbors and close relatives. In Chanal, household heads claimed to borrow and/or loan pottery one to six times per year. Informants said that these transactions occurred more often through family ties or with *compadres* (godfathers) than among neighbors.

In Aguacatenango, the procedure for borrowing pottery was relatively standardized. The borrower took a cup of coffee and piece of bread to the home of the anticipated loaner and asked to borrow some pottery vessels. If the loaned vessels were used for cooking, when the food was prepared in the vessel, a portion was taken back to the loaner as a gift. If the vessel should break, the borrower repaid one-half of its value to the loaner. All types of vessels might be loaned and borrowed for short periods, especially the ritual unrestricted bowl *(borcelana)*, large wide-mouth jar *(oxom grande)*, un-

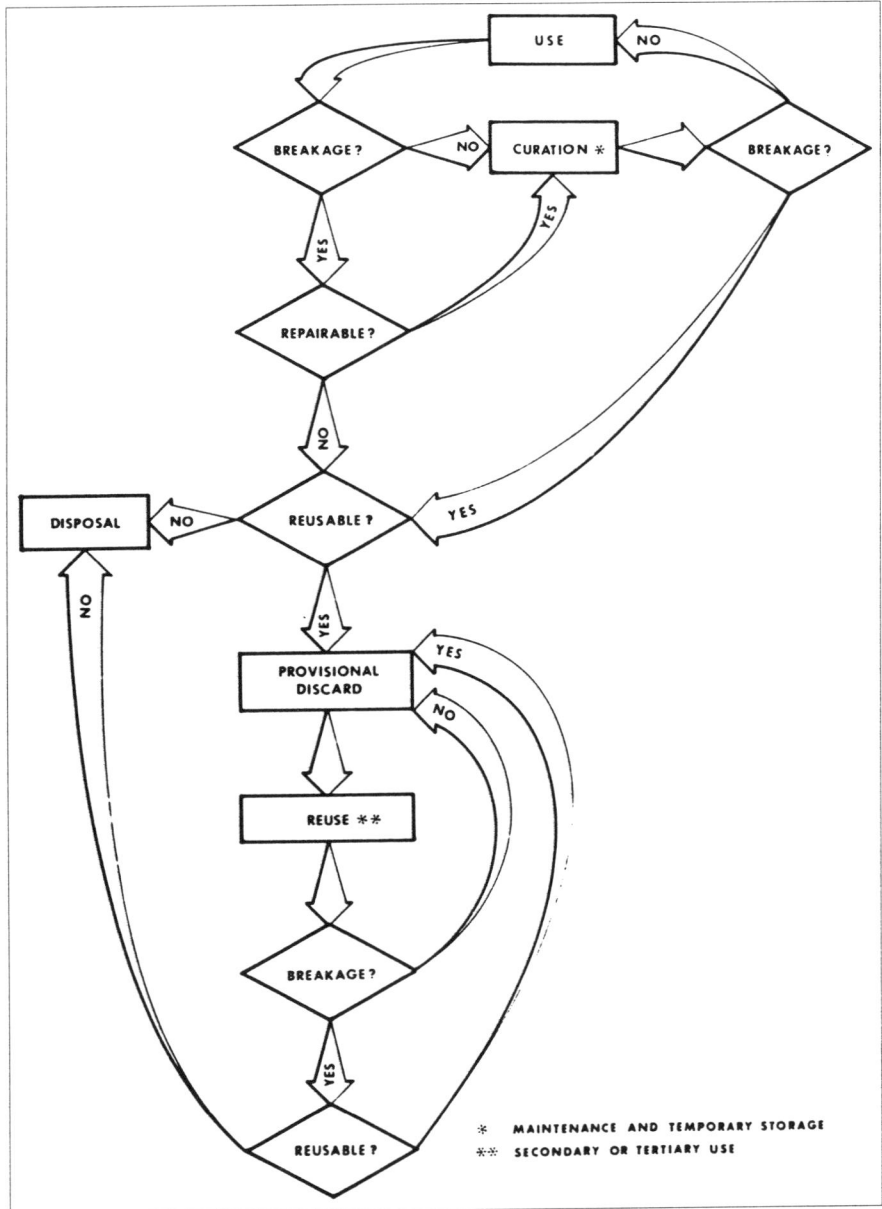

Fig. 4.1. Relationship between use cycle, reuse cycle, and provisional discard.

restricted plate *(samet)*, unrestricted bowl *(poket)* and narrow-mouth jar *(kib)*. The only commonly loaned or borrowed industrial replacement type was the metal cup.

The exchange of goods and services was the most important mechanism in provisioning Tzeltal households with pottery. A medium sized cooking jar or tortilla griddle could be acquired for one bowl *(borcelana)* of beans or maize. On the intracommunity level a potter usually interacted directly with her customers. Customers might visit her home and negotiate an exchange of commodities, which usually meant produce for pottery. A similar form of "balanced" exchange was recorded among the Kalinga (Stark 1994:140). There was very rarely an exchange of cash at this level. Potters could

Fig. 4.2. Woman purchasing narrow-mouth jar *(kib)* at pottery shop in Indian market, San Cristóbal de las Casas.

also peddle their wares in the barrios or in other communities. Peddlers would call from the street to ask if pottery was needed. A few potters even distributed their pottery indirectly through middlemen. This arrangement is a wholesale/retail type of enterprise, in which the middleman earned a commission of cash and/or commodities (also see Balfet 1965:171). The relative intensity of this kind of interaction varied according to the degree of specialization and rate of production within the potter's community, and the accessibility of pottery within the middleman's community. For the latter, it might continue on a full-time basis since he or she would deal with more than one potter. For the customer, the intensity was more sporadic, since it would take place only when the need for provisioning occurred. The relative success of these exchange mechanisms affected the distribution of the wares of individual potters within the community.

On the intercommunity level, currency and/or commodities were exchanged for pottery at local markets, such as San Cristóbal de las Casas and Comitan, and at weekly markets in some smaller communities (Figure 4.2). At the major pottery-making center of Amatenango, many people visited the community on specific fiesta days to obtain pottery. For example, many Aguacatenangueros visited the community on the festival of Santa Lucía (Dec. 13th), although they sometimes stopped there on their way to the Teopisca market to either buy pottery, or exchange calcite temper or foodstuffs for pottery (J. Nash 1959:11). One Aguacatenango informant claimed to visit Amatenango twice a year to exchange one liter of ground calcite for three or four cooking jars. This type of

TABLE 4.3.
Tzeltal Ritual Pottery Activity Set.

(11) Bowl, large hemispherical *(poket grande):* used for beer mixing, hand-washing.
(12) Bowl, small unrestricted *(borcelana):* used for serving vegetables or corn gruel; offering fruit, vegetables, or coffee on altar; serving guests on ritual occasions.
(13) Bowl, single-handle *(neochab):* used for making wax candles.
(14) Bowl, pedestal-based *(chikpom):* used for offering incense.
(15) Cylinder, pedestal-based *(somjebal cantela):* used for offering candles.
(16) Jar, large wide-mouth *(oxom grande):* used for cooking vegetables or preparing corn gruel for large gatherings.
(17) Jar, large composite *(tenosha grande):* used for beer mixing and fermenting, dry storage.
(18) Jar, perforated *(chixnajab'il chica):* used for straining corn gruel.
(19) Jar, pedestal-based *(florero):* used for offering flowers.

TABLE 4.4.
Storage Locations of Formal/Functional Types, by Activity Sets, for Chanal.

Activity Set:	Domestic	Ritual Offering	*Borcelana**	Cooking/ Brewing	*Kib*	Other
Storage Location:						
House Altar	21	90	37	2	4	2
House (General)	287	24	60	123	49	53
House/Kitchen	96	2	10	4	10	6
Kitchen	1036	3	127	64	79	21
Storage Building	41	2	27	26	6	7
Sweatbath	44	0	0	8	9	1
Corn Bin	6	0	0	2	0	0
Workshop	0	0	0	1	0	0
Shop (for sale)	0	2	24	0	0	0
Abandoned Building	3	0	0	0	0	0
On/Around Patio	45	1	2	4	56	1
Total (n=2528):**	1579	124	287	234	213	91

*The unrestricted bowl *(borcelana)* is generally part of the ritual activity set but is occasionally reused for domestic functions or serves both ritual and domestic functions in some households.
**The exact location was not recorded for all inventoried vessels.

exchange is generally more formal, and several factors might affect the intensity of the exchange. These include availability of transportation, frequency of provisioning needs, local availability of specific vessel forms, relative family wealth (i.e., in terms of pottery versus industrial needs) and the social status of the family. In the latter case, certain *cargo* positions involved purchasing many vessels, often of unusual size and form, for specific feasting occasions (see Chapter 2).

MODERN HOUSEHOLD
REQUIREMENTS: THE USE CYCLE
The following discussion outlines the use and reuse cycles in more detail. The use cycle is

TABLE 4.5.
Storage Locations of Formal/Functional Types, by Activity Sets,
for Aguacatenango.

Activity Set:	Domestic	Ritual Offering	*Borcelana**	Cooking/ Brewing	*Kib*	Other
Storage Location:						
House Altar	84	24	7	13	3	8
House (General)	289	19	172	50	24	18
House/Kitchen	233	8	51	17	13	15
Kitchen	622	55	134	35	11	18
Storage Building	101	4	27	19	5	0
Sweatbath	54	0	2	4	1	0
Animal Pen	55	0	0	2	6	2
On/Around Patio	759	4	4	67	201	6
Total (n=3246):**	2197	114	397	207	264	67

*The unrestricted bowl *(borcelana)* is generally part of the ritual activity set but is occasionally reused for domestic functions or serves both ritual and domestic functions in some households.
**The exact location was not recorded for all inventoried vessels.

discussed in terms of variation in vessel function and activity sets, and individual household needs. The latter includes variations due to storage requirements, the substitution of gourds or industrially made vessels for pottery, vessel uselife variation and replacement rates, and current household socioeconomic conditions.

FUNCTIONAL VARIATION AND ACTIVITY SETS

Pottery items satisfied many domestic and ceremonial requirements of the Tzeltal household. Each vessel form was associated with a specific range of functions. Certain groups of vessels were seen to embody distinct "activity sets." An activity set consisted of a group of vessels that served a specific activity, were associated with a specific activity area, and were stored together near their area of use. Carr (1984:113–117) considers the reconstruction of past activity sets and activity areas to be the major goal of spatial analysis at archaeological housesites (see also Kent 1984), and he suggests a number of middle-range concepts to help bridge the gap between systemic and archaeological contexts. Archaeological pottery activity sets

would appear at the most basic level in his model (see Carr 1984:Figure 3.2).

Three major activity sets could be found in any Tzeltal household, including vessels for food preparation and serving, water procurement and storage, and ritual activities. The Tzeltal food preparation and serving set consisted of nine vessel forms in Chanal and Aguacatenango, including five general purpose bowl and jar forms and four vessel forms with restricted functions (Table 4.2; Figures 4.3–4.4). Of these nine vessel forms, the basic activity set consisted of at least one serving bowl, a wide-mouth jar and an unrestricted plate. All forms were generally used and stored within the kitchen structure (Tables 4.4–4.5), while new vessels were stored in the rafters. For entertaining, meals might be eaten in the living house, in which case serving bowls would be used to transfer prepared foods between the two structures.

The second activity set consisted of only one vessel form (type 10), the narrow-mouth jar *(kib)*. This vessel served primarily for the transportation of water from water source to kitchen, where it also served as a water storage container (Figure 4.5). Some households sat up drainage troughs beside

TABLE 4.6.
Distribution of Non-Pottery Storage Containers per Household in
Chanal and Aguacatenango.

Community:	Chanal			Aguacatenango		
Container Type:	Maximum	Mean	s.d.	Maximum	Mean	s.d.
Burlap Bag	24	5.23	5.6	17	4.10	5.3
Cordage Bag	28	8.87	5.9	26	7.74	5.8
Plastic Shoulder/Hand Bag	60	4.56	8.4	20	5.30	4.2
Armadillo Carapace Bag	8	0.49	1.5	4	0.44	0.9
Animal Hide Bag	9	0.72	1.5	1	0.04	0.2
Bull Testicle Bag	—	—	—	2	0.14	0.4
Basket	44	13.17	9.4	22	10.16	5.3
Wooden Box	28	5.87	5.0	17	2.90	3.3
Cardboard Box	55	3.38	8.1	38	5.30	6.2
Barrel	1	0.02	0.1	1	0.10	0.3
Metal Chest	3	0.51	0.7	2	0.26	0.6
Large Tin Cans	2	0.26	0.6	13	1.50	2.6
All Types	—	43.08	—	—	37.96	—

structures with a *kib* at the lower end to collect rain water. Smaller narrow-mouth jars were used to hold water in the sweatbaths, and for training young girls to carry water. Generally each household would have at least one of these vessels, and many households stored extra vessels of this type in case of breakage.

The ritual activity set consisted of nine vessel forms (Table 4.3), most of which were restricted in function. Of these vessel forms, the basic activity set included a pedestal-based bowl for offering incense, a large wide-mouth jar, and one or more serving bowls (Figure 4.6). Some people purchased beer *(chicha)* from bootleggers and therefore did not require the large beer-making vessels. The single-handle bowl *(neochab)* was only used in Chanal, although a very similar vessel form was reported earlier in this century in the Tzeltal village of Cancuc (Blom and LaFarge 1927:390). It was a very specialized item, which was commissioned by a person holding the First *Alferez cargo* position (see Chapter 5). It was used only once to make beeswax candles for a certain ritual offering. This vessel was generally saved by the family as an heirloom.

The preparation of large quantities of food in the *oxom grande* was sometimes done on special festival hearths, constructed on or around the family patio. These and other large ritual vessel forms were stored in any available space, such as in corners, rafters, along outside walls, and in storage buildings where they occurred. Other ritual vessels were primarily used on the family altar and were generally stored on or around the altar (Deal 1988a).

Two vessel forms from this classification (Types 30 and 31) were traditional vessel forms that were no longer produced. One was the Chanal cylindrical jar *(balal oxom)*, which according to one informant was once popular for carrying hot liquids to the *milpa*. The three specimens recorded were being used for cooking beans, storing beans, and storing peaches. The other type, the Aguacatenango pedestal-based bowl *(chinpin)* served as a support for a serving bowl. One other traditional pottery item, the spindle-whorl *(pe'tet)*, was generally found in households with weavers. Some of these were made locally, while others were bought in San Cristóbal de las Casas or Comitan, and probably originated in Oxchuc.

TABLE 4.7.
Tourist Pottery Types Recorded in Chanal and Aguacatenango.

(21) Bowl, tripod, and pestle (*molcajete* and *majodor*): used for grinding chile pepper.

(22) Effigy vessel *(alcancia)*: used for child's money bank.

(23) Figurine *(figurilla, animalito, estatuilla)*: used for child's toy.

(24) Jar, small composite *(tenosha chica)*: used for child's toy.

(25) Dish, flaring-mouth *(cenicero)*: used for ashtray.

(26) Cup, single-handle *(vaso)*: used for serving liquids.

(27) Vase, wide-mouth *(maceta)*: used for flower pot.

(28) Bowl, loop-handle *(mochelum)*: used for general dry storage, decoration.

(29) Bowl, incurving rim *(batea)*: used for general utility, clothes washing.

TABLE 4.8.
Tzeltal Gourd Container Types.

(1) Bowl, restricted-mouth: used for storing tortillas. On ritual occasions a special support *(pechech),* made from maguey cordage, with strings for suspension, was used to support the tortilla server. A ceramic version of this support (called *kobile'ta*) used to be manufactured in the northern Tzeltal village of Sivaca (Becquelin and Baudez 1979:301, Figure 205b).

(2) Bowl, open-mouth: used for general dry storage.

(3) Ladle: used to ladle dry foods (especially beans or kerneled corn) or water.

(4) Bottle: used for storage and transport of liquids and usually closed with a cork made from a corn cob or husks.

(5) Cup: used for serving liquids (*trago* or *atole*) on ritual occasions. These gourds are also used to make ceremonial rattles (see Hayden and Cannon 1984a:96–99).

(6) Bowl, perforated for suspension: used for carrying corn kernels for planting. Bags made from armadillo carapaces also served this function.

STORAGE REQUIREMENTS

In sedentary communities, storage occurs in both formal and informal contexts. Formal storage, which is characterized by specialized compartments such as bins, adjunct rooms, and separate storage structures (Hunter-Anderson 1977), is commonly identified in archaeological situations (e.g., Bawden 1982: 168, 173; D'Altroy and Hastorf 1984; Healan 1979:145; Smyth 1989; Zier 1979:139). By contrast, informal storage is dispersed in nature, and therefore more likely to be confused with activity and disposal locations when encountered on archaeological sites (e.g., Deal 1985, 1987; Hally 1983a: 117, 121; Sullivan 1983). Pottery vessels prevent the dispersion of stored materials but do not provide them with sufficient protection (see Hunter-Anderson 1977:301), and, therefore, must themselves be informally stored, often within formal storage facilities such as storerooms or separate storage structures. Because of this, pottery storage is also intimately associated with the informal storage of a variety of other materials in sedentary communities. Further, due to its tendency to break into numerous fragments, pottery is highly visible in archaeological situations and is therefore an important artifact class in any investigation of informal storage strategies and associated site structure.

Chanal and Aguacatenango households did not acquire any specific vessel forms primarily for use as storage containers, yet any jar, bowl, or cup was a potential temporary storage container (also see Rice 1987:295).

Fig. 4.3. Domestic scene in Chanal, including wide-mouth cooking jars *(oxom)*, at left and under table, large plate *(comal)* at left end of table, and large bowl *(poket grande)* being reused to catch waste from a corn grinder. Also note metal *comal* at left, gourd bowl at center, and metal buckets on and under table.

Fig. 4.5. Cancuc women using Tenango style watercarrying jars *(kib)*, 1979.

Fig. 4.4. Chanal woman serving cooked vegetables from wide-mouth jar *(oxom)* to glazed bowl *(borcelana)*.

Significantly, over 60 percent of the vessels being used for storage at the time of our study were under 25 cm in height. However, proportionally more large vessels than small vessels were being used for temporary storage of dry goods and consumable foodstuffs. In the Pompeii-like situation at the prehistoric Maya site at Cerén, El Salvador, Beaudry-Corbett (1992:3) notes that the pottery inventories in adjunct storerooms exhibited considerable variation in the size and shape categories of vessels. This suggests that an informal pottery storage pattern, involving a variety of vessel forms and sizes, may be typical of traditional domestic contexts, even within adjunct or separate storage facilities.

Fig. 4.6. Ritual scene in Chanal, including incense burner *(chik'pom)* and candleholder *(somjebal cantela)* in foreground.

This pattern may not apply to more formal state level storage situations. For example, at the Inca center of Huanuco Pampa, Morris (1974b:138–143) also notes a considerable variation in vessel forms associated with domestic structures, yet a specific form of stor-

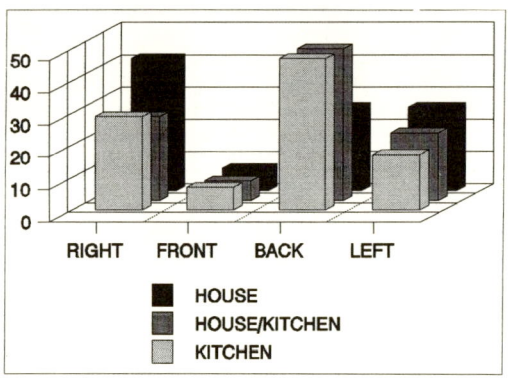

Fig. 4.7. Pottery storage locations along the inside walls of Aguacatenango structures.

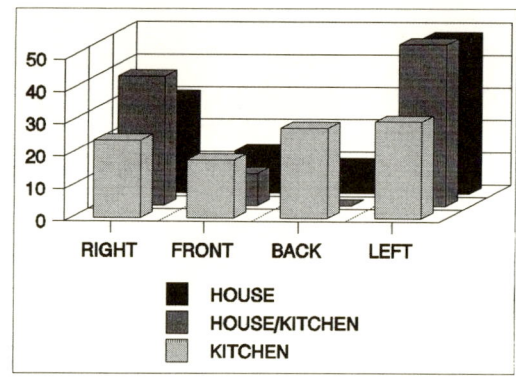

Fig. 4.8. Pottery storage locations along the outside walls of Aguacatenango structures.

age jar was almost exclusively associated with specialized state run storage facilities.

Other informal storage facilities used for long term storage at Aguacatenango include a variety of hide and cordage bags, baskets, wooden boxes, and in recent times, plastic bags, metal chests, cardboard boxes, and large tin cans (Table 4.6; also see Thompson 1958:146). The most commonly stored materials were consumable liquids such as water, honey, corn beer, and corn gruel, consumable foodstuffs such as beans, eggs, corn kernels, peppers, avocados, salt and tortillas, dry goods such as lime, rope, kindling, soap and clothing, and for ritual items such as glass bloodletting tools, serving bowls, and offerings of incense, candles, and flowers.

If we consider storage location in relation to the patio entrances of structures, then Figure 4.7 gives a good indication of the distinction between informal pottery storage in living houses, kitchens, and the combined house/kitchens for Aguacatenango. In terms of internal storage arrangements, the kitchen and combined house/kitchen exhibit a similar pattern. This pattern reflects the preference for locating the food-processing tables against the back walls of these structures, and the close association of domestic pottery storage with these facilities (also see Wauchope 1938:plates 32 and 33). The other major form of inside storage is the clustering of vessels on low benches or racks in any available space, away from other facilities. By

contrast, there is relatively more right and left wall pottery storage in separate house structures. This pattern reflects the practice of locating the house altar along these walls in the house porch. Most ritual pottery is used and stored in the living house, and most of this is stored on and around the house altar. These include vessels used for serving, brewing, and drinking alcohol, handwashing, straining corn gruel, and cooking, and smaller numbers of domestic cooking vessels (Deal 1987).

In terms of informal pottery storage along the outside walls of structures, houses and combined house/kitchens seem to share a similar pattern, while kitchen storage is more generalized (Figure 4.8). Most of the cases recorded here were vessels washed after a meal that were being dried before storage inside structures. This is not surprising, since our visits were generally prearranged and occurred shortly after the morning meal. In some households, however, permanent drying racks were constructed around the patio (also see Baer and Merrifield 1971:144; DeBoer and Lathrap 1979:124). Further, almost every household stored watercarrying jars outside, generally on low benches beside structures (Figure 4.9). They were rarely stored inside because of the potential inconvenience that would result from breakage.

The nature of pottery storage is further conditioned by both the monetary and sociocultural value of the vessel (also see Moore

Fig. 4.9. Watercarrying jar *(kib)* storage in hollows along patio, Chanal Household 40.

Fig. 4.10. Amatenago pottery alligator made for tourist trade. According to local archaeological lore, the original model was made for Susanna Ekholm when she was working at the site of Lagartero.

1982: 76). For example, ritual vessels and heirlooms are more carefully stored than domestic vessels. Further, decisions concerning whether storage should be high or low are partially determined by vessel size; larger vessels are more likely to be stored on the ground. Obviously, vessels in low storage are more likely to be damaged than those on tables and wall racks or stored on rafters (also see DeBoer 1986). Both of the above considerations (i.e., vessel value and size) seem to be evident in the storerooms at the Cerén site, where painted serving vessels received protective storage, while utilitarian jars were normally placed on the floors (Beaudry-Corbett 1992:3).

TOURIST POTTERY

The remaining vessel forms (and vessel equivalents) must be considered in light of two recent trends related to pottery production in both Mesoamerica and the Southwest

(see Nicklin 1971:21). One is the increase in non-utilitarian pottery vessels for the tourist trade (Figure 4.10), and the other is the decline in traditional pottery with the arrival of modern industrial equivalents. Nine vessel forms recorded in Chanal and Aguacatenango are considered tourist types (Table 4.7). These types were very rare in both communities (see Table 1.1). In Chanal they represented only 30 vessels, or .9 percent of the total community inventory, while in Aguacatenango there were 61 vessels, representing 1.4 percent of the total inventory. These vessels were most often stored inside the main living structure.

GOURD CONTAINERS

Throughout modern Mesoamerica, gourd containers can substitute for certain pottery types and therefore can affect the diversity of a household's pottery inventory. The use of gourd containers is a tradition dating back at least 9000 years in various parts of Mesoamerica (Lathrap 1977:725; Lowe 1971; Whitaker and Cutler 1967). Moreover, a variety of gourd containers (including certain thick-rind pumpkins and squashes) probably served as prototypes for the form, surface finish, and decoration in the Mesoamerican "basal" pottery tradition, which emerged about 3600 years ago (Joesink-Mandeville 1974). The production and functional variation of gourd containers among modern Maya groups has been well documented

TABLE 4.9.
Distribution of Gourd Vessels per Household in Chanal and Aguacatenango.

Community:	Chanal			Aguacatenango		
Measurement:	Maximum	Mean	s.d.	Maximum	Mean	s.d.
Gourd Container Type:						
Restricted-Mouth Bowl	42	7.79	8.4	22	7.20	3.8
Unrestricted Bowl	13	1.32	2.5	12	1.70	2.3
Cup	30	1.30	4.3	18	0.62	2.6
Ladle	9	1.55	2.3	0	0.00	0.0
Bottle	14	2.96	3.4	21	6.42	4.8
Suspended Bowl	1	0.02	0.4	12	1.38	2.3

(e.g. Baer and Baer 1950:13–14; Berlin et al. 1974:128–131; McBryde 1947:57, 138; Wisdom 1940:144–145).

In modern Chanal and Aguacatenango households, while the open-mouth gourd bowl could be substituted for any pottery utility bowl, other gourd vessels had restricted functions that generally did not overlap with pottery vessels. Gourd vessels were often associated with ritual activities (Figure 4.11), especially the restricted-mouth bowl *(pompo)* and the gourd cup *(jicara)*. In particular, the use of gourd vessels in funerary rites has often been reported (Menget 1968:54; Wisdom 1940:304), and they have been found in early burials (McBryde 1947:138). Six types of gourd containers were recorded in Chanal and Aguacatenango (Tables 4.8–4.9).

INDUSTRIAL REPLACEMENTS

In some areas of the world the industrial replacement of pottery vessels is almost complete (e.g., Woods 1984). While the situation in Chiapas was not as serious, the purchase of industrial vessels can greatly alter the size and diversity of a household's pottery inventory. Metal, glass, and plastic containers were moderately priced alternatives to many pottery types, and especially those used for food serving and water transport. As among the Huichol (Weigand 1969:20) of northern Mexico, some Tzeltal families used metal and plastic buckets for transporting water from

wells and obtaining water from deep wells. It was even socially acceptable for a man to carry water if he used a bucket rather than a pottery vessel. The most commonly replaced vessels were food serving bowls (see Table 4.10). When asked why industrially made bowls were often preferred to pottery ones, the consistent reply from informants was that the metal ones lasted longer. The same reason has been suggested for the preference of metalware over pottery in the Kathmandu valley of India (Birmingham 1975:385) and among the Bariba of Bénin (Sargent and Friedel 1986:192). Pottery vessels are still important among the Bariba for the preparation of medicines, which indicates their value to traditional curers and their patients (Sargent and Friedel 1986:192). This may also be true of Tzeltal Maya curers, who still use special undersized pottery vessels for preparing medicines.

As with metal bowls, metal cooking vessels were used because they lasted longer, and because they heated up faster. These included metal pots, cooking pans, frying pans, metal *comales*, recycled tin can pitchers, reused tin cans with wire handles and metal buckets. Metal buckets were suspended over the hearth (Figure 4.12). Pottery, however, was universally believed to leave a better taste in cooked food. Often a metal vessel was only used if a ceramic one was broken, or if the cook was in a hurry. Furthermore, metal tortilla griddles, although they required less

Fig. 4.11. Gourd bowls containing *atole*, on serving table at San Bautista fiesta, Chanal, 1977.

Fig. 4.12. Domestic scene in Chanal, illustrating the industrial replacement of cooking jars by metal buckets. Also note metal version of single-handled jar in background.

fuel, were accused of heating too fast, and thus burning the tortilla around the edges while leaving a soggy, bad tasting center. Most households had at least one of these, however, for reheating tortillas. This type, in particular, was an addition to the inventory rather than a replacement for its pottery equivalent.

Except for caches of metal bowls and cups that were generally found around the family altar, few industrially made items were used for ritual purposes. Some households had metal or homemade wooden candleholders, while others had metal or glass flower vases. Tin cans were quite often used for offering flowers on family altars, and as containers for planting young seedlings. A large glass bottle *(garapon)* was often used for fermenting corn alcohol *(trago)*, while beverage bottles were used for distributing smaller portions.

As long as cash continues to be scarce and pottery vessels remain cheaper and more accessible than industrial equivalents, there will be little danger of pottery disappearing from Tzeltal households. Furthermore, pottery can be made in the household, received as gifts, or bartered for produce.

VESSEL USELIFE

The differential uselives of functional types of pottery vessels is an important factor in determining the frequencies of each type observed in the archaeological record of given

household compound (see David 1972; De-Boer 1974:335). Specifically, functional types with short uselives should have a more rapid turnover rate and thus contribute an increasingly larger proportion of vessels to a household's pottery refuse over time. Some major factors related to a vessel's longevity have been identified, including basic strength, function, frequency of use, storage and drying practices, and causes of breakage (Bedaux 1987; Calder 1972; David 1972:141; DeBoer 1974; Foster 1960:606; B. Nelson 1991; Neupeort and Longacre 1994; Pastron 1974:109). Recent research by Michael Shott (1996) suggests that various aspects of vessel size (height, weight, diameter, etc.) may also be significant factors in vessel uselife. Moreover, the repair of vessels for both use and reuse functions must also be considered as a factor in extending vessel uselife, as well as replacement cost (P. J. Arnold 1988).

Basic strength refers to the relative "hardness" of vessel walls, in terms of serviceability, and wall thickness in proportion to vessel size (also see Foster 1960:606). The relative hardness of a vessel depends in part on paste composition, surface treatment (especially glazing), and firing conditions. The relative skill of the individual potter must also be considered an important factor. As a rule, the potters of Chanal tended to be much less proficient than potters of the larger centers such as Amatenango and Yocnajab. The paste composition of Tzeltal vessels, in terms of amount and kinds of temper used, was related to intended vessel function. For example, in Amatenango, large amounts of coarse calcite temper were added to vessels to be used on the hearth, which required a more porous paste. Such pastes are quite soft after being fired. In contrast, serving vessels, not intended for the hearth, had a sand temper that created a finer paste and was relatively hard after being fired.

Glazed, kiln-fired vessels made in San Ramon and Chiapa de Corzo were the most durable pottery vessels in a Chanal inventory followed by the slipped, open-air fired Amatenango vessels. The relatively low uselives estimated for the imported glazed vessels was probably indicative of their function, frequency of use, and storage practices rather than of their durability. The locally produced plainwares, being crudely formed, heavily tempered with calcite, and fired at low temperatures, were considered the least durable.

Closely related to basic strength is differential vessel wall thickness. For example, the relative wall thickness of large ritual cooking jars and beer mixing bowls (often more than one cm) partly compensated for their high calcite content and thus contributed to their longevity (also see Rye 1981:59). Furthermore, such large, thick-walled vessels were heavier and less portable than other vessels in the household inventories and, therefore, were less likely to be broken in transport.

Shott (1996:471–473) recently reevalu-

ated the Tzeltal uselife data as part of a detailed cross-cultural study of uselife and vessel size (also see Chapter 6). His analyses identified orifice diameter as an important factor in the uselives of utilitarian vessels, at least for the globular to conoidal forms, while the effects of vessel height were not significant. This may be difficult to translate into behavioral terms, although orifice diameter is certainly closely associated with vessel size and difficulty in handling. Shott also points out that Foster's contention that non-producers will be more careful with their pottery, thus increasing their uselives, does not seem to hold for Chanal and Aguacatenango. Although Chanal produces most of its own pottery, higher uselife estimates are consistently given for Chanal pottery compared to Aguacatenango pottery. The fact that Chanal is a poorer and more isolated community than Aguacatenango could account for the higher value placed on ceramic vessels and the more careful use of vessels. The people of Aguacatenango had a ready supply of inexpensive pottery in nearby Amatenango, while better quality wares were shipped into Chanal by bus and sold by middlemen at higher prices. Even the locally made vessels were quite expensive. Many Chanal potters who made vessels for home use considered pottery making a burden rather than a moneymaking opportunity.

Differences in vessel function and frequency of use are related to variation in the breakage frequencies for vessel types. Food preparation and serving vessels were used much more often than ritual vessels, and this was reflected in relative uselife. Estimates of uselife given by Chanal and Aguacatenango informants confirm this (Table 4.11). In both communities, the three vessels used daily on the hearth (*oxom*, *samet*, and *chikbin*) were considered to be among the shortest-lived functional types, while most ritual vessels were given longer uselives. For example, the estimated uselife of a tortilla griddle was about six months. Hendry (1992:49) reported a similar lifespan for tortilla griddles at Atzompa, Oaxaca, but indicated that most families had to replace them in a month of so. Uselife estimates for certain types probably showed some variation due to differential sizes of household pottery inventories, that is, a household using only one *oxom* would be likely to give a shorter uselife estimate for that type than a household that uses nine of these vessels interchangeably. Elsewhere, both David (1972:41) for the Fulani and Pastron (1974:109) for the Tarahumara, include cooking vessels at the low end of the scale followed by serving bowls and storage vessels. Foster also included cooking vessels at the low end of the scale for Tzinzuntzan, followed by water storage vessels and fiesta pottery (1960:608).

In Chanal and Aguacatenango, one type of ritual serving vessel (the *borcelana*) was given a relatively short uselife. This probably reflected the effects of Tzeltal drinking habits, in that in many households they were used only on occasions that featured ritual drinking. Similarly, DeBoer and Lathrap (1979:128) gave the shortest uselife among Shipibo-Conibo vessel types to the beer drinking mug. In Chanal and Aguacatenango, vessels used in the preparation of beer (mixing bowls and brewing jars) were used before, but not during, fiesta gatherings and tended to have long uselives. Similarly, Shipibo-Conibo serving and brewing jars were estimated to have long uselives (DeBoer and Lathrap 1979:128).

Differential drying and storage practices also affected relative uselife. Vessels not frequently in use were often given more protective storage. On one hand, ritual beer mixing bowls, *atole* colanders, and serving bowls were often stored in wooden boxes or in the rafters of the main house structure, while incense burners, candle holders, flower holders and occasionally serving bowls were stored on or under the family altar. On the other hand, food preparation and serving vessels were often stored along the interior walls (or exterior walls when drying) of the kitchen where there was considerably more risk of damage. Furthermore, watercarrying jars, which were constantly in transit, were

very susceptible to breakage and, therefore, tended to have a shorter uselife.

Causes of breakage were closely connected with drying practices and locations of use and storage. Food preparation and serving vessels drying or stored along walls were susceptible to accidental breakage by animals and small children. Dogs and poultry were commonly quoted as a frequent cause of breakage in Tzeltal kitchens. Many vessels were damaged while being transported from use locations to storage locations. In the case of watercarrying jars, breakage generally occurred at the water source or along the trail. Handles often snapped off when a woman hoisted her jar onto her back or when she slipped on a wet trail. Vessels used on the hearth were most frequently broken while in use on or around the hearth. Vessels often cracked on the fire because they were filled too full or because the fire was too high. Sometimes a vessel was knocked into the fire or off their firedogs by a person or animal, or occasionally someone simply dropped a vessel because it was too hot to handle. Breakage also occurred on and around the household patio. Ritual serving bowls were often broken during fiestas by clumsy drunks. Others were knocked off storage benches or occasionally damaged when firewood was dropped on them. Colanders were often broken by too vigorous corn washing.

Vessel uselife could sometimes be extended through repair. The decision of whether to repair a pottery vessel depended upon the nature and extent of the damage and the relative reuse value of the vessel. If a vessel was only slightly chipped or cracked, it would usually continue to serve its original function. If the damage was more extensive, a decision had to be made whether it could be temporarily mended. If the repair was unsuccessful or not attempted the vessel would be put in a provisional discard location (see Chapter 5). If needed, the vessel might eventually be repaired or reused for a different function.

If repair was attempted, there were several commonly used techniques, depending upon

TABLE 4.10.
Distribution of Industrial Replacement Vessels per Household
in Chanal and Aguacatenango.

Community:		Chanal			Aguacatenango	
Measurement:	Maximum	Mean	s.d.	Maximum*	Mean	s.d.
Industrial Container Type:						
Food Preparation/Serving						
Metal Bowl	18	6.19	4.2	26	9.52	5.4
Plastic Bowl	11	2.15	2.8	18	4.06	3.6
Glass Bowl	23	0.62	3.2	10	1.46	2.2
Metal Plate	20	1.62	3.7	3	0.30	0.7
Plastic Plate	4	0.31	0.7	3	0.14	0.5
Glass Plate	18	0.62	2.6	5	0.28	0.8
Metal Tray	2	0.13	0.4	2	0.08	0.3
Plastic Colander	0	0.00	0.0	2	0.04	0.3
Metal Cooking Pot	9	1.11	2.0	9	1.96	1.8
Tin Can with Wire Handle	12	1.23	2.3	7	1.00	1.9
Tin Can Heating Pitcher	5	1.21	1.5	16	6.94	4.0
Metal *Comal*	5	0.25	0.8	3	1.58	1.0
Metal Frying Pan	5	0.85	1.1	5	1.82	1.3
Metal Cooking Pan	10	0.21	1.4	1	0.02	0.1
Metal *Sarten*	0	0.00	0.0	3	0.18	0.5
Metal Potlid	8	0.66	1.6	8	1.02	1.7
Homemade Potlid	6	0.26	1.0	8	0.88	1.8
Serving/Storing Liquids						
Metal Cup	25	3.53	4.3	55	6.70	8.3
Plastic Cup	47	3.39	7.7	17	3.90	4.0
Glass Cup	9	0.47	1.9	6	0.60	1.3
Plastic Tumbler	0	0.00	0.0	10	0.44	1.5
Glass Tumbler	20	2.15	3.7	23	2.50	4.1
Shot Glass	10	0.68	1.7	20	0.92	3.2
Plastic Pitcher	1	0.04	0.2	4	0.24	0.7
Glass Pitcher	2	0.08	0.3	0	0.00	0.0
Coffee/Teapot	3	0.34	0.6	3	0.28	0.6
Metal Decanter	0	0.00	0.0	3	0.18	0.6
Thermos	5	0.15	0.7	1	0.06	0.2
Plastic Canteen	20	2.36	3.0	4	0.92	1.2
Glass *Trago* Bottle	2	0.32	0.5	10	0.94	2.5
Glass Beverage Bottle	18	2.94	3.1	39	5.90	7.3
Watercarrying/Storage						
Metal Bucket	17	3.96	3.1	14	3.02	2.3
Plastic Bucket	10	0.87	2.0	3	0.98	0.9
Storage/Utility Containers						
Glass Container	0	0.00	0.0	8	1.56	2.3
Plastic Container	0	0.00	0.0	5	0.64	1.2
Tin Can	45	9.89	9.5	67	16.76	12.9
Glass Jar	8	0.89	1.8	0	0.00	0.0

Community:		Chanal			Aguacatenango	
Measurement:	Maximum	Mean	s.d.	Maximum*	Mean	s.d.
Industrial Container Type:						
Hand-washing						
Metal Basin	6	0.60	1.1	3	0.52	0.7
Plastic Basin	5	0.13	0.7	4	0.96	1.1
Ritual Offering Vessels						
Candleholder	6	0.51	1.3	18	2.86	3.2
Glass Flower Holder	2	0.09	0.4	5	0.78	1.3
Metal Flower Holder	0	0.00	0.0	3	0.24	0.7

*Minimum number per household is one for metal cups and beverage bottles in Aguacatenango.

the nature and extent of the damage to the vessel. The types of damage most often observed to be repaired were cracks or holes in the upper body, neck or rim of a vessel (Figure 4.13). The most popular method of repairing cracks was to apply a sticky pitch made from pine resin. Sometimes a small piece of cloth impregnated with this resin was used as a patch. An alternate method involved the application of a coat of powdered lime in a water solution. This lime coat would be hardened over the fire and serve as a temporary patch. A popular method of temporarily repairing cracked vessels that were not used on the fire, was to melt wax (and in one case plastic!) over the crack. Also, some potters would repair a cracked vessel with new clay and refire it over the kitchen hearth.

If a crack occurred in the rim or neck of a vessel, a rope or wire strapping might be used to prevent the crack from extending lower on the vessel. Occasionally, if a rim were badly chipped, the rim might be sanded smooth or sawed off and then sanded. Holes were also occasionally repaired with pine pitch, lime or clay, but more often a stopper was used. The most commonly used material for stoppers was a dried, dekerneled corn cob. Other kinds of stoppers observed included wooden corks, sections of corn stalk, rolled plastic, and in one case the distal end of a feather.

Fig. 4.13. Watercarrying jar *(kib)*, repaired with lime and reused for collecting rain water, Chanal Household 3.

VESSEL REPLACEMENT RATES

The number of vessels broken per year rarely equals the number of vessels acquired per year. While the uselife of a vessel type remains more or less constant over time, replacement rates are more sensitive to changes

TABLE 4.11.
Uselife Estimates, in Years, for Chanal and Aguacatenango Pottery Types.*

Community:	Chanal		Aguacatenango	
	Mean	s.d.	Mean	s.d.
Food preparation and serving vessels:				
Small cooking jar *(oxom)*	0.58	0.64	0.61	0.93
Tortilla griddle *(samet)*	0.49	0.31	0.67	0.71
Boiling pitcher *(chikpin)*	1.68	1.25	0.55	0.24
Serving bowl *(sets')*	2.17	1.04	0.54	—
Watercarrying jar *(kib)*	2.29	1.62	1.15	1.23
Serving bowl *(poket)*	2.57	2.16	0.86	0.85
Frying bowl *(chalten)*	2.83	3.07	1.56	1.44
Maize colander *(chixnajab'il)*	—	—	1.25	0.50
Ritual vessels:				
Serving bowl *(borcelana)*	1.26	1.13	0.96	1.10
Large cooking jar *(oxom grande)*	3.72	1.45	1.99	2.13
Atole colander *(chixnajab'il)*	3.20	2.79	1.19	1.05
Incense burner *(chik'pom)*	5.80	4.78	1.67	1.67
Candleholder *(somejebal cantela)*	10.00	—	2.46	2.35
Beer mixing jar *(tenosha)*	12.50	3.54	2.92	4.47
Beer mixing bowl *(poket grande)*	20.00	14.14	8.50	9.19
Flower holder *(Yahuil nichim)*	—	—	3.00	2.83

*Excludes types for which estimates were not recorded. Values in italics are based on only one estimate.

in family social and economic position, as well as family makeup and seasonal variations in the availability of pottery (also see DeBoer 1974:341). Increases in family size due to births, or the addition of new wives or members from other families, and decreases due to death, children moving away, and family disagreements all appear to have some effect on vessel replacement rates. Changes in diet or household subsistence economy will undoubtedly affect replacement rates (especially in poorer households) by the supplementing or deleting of vessel types to fit the change in lifestyle.

Chanal and Aguacatenango informants were asked to estimate the approximate number of each type they would replace each year. The mean values of replacement rates for the two communities (see Table 4.12) shows the similarity in their vessel requirements. The bulk of vessels replaced were those used for food preparation and serving

(i.e., 80.78% for Chanal and 78.26% for Aguacatenango). The fact that Aguacatenango households tended to replace fewer vessels per year than Chanal households probably reflects the greater dependence on industrial vessels, and especially ritual serving vessels, in that community as well as the higher proportion of better quality Amatenango pottery to local wares in household inventories.

Households that farm *milpas* at some distance from the community also kept a small pottery inventory at their *milpa* houses. Based on information from 14 Chanal households, these inventories consisted of one to three unrestricted plates, one to four widemouth jars, one to three narrow-mouth jars, one to four single-handle jars, and about half a dozen bowls. Possible industrial replacements at *milpa* houses included a tin can with a wire handle, a metal bucket and a drinking glass.

TABLE 4.12.
Mean Annual Vessel Replacement Rates for Chanal and Aguacatenango.

Community:	Chanal		Aguacatenango	
Vessel Type:	Mean Replacement Frequency/year	Percentage Inventory	Mean Replacement Frequency/year	Percentage Inventory
Food Preparation:				
Bowl *(poket)*	1.36	3.66	2.80	10.92
Bowl *(chalten)*	0.31	1.86	1.10	2.08
Bowl *(poket/sets')*	0.35	5.04	0.10	0.19
Jar *(oxom/chikbin)*	16.63	45.98	8.50	52.84
Jar *(chixnajab'il)*	—	0.04	0.20	2.23
Jar *(kib)*	3.62	10.38	2.90	9.24
Plate *(samet)*	4.67	6.58	2.40	2.70
Food Preparation Subtotal:	26.94	73.54	18.00	80.20
Ritual:				
Bowl *(borcelana)*	3.17	9.65	0.40	9.53
Bowl *(ckik'pom)*	0.69	3.57	1.20	1.37
Jar *(oxom grande)*	2.50	5.12	1.40	1.91
Jar *(tenosha)*	—	0.73	0.50	1.74
Jar *(chixnajab'il)*	0.04	1.26	1.40	0.89
Cylinder *(somjebal cantela)*	—	0.59	0.30	0.07
Ritual Subtotal:	6.40	20.92	5.20	15.51
Other:	—	5.54	—	4.29
Total:	33.34	100.00	23.20	100.00

SOCIOECONOMIC CONDITIONS OF
POTTERY CONSUMPTION

Matson (1965) suggested that the diversity of available types of pottery in the possession of a given household at any one time was largely dependent upon current socioeconomic and demographic conditions of the household, such as family size, group needs, and certain social conditions and replacement factors (i.e., vessel uselives and replacement rates). The Chanal and Aguacatenango data provided a useful opportunity to study the relationships between such factors and pottery variability in ongoing households. Unless these relationships were strong, the use of archaeological pottery assemblages to infer any of these conditions about archaeological housesites in the Tzeltal area might be seriously questioned. In the present study, a series of graphs were generated which compared various aspects of household socioeconomic and demographic conditions with vessel frequency and type diversity. The socioeconomic variables represented are family size, economic rank, social rank, and religious and civil *cargo* rank.

When viewed at the level of the individual household, inferences concerning pottery fre-

TABLE 4.13.

Pottery Frequency and Diversity Trends in Relation to Certain Ranked Socioeconomic and Demographic Variables for Chanal and Aguacatenango.*

Chanal Ranks	Economic	Social	Civil *Cargo*	Ritual *Cargo*
Pottery Frequency	Indeterminate (4.18)	Positive (4.23)	Positive (4.27)	Positive (4.31)
Pottery Diversity	Indeterminate (4.18)	Positive (4.23)	Indeterminate (4.27)	Positive (4.31)
Pottery and Industrial Diversity	Positive (4.20)	Indeterminate (4.25)	Positive (4.29)	Positive (4.33)
Ritual Set Diversity	Positive (4.20)	Positive (4.25)	Positive (4.29)	Positive (4.33)
Food Set Diversity	Positive (4.21)	Indeterminate (4.26)	Indeterminate (4.30)	Indeterminate (4.34)
Imported Type Diversity	Indeterminate (4.21)	Positive (4.26)	Positive (4.30)	Positive (4.34)
Aguacatenango Ranks				
Pottery Frequency	Indeterminate (4.19)	Indeterminate (4.24)	Indeterminate (4.28)	Positive (4.32)
Pottery Diversity	Indeterminate (4.19)	Positive (4.24)	Indeterminate (4.28)	Indeterminate (4.32)

*Indeterminate and positive designations represent the trends indicated by the graphs in figures 4.18–4.21 and 4.23–4.34. A positive designation indicates a positive relationship between the two variables, based on their average values. An indeterminate designation indicates a trend in average values that is neither positive nor negative.

quency or diversity appeared to be highly unreliable when socioeconomic factors were used as the predictive basis. However, when the average values of pottery variables by rank were examined, underlying relationships among households became clearer (also see Hayden and Cannon 1984a). The average values for each rank were linked by a line to give an indication of the trend of the relationship (see summary in Table 4.13).

In Chanal, besides vessel frequency and type diversity, four additional pottery variables were used to characterize household pottery assemblages: (1) ritual set diversity, (2) food preparation and serving set diversity, (3) imported type diversity, and (4) pottery type diversity with industrial equivalents added. Tourist types that were occasionally being used for domestic or ritual functions in a household were also added to that household's food preparation and serving or ritual activity set. Imported type diversity included all pottery items (including tourist types) known to be made outside the peripheral distribution zone. The following discussion outlines the criteria for the variables used and reviews the graphed relationships in more detail.

Family size
This variable represents the total number of individuals recorded for each household.

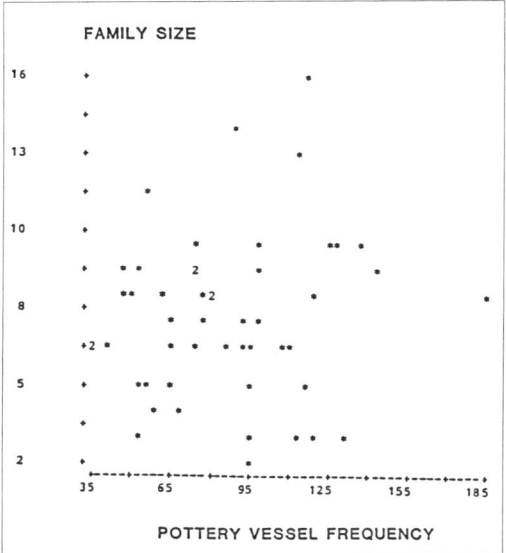

Fig. 4.14. Chanal: Graphic relationship between family size and vessel frequency.

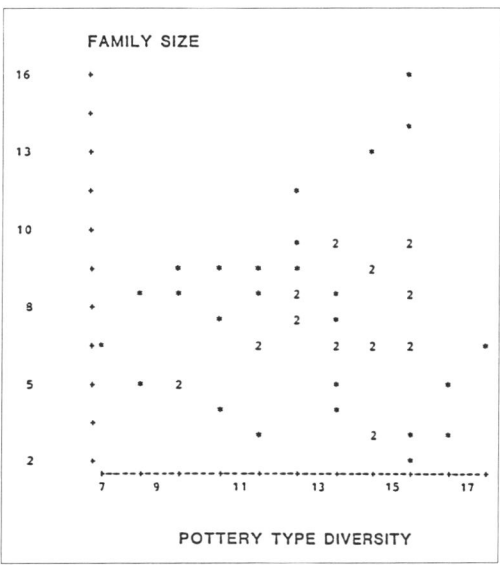

Fig. 4.16. Aguacatenango: Graphic relationship between family size and vessel frequency.

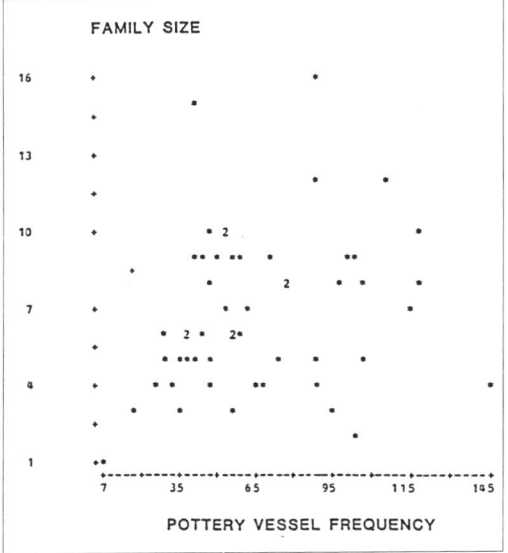

Fig. 4.15. Chanal: Graphic relationship between family size and pottery type diversity.

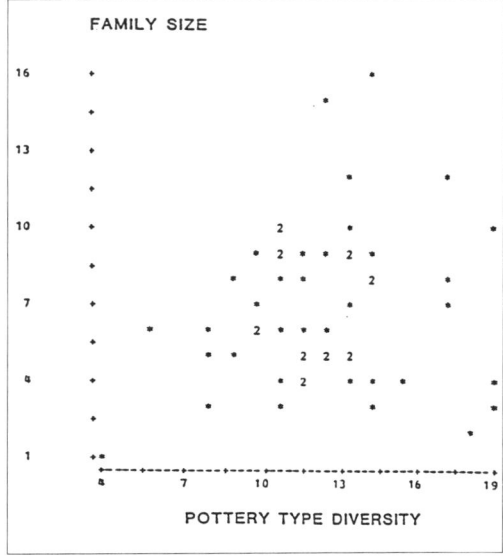

Fig. 4.17. Aguacatenango: Graphic relationship between family size and pottery type diversity.

Studies of prehistoric demographics have sometimes assumed a close relationship between pottery vessel size or frequency and family size (e.g., Cook 1972; Turner and Lofgren 1966). However, recent ethnoarchaeological studies among the Chuj Maya (B. Nelson 1981), as well as the Shipibo-Conibo (DeBoer and Lathrap 1979) and the Hopi (Stanislawski 1980) have not found good correlations between vessel size and number and household size or composition. The Tzeltal data tended to support the latter

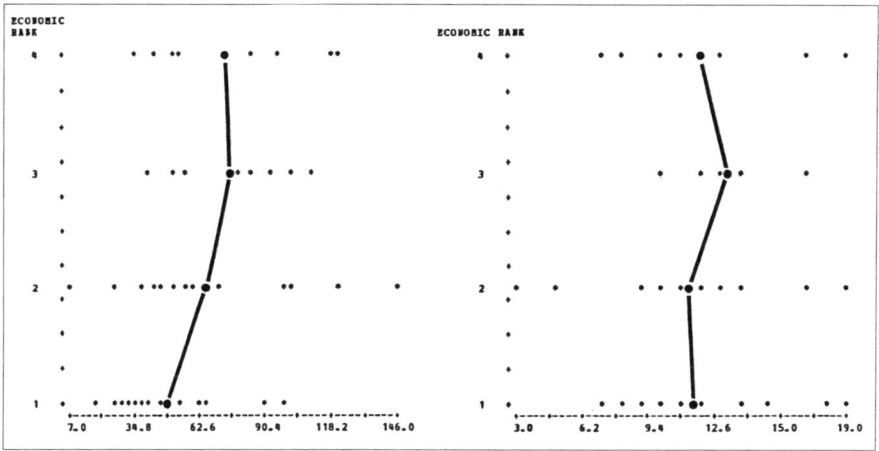

Fig. 4.18. Chanal: Graphic relationship between economic rank and (1) vessel frequency (left), and (2) pottery type diversity (right).

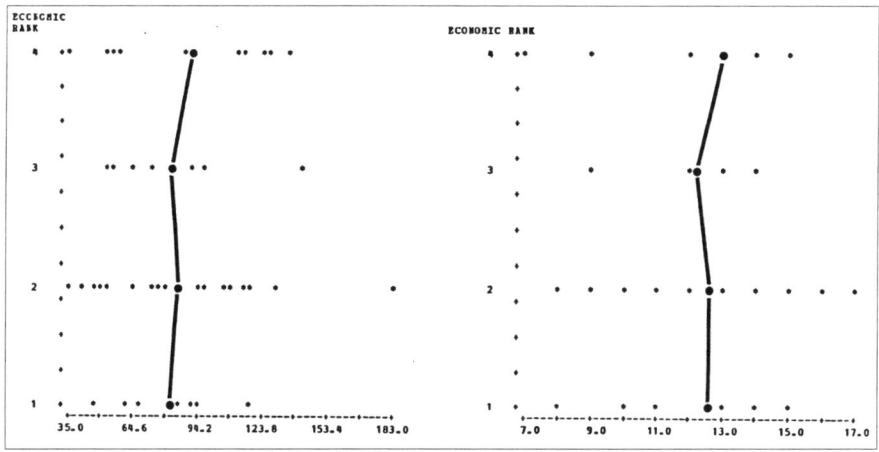

Fig. 4.19. Aguacatenango: Graphic relationship between economic rank and (1) vessel frequency (left), and (2) pottery type diversity (right).

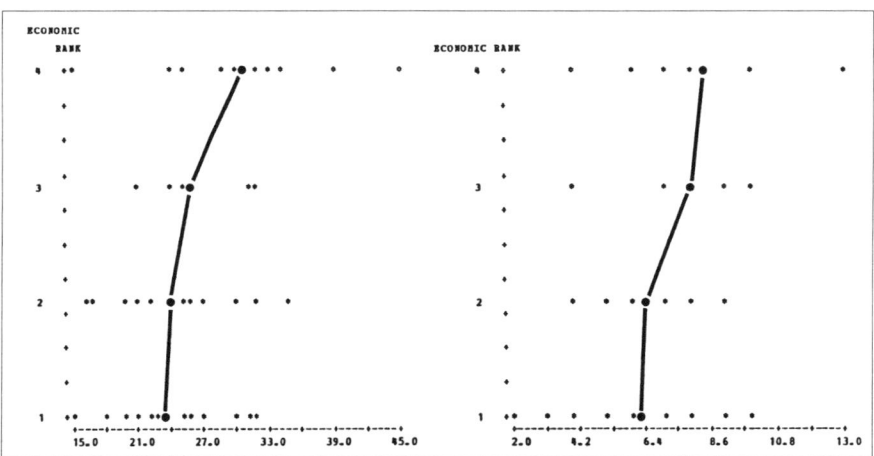

Fig. 4.20. Chanal: Graphic relationship between economic rank and (1) pottery and industrial type diversity (left), and (2) ritual set diversity (right).

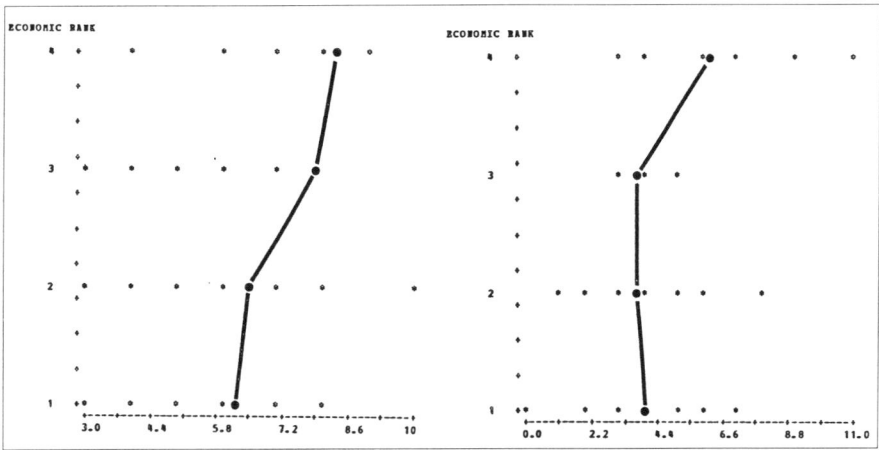

Fig. 4.21. Chanal: Graphic relationship between economic rank and (1) food preparation and serving set diversity (left), and (2) imported type diversity (right).

studies. In Chanal and Aguacatenango, both pottery frequency and type diversity showed a random association with family size (see Figures 4.14–4.17).

Of particular interest here was the fact that many small families had large pottery inventories. For example, many smaller sized families consisted of older couples whose children had moved away. In such cases, it seemed that the pottery inventory was more

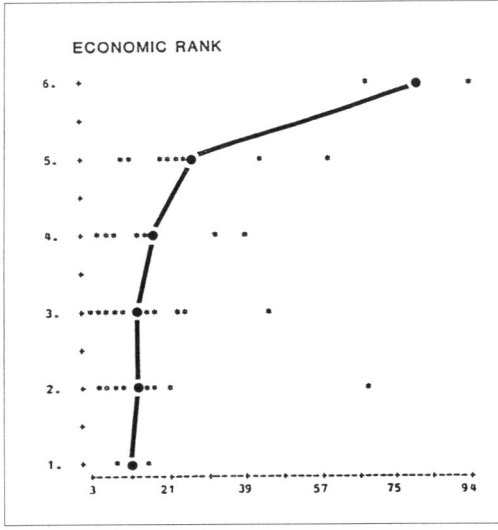

Fig. 4.22. Chanal: Graphic relationship between economic rank and the number of industrial replacements for pottery bowls.

characteristic of the stage of family development when children were present, and that the pottery used in that stage was simply maintained. However, when two variables reflecting the stage of family development (namely, the maximum size attained by the household, and the age of the household head) were graphed against vessel frequency and type diversity, random relationships again were indicated. While family size at any given time obviously affects the size and diversity of a household's pottery inventory, these relationships must be masked by other factors which exert considerable influence upon household pottery variability over time.

Economic rank

The economic ranking used here was based on potential household income. It was decided that the sum of a household's income from various economic activities was a reliable indicator of a family's current economic state (see Hayden and Cannon 1984a:129). Estimates given by informants could be roughly reevaluated from recorded observations. Potential income was determined from the value of all livestock, earnings from *finca* and other wage labor, specialized and part-time money earning activities such as butchering or operating a cantina, and sales from *milpa* surplus (e.g., fruit, vegetables, and firewood). The final value was consid-

TABLE 4.14.
Social Rankings for Chanal and Aguacatenango.

Rank 1: widower household heads, drunkards.

Rank 2: young household heads, persons not high in lineage authority, low *cargo* positions.

Rank 3: elder household heads, near top of lineage authority, although low *cargo* positions.

Rank 4: medium level *cargo* positions to which many people pay deference (such as treasurer or lower *Alferez* position).

Rank 5: older individuals with much deference and moderately high *cargo* position (such as judge, high *Alferez*).

Rank 6: oldest and highest members of *cargo* ladder (church President, civil President, or retired Presidents).

ered a fair estimate of the value of a family's land holdings, since not all land was used at a given time for produce and the relative quality of land holdings varied considerably.

It was assumed that wealthier households would have more pottery and a greater diversity of pottery types than would poorer households. To a certain extent the generated graphs confirmed this assumption (see Figures 4.16–4.21). As economic rank increased, in Chanal, there was an increase in average ritual set diversity, food set diversity, and pottery (including industrial type) diversity. The wealthiest Chanal households (Table 4.14: rank 4) tended to have a greater diversity of imported types, while all other ranks had about the same number of imported types.

For both communities, average pottery frequency and type diversity (excluding industrial equivalents) showed an indeterminate relationship with economic rank. Actually, for economic ranks, values for type diversity in any one rank only varied between 11 and 13 for Chanal and between 12 and 14 for Aguacatenango. Average pottery frequency in Chanal increased between rank 1 and 3 and then decreased slightly in rank 4 (Figure 4.18). This situation probably reflects a greater dependency on industrial equivalents among higher ranking households in Chanal, since there was a strong positive trend between economic rank and pottery and industrial type diversity together. The most commonly occurring industrial

equivalents (bowl forms) definitely showed an increase in the higher economic rank (Figure 4.22).

Social rank

In each household, the household head was given a social rank based on the criteria of age, position in the civil or religious *cargo* system, deference, public drunkenness, and position in lineage. Six ranks were established (Table 4.14). However, for graphing this data, ranks 1 and 2, and 5 and 6, were collapsed to make four ranks of comparable size.

As with household wealth, households of higher social status were expected to have larger, and especially, more diverse pottery inventories, the latter due to religious or civil obligations involving gatherings at their homes. Unlike the relatively weak and often indeterminate relationships with economic rank, most graphs using the social rank variable showed a positive trend (see Figures 4.23–4.26). Only average pottery and industrial type diversity (Figure 4.25–1) and food preparation and serving set diversity (Figure 4.26–1) showed an indeterminate association with social rank in Chanal. Both graphs showed a decrease in the highest rank. In general, there seemed to be a closer relationship between social rank and the diversity of ritual and imported types, as opposed to domestic types. Most pottery, as well as industrial types, had domestic functions. The

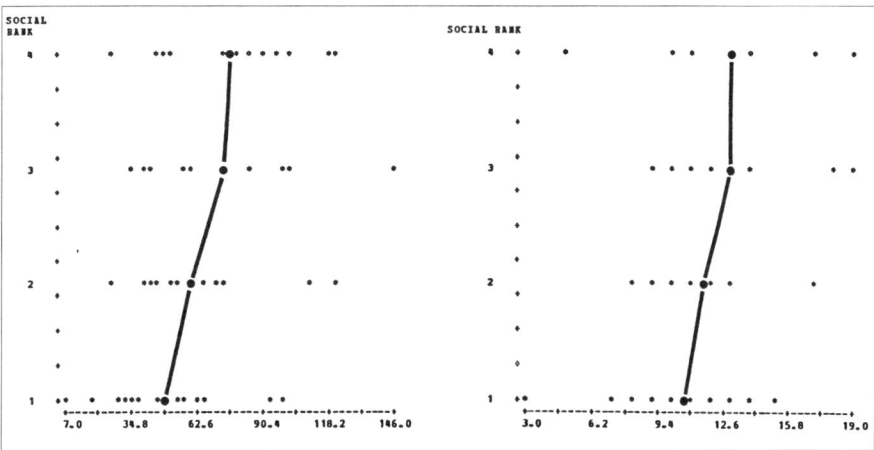

Fig. 4.23. Chanal: Graphic relationship between social rank and (1) vessel frequency (left), and (2) pottery type diversity (right).

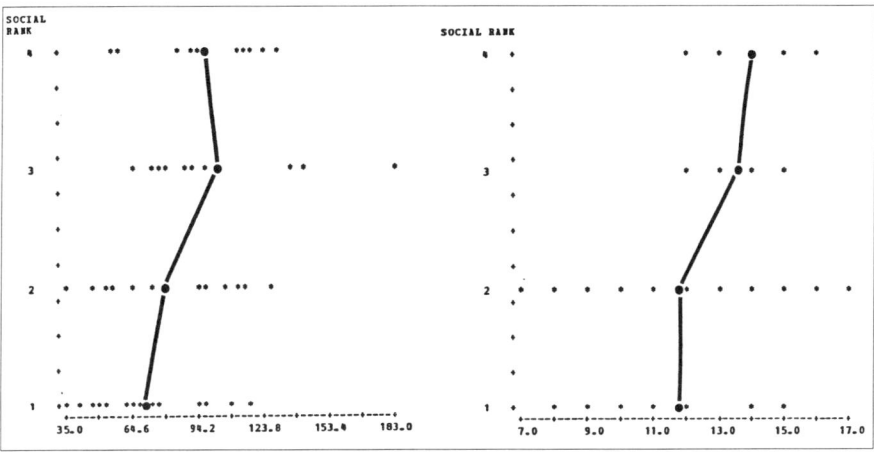

Fig. 4.24. Aguacatenango: Graphic relationship between social rank and (1) vessel frequency (left), and (2) pottery type diversity (right).

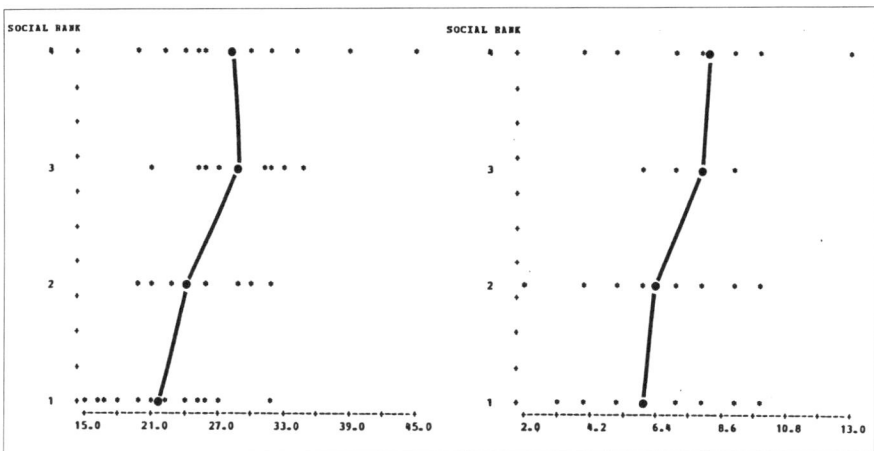

Fig. 4.25. Chanal: Graphic relationship between social rank and (1) pottery and industrial type diversity (left), and (2) ritual set diversity (right).

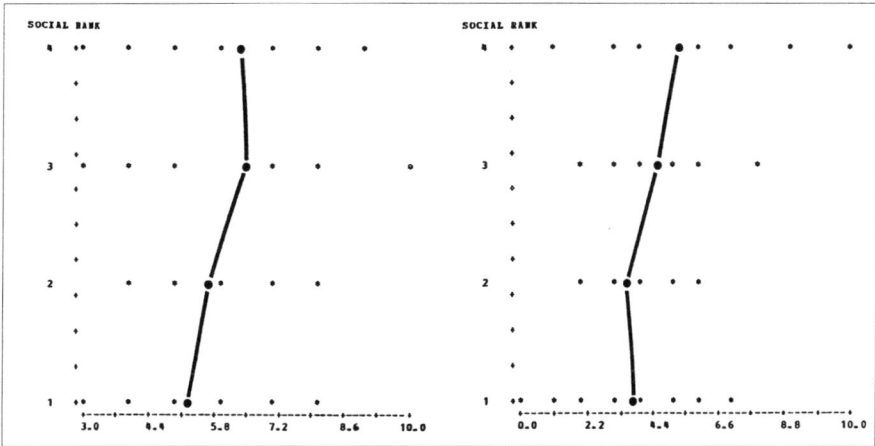

Fig. 4.26. Chanal: Graphic relationship between social rank and (1) food preparation and serving set diversity (left), and (2) imported type diversity (right).

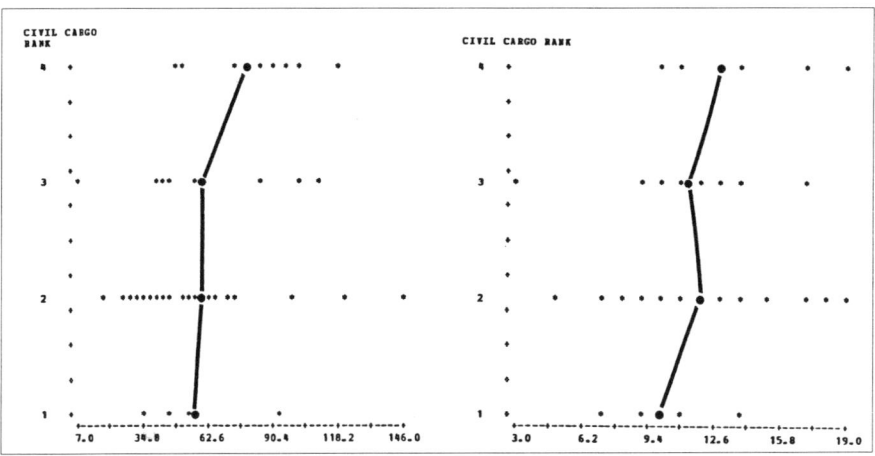

Fig. 4.27. Chanal: Graphic relationship between civil cargo rank and (1) vessel frequency (left), and (2) pottery type diversity (right).

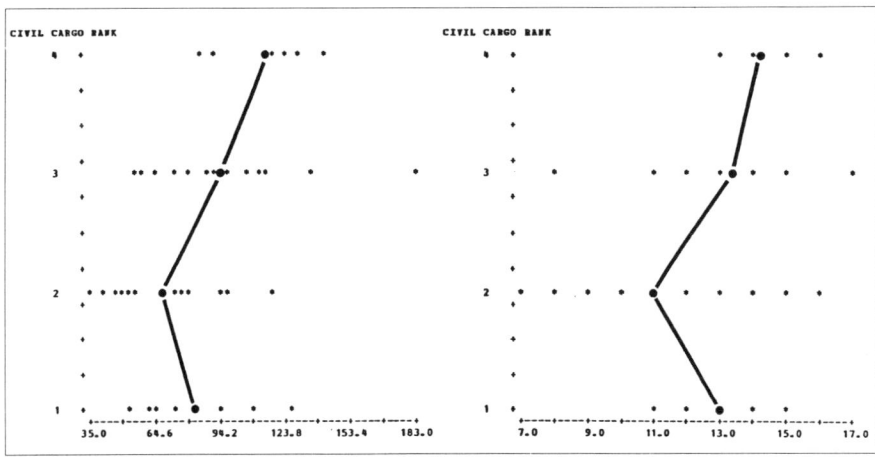

Fig. 4.28. Aguacatenango: Graphic relationship between civil cargo rank and (1) vessel frequency (left), and (2) pottery type diversity (right).

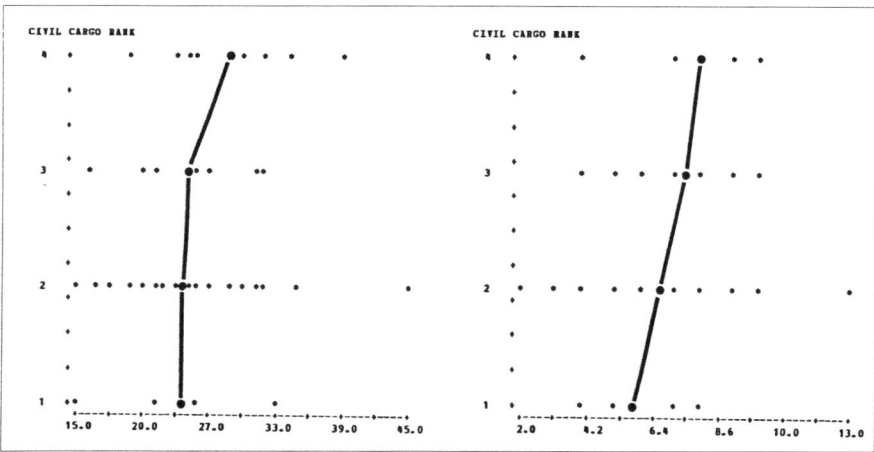

Fig. 4.29. Chanal: Graphic relationship between civil *cargo* rank and (1) pottery and industrial type diversity (left), and (2) ritual set diversity (right).

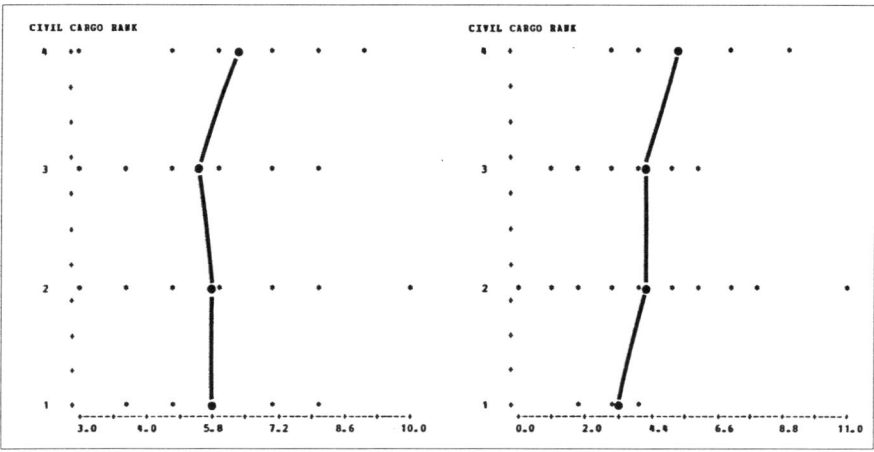

Fig. 4.30. Chanal: Graphic relationship between civil *cargo* rank and (1) food preparation and serving set diversity (left), and (2) imported type diversity (right).

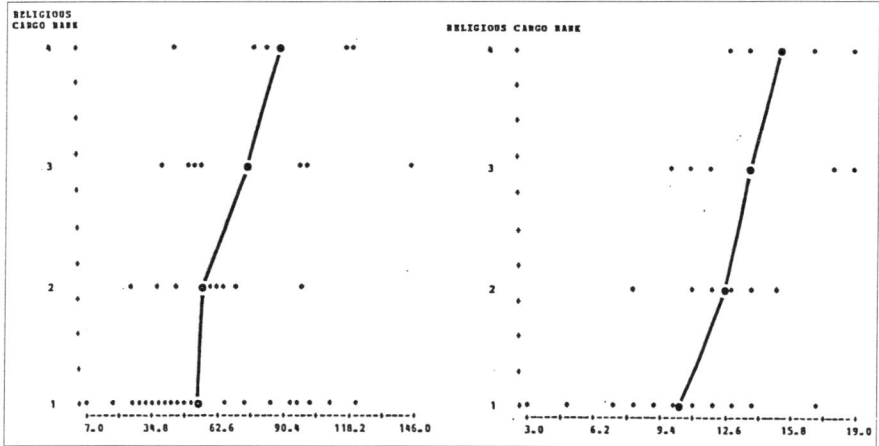

Fig. 4.31. Chanal: Graphic relationship between ritual *cargo* rank and (1) vessel frequency (left), and (2) pottery type diversity (right).

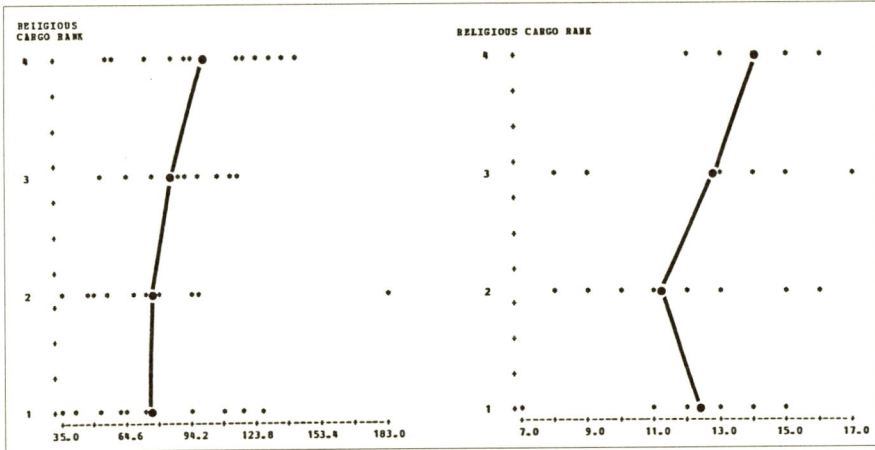

Fig. 4.32. Aguacatenango: Graphic relationship between ritual *cargo* rank and (1) vessel frequency (left), and (2) pottery type diversity (right).

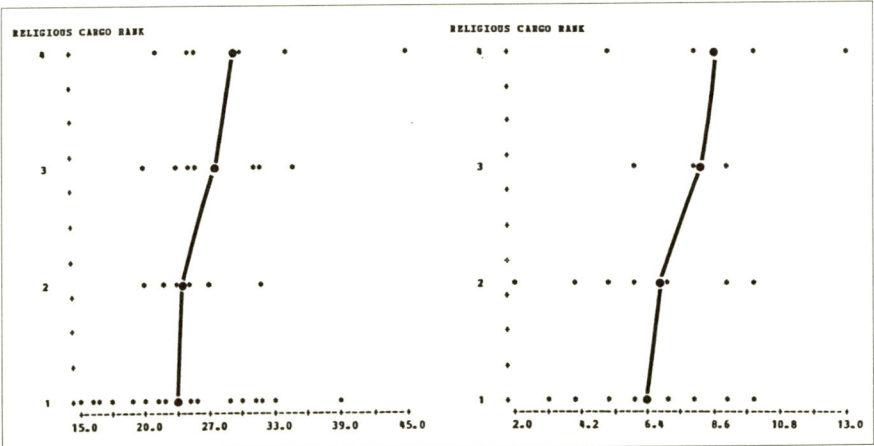

Fig. 4.33. Chanal: Graphic relationship between ritual *cargo* rank and (1) pottery and industrial type diversity (left), and (2) ritual set diversity (right).

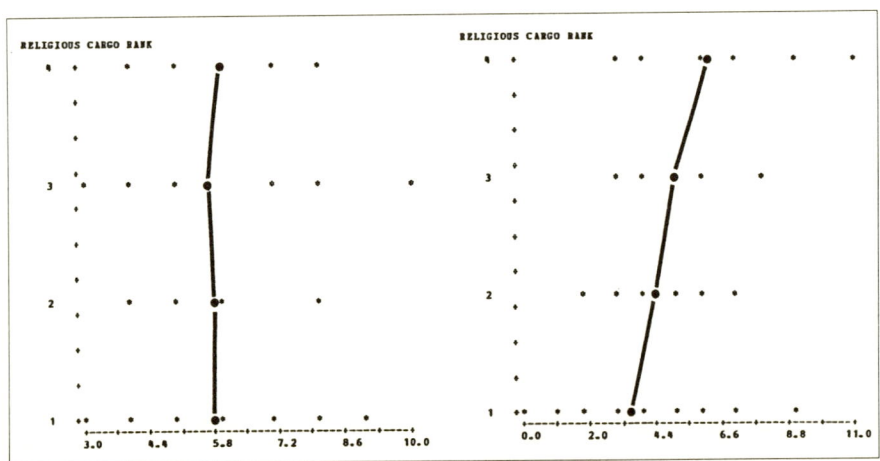

Fig. 4.34. Chanal: Graphic relationship between ritual *cargo* rank and (1) food preparation and serving set diversity (left), and (2) imported type diversity (right).

positive trend of type diversity and social rank could largely be attributed to ritual, rather than domestic type diversity. The same may also be true of the positive trend of type diversity and social rank of Aguacatenango. The decrease in average pottery frequency in Aguacatenango, where the *cargo* system had a much weaker presence, may reflect a greater dependency on industrial types and the reduced pottery requirements of the *cargo* system in that community.

Cargo *rank*

The ranking for social status used above took into account the civil or religious *cargo* status of the household head. However, in order to determine the relative affects of civil versus religious *cargo* status on the relationship between social status and pottery variability, civil and religious *cargo* statuses were also treated separately. As with social status, each household head was given a rank from one to four (see Figures 4.27–4.34).

In Chanal, all but one of the pottery variables showed a positive trend as religious *cargo* rank increased, while average ritual set diversity, average imported type diversity, and average pottery and industrial type diversity showed positive trends as civil *cargo* position increased. Average pottery frequency and food set diversity all showed a decrease in rank 3 followed by an increase in rank 4. In Aguacatenango, average pottery frequency and average pottery diversity showed a decrease between ranks 1 and 2, then increased through rank 4 for both civil and religious *cargo* status (Figures 4.28, 4.32). As mentioned above, the traditional form of *cargo* system has deteriorated considerably in Aguacatenango in recent years, so that fewer people assume *cargo* positions. This includes many wealthier families, who might have the lowest *cargo* rank but have relatively large and diverse pottery inventories (thereby increasing the average pottery frequency for that rank). In general, both civil and religious *cargo* ranks showed similar relationships with pottery frequency and type diversity, and both closely correspond to the results recorded for social status. How-

ever, civil *cargo* rank did differ from social status and religious *cargo* rank when compared to pottery type diversity (excluding industrial types), and social status differed from both *cargo* rankings when compared to pottery plus industrial type diversity.

Clearly socioeconomic factors play an important role in pottery variability. In Chanal and Aguacatenango, household pottery diversity and vessel frequency seem to be most closely associated with the social status of the household head (especially where this reflects religious *cargo* rank). In Chanal, ritual set diversity is seen to be sensitive to all of the socioeconomic variables considered. The Chanal sample also indicates that the diversity of pottery and industrial replacements together tends to have different relationships with socioeconomic variables than does pottery diversity alone. In fact, only average food set diversity and pottery plus industrial type diversity show positive associations with economic rank. Current family size in both communities does not appear to be closely related to pottery variability.

The results of this exercise indicate that pottery vessel frequency or type diversity alone are not good indicators of any of the socioeconomic or demographic factors considered. However, ritual set diversity may be a reliable indicator of the ritual status of the household head. While household social and economic levels obviously account for some of the pottery variability, other factors, which are more difficult to quantify, must also be important. These probably include the idiosyncratic tastes of household occupants, changing household composition, replacement factors, borrowing and loaning practices, *milpa* inventories, and various production considerations (see Chapter 2). The problems associated with the use of pottery data to infer socioeconomic condition in archaeological housesites is treated in more detail in Chapter 5.

HOUSEHOLD REQUIREMENTS: THE REUSE CYCLE

The reuse cycle differed from the use-curation cycle in at least three important

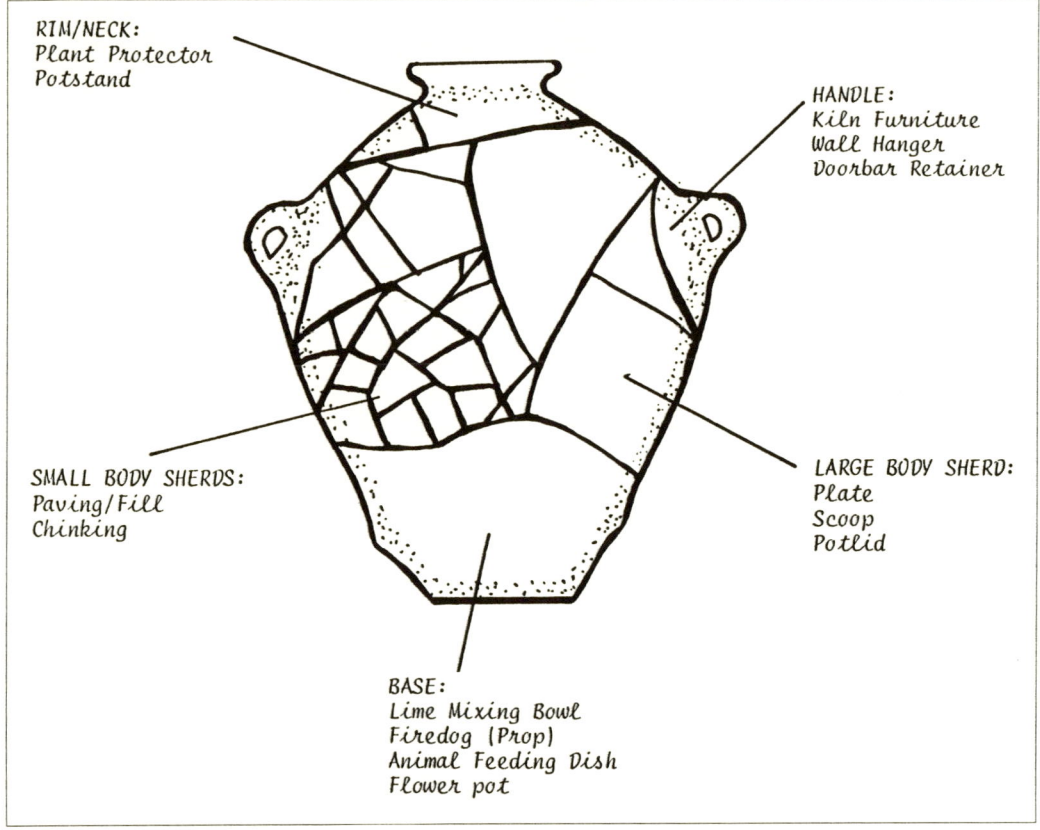

RIM/NECK:
Plant Protector
Potstand

HANDLE:
Kiln Furniture
Wall Hanger
Doorbar Retainer

SMALL BODY SHERDS:
Paving/Fill
Chinking

LARGE BODY SHERD:
Plate
Scoop
Potlid

BASE:
Lime Mixing Bowl
Firedog (Prop)
Animal Feeding Dish
Flower pot

Fig. 4.35. Typical breakage patterns for a watercarrying jar *(kib)* and possible reuse functions for specific breakage forms.

characteristics. First, when a vessel was reused it went through an activity set transformation. Generally, it could no longer be used for its original function and was therefore reused as part of an activity set which included only broken vessels. These broken vessels would include mostly vessels from classes with shorter uselives. Secondly, use location and storage location were generally the same. Thirdly, once a vessel entered the reuse cycle its value decreased. If a vessel was broken while in reuse it would not likely be repaired. Furthermore, whether it was damaged while being reused or not, when the compound or feature with which it was associated was abandoned, it would almost certainly be abandoned.

The decision to reuse a given vessel for a specific activity was determined by the nature of the surviving portion, such as a rim segment, a large sherd, or a bottomless vessel, rather than by its original value, quality, or morphology. In the Tzeltal study, 56 types of damage were observed (see Deal and Hagstrum 1995). Certain vessel fragments (e.g., rim, handle, or base) were consistently being reused for a few functions (Figure 4.35). Some vessels might even be reused a second or third time. For example, small wide-mouth jars or single-handle jars that had been reused for lime-mixing containers, might be broken again and reused as firedogs or as enclosures for seedlings.

The average proportion of vessels being reused in Chanal and Aguacatenango households at the time of our surveys was 21% of the household inventory for both communities. This translates to 13 vessels per household in Chanal and 18 vessels per household in Aguacatenango. In Chanal, potters tended

Fig. 4.36. Secondary reuse of broken wide-mouth jar *(oxom)* as firedog to support *comal*.

Fig. 4.37. A cooking jar *(oxom)* base being reused as a feeding dish for chickens, Chanal.

Fig. 4.38. Modified cooking jar *(oxom)* reused to protect a seedling in a Chanal kitchen garden.

Fig. 4.39. Upper portion of watercarrying jar *(kib)* reused as chinking in sweatbath chimney.

to reuse twice as many vessels as nonpotters (an average of 16 vessels per household for potters and eight vessels per household for nonpotters). These reused vessels represented a diversity of four types per household in Chanal (with five types for potters and three types for nonpotters) and six types per household in Aguacatenango.

At least seven reuse activity sets were recognized in Chanal and Aguacatenango pottery inventories (actual counts for cooking and watercarrying jars are presented in Deal and Hagstrum 1995:Table 2):

1. Food preparation/kitchen maintenance: functions, included potlid, propping up a tortilla griddle over the hearth (Figure 4.36), cutting board, collecting corn grinder or colander waste, lime-mixing container, removing ash or garbage from kitchen, and marking the location of lime storage pits.

2. Animal husbandry: functions included nests for poultry (chickens and turkeys),

TABLE 4.15.
Functional Diversity of Precolumbian and Historic Vessel Forms for Tzeltal Maya of the Central Highlands of Chiapas (After Culbert 1965) and the Colonial Coxoh Maya of the Chiapas Lowlands (After Lee 1979a).

Phase:	Kan (Early Classic)	Tsah (Late Classic)	Yash (Early Postclassic)	Lum (Late Postclassic)	Colonial Coxoh	Historic Tzeltal
Functional category:						
Small bowl	6	2	1	3	2	6
Large bowl	1	4	1	2	?	1
Wide-mouth jar	1	1	3	1	1 (?)	6
Narrow-mouth jar	3	1	?	1	2	1
Perforated jar	—	—	—	1	1	2
Unrestricted plate	—	1	—	—	1	1
Cylindrical vase	1	1	1	1	—	—
Censer	1	1 (?)	1	1	2	1
Basic Inventory:	13	11	7	10	9	18
Rare/Other	3	2	—	2	5	13
Total diversity:	16	13	7	12	14	31

feeding dishes (Figure 4.37), and containers for preparing medicine for animals.

3. Gardening: functions included enclosures for protecting seedlings, (usually a rim or bottomless vessel; Figure 4.38), containers for watering plants, and trays for seed drying.

4. Construction and general maintenance: functions included paving material for patios or pathways, chinking in chimneys of sweatbaths (Figure 4.39) or wattle-and-daub walls, roof slating, props for poultry coops, retaining walls for ash dumps, storage containers for construction materials (mud, sand, cement, string), and containers for mixing pine pitch sealant.

5. Pottery making: functions included storage containers for raw materials (clays, tempers, paints, slips), mixing containers for paints and slips, and containers for water for hand wetting and clay smoothing while potting.

6. Ritual: functions included holders for candles, stands for candles in glass containers, containers for afterbirth burial,

and items of religious significance (such as broken incense burner parts or Precolumbian sherds).

7. Personal: functions included vessels used to hold bath water and soaproots in the sweatbath, vessels used to make home remedies, and children's toys.

The use of pottery vessels as containers in which to bury afterbirths is of particular interest to archaeologists because of the potential archaeological visibility of these vessels. This practice was more common in Aguacatenango than in Chanal. Informants in 13 households claimed to have buried placentas in pottery containers from as many as eight births. In each case a small wide-mouth jar was used. A pit between 20–60 cm deep and 20–40 cm in diameter was dug within the compound (sometimes near the house), and the same pit was used for successive births.

The practice of burying the afterbirth in pottery vessels has been recorded in various parts of Mesoamerica. For example, Parson (1936:76) reported variations of this custom in several Zapotecan communities. Among the Zapotecs, the afterbirth might be wrapped in a cloth (or banana leaf), placed in a new jar and buried at the corner of the house, in the patio, or in a "shaded place" in the house (Parsons 1966:76). More recently Vivian Gotthilf (personal communication, 1983) recorded this practice in three Oaxacan villages (San Matio Cajones, San Pablo Yaganitza and Santo Tomas), as well as Nenton, in the Chiapas Depression, and three Guatemala Highland communities (Barillas, Santa Eulalia and San Mateo Ixtatan). Some households in Santa Eulalia and San Mateo used lidded jars. One of our San Mateo informants claimed that an inverted new bowl (*jom lum*) was ritually killed when burying the afterbirth. In the Mixteca community of Cuilapam, the "washed" jar containing the afterbirth was placed inside a second jar and buried at the corner of the house (Parsons 1936:76–77, note 31). In the Chorti Maya area, a gourd vessel served this function, and it was buried in a secret "and shaded" place on family land (Wisdom 1940:288).

PRECOLUMBIAN HOUSEHOLD REQUIREMENTS

Ultimately, our ability to use ethnoarchaeological pottery models for the interpretation of Precolumbian pottery assemblages rests on the degree of similarity that exists between our present models and our archaeological data for a given period. To better understand the potential for such comparisons, the following discussion reviews the Precolumbian pottery sequence for the Central Highlands, with special attention to similarities and differences in functional diversity (i.e., subcomplex change) over time.

Considerable diversity in vessel forms has been recorded in the Central Highlands for Early Classic Kan times to the present (Table 4.15). However, Culbert (1965:45) suggests that the most common pottery forms show a great stability throughout this sequence. He attributes this stability to an adherence to certain "rules of basic shape and dimensions" which he believes are based on vessel function. Culbert's study includes an attempt to establish functional classes for Precolumbian pottery in the Central Highlands based on vessel morphology and comparative ethnographic data. Becquelin and Baudez (1979) provide a useful comparative, although less complete, classification for the pottery of Tonina and the Valley of Ocosingo in the northern Tzeltal area. Using Culbert's preliminary classification, the following discussion addresses the problems of broad subcomplex (domestic versus ritual) change through time in the Central Highlands, and the possible effects of these changes on household inventories and activity set composition.

The most common domestic forms are large griddles, large bowls, and a variety of broad-mouth, small-mouth, and perforated jars. About one quarter of the vessel forms identified by Culbert (1965:43) are classified as fine-quality vessels, many of which were recovered from burials and caches. These vessels were predominantly bowls (or dishes) but also included tall cylindrical polychrome vessels. Coe (1973:16) suggests that these vessels, which often appear on Maya pictorial ceramics, were most likely used to hold an intoxicating drink (*balché*) used in ceremonies. Cylindrical vessels are rare in the Central Highlands, yet they appear in the ceramic sequence from Early Classic to Late Postclassic (Culbert 1965:Chart 3, 32, 70). Cylindrical forms are more common in the Tonina and Valley of Ocosingo area during the Early Classic to Early Postclassic (Becquelin and Baudez 1979:Chapter 3). This is not surprising, since this area is much closer to major trade routes for lowland Maya fine paste and polychrome pottery (see N. Hammond 1982:224). Finer quality bowls are still used in ritual contexts by the modern Tzeltal, but cylindrical vessels dropped out of use during the Postclassic. The most obvious ritual vessel form is the censer, which is common throughout the prehistoric and modern sequence and is generally a local ware.

Before the Early Classic Kan phase, little is known of Central Highlands pottery (Culbert 1965:79). The Early Classic period is

TABLE 4.16.
Functional Diversity of Precolumbian and Historic Vessel Forms for Tzeltal Maya of
the Tonina and Valley of Ocosingo Area (After Becquelin and Baudez 1979).*

Phase:	May (Early Classic)	Ixim (Late Classic)	Chenek (Early Postclassic)	Chib (Late Postclassic)	Historic Sivaca**
Function category:					
Small bowl	4	14	9	4	3
Large bowl	?	4	2	?	2
Wide-mouth jar	1	1	2	1	3
Narrow-mouth jar	?	3	2	2	1
Perforated jar	—	—	—	?	1
Unrestricted plate	—	—	—	1	1
Cylindrical jar	1	2	2	—	—
Censer	?	2	1	2	?
Basic Inventory:	6	26	18	10	11
Rare/Other	—	4	2	2	3
Total Diversity:	6	30	20	12	14

*Information is predominantly for the Ixim phase; counts are as follows: May (209 sherds), Ixim (20,592 sherds, 90 complete), Chenek (1,395 sherds, 24 complete), Chib (145+ sherds, 1 complete).
**From three households reported in Becquelin and Baudez (1979:299–303). Two other bowl forms, now obsolete, were recorded for this village by Blom and LaFarge (1927:245–256). No censer form was reported in either survey.

marked by a population increase that proba-bly represents a large-scale migration into the area of peoples speaking the linguistic parent stock for both Tzeltal and Tzotzil (Campbell 1988). Kan pottery includes several ex-amples of fine quality, small, restricted or un-restricted bowl forms, one large unrestricted bowl form, wide-mouth jars, narrow-mouth jars, effigy dish and jar forms, and everted rim censers (Culbert 1965:56–60). The di-versity of Kan bowl forms is consistent with the situation today, and they may have served a similar range of domestic and ritual func-tions. The abundance of fine quality bowl forms in Precolumbian times probably reflects a highly developed ritual system that required most households to keep on hand quantities of finer serving bowls.

The Kan domestic subcomplex probably included wide-mouth jars and smaller large diameter bowls as cooking vessels (Culbert 1965:44). Two food preparation vessel forms that are conspicuously absent in the Kan phase assemblage are the unrestricted plate (tortilla griddle) and the perforated jar (colander). Both forms appear first in the Late Classic (Tsah phase). Culbert (1965:44) sug-gests that the relative scarcity of the former, from the archaeological record of the Central Highlands, may indicate that something else, such as a large stone, served its function. These griddles are also uncommon in archae-ological sites in the Yucatan (R. Thompson 1958:63), but they were in use when the Spanish arrived, as evidenced by their inclu-sion in the Motul dictionary of the late six-teenth century (Joesink-Mandeville 1976: 46). However, this form did occur much ear-lier, in Middle Classic deposits at Kami-naljuyu (Borhegyi 1959; Lischka 1978:230) and Middle Preclassic deposits at Quelepa (Sheets 1982:102). One additional domestic vessel, the narrow-mouth jar, is similar to present-day watercarrying jars and probably served the same function.

Culbert (1965:45) sees no clear distinction

between domestic pottery inventories and the inventories of ceremonial centers throughout the entire sequence, and this may also be true among the Lowland Maya of the Classic period (Smith and Gifford 1965). In general, the Kan ritual subcomplex shows less diversity than that of the present-day Tzeltal. This may be due, in part, to a greater reliance on bowl forms in Kan period rituals, and to the addition of certain distinctive ritual vessel forms during the contact period (such as candleholders and flower-holders). The only certain Kan ritual vessel is a bowl censer, while the effigy dish and jar forms may have had ritual functions. A large unrestricted bowl form is present which may have served the beer-mixing and hand-washing functions of its modern counterpart. Culbert (1965:44) sees this form more as a water storage vessel, similar to those described by R. Thompson (1958:113, 117–118) for the Yucatan. However, the author has not observed any large bowl forms being used for water storage in the Chiapas Highlands. In fact, only a narrow-mouth jar form *(kib)* was being used for water storage in Chanal and Aguacatenango.

The Late Classic Tsah phase is characterized by a denser occupation of the Central Highlands. Tsah pottery, especially large storage bowls and jars, shows closer ties between Central Chiapas and the Maya Lowlands. Imported vessels are rare, as in earlier phases, but are traceable to the Maya Lowlands (Culbert 1965:83). Tsah pottery represents a similar range of vessel forms to that in use during the Kan phase, including small, fine-quality, restricted and unrestricted bowl forms, wide-mouth jars, narrow-mouth jars, and unrestricted plates (Culbert 1965:62–67). One incomplete vessel exhibits exterior applique spikes ("bosses"). Applique spikes are used almost exclusively on ritual vessels, although a wide range of ritual functions is possible (Deal 1982). Tsah pottery differs from Kan pottery primarily by having less diversity of fine bowl forms, greater diversity of large bowl forms, and the use of the unrestricted plate form. By contrast, the pottery invento-

ries for the Late Classic Ixim and Early Postclassic Chenek phases in the Tonina and Valley of Ocosingo are dominated by bowl forms, and the unrestricted plate form does not seem to be present (see Table 4.16).

The Early Postclassic Yash phase of the Central Highlands is characterized by the continued occupation of Tsah phase sites (Adams 1961:352) and a similar pottery inventory. In fact, Culbert (1965:84) views the Yash phase pottery inventory as transitional between the Tsah and Lum phase inventories. Yash vessel forms include large and small fine quality, unrestricted bowl, cylinder, and jar forms, wide-mouth jars and the frying pan type censer (Culbert 1965:69–71). The Yash inventory differs from the previous phases in several respects. It has a lower diversity of large bowl forms and fine-quality bowl forms, although there are more fine-quality vessels of other forms (e.g., cylindrical vessels and jars). It lacks an unrestricted plate form and no vessel has been identified for water carrying. Two distinctive ritual forms, the frying pan censer and fine-quality cylindrical jar, are present. Several fine-quality bowl forms, including one with applique spikes, an effigy whistle, and an unslipped stamp seal were found in a Yash phase tomb at Cerro Ecátepec (Culbert 1965:Figure 15). In general, changes in Yash phase pottery inventories suggest an elaboration in ritual pottery.

The Late Postclassic Lum phase of the Central Highlands is marked by the emergence of larger, more complex and fragmented political units (Adams 1961:352–359; Culbert 1965:86–87), accompanied by an increase in divergence of pottery inventories between eastern and western sectors of the region. In general, the Lum phase pottery inventory included small, fine-quality, unrestricted bowl forms, large restricted and unrestricted bowl forms, wide-mouth jars, narrow-mouth jars, perforated jars, and a dish-censer. Perforated jars, which were presumably used as colanders, and narrow-mouth (vague-neck) jars are more common in the eastern sector, while large bowl forms, wide-mouth jars, and the dish-censer are associated with the western sector. The dish censer may have had detachable bases in the form of large hollow cylinders (Culbert 1965:77). Rare, possibly imported, vessel forms in the western sector also included a miniature jar and a bottle.

Little is known of the Colonial pottery record for the Central Highlands. However, the pottery assemblages from the lowland Coxoh excavations are probably representative of the pottery diversity available throughout Colonial Chiapas. When the Spanish arrived, the Chaipas Highlands was the major route for trading and warring between Central Mexico and the Guatemala Highlands (Adams 1961; Wauchope 1970). Coxoh pottery includes several vessel forms that can be directly linked with the Late Preclassic, including the unrestricted plate, narrow-mouth jar, wide-mouth jar, perforated jar, unrestricted bowl forms, spiked, pedestal-based bowls and ladles, and spindle whorls, as well as exotic (glazed) Spanish vessels, such as soup dishes, pitchers, cups and candle holders (Lee 1979a:102–103, 1980:23). The imported, glazed Spanish pottery is always rare but some appeared in "even the most humble indigenous house" (Lee 1979a:102). These imported bowls probably replaced earlier fine-quality Maya bowl forms and may have served both domestic and ritual functions, as in modern indigenous households. Coxoh pottery assemblages differ from the Lum phase pottery of the Central Highlands mainly by the addition of Spanish vessel forms.

Based on Culbert's study of Central Highland pottery, at least 16 basic formal variants of pottery vessels were available during the Kan phase, 12 during the Tsah, 7 during the Yash and 11 during the Lum (Table 4.15). In addition, at least 14 formal variants were available to the Colonial Coxoh. Prehistoric inventories for Tonina and the Ocosingo Valley area are similar except for the greater variety in bowl forms during the Late Classic Ixim and Early Postclassic Chenek phases (Table 4.16). The prehistoric estimates are generally far less than the 31 vessel forms in Chanal and Aguacatenango; however, the adoption of certain European ritual forms and the tourist trade items accounts for much of the vessel diversity of present-day Tzeltal inventories. In fact, the basic native inventory consists of only 18 vessel forms. Most of the essential Precolombian vessel forms have persisted and probably served the same range of functions as their modern morphologically similar counterparts. The relative lack of ritual types may merely reflect a greater reliance on bowl forms in Precolumbian times and the fact that few housesites have been completely excavated. If these changes are considered, the potential for comparing models based on modern Tzeltal pottery with Precolumbian pottery assemblages should be considerable.

We also know from the recent excavations at Cerén, El Salvador, that the Maya have been reusing pottery vessels since at least the Middle to Late Classic period (Sheets 1992:45, 49–50; also Beaudry-Corbett 1992). At Cerén there are several preserved instances of ceramic and *metate* reuse, as well as examples of the storage of broken (rimless) vessels for future reuse. In particular, large sherds had been reused as crude plates, and handles from large broken storage jars were mounted in adobe walls for reuse as hangers and inside doorways to secure doorbars (Sheets 1992:45). As Sheets (1992:45) has noted at Cerén, reused vessels are occasionally modified to serve new functions. This is also consistent with modern practices, since the Tzeltal will smash out the base of an already damaged jar to put over a seedling as protection from animals.

5

Household as Depositional Unit

To a large extent, ethnoarchaeology is the ethnographic study of processes of human discard. (Gould 1978:259)

The models of pottery production and use-reuse presented in the previous chapter operated within the predepositional context. Pottery, from raw material to reuse, was in direct association with its producers and users, and areas of production and use, and it participated in an ongoing cultural system. Household pottery variability and patterning within this context was geared to the functional requirements of the household. Initial household requirements and replacement rates are believed to be influenced by changing socioeconomic and demographic conditions (especially social and ritual status) of the household. When socioeconomic and demographic conditions remain constant, the rate of vessel breakage (uselife) associated with different functional types becomes an important factor in determining pottery refuse volume and diversity.

In the present chapter, pottery deposition is addressed in terms of cultural (behavioral) processes involved in the formation of archaeological housesites. Much of the current knowledge of the cultural and natural processes associated with site formation has been summarized by Michael Schiffer (1972, 1983b, 1987), and is now typically applied to archaeological interpretations (e.g., Mehrer 1995:20). Schiffer distinguishes between the ongoing behavioral (ethnographic) system *(systemic context)* and the nonbehavioral system *(archaeological context)*. Material cul-

ture transformation from the systemic to the archaeological context is referred to as cultural deposition (Schiffer 1976:28). In an elaboration of Schiffer's scheme, Sullivan (1978:195–197) characterizes the ongoing behavioral system as three distinctive contexts relating to materials and activities during use *(interactive)*, between use events *(disposal)*, and in disuse *(discard)*. His depositional context is based on the notion that not all materials and activities can be in use simultaneously. For example, a pottery vessel not in direct association with its producers or users, as in storage, would be in depositional context (Deal 1985:249). By contrast, a broken vessel propped against an outside wall of the kitchen is considered to be in the discard context unless its location is altered by human activity. Here, vessel *use* involves a transformation from depositional context to interactive context, while vessel *reuse* involves a transformation from discard context to interactive context.

Pottery is a particularly useful artifact category around which to develop a discussion of depositional behavior because it is relatively indestructible and therefore highly visible in the archaeological record. Further, the disposal behavior associated with pottery seems to be representative of disposal behavior for many other durable items. The discussion that follows is divided into three sections concerning (1) the recognition, defi-

TABLE 5.1.
Tzeltal Pottery Disposal Modes in Relation to Refuse Type, Artifact Condition,
Spatial Patterning and Associations (After South 1979:221).

Refuse Characteristics: Disposal Mode:	Refuse Types	Artifact Condition	Spatial Patterning (associated feature)
Provisional Discard:			
Single Vessels	Secondary	Fragmented or Damaged	Individual Items (floor)
Vessel Clusters	Secondary	Fragmented or Damaged	Cluster (edge of mound platform)
Maintenance:	Secondary	Fragmented (small size)	Cluster (circum-patio; drainage ditch)
Loss:	de facto	Whole, Fragmented, or Damaged	Individual Items or Cluster (away from structures)
Pathway Breakage:	Primary	Fragmented	Individual Items (pathway)
Dumping:			
Discrete	Secondary	Fragmented or Damaged	Cluster (circum-patio toft)
Broadcast	Secondary	Fragmented or Damaged	Individual Items or Cluster (circum-patio toft)
Tossing	Secondary	Fragmented or Damaged	Individual Items (toss zone)

nition, and classification of phenomena (processes, stages, etc.) of the depositional context at the household level of analysis; (2) a discussion of the Tzeltal Maya data upon which the classification is based; and (3) the usefulness of the ethnographic model of Tzeltal depositional behavior for the interpretation of the archaeological patterning of pottery refuse.

HOUSEHOLD POTTERY DEPOSITION

Pottery deposition, in terms of both depositional and discard contexts, is viewed here as an evolutionary process associated with the prevailing state of household abandonment. Three stages of household abandonment are recognized: preabandonment, abandonment and postabandonment (Stevenson 1982). Each of these stages results in distinctive and recognizable changes in the frequency, type diversity, and spatial patterning of discarded

pottery within the household assemblage (see Figure 5.1).

The initial, preabandonment stage is characterized by various types of disposal behavior, termed "disposal modes" (after Binford 1978:344). In terms of pottery, variation in depositional behavior is intimately connected with the internal arrangement of structures, gardens, and specific activity areas within a household compound. The spatial distribution of discarded items within an ongoing household is also seen to be affected to some degree by the cycle of structure reuse and renovation and the concomitant movements of pottery-related activities.

The abandonment stage involves not only abandonment but the physical conditions of abandonment which may vary over the uselife of a given compound. Housesite abandonment includes four basic modes which reflect the speed of abandonment and the

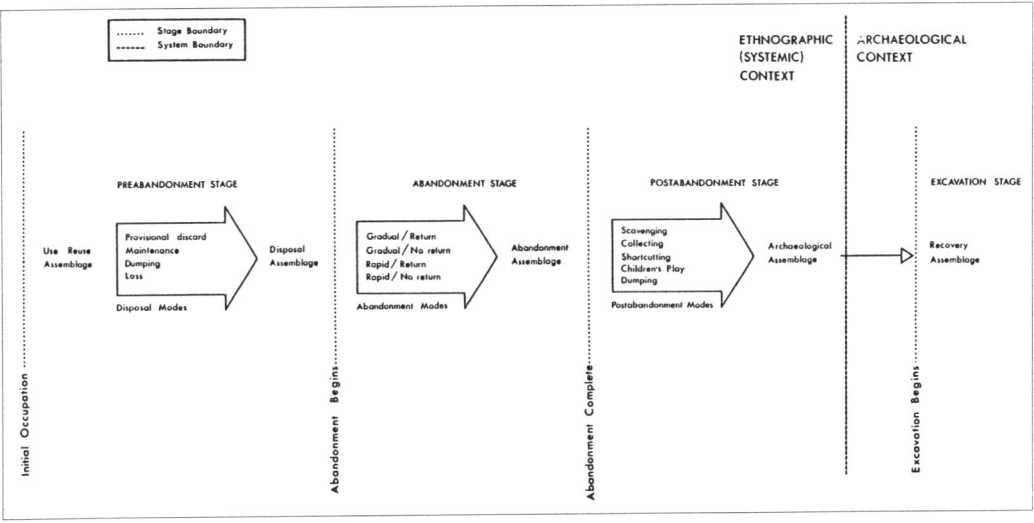

Fig. 5.1. Pottery deposition model, with emphasis on assemblage change within the depositional context.

probability of reoccupation of the compound site. Each abandonment mode has different effects on the content (i.e., nature, size, and distribution) of the items and features remaining at the abandoned housesite. When the structure reuse and renovation cycle ceases, a compound becomes an open or closed (e.g., fenced) vacant lot.

The postabandonment stage is characterized by several cultural processes that alter the content of discarded and abandoned items and features on sites deserted within an ongoing community. The extent of the alterations are believed to be greatly influenced by the conditions of the abandonment (i.e., reflected in the content of abandoned items and features) and the state of abandonment (i.e., open or closed lot), and the proximity of the abandoned compound to the center of the community.

THE PREABANDONMENT STAGE

In order to understand the variability and patterning of archaeological pottery assemblages, it is first necessary to examine the behavior associated with pottery disposal and abandonment and the resulting spatial patterning of pottery remains within a typical, ongoing Tzeltal compound (see Figure 5.2).

In the preabandonment stage, Tzeltal pottery disposal can be characterized by five distinctive modes including provisional discard, disposal resulting from housesite maintenance (i.e., maintenance disposal), dumping disposal, loss, and breakage. Table 5.1 outlines the predicted variation in the nature of pottery refuse, vessel condition, and feature association related to each of these disposal modes. The first three modes are intentional strategies for the disposal of refuse, while the latter two modes are examples of unintentional refuse disposal. In addition, the spatial patterning of discarded pottery can be altered due to trampling activity and gardening.

Based primarily upon Tzeltal and Chuj informant responses, Hayden and Cannon (1984b) have identified three general principles that are related to intentional refuse disposal in terms of how refuse is sorted and where it is dumped. These are economy of effort, the temporary retention of potentially reusable materials, and hindrance minimization. Each of these principles seems to operate differently in relation to dissimilar disposal modes and under different household conditions, such as reuse requirements and compound location.

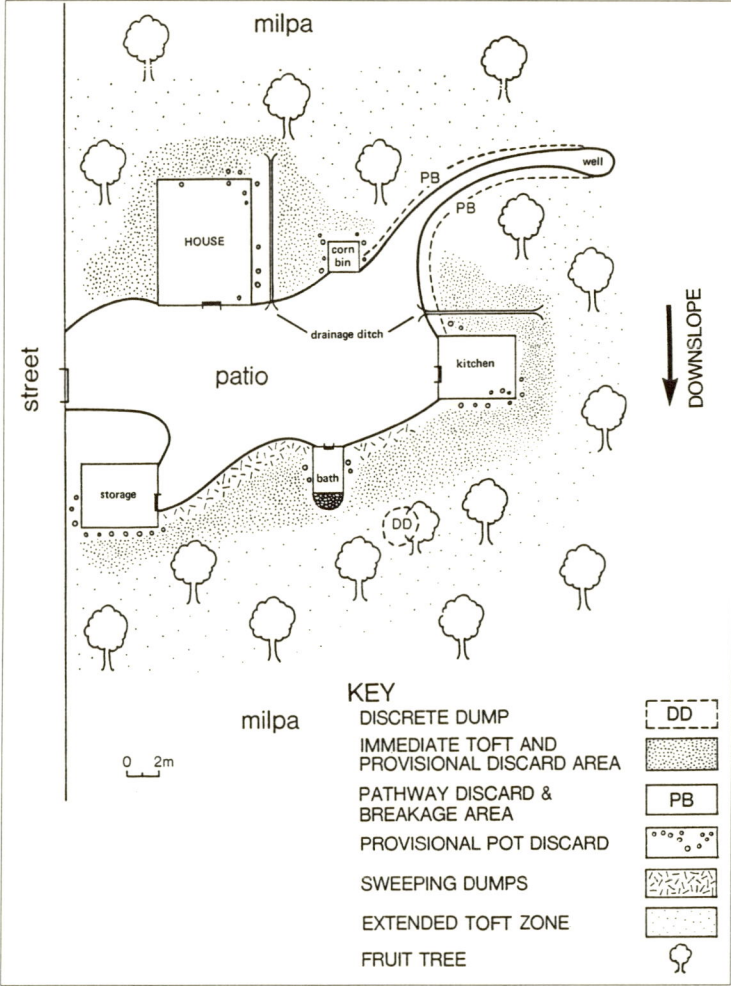

Fig. 5.2. Tzeltal refuse pattern.

Intentional Disposal Modes

The provisional discard of damaged vessels and other inorganic items may prove to be the most important disposal mode for understanding the spatial patterning of archaeological pottery assemblages. Provisional discard among the Tzeltal was represented by two distinctive strategies. The first strategy involved the isolated storage of material item fragments. Among the Maya it took the form of provisional storage, often in difficult-to-get-at places, of damaged material items in anticipation of potential future repair and/or reuse. The second strategy involved the discrete storage of damaged or partly damaged pottery vessels. The resulting clusters, or

caches, of broken pottery were features of most Tzeltal Maya compounds. The basic difference between the two strategies was that the former was a less structured activity which featured the storage of items singly, or in disordered association, rather than in tightly bounded clusters. The locations of these singly stored items could soon be forgotten, while a cluster of broken pottery represented a continually used household facility. In a recent ethnoarchaeological study in Buhera, Zimbabwe, Lindahl and Matenga (1995: 106) noted that this form of provisional discard was observed in practically every homestead. In Buhera, broken vessels, along with seldom used complete vessels,

TABLE 5.2.
Locational Distribution of Whole and Fragmentary Pottery Vessels Not in Use.*

Discard Mode: Chanal Locations:*+	Single Vessel Provisional Discard	Vessel Cluster Provisional Discard	Misplacement/Loss (whole vessels)**
Main Structure	—	7	4
Kitchen	3	6	7
Sweatbath	1	2	2
Storage structure	3	2	—
Abandoned Structure	2	—	—
On and Around Patio	2	3	2
Corn Bin	1	—	—
Street	—	—	1
General Compound	—	—	—
Not Specified	—	—	5
Subtotal:	*12*	*20*	*21*

Discard Mode: Aguacatenango Locations:	Single Vessel Provisional Discard	Vessel Cluster Provisional Discard	Misplacement/Loss (whole vessels)**
Main Structure	10	21	—
Kitchen	10	17	—
Sweatbath	2	4	—
Storage Structure	3	8	—
Abandoned Structure	—	1	—
On and Around Patio	16	15	3
Corn Bin	—	—	—
Street	—	—	—
General Compound	12	23	9
Not Specified	3	3	3
Subtotal:	*56*	*92*	*15*

*Each value represents the number of households in which a given disposal mode resulted in the placement of pottery in a given location.
**Includes vessels displaced by children.
*+Recorded only for the 33 households in which the author worked.

were stored under raised granary floors, which provided protection from domestic animals. Sommer (1990:52) makes a useful distinction among activity areas, provisional discard locations, and passive areas. Passive areas are spaces that are not intentionally used and do not normally generate refuse, such as sleeping areas, storage rooms and any other spaces that are difficult or impossible to access.

In terms of the first strategy, various damaged items or their fragments, including machete blades, axes, bottles, odd shoes, toys, corn grinder parts, metal and plastic sheeting, metal bars and pipes, and pottery vessels, could be observed lying along the base of interior or exterior walls, in corners, and under tables, beds and corn bins, hanging from beams, or tossed into the rafters. Because these items had little immediate value

Fig. 5.3. Broken vessel storage (provisional discard) location along a kitchen wall, Chanal.

and were likely to be left behind upon abandonment, one could readily see how this type of disposal behavior could lead to misleading interpretations of activity areas within structures. For example, two or more items with potential functional association (i.e., that could have been used for the same craft or specific activity) might be loosely placed in provisional discard locations in general proximity to each other, such as under the same bench, or along the same wall, yet they might wrongly be interpreted as evidence of a certain past activity in that locality. In fact, in Maya households this kind of short term refuse storage was much more likely to account for artifacts being associated with living floors than was primary disposal.

In terms of the second strategy, clusters of damaged or partly damaged vessels were often found along the outside walls of structures (Figure 5.3), along the edges of the patio, occasionally on the roofs of sweatbaths or other buildings, in structures which were used for storage, or in abandoned structures (see Table 5.2). Elsewhere, Weigand (1969:23) reported that among the Huichol "Nearly every sherd which is a potential container is stored, most often in a corner of the kitchen, even if it cannot be put to immediate use." Similarly, Reina and Hill (1978:247) described five broken vessels being stored along the outside wall of a new kitchen in a Quiche household in Zunil. As with the loose provisional storage of single items, clustering of broken vessels along house walls in this manner might

wrongly be construed as evidence for pottery-related activity in archaeological housesites.

The second provisional disposal strategy can be equated with Binford's category of "placing" (or "positioning"), which is characterized by artifact clustering in locations where they can be easily retrieved, but at the same time, are not in the way of ongoing activities (1978:346). Similarly, Hayden and Cannon (1983) have suggested that this kind of storage is related to the principle of least effort, since collecting refuse together for periodic trips to dumping locations is much more efficient than making trips to dumps every time a vessel is broken. They add that the length of storage time for a given item will depend primarily on its original value, its reuse potential, the degree of further breakage while in storage, and its hindrance value to other activities.

Maintenance disposal refers to the efforts made to keep a clean living and working space. This was achieved by regular sweeping of house, kitchen, and patio living areas. Most household activities occurred in the kitchen, therefore the kitchen floor was usually swept clean each morning. The house floor and patio, however, were only swept about once every two or three days. Frequently, difficult to reach places such as under tables and benches, around hearths, along walls and in corners were left unswept. Such places were likely to become artifact traps for small items, including potsherds (H. Green 1961b:91; Weigand 1969:26). Due to the frequent sweeping, primary refuse from household activities tended to be removed. Sweepings, including mostly organic materials and dust with some small pottery sherds, were either dumped in an area reserved for refuse (e.g., often at the edge of the patio) or hoed into the garden as a form of compost (Figure 5.4). Patio refuse was often merely swept off the edge of the patio, and it was sometimes burned before disposal.

The drainage ditches along the outside of house and kitchen walls also served as artifact traps. The movement of animals, people, and rainwater along the edge of the patio carried the smaller items (often from sweepings)

Fig. 5.4. Chanal couple distributing domestic refuse in kitchen garden.

into the ditches where they accumulated. Damaged pottery vessels that were temporarily stored along the walls of structures would also contribute small pottery fragments to these traps as the vessels deteriorated.

Probably the bulk of material items contributed to the archaeological record of sedentary communities are the direct result of the intentional dumping of refuse. In Tzeltal Maya communities this could take place in discrete dumping locations, as well as in areas of dispersed (or "broadcast") refuse. Dumping locations included household compounds, neighborhood dumps, and community streets.

According to some informants in Chanal, potsherds dulled their hoes if left in the compound garden area, and therefore, they were removed from the compound. Howry believed this to be a general rule in most Maya households (1973:28). However Aguacatenango and the Tzotzil community of Chamula seemed to be exceptions to this rule. In Aguacatenango, while larger items and glass were often taken to neighborhood

dumping areas, and cobbles and smaller refuse often ended up in the streets, potsherds were generally scattered about the compounds. This differential disposal of pottery seems to be associated with the lack of intensive gardening in Aguacatenango compounds. In Chamula, this practice was more likely related to the long distance to wooded disposal areas (Howry 1973:28).

Frequently, within compounds, some inorganic refuse was either dumped, tossed, or dispersed by children within a household "toft" area. Following Lewis (1976:101), a toft is the immediate site of a dwelling and its outbuildings. It is also the location of most activities associated with the dwelling, and its size and form are not fixed (i.e., it may vary according to the nature of the dwelling and its associated features). By definition, the toft is also the principle area of domestic refuse disposal (Hurst 1971:116; Lewis 1976:105).

In Chanal and Aguacatenango, the nature of toft refuse varied according to major features, such as patios, kitchens, and other structures. These toft areas bordered upon compound gardens and orchards. The patio toft was characterized by dispersed (i.e., broadcast) refuse, patio sweepings accumulated along the patio edge, one or more small discrete dumping locations (e.g., often under a tree or bush) and a "toss zone" (Binford 1978:345) toward its outer limits. In general, within a patio toft, the highest density of refuse occurred along the edge of the patio and between structures and decreased as one moved away from the patio edge. The toss zone was merely a broad area at the outer limit of the patio toft which collected larger unwanted inorganic items such as tin cans, old shoes, and large potsherds, as well as items left by children. These were usually tossed from the patio after use or thrown from their provisional discard locations by playing children. Households with sweatbaths generally had a small discrete dumping location nearby where fire-cracked rock, ash and charcoal, and sherds from vessels used to hold bathwater were discarded.

Where kitchens constituted separate structures, the toft area directly around the kitchen generally had a somewhat different appearance from the patio toft since it consisted mainly of organic wastes from food preparation and consumption. These were dumped once or twice a day, or, occasionally, kitchen refuse was thrown through convenient holes in the kitchen walls. Potsherds found in kitchen tofts were almost exclusively from domestic food preparation and serving vessels.

Pits were seldom used for refuse disposal, yet in a few cases pits had been dug for other purposes (such as wells or fruit ripening) and were eventually refilled with dirt and refuse from the toft areas (also see Gotthilf 1982; Hayden and Cannon 1983), sweepings from structures and the patio areas, or even refuse related to the excavation and use of the pit (see Green 1961a). If a structure was slowly being dismantled within an ongoing household it might become a dumping location for large inorganic items, and especially pottery (also see Butzer 1982:90–92).

Unintentional disposal modes

Loss cannot be considered a major disposal mode in terms of pottery. Large objects such as whole vessels have a low loss potential (see Fehon and Scholtz 1978:271; Hildebrand 1978:277) and conversely, a high rate of recovery from loss. In Chanal compounds, when whole or damaged vessels were lost (e.g., resulting from the play of small children) and not subsequently damaged by animals, they would undoubtedly be found again by adults. Even vessels not found before the compound was abandoned would likely be found by people scavenging the site for reusable items.

A common disposal behavior associated with the watercarrying jar *(kib)* was accidental breakage along pathways between kitchen and water source. Vessels were often dropped while being handled at the well or at a storage location around the kitchen. On other occasions the carrier might slip, or lose her balance, and drop the vessel along the pathway. When this happened the larger sherds were either saved for reuse or swept to the sides of the pathway.

The vertical, and to some extent horizontal, dispersal of refuse in occupation areas is often attributed to trampling activity (e.g., Bradley and Fulford 1980; Green 1961b: 52; Hughs and Lampert 1977; Matthews 1965:295; Nielson 1991; Stockton 1973). Stockton (1973) has conducted experiments to determine the effects of trampling on artifact movement. His study emphasizes the importance of surface composition to artifact movement. In general, small artifacts are more likely to move downward in less compact deposits, such as sandy or loamy surfaces, while large objects tend to move upward. In terms of Tzeltal pottery, preabandonment trampling should be most intense on house floors, patios, and pathways. Small sherds missed during the maintenance of these areas after vessel breakage were likely to be kicked about and trampled into these compacted surfaces. Vertical movement in these surfaces would vary seasonally, with little movement during the dry season, when

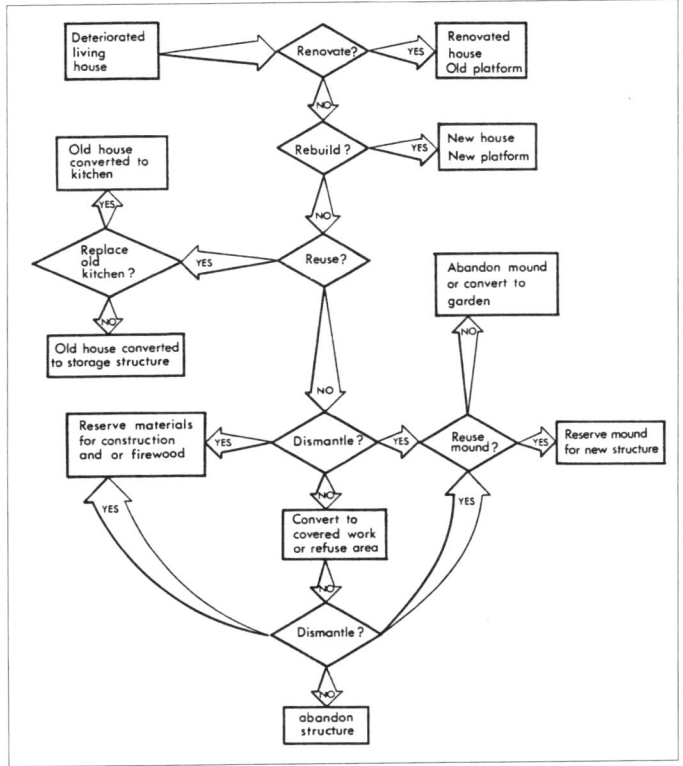

Fig. 5.5. Idealized model of Tzeltal main structure renovation and reuse.

the surfaces are hard, and maximum movement during the wet season, when the same surfaces varied from soft to soupy mud (also noted by Lindahl and Matenga 1995: 103–104). Trampling was less likely to be associated with discrete dumping locations, while broadcast refuse in compound toft areas would receive some random trampling.

Gardening activities caused substantial horizontal and some vertical movement of sherds during the preabandonment stage. Since compound gardening was more intense in Chanal then in Aguacatenango, it might be expected that gardening activity would be more likely to affect pottery patterning in Chanal. However, this was somewhat compensated by the informal "taboo" in Chanal against dumping large sherds in gardening areas. Children could also act as dispersing agents for broken vessels and sherds (also see Weigand 1969:24). In Tzeltal households,

sherds were popular as place markers for games and as missiles. Damaged vessels were also used in housekeeping play.

THE REUSE AND RENOVATION CYCLE OF STRUCTURES

During the occupation of a given household there is a continuing cycle of reuse and renovation of individual structures within the household compound (also see David 1971; Lind 1979; Rock 1974). This cycle ends for each structure when it is completely abandoned, or when it is used only for refuse disposal, or for dismemberment in order to recycle the materials in the construction of another building, or for destruction in order to reuse the land as pasture or garden. The cycle ends for the compound when the entire household cluster of buildings are abandoned. During the cycle, separate structures may change function as new structures are

TABLE 5.3.
Domestic Structure Reuse and Abandonment Recorded for
33 Aguacatenango households.*

Structure Type: Condition:	House	House/Kitchen	Kitchen	Sweatbath	Total
Replaced or Incorporated (new house in same position)	8	4	5	—	17
Replaced or Incorporated (new kitchen in same position)	3	—	4	—	7
Replaced by House/ Kitchen	1	—	—	—	1
Replaced by Storage Unit (in same position)	1	—	—	—	1
No Surface Remains	3	—	—	—	3
Converted to Garden**	2	1	1	—	4
Converted to Patio	3	—	4	—	7
Platform Mound only	4	2	—	1	7
Covered by Woodpile	1	1	—	—	2
Abandoned and still erect	—	—	1	1	2
Total	26	8	15	2	51

*In the remaining 17 households the families were using only the original structures.

**Three of these cases represent the movement of a single household cluster (two houses and one kitchen).

added to the compound (Figure 5.5). For example, an old kitchen may become a storage building when a new kitchen is built, or houses which served both as kitchens and living quarters might become strictly sleeping and storage structures upon the addition of a structure for cooking. Alternatively, structures can retain their original function throughout the entire history of the compound and merely be renovated or rebuilt. According to Tzeltal informants a structure lasts about 20 years.

Since a given compound may enter the abandonment stage at any moment during this cycle, "an element of confusion" may be added to the interpretation of the archaeological situation if there has been a change in position, number, or function of structures within the compound (David 1971:123; also see Meggers and Evans 1957:248; Stanislawski 1973:380). In Chanal, this situation is further complicated by the practice of relocating structures in different areas of the compound in order to use previous locations of structures for gardening. Similarly, in Chamula, when a housesite was abandoned the house structure was dismantled or burned, and the levelled platform was left fallow and eventually cultivated (Howry 1973:29).

An additional problem occurs in households with wattle-and-daub or mud brick structures since wall clay that accumulates over former living floors generally retains the color and texture of the surrounding soil (see Fitch and Branch 1960; Gullini 1969; McIntosh 1974, 1977). Also the pits from which the clay is obtained become artifact traps and are occasionally used for refuse disposal. In terms of pottery, sherds from previous occupations are excavated and used in wall construction (Figure 5.6) while more recent

TABLE 5.4.
Pottery Abandonment at Tzeltal Maya Housesites (Format Adapted from
Stevenson 1979:226).

Condition of Abandonment:	Rapid	Rapid	Gradual	Gradual
Anticipation of Return:	No	Yes	No	Yes
Probability of Material State:				
Vessels in Association with Activity Loci	High	High	Low	Low
Vessels in de facto State (or due to death)	Mod/High	Mod/High	Low	Low/Mod
Vessels in Manufacture	Mod/High	Mod/High	Low	Low
Vessels in Storage	Low	Low/Mod	Low	High
Vessels of Socioeconomic Value	Mod/High	Moderate	Low	Low

sherds are trapped or dumped into the pits from which the clay was taken. Further, the size and number of structures within some compounds may be in a constant state of flux due to changes in family size and economic position. Most importantly, as the cycle of structure change progresses there may be concomitant changes or reorientation in the areas of pottery-use activities, storage, and disposal of pottery and other durables within the compound.

The difficulties of conceptualizing an ideal cycle of structure change are reflected in the record of domestic structure reuse and abandonment for Aguacatenango (see Table 5.3). Occupants of 33 households had reused or abandoned one or more structures while they had occupied their compounds (all within the last 60 years). Of the 51 structures recorded, in 26 cases (51%) new structures had been built on the platform mounds of dismantled structures or portions of the old structures had been incorporated into new ones. In all other cases new structures with new platforms were built in different locations from the old structures, although they were generally built near to the old structures. Similarly, Wauchope (1938:152) reported that Maya in the Yucatan generally built a new house to one side of the old one. In 14 (28%) of the Aguacatenango cases, all traces of a previous structure and platform were destroyed by gardening, patio construction, or some unremembered activity. In the remaining 11 cases (22%), some structural remains, the platform mound, or a hearth feature from a previous structure were clearly visible.

Among the households surveyed in Aguacatenango, only two structures, a kitchen and a sweatbath, remained relatively intact after abandonment. Both of these had been abandoned within the last six years. Only five erect, recently abandoned structures were recorded among the households surveyed in Chanal. Abandoned structures were observed in some households visited but not surveyed in both communities. In general, it seemed that abandoned structures were relatively rare in growing communities, and if they were left erect for any length of time they often served as refuse dumps, animal shelters, play areas for children, or as a convenient covered activity area, such as a sheltered area for woodworking.

Changes in structure location may disrupt artifact patterning in toft areas, they will generally destroy artifact patterning from previous structure configurations resulting from provisional discard and loss. However, there may be little or no effect on pathway, maintenance, or dumping behavior. Because loss accounts for such a small percentage of items, the effects of this mode on overall refuse patterning will probably be negligible in Maya sites. Thus, except for possible remnants of the previous toft areas, refuse patterning should reflect the last use configuration of structures. As long as structure reorientation and reuse occur in the same patio context, the overall refuse patterning should not be

Fig. 5.6. A wattle-and-daub structure in Aguacatenango. Pottery sherds are often incorporated in the daub when it is excavated from previously occupied areas of the compound.

too badly distorted. Clearly, the best context for examining modern refuse patterning is in semi-sedentary communities which occupy land for only a few years or up to one generation.

ABANDONMENT STAGE

Whatever the reason for the desertion of a compound (i.e., household cluster), the primary behavioral factors determining the nature of the material items (e.g., size, condition, value, location) left at the site will include the rapidness of the departure and the anticipation of returning or not returning to the site at some future date (Baker 1975; Cameron 1991, 1993; Lange and Rydberg 1972; Stevenson 1979, 1982; see Table 5.4). At least four compound abandonment modes can thus be recognized, including gradual abandonment with return anticipated, gradual abandonment with return not antici-

pated, rapid abandonment with return anticipated, and rapid abandonment with return not anticipated.

GRADUAL ABANDONMENT MODES

Most archaeological housesites are believed to have been abandoned gradually, with or without anticipation by the occupants of returning at a future date. Under such conditions, special-purpose structures, such as kitchens, may have a higher likelihood of activity area survival than do more general-purpose structures, such as houses (Joyce and Johannessen 1993). Among the Tzeltal, housesites may be abandoned for a number of reasons, such as improved social ranking of the family, increased wealth, a death in the family, or a move to a community closer to the family *milpa*. Decisions to abandon a group of related households in this way may be caused by village factionalism, religious disputes, conflicts over rights to resources, health problems, or poor agricultural conditions (e.g., Heizer 1962; Stanislawski 1973). For example, many of the *pueblos de Indios* established by the Spanish after the conquest eventually had to be abandoned because the locations were unhealthy, had inadequate farmland or lost viability due to trade restrictions (Markman 1972:199).

Under gradual abandonment conditions, pottery of significant social or economic value, together with vessels in a state of manufacture and vessels in association with activity areas are not likely to be deserted (see Lange and Rydberg 1972:430; Robbins 1973:212). In cases where return is not anticipated, refuse that would normally be removed from living and working areas might be allowed to accumulate during site abandonment (Stevenson 1982:246). In cases where return is anticipated there is more likelihood that usable items will be left at an abandoned site. It has been suggested that an orderly versus random arrangement of useful materials may reflect anticipated return to a site (Baker 1975). Caching of whole and functional items also implies anticipated return (e.g., Gould 1980:10; Stevenson 1982:253).

An abandonment practice relatively common among the Tzeltal Maya that results in a situation resembling anticipated return, but which is actually quite different, is the orderly abandonment of a living house after a death in the family. This practice can be traced through Landa (Tozzer 1966:130 [1941]) to at least the early Colonial period (16th century). According to Wauchope, houses are generally deserted after there have been one to three deaths, depending upon the size of the family occupying the house (1938:152).

A modern example of a compound abandoned due to a death in the family was reported in the Huistan *paraje* of San Pedro in 1977. Unfortunately, it was not clear whether items used primarily by the deceased individual constituted the principal material left in the house. In the San Pedro compound, the kitchen structure of the compound had been largely dismantled and usable items scavenged, while the living house was relatively intact, and some of the household ritual paraphernalia was still stored in the rafters. These included two large fiesta cooking jars, a large fiesta tortilla griddle, and a gourd tortilla-storage bowl.

RAPID ABANDONMENT MODES

Instances in which a site is abandoned rapidly, and especially when the occupants have no anticipation of returning, are probably less common than those of gradual abandonment except in the cases of the immediate threat of attack, an epidemic, or an impending natural disaster (e.g., earthquake, fire, or volcanic activity). However, Friede and Steel (1980) suggest that most occupation floors excavated in prehistoric African settlements represent huts which have been burned down. Their experiments with burning down abandoned huts shows that one effect of fire is a measurable change in the magnetic properties of supporting soils. Because of these changes it may be possible to infer the rapid abandonment of households in cases of fire.

The Classic site of Cerén, El Salvador that was buried by volcanic activity (Sheets 1979; 1992), creates an ideal kind of situation for archaeological interpretations, since pottery and other artifacts are left in association with activity and storage areas under such conditions. Further, as a result of rapid abandonment, more complete and valuable vessels, which are normally removed, may be left in the structure. The effects of rapid abandonment are similar whether or not return is anticipated, with the possible exception that the latter situation would result in the removal of some vessels with social value, such as heirlooms, or economic (i.e., resale) value.

Other factors which may contribute to determining the nature of items left at a site include their portability, the means of transportation, distance to the new site, season of movement and relative functional utility of the items (Stevenson 1979). Pottery vessels are not highly portable and the normal mode of transportation is by foot, with baggage supported by a tumpline. Thus under conditions of gradual abandonment, most vessels, and especially larger ones, might be given to relatives, or sold if the new site is at any distance away or if the move takes place during the rainy season. Under rapid abandonment conditions, it is highly unlikely that any but the most valuable vessels, such as polychromes or heirlooms, would be removed. Pottery being stored for potential repair or reuse would almost certainly be left under both gradual and rapid abandonment conditions.

While various stages of abandonment have been discussed, it should also be stressed that there are a number of optional movements between these stages and the final archaeological record. Once the compound is abandoned it might remain a closed (or fenced) compound with limited access, an open site (vacant lot) with unlimited access, or it might enter the archaeological record directly due to catastrophic events, or the relocation of entire communities, as among the semi-nomadic Lacandon. In the latter case, compounds would not be exposed to significant cultural postabandonment activities. A closed site may be reoccupied, or converted to a garden or pasture; it may be opened by removal of fences, or it may enter the archaeological record without becoming open. Once a compound becomes an open (vacant) lot it may be reoccupied, converted to a garden or pasture, or enter directly into the archaeological record. Finally an archaeological site may be reoccupied after being left isolated from human activities for many years. Thus there are many possible pathways or sequences between occupation and the archaeological context, each with slightly different archaeological consequences for the patterning and content of items and features. Obviously, sites directly entering the archaeological record, or sites which remain closed until the community is abandoned, hold the most promise for archaeological interpretation.

POSTABANDONMENT STAGE

Much of the "smearing and blending" of cultural remains that occurs after a site is abandoned can be attributed to natural processes, such as soil erosion and the deterioration of the perishable ecofacts (e.g., Butzer 1982; Foley 1981; Schiffer 1983b; Wood and Johnson 1978). However, as Ascher (1977:237) points out "there are also contributing human factors in the first stages of smearing and at every stage in its progression." These factors include several activities associated with the open (or vacant lot) stage experienced by many housesites in Tzeltal communities. This stage is characteristic of housesites which are left open to general public traffic and are thus accessible for various activities comparable to those conducted in open housing lots in our own towns and cities (see Wilk and Schiffer 1979). By comparison, abandoned lots which are not readily accessible to everyone, such as those in fenced compounds, are referred to here as "closed." Both open and closed compounds are, of course, exposed to the same kinds of postabandonment activities; however, one would expect those activities to be conducted with considerably less intensity in closed abandoned lots. Major postabandonment processes include scavenging, shortcutting, children's play, and postabandonment dumping disposal.

Scavenging activities are generally associated with the early abandonment stage. Many sites may already be devoid of reusable items before they become vacant lots. The intensity of scavenging at a given abandoned housesite is directly dependent upon the kinds and quantities of materials left during the abandonment process. Logically, there will be "better pickings" at rapidly abandoned housesites. Usable pottery, as well as ground stone items, such as *metates*, would be "choice" items for scavenging. Larger pottery fragments might also be taken depending partially upon the relative availability of pottery within the community as a whole.

Scavenging is also affected by the population flux of the community. The shorter the period of time in which the entire community is being abandoned the lower the intensity of scavenging. For example, one would not expect a great deal of scavenging to occur at the abandoned Arab village reported by Nisson (1968), where virtually the entire population departed *en mass* when their water supply was closed-off. Further, the seminomadic Lacandon and other swidden horticulturalists are known to regularly change village locations. Scavenging activity is more intense in communities that are growing, that maintain a constant population level, or that are gradually abandoned.

The scavenging of artifacts from known Precolumbian sites (i.e., the reclamation process) was also relatively common in the Tzeltal Maya area. In Aguacatenango, a fine quality, three-legged bowl which dates to the Classic period was being reused as a dog's drinking dish in one household (Figure 5.7). *Manos* and *metates* were commonly reclaimed for grinding temper. This practice has also been recorded in the American Southwest (Harvey 1964:58). Similar examples occurred in Chanal. In one Chanal household, a fine, long-necked vase being used as a flower holder and a shallow bowl being used as a spindle-dish were probably both of Precolumbian origin. In another household, prehistoric sherds and adze blades taken from a nearby cave were stored in a place of reverence on the family altar. A

Fig. 5.7. Fine Orange bowl reused as dog feeding dish at an Aguacatenango compound. This vessel is now in the collection of the New World Archaeological Foundation.

further example, involving the reclamation of pottery burial vessels from an archaeological site, was reported by Blom (1954:125), in which " . . . a cave that contained more than two dozen pottery vessels all in such excellent state of preservation that the finder took them to his house where the women used the pots for carrying water and cooking food until at last all the pieces were broken."

Once an abandoned compound was freely accessible to the entire community the probability of the preservation of the original pathways decreased. The use and preservation of such pathways was also dependent upon the nearness of the site to the community center where the bulk of human traffic converged. New pathways were formed if they provided a speedier transect of the lot. After a short time it was difficult to distinguish these new shortcuts from the original pathways within the compound. Moreover, pathway breakage and dumping often occurred along the edge of these communally used pathways, which could cause considerable distortion of the refuse patterning associated with the original compound occupation.

Abandoned housesites were also popular play areas for children, and especially if there were partially standing structures and material fragments about to serve as play equipment. Pottery vessels or fragments were essential housemaking equipment for children in their own households and were probably equally important when playing at aban-

doned housesites. In fact, children might bring pottery from their own household to their "playhouse" at an abandoned lot. Wilk and Schiffer (1979) and Hammond and Hammond (1981) treat the subject of the effects of children's play on abandoned lots in more detail.

Disposal behavior patterns associated with vacant lots tended to vary considerably from those of in-use compounds and was characterized by a dumping disposal mode often accompanied by small fires (e.g., for disposal of organics). In ongoing compounds, decisions concerning where to throw refuse within a compound were made in relation to the location of structures, patio and other features, and activity areas, while disposal behavior in abandoned lots seemed to be most closely associated with pathways, boundary fences, and other structures that provide depressions or concealment of trash. Similarly, Wilk and Schiffer (1979) reported that refuse disposal in modern vacant lots in Tucson, Arizona often took place along and at the ends of terminating paths.

ARCHAEOLOGICAL CONSIDERATIONS
While abandonment and postabandonment behaviors are not rigidly bounded there is a distinguishable set of disposal patterns within the Tzeltal Maya area. Although some degree of variation seems to occur between communities, it appears that these patterns represent economical, sensible solutions to common problems of spatial organization (also see Hayden and Cannon 1983). A better understanding of these patterns should enable archaeologists to identify relatively undisturbed compound areas, as well as the conditions of abandonment. For example, archaeological remains at the early historical Coxoh site of Coneta point to rapid abandonment (Lee 1979b). The following discussion reviews some of the more interesting archaeological assumptions relating to the present study and outlines some examples of likely archaeological refuse patterns and inferences concerning abandonment and postabandonment activities associated with them.

TABLE 5.5.
Six Descriptive Models of Pottery Refuse Patterning.

Model 1:
Characteristics: discernable patio and pathway tofts.
provisional discard present.
usable whole vessels present.
Assumptions: no or minimal postabandonment activity.
return was probably anticipated after abandonment but not achieved; or rapid abandonment occurred, and return was not anticipated.
single occupation.

Model 2:
Characteristics: discernable patio and pathway tofts.
provisional discard present.
no whole vessels present.
Assumptions: minimal postabandonment activity; possible scavenging of whole vessels.
return was anticipated and whole vessels were left and eventually scavenged; or return was not anticipated, whole vessels were taken upon abandonment, and postabandonment activity was minimal.
single occupation.

Model 3:
Characteristics: discernable patio and pathway tofts.
provisional discard present.
no whole vessels present.
intrusive pathway present.
small dumps along boundaries and intrusive pathway.
Assumptions: considerable postabandonment activity, especially shortcutting, minor dumping, and scavenging.
return was not anticipated; or return was anticipated and not achieved, and whole vessels were scavenged.
single occupation.

Model 4:
Characteristics: blurred but discernable patio and pathway tofts.
no provisional discard present.
no whole vessels present.
intrusive pathway present.
extensive dumping along boundaries and intrusive pathway.
Assumptions: extensive postabandonment activity, especially dumping, shortcutting, and scavenging.
abandonment situation unclear.
single occupation.

Model 5:
Characteristics: very blurred patio and pathway tofts.
no provisional discard present.
no whole vessels present.
moderate sherd density over entire site.
Assumptions: postabandonment gardening discernable.
abandonment situation unclear.
single occupation.

Model 6:
   Characteristics: very blurred patio and pathway tofts.
                          no provisional discard present.
                          no whole vessels.
                          high sherd density over entire site.
   Assumptions: postabandonment gardening extensive.
                          abandonment situation unclear.
                          successive occupations of site.

Several authors have suggested that artifact clustering in archaeological sites may be produced by disposal behavior rather than representing activity areas (e.g., Binford 1978:356; Murray 1980:398; Schiffer 1983b). Wilson (1994) provides a valuable examination of localized, high-density secondary refuse situations, or "secondary refuse aggregates," in terms of the household socioeconomic conditions and refuse-producing activities. Among the Tzeltal, both dumping and provisional discard can result in such clustering and might wrongly be associated with activity areas inside of structures. If clustering seems to be activity-related it is more likely the result of provisional discard or postabandonment behavior, rather than predepositional activities. Maintenance disposal practices add to the visibility of work areas such as the household patio, by concentrating refuse around these areas. A recent study by Philip Arnold (1990) suggests that the composition and distribution of refuse items across patio areas is conditioned by patio size. In Sierra de los Tuxtlas, Veracruz, he identified a higher degree of waste management with larger discrete dumping areas in association with smaller patios (Arnold 1990).

A characteristic of the patio toft is a general size sorting of discarded items, with larger items being tossed to the outer limits of the toft. This characteristic may be useful for delimiting compound refuse areas based on the distribution of larger items of refuse relative to structural features. Children are also important dispersing agents.

The intensity of compound gardening is an important factor in decisions concerning where to dump refuse, and especially inside versus outside the compound, and also the dispersion of sherds that do become incorporated in garden plots. The removal of large fragments of pottery from the compound for hindrance minimization will have a considerable effect on the nature of the household pottery assemblage in terms of the relative proportion of the pottery refuse produced by the household which remains in association with the compound after abandonment. A detailed treatment of the relationship between agricultural activities and residential site structure and refuse management is presented by Killion (1990).

Several abandoned structures in Chanal and Aguacatenango were closed to general access. In the past, in instances where structures had remained closed until the entire community was abandoned, their pottery assemblages would be less likely to have experienced postabandonment alterations. Obviously, the less a housesite was affected by postabandonment processes, the higher the probability of making accurate interpretations concerning the original occupation.

Postabandonment refuse disposal, and especially pottery disposal, differs from preabandonment refuse disposal primarily in terms of location of dumping areas within the compound. Postabandonment dumping results in concentrations of refuse along fences and pathways or in household depressions rather than near the household cluster.

Reusable items, such as *manos, metates,* and nearly whole vessels are usually scavenged after housesite abandonment. The frequency and condition of such artifacts left on a site may therefore be useful for interpreting the conditions of site (or community) aban-

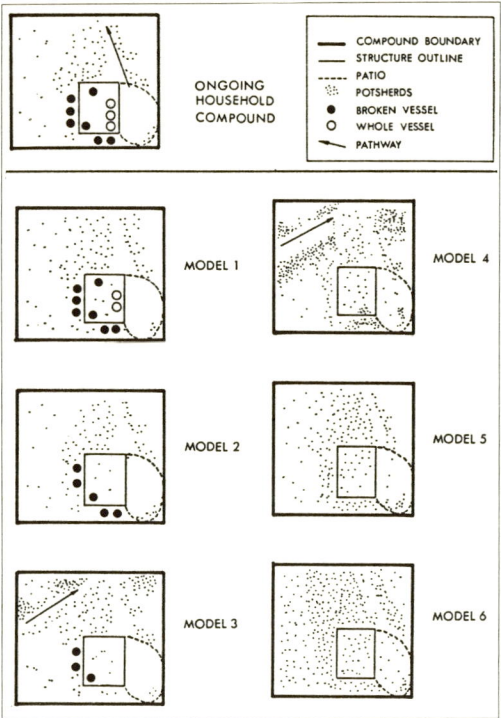

Fig. 5.8. Six hypothetical, archaeological models of Maya pottery refuse patterning.

donment in terms of the speed of abandonment and the intensity of postabandonment activity.

In order to explore the archaeological implications of the Tzeltal observations in more detail, the ways in which abandonment and postabandonment activities might combine to produce distinctive archaeological patterning must be considered. Table 5.5 outlines some of the most likely combinations of depositional events that might affect a common refuse pattern in the preabandonment stage as well as the resulting archaeological patterns. Special attention is given to certain patterns with high potential for archaeological visibility, that is, patio, pathway, and toft refuse, provisional discard, and deserted usable whole vessels. These archaeologically relevant patterns have been presented elsewhere as six simple models (Deal 1985: 273–280; Figure 5.8).

During the 1979 field season, one of the Coxoh Project crew members conducted a surface collection of artifacts from two abandoned Aguacatenango housesites (Bru-

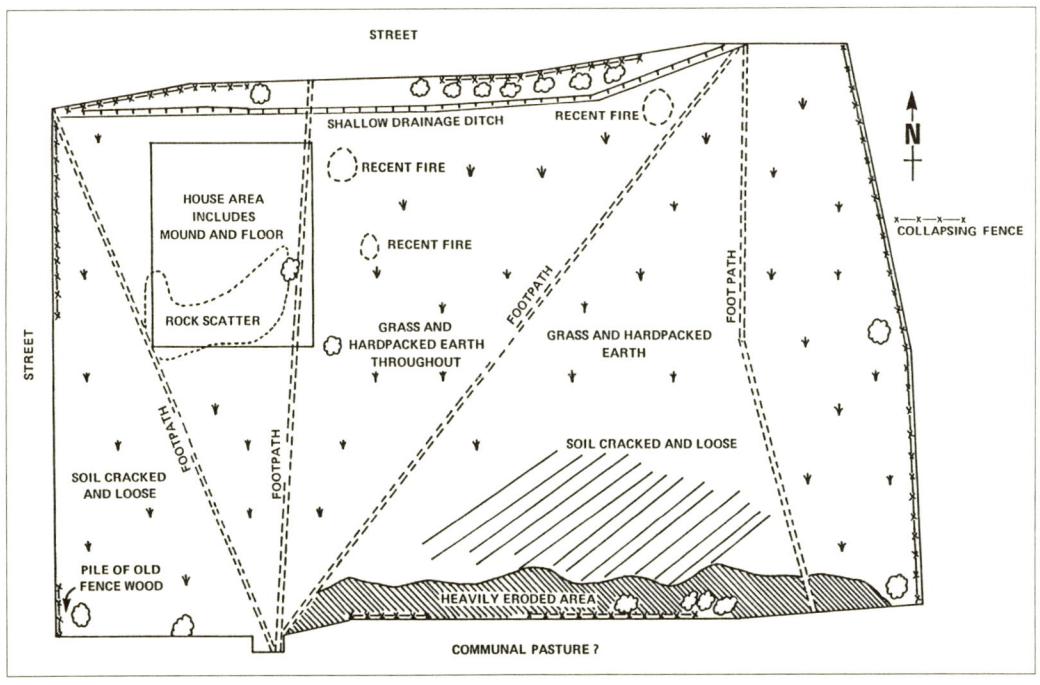

Fig. 5.9. Feature map of abandoned housesite 1, Aguacatenango.

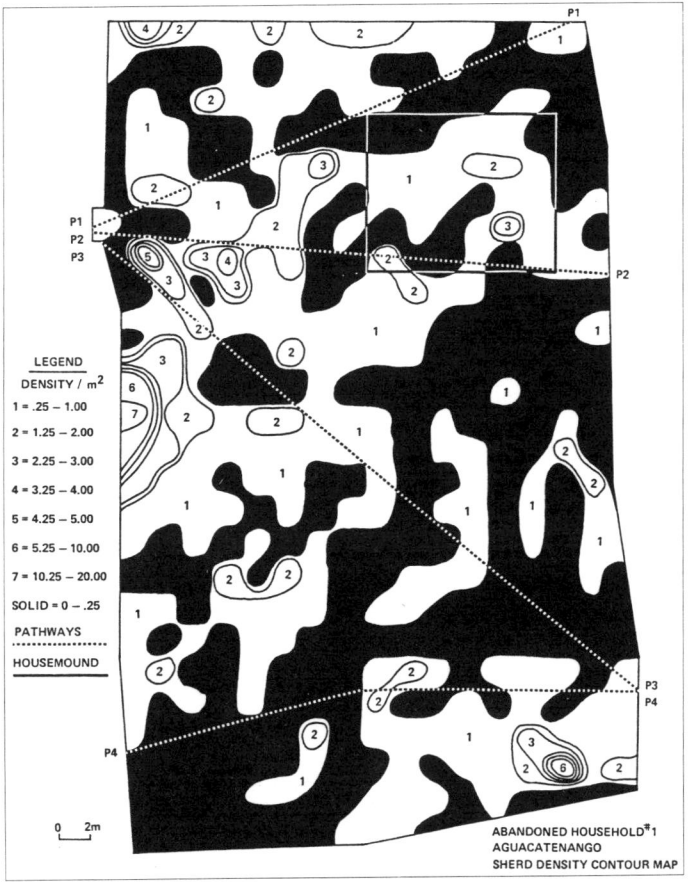

Fig. 5.10. Sherd density contour map of abandoned housesite 1, Aguacatenango.

lotte 1979). Brulotte's data is used here to demonstrate how the Tzeltal depositional model might aid the interpretation of archaeological refuse patterning. One of the most striking characteristics of the two abandoned housesites is the relatively low potsherd densities associated with the house platforms, which are both presumably house and kitchen combined (see Figure 5.9–5.12). In order to understand why such a situation would occur, a number of relevant factors are considered. These include various aspects of the deposition related to depositional behavior as it affects the density of pottery refuse, and its spatial distribution within a compound and the general physical characteristics of abandoned compounds that reflect the intensity of postabandonment activity (e.g., location, open or closed state).

To begin with, how do each of the recognized disposal modes and processes contribute to the accumulation of pottery refuse on and around a house platform (i.e., within one or two meters from the outside walls)? Maintenance and provisional discard disposal are probably the most important relevant factors in this regard. Frequent sweeping of house and kitchen floors, as well as associated patio areas, removes almost all accumulations of sherds in structures and in patio areas, although such sweeping results in concentrations of small sherds and other small items in the drainage ditches and along the edges of the patio near dwellings. Thus, during the predepositional stage, virtually all

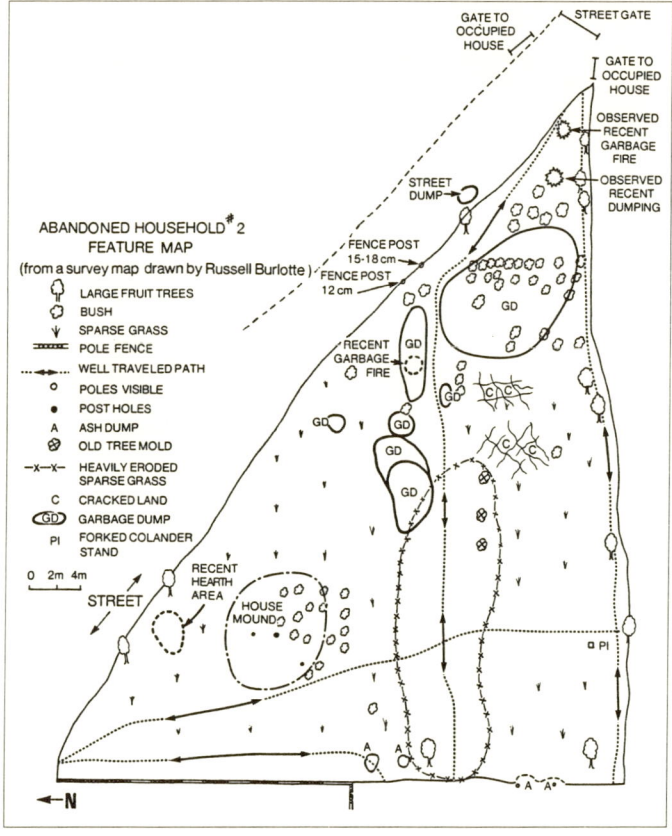

Fig. 5.11. Feature map of abandoned housesite 2, Aguacatenango.

large pottery refuse associated with a house or kitchen platform results from provisional discard and, to a lesser extent, trampling activity after maintenance.

In Aguacatenango, cases of provisional discard of single damaged vessels were associated with the house structures of 21 households (42% of sample) and with the kitchens of 17 households (34% of sample). This could be compared with the provisional discard of clusters of broken pottery, which occurred along the outside walls of houses in 10 households (20% of sample) and likewise along the walls of kitchens in 10 households. Singly stored broken vessels and vessel fragments generally occurred inside while clusters of broken pottery rarely occurred inside structures. Thus, many households would not have had large sherds even in provisional

discard around structures, and even if such objects were left upon abandonment they might quickly be removed due to various postabandonment processes.

All other disposal modes, and to some extent provisional discard, resulted in the accumulation of discarded potsherds throughout the compounds, and especially broadcast patterning. Since the toft, garden, and orchard areas within Aguacatenango compounds were not regularly cleaned, as were the floors of structures and patio areas, a greater buildup of refuse in these areas relative to structures and patio areas over time might be expected. However, at least two preabandonment practices unrelated to household economic activities could have contributed considerable sherdage to abandoned house platforms. The first was the

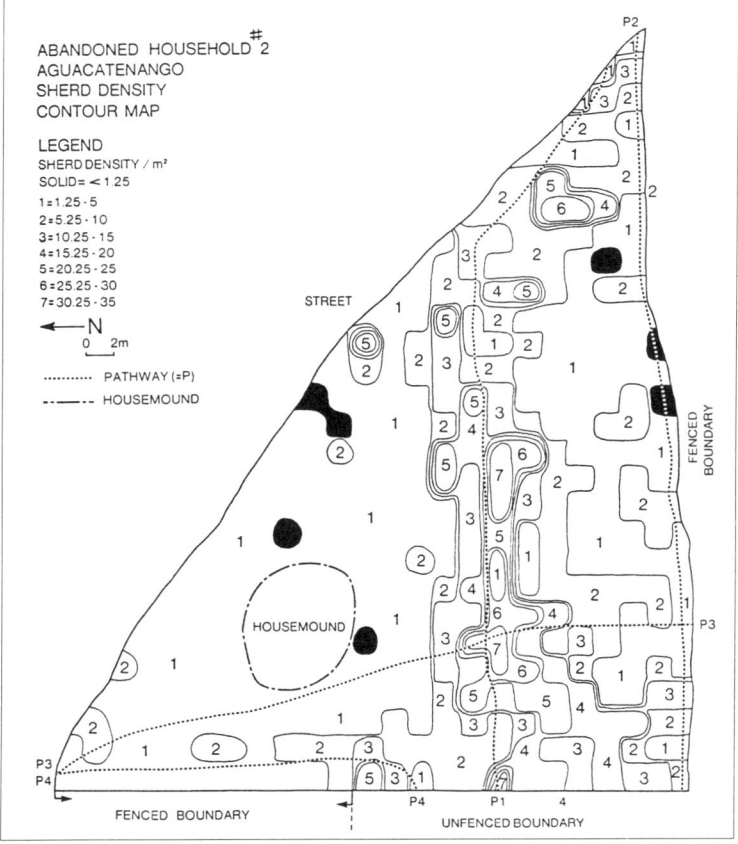

Fig. 5.12. Sherd density contour map, abandoned housesite 2, Aguacatenango.

practice of constructing wattle-and-daub structures and the second was the use of abandoned structures for the dumping of refuse. The latter practice was only rarely observed in Aguacatenango, but the use of wattle-and-daub was very common. Further, the relative amount of sherdage incorporated in the wall fill was observed to increase with proximity to the community center.

In terms of the abandonment modes discussed above, one might expect low potsherd densities on and around house platforms to reflect a gradual rather than rapid rate of abandonment, and especially if return was not anticipated. In general, as the speed of abandonment decreases, the frequency of deserted whole or damaged pottery vessels, and potential sherdage, is likely to decrease. Similarly, as the probability of return decreases, the likelihood of deserted vessels decreases. After abandonment in an ongoing community, certain postabandonment processes, if they come into effect, may greatly alter relative sherd densities within an abandoned compound. Specifically, scavenging and children's play may remove any deserted vessels, including large fragments, associated with the structure (e.g., provisional discard), and postabandonment dumping activity may create new high density concentrations of sherds along pathways and fences away from structures. The location of new pathways may be crucial in this regard.

The two abandoned Aguacatenango compounds were extensively surface collected, over a six week period. Both compounds represented the open (or vacant lot) state of abandonment. Each lot was partially fenced, but open to through traffic. Brulotte (1979) observed intensive postabandonment activity on both sites during his survey. This took the form of continual traffic along old and new pathways and dumping refuse, and especially small organic refuse fires, along pathways and fences. The general effect of such activities was to increase the sherd densities in these areas relative to the house platform area. The system of pathways on both lots was extensive. One new pathway (P2 on Figure 5.9) cut across the house platform of housesite #1 and the two highest density areas within the mound seemed to be associated with it. In fact, the relative high density of one survey unit (i.e., three sherds/m²) seemed to be the direct result of a single event of pathway breakage, in which a watercarrying jar *(kib)* was dropped on the platform mound and survived as a cluster of nine sherds.

Secondly, the materials from which the houses were constructed were of importance. In both cases only the platform mound remained from the original structure. Presumably both structures were dismantled during or after abandonment of the compounds. The structure in housesite #1 was of *corazon de piedras* ("heart of stone") construction, evidenced by the scattering of small stones on the house floor and by small diameter postholes. The structure in housesite #2 was of wattle-and-daub construction, evidenced by 26 daub fragments (Brulotte 1979). As mentioned above, potsherds formerly mixed into the daub walls might account for the slightly higher density associated with the house platform of housesite #2. Prehistoric plainware sherds in walls might be indistinguishable from modern plainware sherds. Surface sherds derived from wall fill were absent at housesite #1.

Lastly, the proximity of each compound to the center of the community was taken into consideration. Since housesite #2 was more centrally located than housesite #1, it was open to much more foot traffic and had become a more popular disposal area. This latter fact was reflected in the tremendous difference in surface sherd densities between the two sites (see Figures 5.10, 5.13).

At least 10 factors can be identified that could have affected the differential potsherd densities of house platform versus compound areas for the two abandoned Aguacatenango compounds, including:

(1) A combination of the frequency of occurrence of house, kitchen, and patio maintenance disposal, and especially the sweeping of structure interiors, and the increase in refuse concentration in toft areas over time.

(2) The likelihood that most pottery left on and around the house or kitchen structure upon abandonment would consist of singly stored fragmentary vessels along the interior walls and/or a cluster of fragmentary vessels around the exterior of the structure.

(3) Disposal behavior, other than provisional discard disposal, resulting in refuse dumping (i.e., broadcast or discrete patterns) away from structures, and probably outside of the compound.

(4) The use of abandoned structures for refuse disposal as a relatively rare occurrence in ongoing communities.

(5) The use of wattle-and-daub wall construction affecting relative potsherd densities on housemounds (e.g., the relatively higher density of potsherds associated with household #2).

(6) The likelihood that the amount of pottery refuse left upon abandonment, on and around the house platform, would decrease or increase under different abandonment conditions. Decreases would occur especially under gradual abandonment conditions with no anticipation of return. Under such conditions, no items of value would likely be left, including usable (or reusable) pottery vessels.

(7) Open abandoned lots in ongoing communities being more susceptible to postabandonment cultural processes than closed abandoned lots.

(8) Intensity of postabandonment activity (especially the processes of shortcutting and dumping) increasing with proximity to the community center.

(9) Scavenging and children's play in open lots removing any items of value for adults or children (e.g., fragmentary pottery, *manos, metates*) left upon abandonment.

(10) Relative potsherd densities on open lots being greatly distorted by postabandonment dumping along pathways and borders.

Under varying sets of conditions, most of these factors could play important roles in creating low or high potsherd density, although preabandonment maintenance behavior, as well as the intensity of postabandonment dumping must be given priority in initial examination of the topic. When such conditions are taken into consideration, the accurate interpretation of relative potsherd density on abandoned Aguacatenango, and possibly any Tzeltal, house platforms appears to be highly probable. Of the six refuse models outlined in Table 5.5, both abandoned Aguacatenango sites seem to be most comparable to model 4.

QUANTIFYING DISCARD

Considering the complexity of Tzeltal pottery disposition, what kind of expectations can we have for predicting the size and diversity of household pottery assemblages over time? Currently, the preferred way of addressing this question is to mathematically simulate household pottery inventory change (e.g., Mills 1989). This can be easily done using Schiffer's (1976:60) total discard equation. This formula can be used with ethnographic pottery inventories to make predictions of changes in the relative proportions of pottery types within inventories over time, as well as changes in size of inventories over time. Recent computer simulations of cooking pot assemblage formation by Varien and Potter (1997) lends support to the continued use of the total discard equation. These authors

use the term "accumulation studies" to refer to the branch of formation studies that deals with relationships between time, population, and material culture accumulation. Varien and Mills (1997) present an accumulation approach to the refinement of occupation span measurement of sites in the American Southwest.

In order to include as many recognized pottery types as possible in the simulation, an average household inventory for each community was established, using the mean frequencies for each pottery type for which uselife estimates were collected. No individual household inventory included all of the types used in the simulation. The following discussion outlines the information required by the equation, and Tables 5.6 and 5.7 give summaries of all values observed and generated for each pottery type in the average household.

The equation for calculating total discard (Schiffer 1976:60) is expressed as:

$$TD = St / L$$

where: TD = total discard per unit;

S = the average number of a given item (vessel) type normally in use at a given time;

t = the time span over which a given item (vessel) type is in use;

L = lifespan (or uselife), expressed in units of time (t).

To facilitate the simulation, the frequency of each type (S) and the uselife of each type (L) are assumed to remain constant over time. That is, each time a vessel is broken it is immediately replaced. In reality, replacement rates tend to vary considerably from household to household over time according to changes in household socioeconomic and demographic conditions (see Chapter 4). With vessel number and uselife held constant, the estimates of type proportion (i.e., percentage of inventory) over time will become constant immediately upon replacement of the origi-

TABLE 5.6.
Total Discard Model for Chanal.

Emic Types:	Uselife	Original Frequency	Total Discard after 20 Years	Percentage of Original Vessels	Percentage of 20 Year Total
Samet	0.49	2.64	107.76	5.40	10.26
Oxom	0.58	20.49	706.55	41.94	67.28
Chikpin	1.68	3.19	37.98	6.53	3.62
Sets' (local)	2.17	0.66	6.08	1.35	0.58
Kib	2.29	4.71	41.14	9.64	3.92
Poket	2.57	3.45	26.85	7.06	2.56
Chalten	2.83	0.66	4.66	1.35	0.44
Total Domestic		35.80	931.01	73.27	88.66
Borcelana	1.26	5.43	86.19	11.11	8.21
Chixnajab'il	3.20	0.75	4.69	1.53	0.45
Oxom Grande	3.72	3.77	20.27	7.72	1.93
Chik'pom	5.80	1.78	6.14	3.64	0.58
Somjebal Cantela	10.00	0.36	0.72	0.74	0.07
Tenosha	12.50	0.24	0.38	0.49	0.04
Poket Grande	20.00	0.73	0.73	1.49	0.07
Total Ritual		13.06	119.12	26.72	11.34
Total Inventory		48.86	1050.13		

nal inventory. However, the difference between the original and subsequent inventory proportion is of considerable interest.

According to Tzeltal informants, the average life expectancy for a traditional plank-wall, thatched roof structure is about 20 years (also see Howry 1978:256). Using Chanal data as an example, the predicted discard rate for the most common vessel type in Chanal, namely, the unslipped, wide-mouthed jar *(oxom)*, for a single occupation of 20 years, can be expressed as:

$$\text{Tjar} = \frac{20.49 \text{ jars} \times 20 \text{ years}}{.58 \text{ years}} = 707 \text{ jars}$$

A comparison of total discard rates for the entire inventory indicates the effect of different uselives on the proportion of the origi-

nal inventory. For example, in our average household inventory for Chanal, unslipped, wide-mouth jars represent 41.94 percent of the total inventory, while over a 20 year period these jars will constitute 67.28 percent of vessels contributed to the pottery refuse of the household. This increase is directly attributable to the relatively low uselife of this type. In fact, in Chanal, only two of the major domestic types, the unslipped, wide-mouth jar *(oxom)* and the unrestricted plate *(samet)*, actually increased in percentage proportion of the projected pottery assemblage, while the percentage of all other types decreased. In Aguacatenango, an increase is also seen for the single-handled jar *(chikpin)* and restricted-mouth bowl *(borcelana)*.

In terms of activity sets, an increase in short-lived domestic types and plainwares in

TABLE 5.7.
Total Discard Model for Aguacatenango.

Emic Types:	Uselife	Original Frequency	Total Discard after 20 Years	Percentage of Original Vessels	Percentage of 20 Year Total
Samet	0.67	1.48	44.18	2.23	2.46
Oxom	0.61	6.67	218.69	10.06	12.17
Chikpin	0.56	26.64	951.43	40.16	52.93
Sets' (imported)	0.50	1.04	41.60	1.57	2.31
Kib	1.15	5.76	100.17	8.68	5.57
Poket	0.86	7.76	180.47	11.70	10.04
Chalten	1.56	1.70	21.79	2.56	1.21
Chichina	1.25	1.48	23.68	2.23	1.32
Total Domestic		52.53	1582.01	79.19	88.01
Borcelana	0.96	8.08	168.33	12.18	9.36
Chichina chica	1.19	0.72	12.10	1.09	0.67
Oxom Grande	1.99	1.04	10.45	1.57	0.58
Chik'pom	1.67	1.14	13.65	1.72	0.76
Somjebal Cantela	2.46	0.02	0.16	0.03	0.01
Tenosha	2.92	0.72	4.93	1.09	0.27
Poket Grande	8.50	1.84	4.33	2.77	0.24
Yajuil Nichim	3.00	0.24	1.60	0.36	0.09
Total Ritual		13.80	215.55	20.81	11.98
Total Inventory		66.33	1797.56		

general, is apparent over time, along with a concomitant decrease in the longer-lived ritual types. This is consistent with the relatively high proportion of plainware sherds usually associated with domestic house excavations (see Wauchope 1938:120). The percentage proportion of domestic vessels is seen to increase from 73 percent to 89 percent of the household inventory over a 20 year period in Chanal, while the proportion of ritual vessels drops from 27 percent to 11 percent over the same period. In Aguacatenango similar, although less dramatic, results are indicated, with the percentage proportion of domestic vessels rising from 79 percent to 88 percent, while the proportion of ritual vessels drops from 21 percent to 12

percent of the household inventory over a 20 year period. It is important to note that the predicted proportions for each community are virtually the same for domestic and ritual vessels (i.e., 89 percent versus 11 percent for Chanal, and 88 percent versus 12 percent for Aguacatenango).

Summing the values of the total discard variable over a 20 year period (or one occupation) produces an estimate of 1050 vessels for the average Chanal household (i.e., 22 times the original inventory) and 1798 for the average Aguacatenango household (i.e., 27 times the original inventory). Assuming that these values are a reasonable approximation of reality, then the average Chanal household can be expected to discard about

53 vessels per year for the 20 year period, while the average Aguacatenango household would discard about 90 vessels per year in the same period. In each community, the average family size is approximately seven persons. Therefore, according to the simulation model, the per capita discard rate for Chanal would be about eight vessels per year while the per capita discard rate for Aguacatenango would be about 13 vessels per year.

Simulations of this kind are useful for illustrating the variation in pottery assemblages caused by differential lengths of household occupation. But before such a model can be used for archaeological interpretation, a better understanding is needed of uselife estimates for more exotic types, the relationship between replacement rates and changes in household socioeconomic and demographic conditions, and factors affecting inside versus outside compound disposal (e.g., concerning the latter see Hayden and Cannon 1983).

SUMMARY

In terms of pottery and other durable elements, the locations of storage and disposal behavior seem to be the most important factors in the ethnographic context which contribute to their eventual spatial distributions in the archaeological record. Of recognized disposal modes, provisional discard locations are probably the most sensitive to the transformation stages of structures within a compound, while maintenance disposal, dumping, and pathway breakage may escape alteration due to such transformations.

In terms of abandonment and postabandonment behavior within a large residential archaeological site, one might find housesites reflecting varying conditions of abandonment, from households abandoned rapidly (e.g., due to fire) with relatively little post-abandonment activity to gradually abandoned households with a high degree of postabandonment activity. In order to make comparisons between household assemblages meaningful, only households exhibiting the same kind of abandonment and postabandonment conditions should be compared. Generally the last structures in use prior to abandonment of a given compound will be the ones most intact in the archaeological record. Households that have been converted to gardens may be so obliterated as to escape detection during surface surveys except as refuse scatters, while others may have suffered little from postabandonment activities.

Unless abandonment of the compound is rapid, all except the least valuable vessels are likely to be taken from the site and either curated to the new site or sold or given to neighbors and relatives. Whatever survives to the abandonment stage may become exposed to further cultural and natural processes. The frequent scavenging of reusable vessels and vessel fragments and the use of the site for refuse disposal from other compounds probably have the most devastating effects on the final pottery record of a housesite. Although the overlapping of such disposal patterns makes the analysis of depositional behavior more difficult, it does not preclude it, and is an essential consideration when interpreting the use context of items found on floors of structures.

These few general observations concerning the formation of pottery assemblages in Tzeltal Maya housesites may not be widely applicable outside the Maya Highlands, however, some understanding of the regularities of pottery-related depositional behavior, regardless of geographical location, must form the baseline of any statement concerning the social nature of a given pottery assemblage.

6

The Prediction of
Household Socioeconomic Conditions

Classification is long and life is fleeting. (Willey 1961:230)

In the previous chapters, ethnographic pottery information was used for theoretical model building, however, such information is also useful for testing and evaluating standard archaeological methods of analyzing pottery assemblages from excavated sites. The most common archaeological method involves the measurement of the frequencies (or proportional frequencies) of vessels, vessel types and vessel wares comprising an assemblage. One of the ultimate goals of such analyses is, or should be, the interpretation of socioeconomic information from the pottery assemblages. However, obtaining reliable measurements of vessel frequency is a major problem for archaeologists (Orton 1980:156). Moreover, analyses using whole vessels tend to have different interpretative goals than analyses using sherd counts, the former relating to subsistence patterning and the latter to settlement patterning (Mills 1989).

Before considering the interpretation of the socioeconomic conditions of a given housesite one must first be confident that there is negligible postabandonment disturbance of the assemblage, or that any physical remnants of postabandonment activities can be identified (see Chapter 5). With the above goal (and restriction) in mind, the aim of the present chapter is to outline the methodological problems surrounding the use of frequency measures for characterizing pottery assemblages, to suggest an alternative quantification measure, that of type diversity, and to explore the variability in socioeconomic inferences that can be made at the household and village levels based on Tzeltal pottery data.

A METHODOLOGICAL MORASS

As stated previously, if ethnologists (or ethnoarchaeologists) and archaeologists wish to compare data sets based on observations of the same variables, then similar methods of measuring and analyzing these variables should also be used whenever possible. One area in which problems arise when comparisons are made between ethnographic and archaeological data sets concerns the methods used to measure the relative frequency of pottery vessels, types, or wares. The difficulties arising with pottery type frequency measures results from the fact that such measures are based primarily on whole vessel counts in the functioning ethnographic context while they are made primarily on incomplete vessel fragments in the archaeological context. If we are concerned with quantifying ethnographic data for the development of predictive models of the relationships between material culture frequency and socioeconomic conditions, or if we merely wish to compare descriptive statistics of such relationships between two excavation units, then it would be useful (even necessary) to use similar methods of measurement. Logically, it would be better in practice for the archaeologist to try to convert his potsherds into whole vessels rather than for the ethnoarchaeologist to destroy the pottery of his unsuspecting informants for the purpose of making sherd counts. However, the conversion of archaeological sherdage into whole vessels is a thorny problem since the methods presently in use may not be adequate to the task.

While debate over methods used to measure taxonomic frequency within faunal assemblages seems to abound in the archaeological literature (Grayson 1980), there seems to be little concern over the methods used to measure pottery type frequency (notable exceptions include Millett 1979; Orton 1975, 1982, 1993; Orton et al. 1993). However, some of the methods used to measure the frequency of pottery types are comparable to those used by faunal analysts and they share many of the same methodological weaknesses. The lack of attention being paid to the methods used in pottery analysis can undoubtedly be attributed to the kinds of problems for which pottery data have traditionally been used to solve.

Archaeologists have long recognized the utility of faunal remains for understanding human subsistence behavior and historical biogeography, and that the quantification of taxonomic diversity and relative frequencies is basic to these ends (Grayson 1980:199). Pottery data, on the other hand, have traditionally been used for the development of regional chronologies, the relative dating of features within sites, and the description of pottery types and their proportions. In all of these situations the accuracy of type frequency values is not necessarily important beyond the determination of whether type A is more common than type B in components being compared. Even so, the use of type frequencies based on sherd counts alone for measuring chronology (ie., seriation) has been brought into question (for discussion see Sullivan 1978:209). Recently, a number of researchers have attempted to use pottery assemblages for investigating the relative socioeconomic conditions of sites or between sites (e.g., Bawden 1982:172; Deetz 1965; Dickens and Chapman 1978; Finsten 1995;

Fry 1970; Lischka 1978; Michaels 1979; Redman 1979:78; Upham et al. 1981). In this study, it is argued that traditional methods of treating pottery assemblages, while probably adequate for the original culture historical problems they were meant to deal with, have not been appropriate for investigations of socioeconomic conditions at the level of the individual household.

It seems obvious from the archaeological literature that the methods of pottery analysis, including methods of measuring type frequency chosen by a given archaeologist, depend largely upon the kinds of methods used previously by other archaeologists working in the same area. Methods are often used without being given any critical thought as to whether or not they are the most efficient ones available or are more relevant to the kinds of problems being investigated. Some of the more commonly used methods for measuring type frequency are outlined below and their limitations and relative usefulness are discussed.

NUMBER OF INFERRED VESSELS (NIV)
The majority of methods presently being used by pottery analysts to determine type frequency result in a measure which represents the Number of Inferred Vessels (hereafter, NIV) for each type (also referred to as "evrep" or estimate of vessels represented, Orton et al. 1993:172). Whether the analyst is using the total sherdage from a site, or using only the rim sherds, some attempt is generally made to combine any sherds that can be assigned (with relative certainty) to individual vessels. This is sometimes called the "batch" method. The NIV measure should not be confused with the "Number of Individual Specimens" (NISP) measure used by faunal analysts, which can be viewed as equivalent to raw sherd counts. Rather, the NIV measure is the analog of the Minimum Number of Individuals (MNI) measure used by faunal analysts. Further, it should not be confused with Orton's "Maximum Number of Vessels" (1975:31), which does not infer two given sherds to be from the same vessel unless they can be joined (that is, unless it

TABLE 6.1.

Example of Three Methods Used for Measuring Minimum Number of Pottery Vessels per Type for a Hypothetical Gamma-Gamma Village Site.*

Method:	Total Rims NISP	Method 1: Rims NIV	Method 2: Bases NIV	Method 2: NIV Rims and Bases	Method 3:** Rims/Mean Rims per Vessel
Type a					
Stratum 1	100	97	32	97	20
Stratum 2	76	52	1	52	15
Stratum 3	63	46	73	73	13
Total:		195		222	48
Type B					
Stratum 1	375	42	4	42	75
Stratum 2	56	48	9	48	11
Stratum 3	429	62	48	64	86
Total:		152		154	172
Type C					
Stratum 1	84	22	68	68	17
Stratum 2	319	64	50	64	64
Stratum 3	323	209	25	209	65
Total:		295		341	146

* Raw rim-sherd counts, NIV values for rim and basal sherds, and total NIV were taken from a table of random numbers (Blalock 1972:554).
** This value equals the raw rim-sherd counts divided by the average number of rim sherds for reconstructible vessels (arbitrarily set at five sherds per vessel).

can be demonstrated). In other words, Orton's measure represents a step between raw sherd counts (or NISP) and the number of inferred vessels (NIV).

The reduction of entire collections of sherds to whole vessel counts (McPherron 1967; Newell and Krieger 1949), or merely the reduction of decorated rim and body sherds to whole vessel counts (Brose 1970), can be a very tedious and time consuming task (many years in some cases) and requires a large continuous excavation unit (preferably an entire site) in order to be effective (Barker 1977:179; Baumhoff and Heizer 1959:309; Ford 1951:93). Additional difficulties arise when the sorting of sherds into vessel batches involves assemblages in which designs are relatively simple, formalized, or repetitive (Ford 1951:93).

To get around the problems of reducing huge sherd collections to whole vessel counts

in many areas, it has become a common practice to use only rim sherd counts for deriving NIV measures which are then used directly to determine type frequency (e.g., Deetz 1965; Fry 1970; Lischka 1978; Pearce 1978). An alternative method proposed by Wright (1974) predicts whole vessel type frequency by dividing the number of rim sherds per type by the average number of rim sherds represented in vessels which could be reconstructed from the assemblage.

In a recent pottery analysis at Jalieza, Oaxaca, Finsten (1995:43) used NIV counts from vessel batches to examine the frequency and distribution of functional vessel forms. She also looked at vessel size distributions among terrace residential groups (i.e., elite and non-elite residences and civic-ceremonial cores), using rim sherds to establish vessel size categories and vessel diameters. This approach led to a surprisingly robust interpretation of socioeconomic conditions for Early Classic and Early Postclassic components at this site (Finsten 1995:89–90).

In order to illustrate the inherent variability in the above methods the pottery assemblage from a hypothetical gamma-gamma village site (see Ford 1954) is presented in Table 6.1. The assemblage was found to consist of three distinctive types. The minimum number of vessels per type per strata was determined using three different methods. Method one merely used the NIV values based on the combination of as many rim sherds as possible, to represent the actual type frequency per strata. In method two the NIV values for rim sherds were compared to the NIV values for basal sherds for each level. The highest of the two values was taken to represent the final number of inferred vessels per type. Method three converted the raw counts of rim sherds to an approximation of whole vessel frequency by dividing the raw counts by the average number of rim sherds found in vessels that could be reconstructed.

Although this is a hypothetical case, it is easy to see how these three different methods can give vastly different estimates of vessel frequency per type. In fact, there are a number of problems and limitations concerning the use of NIV or NISP measures of type frequency. To begin with, at given housesites, and over an entire site, practices of differential vessel use and reuse, pottery disposal, as well as site abandonment activities greatly affect the relative frequencies of vessel fragment types (rims versus bases, etc.). In Chanal, for example, the section from rim to neck of a broken vessel was often saved for reuse as an enclosure for seedlings while the body and base of the vessel were often discarded outside the compound.

Another problem concerning the use of NIV or NISP measures of type frequency is that they assume that all specimens (and all types) are equally affected by chance or deliberate breakage. This assumption does not account for the relative quality of vessel types, largely determined by characteristics of vessel fabric, morphology (such as structural strength), and function, which may pre-

vent one sherd from breaking in a situation in which a less "robust" sherd might. In addition, breakage rates of vessels in Chanal and Aguacatenango were believed to be affected by a number of demographic factors, such as family size and the number of small children and dogs. Furthermore, fragmentation of pottery can result from random hazards at each depositional locality (Jelinek 1967:84), such as areas of shortcutting.

Orton (1980:163) estimates the number of vessels represented by two types from the sherdage of a hypothetical archaeological assemblage by dividing the number of sherds of each type by a constant that represents the number of sherds into which a vessel of each type is always assumed to break. Orton's method, which is basically similar to that used by Wright (1974) on rim sherds from a real assemblage, illustrates that, if a number of types exhibit differential breakage characteristics, the estimates of relative proportions of the types is seriously affected by the proportion of the entire site which is excavated. There is a tendency for vessels which break into more pieces to represent a larger proportion of an assemblage (and higher type frequencies) as the percentage of the total-site-excavated decreases.

Using Schiffer's Total Discard Equation (see Chapter 5), Tzeltal vessel types with shorter uselives such as the small widemouth jar, were predicted to constitute greater proportions of a given household's pottery assemblage after the original assemblage had been completely replaced (also see David and Hennig 1972:20; DeBoer 1974). Such frequently used and easily broken vessels will probably increase in proportion to other vessel forms over time.

Another problem with using NIV or NISP measures of type frequency involves variable sherd size. Doran and Hodson (1975:114) have stressed the necessity of fixing a lower limit to the size of items (sherds or flakes) counted which is consistent with techniques of excavation in use. Collection techniques emphasizing different limits of sherd size may also greatly affect relative proportions of vessel types and especially NISP measures.

Screening techniques developed to collect "microsherds" and lithic "microdebitage" is one example of this situation (Fladmark 1982; Keighley 1973; McPherron 1967). Although screening has the benefit of being an unbiased approach, it is not an easy task to count sherds which are often too small to be diagnostic, and painted motifs are often unrecognizable (Keighley 1973:135; Sullivan 1978:209). Therefore the use of microsherds for estimation of type frequency may not be warranted.

The greatest problem with using raw counts of sherds (NISP) as estimates of relative type frequency is the inherent interdependence of sherd specimens which even the most careful analyst may not be able to accurately assess. If two rim sherds from a given vessel are not recognized as being from the same vessel they will likely be counted as representing two separate vessels. In other words, the method precludes their being classified as a single observation. As Grayson points out (1980:202), statistical methods used to analyze samples based on NISP measures (i.e., raw counts) assume that the specimens used, whether bone fragments or sherds, are representative of the sample population and that each is independent of every other one. Therefore the application of such methods to NIV measures becomes inappropriate if it cannot be ascertained that sherds are derived from the same vessels. The same reasoning also applies to NIV measures of type frequency.

The second NIV method is more comparable to the MNI method used by faunal analysts. However, anyone who might be considering the use of this method should refer to Grayson's detailed criticisms of the use of the MNI method on faunal studies (1980). According to Grayson, because the relationship between MNI values and actual frequencies is never known and because different aggregation techniques can give MNI results for a single collection which are not necessarily comparable, MNI cannot provide a valid measure of type frequency that is greater than ordinal in scale. Even an ordinal scale must be empirically determined in each case.

Thus there are several factors which bias estimates of NIV or NISP based on potsherds. These include (1) differential use, reuse, discard, and abandonment practices, (2) vessel quality (robustness), (3) random hazards of different discard locations, (4) percentage of site excavated, (5) sherd size collected, (6) aggregation techniques, and (7) the length of site occupation.

An alternative measure of NIV, devised specifically for pottery analysis, is based on rim arc measurements (see DeBoer 1974; Egloff 1973; Fulford 1973:23–24; Orton 1980:165–167). Using rim sherds representing each recognized vessel type, the length of arc of each sherd is divided by the total rim circumference for the sherd, which is estimated using a graded series of concentric arcs. The values derived by this method for each sherd of a given type are summed, and the resulting sum is used as an estimate of the minimum number of vessels for that type. By adding radii at 5 percent intervals along the circumference of the concentric arcs, Egloff (1973) was able to derive a "percentage factor" equalling the fraction of the vessel orifice represented by each sherd. When the most closely corresponding arc is determined, a sherd is placed on the arc at the 0 percent radius point and the radius closest to the opposite end of the sherd is recorded as the percentage of the total rim which the sherd represents. This technique is popular in the Northeast, where archaeological vessels tend to be highly fragmented.

Orton (1980:164–167; 1982) presents an interesting variation on this method using rim and/or basal sherds which he calls "vessel-equivalent." The vessel-equivalent of a given sherd equals the percentage of the whole vessel which it represents (in terms of weight or surface area). The advantage of this method is that proportions estimated from vessel-equivalents are not hampered by the problems of differential breakage characteristics of types or by the proportion of site excavated. When both rim and basal sherds are used the vessel-equivalents for a given type equal the sum of rim and basal percentages divided by two.

TABLE 6.2.
Percentage of Sherds by Weight and Number, and the Number of Sherds/Ounce by Level from a 3' x 6' Pit at Site 17, Fiji (After Gifford 1976, Tables 17 and 18).

Depth:	6"	12"	18"	24"	30"	36"	42"	48"	74"*
Plain:									
% Weight	79.0	80.0	81.0	82.5	76.5	74.5	47.5	49.5	45.0
% Number	89.0	90.0	91.0	90.0	89.0	82.0	60.0	60.0	60.0
Sherds/Ounce	7.5	8.0	7.0	8.0	8.0	9.0	8.0	7.0	6.0
Incised:									
% Weight	17.0	16.0	14.0	10.5	10.0	3.5	0.5	—	—
% Number	9.0	7.5	4.5	5.0	4.0	1.0	0.3	—	—
Sherds/Ounce	4.0	3.0	2.0	3.0	3.0	4.0	4.0	—	—
Relief:									
% Weight	4.0	4.0	5.0	7.0	13.5	22.0	52.0	50.5	55.0
% Number	2.0	2.5	5.0	5.0	7.0	16.0	39.5	40.0	34.0
Sherds/Ounce	5.0	4.0	6.5	5.0	4.0	7.0	4.0	4.0	3.0

*The interval 48"–74" was not excavated in 6" levels.

Although the rim (or basal) arc method may represent an improvement on the use of NIV measures of type frequency based on sherd frequencies, it also suffers from the differential discard and abandonment of vessel fragments. Fry (1970:202) for example, noted that any socioeconomic inferences made from sherd collections from individual structures and mound groups peripheral to Tikal were hampered by the "rather small number of rim sherds obtained from most groups." Millett (1979:77) also points out that this method would presumably be of little use on extremely fragmentary material and some handmade wares with irregular rims. In fact, from our Maya observations, pottery made by most non-specialists tends to have irregular rim openings and therefore sherds from different points along the same rim may correspond to slightly different rim arcs. Basal arcs might overcome this problem, as long as bases are more regular than rims, and the vessels studied do not have round bases.

WEIGHTS VERSUS COUNTS

Because of the many problems with the use of sherd or vessel counts, many pottery analysts have begun using sherd weights as an alternative or comparative method to making sherd counts. According to Orton and others (1993:169), the proportion by weight of a type in an assemblage reflects the proportion of that type and the relative weight of whole vessels of that type within the total assemblage. In terms of solving traditional problems, weight-oriented studies seem encouraging (examples include Baumhoff and Heizer 1959; Evans 1973; Gifford 1976; Gifford and Shutler 1976; D. A. Hinton 1977; Hulthen 1974; Jelinek 1967; McPherron 1967; Solheim 1960; Willey 1961). The relative sherd size per type accounts for the major difference in percentages derived from the two methods. The advantage of the sherd weight method is that varying sherd size between excavation units does not affect total weight per unit (Baumhoff and Heizer 1959:309). This situation is illustrated in Table 6.2 in which percentages of sherdage per type based on individual sherd counts for Gifford's site 17 in Fiji. A comparison of these percentages with the number of sherds per ounce indicates that the sherd counts for plain versus incised and relief modelled sherds shows a disproportionately high percentage per six-inch level when compared to percentages of sherd weight per level for the same types.

McPherron (1967:251) notes that the relationship between sherd frequency and sherd weights remains relatively constant through time. Microsherds (i.e., those "smaller than a dime") which were too small for attribute analysis could still be used in weight measures (McPherron 1967:46). A regression analysis of microsherd frequency and weight for 100 provenience units containing at least 10 microsherds revealed that microsherd weight was a good predictor of relative frequency of microsherds.

Any attempt to use the relationship between sherd weights and sherd counts as an adjustment factor when estimating actual type frequency is likely to create more problems than it would solve. The major problem created by comparing sherd weights with sherd counts is the likelihood of distortions caused by the weight of sherds from large vessels. Baumhoff and Heizer (1959:312) present an equation for adjusting the weights of sherds from larger vessels, but only if one has control over the size range of the vessels in a given assemblage.

Two articles considering the relative theoretical (Orton 1975), and practical (Millett 1979) merits of different measures of pottery type frequency agreed that the two most important methods are sherd weights and some measure of NIV (e.g., Orton's derived from rims or bases and Millett's from all sherds). Orton favored sherd weights slightly over raw sherd counts and concluded that Maximum Number of Vessels (i.e., those demonstrated rather than inferred) was not recommendable. Millett ranked sherd counts and adjusted sherd weights (Hulthen's method) as third and fourth in his study (1979:76). He went on to conclude that sherd weight will be the most useful for intersite comparison since it is much more easily calculated than the number of inferred vessels. In another article, Orton (1982) used two new models for sherd breakage (i.e., Kirkby processes and recursive sampling) to assess the performance of sherd count, weight, NIV, and vessel equivalents. Of these measures, the vessel equivalent method was predicted to be more often unbiased, while NIV ("vessels represented") should generally give the lowest sampling error. Orton and Tyers (1991) have developed a mathematical technique (the "pie-slice") that converts estimated vessel equivalents (eves) of the types in an assemblage into numbers with the same statistical properties as counts of objects and, therefore, permits the use of statistical techniques designed for counts for comparisons of assemblages. Orton and others (1993:174–175) discuss the potential utility and limitations on this technique.

The present discussion suggests that sherd weight measures are at least as useful as sherd count measures, and Solheim has argued that comparing the two results can yield more information than either method by itself (1960:329). However, in terms of aiding in the estimation of whole-vessel type frequency, weight measures seem to be little more appropriate than the method of raw sherd counts. In a recent study in the American Southeast, Mehrer (1995) uses refitted diagnostic rim sherds to estimate NIV measures for the study of the spatial distribution of pottery, while sherd counts and weights are used to study refuse disposal behavior and site formation processes.

AN ALTERNATE METHOD

As the above discussion indicates, archaeologists are still a long way from finding a practical method of estimating vessel type frequencies. Of the methods discussed, the use of rim or basal arc lengths (and percentage factors) seems to be a reliable way of determining vessel type frequency (Egloff 1973; Orton 1980, 1982) and the Orton and Tyers (1992) "pie-slice" technique shows considerable promise.

Ericson and DeAtley (1976) have presented a detailed method of reconstructing vessel morphology and capacity from a pottery assemblage composed of sherds. Segments of vessels were reconstructed using geometrical formulae and these segments, manifested as geometric solids, were combined to form vessels. Using a 20 percent sample of an experimental assemblage their prediction of vessel morphology was an impressive 76 percent accurate. The identification of shapes and the use of geometrical formulae were somewhat hampered by formal irregularities in some vessels. Similarly, M. F. Smith (1985, 1988) proposed a detailed procedure using geometrical formulae aided by statistical methods to reconstruct vessel size and shape from potsherd assemblages, and predict vessel function from the reconstructed vessels. Interpretations of vessel use, in turn, could be used for making interpretations of socioeconomic conditions associated with the assemblage. The general approach of these methods is promising for estimating formal-functional type frequencies from samples of potsherd assemblages. However, when dealing with large and non-experimental assemblages they are adversely affected by the time and boredom factors characteristic of the "batch" method.

Clearly, a better understanding of the nature of the interdependence among potsherd specimens in archaeological assemblages is needed if archaeologists are to adequately make use of ethnoarchaeological models and descriptive statistics for investigating the relationships between archaeological pottery assemblages and past socioeconomic or other conditions. The present situation calls for more experimentation with, and comparison among, the analytical methods presently being used on our archaeological assemblages. This may include model and computer simulation experiments, as exemplified by Orton (1982), or the controlled monitoring of breakage and deposition in the ethnographic context. The latter, where operationally possible, would be admittedly more time consuming, but is a potentially more objective approach. The remainder of the present discussion concerns an alternative method of treating pottery data in order to obtain socioeconomic information, namely, measuring diversity within pottery assemblages. Under certain conditions, this method appears to be superior to measures of vessel frequency for deriving socioeconomic information.

DIVERSITY MEASURES

Measuring type diversity is an alternate method of treating pottery assemblages, and one which appears to have the potential for more accurately yielding socioeconomic information on households than measurements based on whole vessels. The measure of diversity used here was originally adopted for the study of other classes of Tzeltal material culture (Hayden and Cannon 1984a, b). According to this method each type represented at a given housesite or feature was given a diversity value of "1" without consideration to its relative frequency compared to other types. It is more like a measure of ubiquity (but scoring only type presence and not type absence) than like the more sophisticated measures of diversity used in ecology (Pielou 1977) and paleoethnobotany (Popper 1988). The latter approaches, which have been tried in pottery studies (e.g., Rice 1989), also take into account the evenness of the distribution of artifacts within categories. More complex measures were not used in the Tzeltal analysis because household assemblages did not exhibit any pronounced variability in the evenness of artifact distribution (Cannon 1983: 787).

The relative diversity of vessel types within a given unit appear to be more representative of the social or economic characteristics associated with that unit than are NIV or NISP estimates per type made for the same unit, especially when sherd counts are low (e.g., the rim sherd counts from Fry's mound groups on the periphery of Tikal). For example, a hundred vessels from one unit may represent 20 types while the same number of vessels from another unit may represent only two types.

As a method of quantifying pottery (or any artifact) assemblages, diversity has several advantages. First it is simple to calculate once the assemblage has been broken down into its component types and wares. Secondly, it is not affected by the relative frequency or size of sherds from each vessel type or ware. Thirdly, it is less likely to be affected by disposal behavior, that is, it is more likely that all types will be represented than all vessels. Lastly, it is less affected by variation in collection techniques than are frequency measures.

The greatest disadvantage of diversity measures is that in some areas, such as the prehistoric Great Lakes region, there is relatively little recognizable formal or stylistic diversity in pottery assemblages. This situation probably reflects a relatively low level of socioeconomic differentiation in such areas. This problem is not so acute in the Maya area. In the modern community of Chanal the number of formal-functional types per household ranged from three to 17 and comprises as many as 23 wares when stylistic variants are taken into consideration. High diversity scores for formal-functional types seems to be mostly a function of the variability of ritual types owned by a household. The diversity of food preparation and serving types ranged from three to seven (mean of 4.8) per household while the diversity of ritual types ranges from zero to eight (mean of 4.4) per household. Of the seven other types every household had between two and four types, and two of these can usually be accounted for by the fact that 93 percent of all households had watercarrying jars and 57 percent had one or more spindle whorls.

In order to evaluate diversity measures versus frequency measures as a basis for making predictions of socioeconomic conditions at the household level, correlation coefficients were calculated between two pottery measures thought to be strongly reflected in pottery household assemblages and two dichotomous socioeconomic variables. The two pottery variables were pottery vessel frequency and type diversity and the two socioeconomic variables were presence/absence of a potter and presence/absence of a First *Alferez*. It must be explicitly stated that the object of the exercise was to assess which of the two quantification methods is a stronger indicator of certain socioeconomic conditions believed to be reflected in pottery inventories and not an attempt to demonstrate the feasibility of making inferences concerning these conditions at the household level of analysis.

A description of, and assumptions involved with, the two socioeconomic variables chosen are as follows:

(1) Presence/absence of a First *Alferez*

In Chanal, two persons, entitled First and Second *Alferez*, were selected to sponsor certain religious festivals (see Chapter 2). The main responsibility for the fiesta belonged to the First *Alferez*. This involved organizing and providing ritual paraphernalia, keeping wooden festival idols and presenting them to the public, and providing all food and drink for officials and a general feast at his home. One of the commitments of the First *Alferez* was to provide the large ritual pottery types required for the particular festival he was sponsoring, as well as the special candle-making bowl *(neochab)* which was to be used for one occasion only, after which it was saved as a family heirloom. Some of these vessels might be borrowed from relatives and neighbors, while others might be commissioned from a local potter. Heads of 16 of the households interviewed had held this position.

The assumption involved with this variable was that households whose members had participated in this specialized ritual office, for which specialized ritual pottery types must be procured, would have a relatively large and more varied pottery inventory. Seven of the 11 households for which information could be obtained on pottery purchased by *Alferezes* had purchased at least two vessel types, the candlemaking bowl and the large wide-mouth jars *(oxom)*. Two of these households as well as two others had loaned two or three large wide-mouth jars to other people holding the *Alferez* office, and one former *Alferez* interviewed had borrowed large wide-mouth jars and a large composite jar *(tenosha)* when he held the office. Numerous small unrestricted glazed serving bowls *(borcelana)* and large hemispherical bowls *(pokets)* are also commonly bought for such occasions. The fact that four households either borrowed or loaned pottery for this position may seriously affect the strength of the relationships involved, although typically each *Alferez* purchased at least some portion of the pottery required for the festivals.

(2) Presence/Absence Potter

Twenty-eight Chanal households interviewed had one or more potters in residence. The assumption involved with this variable was that a household in which a specialized activity such as pottery making occurred would contain a relatively high frequency of products of that activity. One might also assume that in a modern Maya community a household with a potter would rely more heavily on pottery as opposed to industrial equivalents than would a nonpotting household. Further, potters might also have a greater variety (diversity) of their specialized products on hand.

METHOD OF COMPARISON

The method used here to compare household pottery frequency and type diversity with the dichotomous variables presence/absence *Alferez* and presence/absence potter, was Kendall's tau used as a nonparametric point-biserial correlation (Marascuilo and Mc-Sweeney 1977:453–454). As in Cannon's study (1983) the parametric point-biserial correlation (for description see McNemar 1962:192–193) was not used here because the continuous variables were not normally distributed in each class of either dichotomous variable. Kendall's tau was calculated for each pair in the following manner:

(1) The continuous variable (Y_1) was rank ordered, beginning with the household with the lowest value, and the presence/absence of the dichotomous variable (Y_2) was assumed to represent a ranking (i.e., absence receiving the lowest rank).

(2) Each ordered pair of values (1&2, 1&3 . . .) in each variable were compared, and those in proper order (low/high) were assigned a score of (+1), while those in reverse order (high/low) were assigned a score of (−1) (see Marascuilo and Mc-Sweeney 1977:439–445). Each score of Y_1 was then multiplied by the corresponding score of Y_2 and the resulting pairs with a score of (+1) were considered to be concordant, while those with a

score of (−1) were considered to be discordant. Kendall's tau (t) represents a measure of the difference of proportion of the concordant and discordant pairs, and was calculated by the following formula:

$$T = \frac{Nc-Nd}{\sqrt{N_2-U_1}\ \sqrt{N_2-U_2}}$$

where,

$$U_1 = \frac{1}{2}\sum_{j}^{k} T_j(T_j-1)$$

and,

$$U_2 = \frac{1}{2}\sum_{j}^{k} U_j(U_j-1)$$

where,

$T_j=$ the number of tied values on the Y_1 variable

$U_j=$ the number of tied values on the Y_2 variable

$Nc=$ the number of concordant pairs

$Nd=$ the number of discordant pairs

RESULTS AND DISCUSSION

The use of type, ware, or attribute diversity in pottery assemblages does not seem to be widely used by pottery analysts at present (some exceptions include Feinman et al. 1981; Rice 1981; Upham et al. 1981; Whittlesey 1974). Cannon (1983), working with data from the Coxoh Project, has tested and evaluated the effects of three different quantification methods (i.e., frequency, proportion, and diversity) upon making inferences concerning the presence of specialized activities, including potting, and their associated artifacts. As in Cannon's study, both frequency and diversity measures showed only a weak to moderate correlation with each dichotomous variable, yet what is important for the purpose of this study, as it was in Cannon's, is that the diversity measure showed the strongest degree of association with each dichotomous variable.

The Kendall's tau value for the association between presence/absence of an *Alferez* position and pottery diversity was .48 (p< .001), compared to .42 (p< .001) using a pottery frequency measure. Weaker associations occurred between presence/absence potter and pottery diversity (t=.23, p<.054) and pottery frequency (t=.08, p<.484), yet diversity again showed a much stronger association. Cannon's comparison of presence/absence of pottery making with measures of frequency and diversity, using only locally made pottery, yielded similar relative associations between presence/absence potter and type diversity (t=.29, p< .019) and between presence/absence potter and vessel frequency (t=.15, p<.184). Although none of the associations were strong, they did demonstrate that the holding of a First *Alferez* position and making of pottery do affect the composition of a household's pottery assemblage.

Of the two quantification techniques used here, diversity of pottery types was a more powerful indicator of the presence/absence of an *Alferez* and of pottery making at the household level. The methodological problems involved with using frequency measures on archaeological data were discussed above. Furthermore, artifact frequency was often affected by other factors, besides functional need, such as accessibility, family development, length of housesite occupation, and idiosyncratic taste (DeBoer and Lathrap 1979:124; Hayden and Cannon 1984a). The use of diversity measures to quantify pottery or other artifact assemblages might not be regarded as the panacea to methodological problems in archaeology, however, they might prove to be more useful alternatives, depending upon the problem being addressed, to quantitative characterizations of household artifact assemblages based on frequency. For our Chanal sample, given a choice between diversity and frequency, the diversity measure was easier to formulate and yielded better results for predicting presence/absence of both *Alferezes* and potters, and presumably, other socioeconomic conditions. By breaking diversity down into subgroupings, such as functional versus stylistic types, locally made versus imported types, or food preparation and serving versus ritual

types, it might be possible to derive even more accurate inferences concerning socioeconomic characteristics at the household level.

THE VARIABILITY OF POTTERY DIVERSITY

Before prescribing the extensive use of diversity measures on archaeological pottery assemblages it would be useful to explore the nature of household pottery diversity, that is, to determine as far as possible which socioeconomic factor or factors contribute most to pottery diversity at the household level. According to Rathje (1979:20), many recent studies of modern material culture have led to the conclusion that there are no direct correlations between material culture and behavior, or in other words, that our stereotypical views of material culture–behavior relationships are oversimplified in the real world.

More recently, a study of modern Tucson households (Schiffer et al. 1981), yielded weak to moderate statistical correlations between the frequency of certain material items (i.e., furniture and appliances) and household stability based on the number of moves in the last 5 years, number of people in the household, and household income (i.e., Spearman's R values of .37, .34 and .53 respectively). Similarly, Hayden and Cannon (1984a), using the Coxoh data, have found weak relationships between individual socioeconomic variables (household wealth, status, etc.) and frequencies of various items of material culture (i.e., luxury items, durable items, and various kinds of tools). Can archaeologists expect comparatively weak relationships between household socioeconomic conditions and diversity in household pottery inventories? The following section addresses this question using modern Maya pottery data, in an effort to identify and account for as much of the variability in household pottery type diversity as possible.

Following the procedures used by Hayden and Cannon (1984a) for analyzing household material item variability for the communities surveyed by the Coxoh Project, multiple regression analysis was chosen as the

TABLE 6.3.
Summary of Contents of Continuous Variables Used for Regression Analysis.

Descriptive Statistics:	Min. value	Max. value	Mean	s.d.	N
Dependent (Pottery) Variables:					
Formal-functional type diversity	3	18	11.1	3.1	53
Pottery ware diversity	4	23	13.0	4.2	38
Imported pottery type diversity	0.00	11	4.3	2.1	53
Pottery plus industrial type diversity	15	45	24.4	6.0	53
Food preparation/serving type diversity	3	7	4.8	1.2	53
Ritual type diversity	0.00	8	4.4	1.0	53
Independent (Socioeconomic) Variables:					
Number of children/household	0.00	8	2.8	1.7	53
Number of economic males/household	0.00	6	2.0	1.3	53
Number of economic females/household	0.00	5	2.0	1.1	53
Annual household income (pesos)	39	1986	589.5	445.9	50
Trips to other communities per year	1	58	11.6	13.3	52
Age of household head	20	99	44.9	18.4	51

potentially most useful method for assessing the mutual relationship between a number of independent socioeconomic variables and each dependent pottery variable. Despite the significant difficulties involved in using this method, a multivariate technique was chosen because of the degree of interdependence between the socioeconomic variables. During the regression, certain independent variables showing some significance when compared individually to a given dependent variable (i.e., in the form of product moment correlation coefficients) were eliminated as redundant or as having little effect on the dependent variable when used with the other socioeconomic variables. Thus, the intent was to impose a greater analytical control over the relationships between the variables used. An attempt was made to monitor sources of variability as differentiated according to (1) household pottery requirements (or need) and (2) household access to pottery (i.e., the relative ability to have greater pottery diversity). Sixteen socioeconomic variables believed to influence either household need or accessibility were chosen for the analysis. Assumptions concerning the "role" of need and accessibility

and a description of the contents of individual variables is outlined below, followed by a description of the regression technique and the results generated.

Pottery-dependent variables capable of describing archaeological assemblages, as well as ethnographic inventories were chosen for the analysis. Six variables were used: (1) formal-functional pottery type diversity, (2) stylistic ware, or surface treatment, diversity, (3) imported type diversity (4) pottery plus industrial equivalent type diversity, (5) food preparation and serving type diversity, and (6) ritual type diversity. The fourth variable was included in an attempt to account for the possible effects on the household inventory of adding to or replacing pottery types with their industrial equivalents (see Chapter 4). A summary of the range and mean values of these variables, along with seven continuous socioeconomic variables appear in Table 6.3.

Independent socioeconomic variables were chosen largely on the basis of reasonably expected relationships with household pottery inventories. Some variables were only deemed meaningful if used in a dichotomous fashion, such as presence/absence potter. One other dichotomous variable, high/low social status, was included along with some of the continuous variables from which it was abstracted on the assumption that it might show greater influence on diversity measures at a more general level, whereas the finer, more continuous, component variables might pick up "noise" from other variables used in the regression. Schiffer et al. (1981:83) has suggested that much of the gross variability in household material culture (i.e., both kinds and quantities) could be accounted for by four factors, including (1) stage of household development (size, composition, etc.), (2) residential stability, (3) time since last move, and (4) relative wealth or income. Chanal equivalents of the first and last of these were included in the present study (variables #7 and #12 below). The other two variables did not tend to vary greatly in Chanal.

VARIABLES EMPHASIZING HOUSEHOLD REQUIREMENTS (NEED)

(1) Number of children per household. The number of children in a household is often believed to affect the kinds and frequencies of pottery vessels required by the household. For example, more or larger cooking vessels would be required to prepare a meal for a large family.

(2) Presence/absence of a lineage head. The presence of a lineage head in a household suggests that the household was often responsible for holding lineage-based gatherings and would require more pottery and more of the larger types for this reason. However, lineage heads tended to loan out more pottery to households of his or her lineage and this might cause considerable fluctuations in the size and contents of the household inventory, as well as that of the borrower.

(3) Presence/absence of a former First *Alferez*. As mentioned previously, the presence of a former First *Alferez* in the household was expected to be particularly significant in terms of the diversity of vessel types, and especially ritual types, owned by a household. General vessel frequency might also be higher since one requirement of this *cargo* posi-

tion was that the holder provide the pottery vessels used during the festival, including certain specialized types. This involved considerable expense for the office holder, and once the festival was completed his household kept the purchased vessels. After holding an *Alferez* position, large vessels might be converted to storage containers or stored away and used again only singly when family or lineage rituals required, or when requested as a loan by relatives.

(4) Presence/absence yearly festivals. If a family held yearly gatherings to celebrate a birthday in the family or to celebrate the corn harvest one would expect such families to have a relatively large pottery inventory and possibly a more diversified one. This depended partly upon the civil or religious nature of the celebration. In addition, household heads might borrow vessels for such occasions from their lineage heads, *compadres*, or neighbors. Conversely, families not holding yearly celebrations might be expected to have smaller and possibly less diversified inventories, especially in food preparation and serving vessels.

(5) Presence/absence of high civil *cargo* positions. People with civil *cargo* positions equivalent to or above the *Alferez* level would be involved in more social interactions and were more likely to hold gatherings at their homes for which the larger vessel types would be required, thus adding more diversity to their inventories.

(6) Presence/absence of high religious *cargo* positions. This variable would be greatly affected by the inclusion of an *Alferez* (variable #3 above) but would also include households with holders of other religious *cargo* positions. These households would be more likely to have both larger and more diversified pottery inventory, especially in ritual types.

(7) Age of household head. The age of the household head was used here as an indirect measure of the stage of household development. The assumption was that

the older the household head the longer the household had been together. The longer the household was in existence the more pottery types the household was likely to have accumulated. For example, the Chanal household with the most pottery (147 vessels) and the second highest diversity (17 types) was occupied by only an elderly couple who had had seven children, five of whom had moved away, while the two still living at home were of marrying age. This information was not obtained for two households.

(8) Family type. The family type variable, dichotomized to nuclear versus extended, indicated relative family size which was assumed to affect the quantity and possibly the diversity of pottery types in a household.

(9) Proportion of income from household produce. Households with a higher proportion of their income coming from agricultural produce were assumed to be more linked to the traditional economy and indirectly were more likely to hold traditional values. In terms of pottery diversity, these households were more likely to hold agricultural festivals for which larger ritual pottery vessels would be required. They might also be more likely to prefer pottery types over industrial equivalents, which were assumed to be associated with the more progressive households (i.e., those linked to the modern cash economy).

(10) Social status. Each household in Chanal was given a social status rank based on a number of sociopolitical conditions as they were perceived during the survey period (see Chapter 4). Ranks increased with higher civil or religious *cargo* position, the age of the household head, and presence of a lineage head, and they were decreased according to negative social attitudes such as chronic drunkenness, involvement in illegal affairs, and lack of respect for authority. The difficulties of forming an objective and meaningful sta-

tus ranking have been well documented (Kelsall and Kelsall 1974:52–61; Price and Price 1972:311–317), especially using archaeological artifact assemblages (a notable exception is Michaels 1979:Chapter 5).

Conceptual problems arose because status was an attribute conferred by others, so that the person in question had limited control over his status or how different people might perceive his status. For example, Chanal *cargeros* would often confer a higher prestige on their own *cargo* position than would other *cargeros*. Such small discrepancies were hopefully minimized in our status ranking by the use of a diverse number of attributes. Furthermore, for the present study the margin of error was minimized by dichotomizing the variable into low (ranks 1 to 3) and high (ranks 4 to 6) status. The relationship between social status and pottery frequencies and diversity must be a complex one due to the diversity of attributes making up the ranks. In general, one might expect higher social rank to involve more social interaction, at both lineage and community levels, which should require both a larger and a more diverse pottery inventory. Although perceived as basically a need-related variable, one might also expect accessibility to pottery to be related to social status, that is, more social interactions might create exposure to more pottery diversity.

VARIABLES EMPHASIZING ACCESSIBILITY

(11) Number of economic males. The number of males contributing to the household income was assumed to be directly connected to the household's ability to afford more pottery and a greater variety of pottery. However, it might also reflect family size (extended versus nuclear family) and therefore also reflect household pottery needs.

(12) Number of economic females. As in variable #11 above, the number of females contributing to the household income was assumed to have an influence on the household's ability to afford more pot-

tery types. Also family size and presence of more kitchen workers might· be involved and thus reflect household pottery needs.

(13) Annual income. Households with high incomes were assumed to be able to afford more pottery and more kinds of pottery. In three cases, where income was believed to be greatly exaggerated by the informant, the cases were dropped from the analysis.

(14) Presence/absence potter (and therefore potting) during the household's existence. As mentioned above, potters were more likely to have a greater diversity of vessels on hand because they produced and stored them for sale, and because they generally relied less on industrial equivalents than did nonpotting households.

(15) Store *(tienda)* owner. Store owners were generally among the wealthier householders and were able to afford a greater variety of pottery types which they sometimes sold from their stores. They were also more likely to have a greater diversity of industrial equivalents since they sold many of these items in their stores.

(16) Number of trips to other communities per year. Household heads who made more trips to other communities were more likely to come into contact with a greater variety of pottery types, especially at festivals in pottery-making centers such as Amatenango. One case was dropped for this variable because we could not obtain this information.

REGRESSION METHOD

Before running the regression analysis the SELECT command option of the MIDAS statistical package (Fox and Guire 1976: 152–153) was used to eliminate all but the strongest "predictors" from among the independent variables. Using the STEPWISE option of this command a variable selection procedure was performed which selects independent variables for the regression model.

Variables were entered into the equation one at a time until a point in the selection was reached when the addition of any further variables would have had a negligible effect on the ability of the previously entered variables to predict response-variable values. The use of this command allowed for the elimination of any independent variables from the final regression that might be highly intercorrelated with other independent variables, and therefore be redundant. Whenever this occurred, random measurement errors in some variables would tend to increase the apparent effects on the dependent variable of those variables with which they were highly correlated (Blalock 1972:450). When the STEPWISE option was specified the following procedure was generated:

(1) A partial t-statistic was generated to determine if the regression coefficient was significantly different from zero. The independent variable with the highest t-statistic was the first to be entered into the equation.

(2) The first variable was held constant and a partial t-statistic was calculated for the remaining variables, and those variables with the highest t-statistic were entered into the equation until all variables whose t-statistic exceeded the specified probability level (.1 was used here) had been entered.

(3) Any subsequent variable whose entry into the equation would cause a significant decrease in the value of the t-statistic of a previously entered variable was automatically deleted from the equation. These variables were considered redundant or as having little effect on the frequency of the dependent variable.

In order to judge the appropriateness of the final regression model, the residuals (the differences between observed and predicted values for the dependent variable) were computed and standardized by dividing each by the standard error of the regression equation. These standardized values of the dependent variable were graphed against the predicted values. By examining the resulting graph, any outliers (i.e., cases with large residuals relative to the residuals for the remainder of the observations) could be observed. Outliers, when they occur could distort the relationship between dependent and independent variables (for discussion see Chatterjee and Price 1977; Hartwig and Dearing 1979: 46–48). In other words, these cases would not fit the model describing the bulk of the sample and could therefore be dropped from the final regression equation. No outliers were observed in the following equations.

The final multiple linear regression analysis was performed using the REGRES command of the MIDAS statistical package (Fox and Guire 1976:211–212). Only the independent variables selected by the SELECT command were used in the equation. The final equation of the regression model is expressed by:

$$Y = a + B_1 (X_1) + \ldots + B_k (X_k)$$

where,

Y = the dependent (predicted) variable
X_1 = the initial independent variable
a = the additive constant
B = the regression coefficient (slope)

The present study was less concerned with accurate prediction of the dependent variable than in determining the relationship between the dependent and other variables. The coefficient of variation was computed to provide a measure of the size of the prediction error relative to the size of the dependent variable being measured (see Younger 1979:327). The coefficient of variation was expressed by:

$$CV = SE/Y$$

where,

CV = the coefficient of variation
SE = the standard error of the regression model
Y = the mean value of the dependent variable

The value of CV represented the average error of predictions made by the regression equation. It provided a nonparametric measure of the predictive ability of the regression equation. In order to assess the relative strength of each independent variable in the equation, the standardized regression coefficients (slopes) were computed and compared. These values (also called beta weights) indicated the amount of change produced in the dependent variable by a standardized change in one of the independent variables when the other independent variables were controlled (Blalock 1972:452–453).

Four of the 6 SELECT runs chose only one or two dichotomous variables for inclusion in the predictive formula. In these four trials, instead of completing the regression analysis, less complicated statistical methods were opted for, namely, the Kruskal-Wallis oneway test of variance by ranks and the Mann-Whitney U test. These two nonparametric tests provided an indication of the tendency for each independent sample (i.e., the group of households in each strata of the dichotomous variables) to have a greater or lesser diversity of the pottery category (ritual types, etc.) being tested. In order to gain some understanding of the degree of association between the dependent variables and the independent dichotomous variables, Kendall's tau was used again as a nonparametric point-biserial correlation. As before, these methods were employed in terms of data exploration.

ANALYSIS RESULTS
Trial #1: Pottery type diversity

As a result of the SELECT procedure only two independent variables were chosen for inclusion in the predictive formula. Interestingly, these were the two variables used above to compare type diversity and vessel frequency measures, namely, the presence/absence of a potter and the presence/absence of a former first *Alferez*. In the present study these variables were believed to be representative of household accessibility and need, respectively. Rather than completing the regression analysis, another method was opted for, namely, the Kruskal-Wallis oneway test of variance by ranks provided by the KSAMPLE command of the MIDAS statistical package (see Fox and Guire 1976: 245–251). KSAMPLE, being a nonparametric command, did not require the assumptions of normality and equal variances, while the Kruskal-Wallis test seemed to be the most efficient of the nonparametric tests for k-independent samples (Siegel 1956:194). The Kruskal-Wallis test assumed that the dependent variable (in this case type diversity) had an underlying continuous distribution and required at least an ordinal measurement of that variable (Siegel 1956). The present study was particularly concerned with the assumption that type diversity was not the same for the four independent samples:

(1) absence potter; absence *Alferez*
(2) presence potter; absence *Alferez*
(3) absence potter; presence *Alferez*
(4) presence potter; presence *Alferez*

The null hypothesis being tested was:

Ho: pottery type diversity was equal for each of the four samples specified (1–4 above).
H1: pottery type diversity was not equal for at least one of the four samples.

Procedure (after Siegel 1956:188):

(1) All observations for the four samples were ranked (1-N) in a single series.
(2) The sum of the ranks (R) for each sample was determined.
(3) Since ties occurred between two or more scores, the following formula was used to compute the value of KW (the Kruskal-Wallis statistic):

$$KW = \frac{\frac{12}{N(N+1)} \sum_{j=1}^{k} \frac{Rj^2}{nj} - 3(N+1)}{1 - \frac{\sum T}{N^3 - N}}$$

where,

k = number of samples
Rj = sum of ranks in jth sample
nj = number of cases in jth sample
N = Σnj, the number of cases in all samples combined

$\sum_{j=1}^{k}$ directs one to sum over the k samples

T = $t^3 - t$ (when t is the number of tied observations in a tied group of scores)

ΣT directs one to sum over all groups of ties

If Ho was true, then KW was distributed approximately as chi-square with df=k-1 as the sample size (N) increased in size.

(4) The method of assuming the significance of the observed value of KW was not very good if k=2 or when k=3 and the number of cases in each of the three samples was five or less. In the present test, k=4 and the number of cases for the four samples were 17, 20, 8, and 8, respectively.

(5) If the probability associated with the observed value of KW was equal to or less than the previously set significance level (α=.01 in this trial), Ho was rejected in favor of H1.

(6) In trial #1, the region of rejection consisted of all values of KW which were so large that the probability associated with their occurrence under Ho was equal to or less than .01

The computed value of KW>20.2, with df=3, had a probability of occurrence under the null hypothesis of p<.0002. Since this probability was smaller than .01, Ho could be rejected in favor of H1, namely, that *pottery diversity was not equal for at least one of the four samples.*

The conclusion according to test results, was that, the four samples differed in diversity of pottery types. Households with either a potter or former *Alferez* tended to have a more diverse pottery inventory, and those with both potter and former *Alferez* tended to have the greatest diversity. The correlation coefficients (Kendall's tau) calculated above suggested that only a moderate degree of association existed between type diversity and presence/absence of *Alferez* (t=.48, p<.001) and a weaker degree of association existed between type diversity and presence/absence potter (t=.23, p<.054). Given these degrees of association, type diversity alone was obviously not a sufficient basis for inferring either the presence of a potter or former *Alferez* for a given household.

Trial #2: Pottery ware diversity

Informants were not always able to differentiate wares representing the peripheral distribution sources, since they exhibited a high degree of formal and fabric similarity. Any households in which ware diversity information was lacking for more than 20% of the pottery inventory were dropped from the regression analysis. This amounted to 15 households or 28% of the sample. Despite this fact, it was important to include ware diversity among the dependent variables, since, unlike formal-functional type diversity it should be sensitive to the variability of more rare or imported vessels which archaeologists generally associate with relative social status.

Only three of the 15 independent variables were chosen by the SELECT runs for the predictive model: number of economic males, presence/absence former *Alferez,* and presence/absence of high religious *cargo* position. The former was believed to be representative of household accessibility to pottery while the latter two were more representative of household need. The regression equation took the form:

$$Y = 9.3 + .92 (X_1) + 5.20 (X_2) + 1.90 (X_3)$$

with SE= 3.00, Mean= 12.95, and where,

  Y = household ware diversity
  X_1= number of economic males
  X_2= presence/absence of First *Alferez*
  X_3= presence/absence high religious *cargo* position

The coefficient of variation (CV) for this equation indicated an average error of 23%. In other words, predictions of the relative ware diversity of a given household would be off on an average of 23% (approximately three types) based on the above equation. The predictive ability of the equation was therefore relatively high. The relative strength of the predictor variables was indicated by the following beta weight values:

(1) presence/absence *Alferez* = .51
(2) economic males = .27
(3) presence/absence religious *cargo* position = .22

Trial #3: Imported type diversity

Imported type diversity included all pottery items known to be made outside the peripheral distribution zone. As in case #1, the SELECT command did not choose any continuous variables, and in fact, only a single dichotomous variable (low/high social status) was chosen. As discussed above, this variable was assumed to be representative of household need. Rather than completing the regression analysis, a less complicated technique was chosen to compare the two variables, namely, the TWOSAMPLE command of the MIDAS statistical package (see Fox and Guire 1976:177–178, 222–224). TWO SAMPLE is an univariate, twosample nonparametric command that provides certain statistics which test the hypothesis that the two samples were from the same underlying population (Fox and Guire 1976:222). The statistic used here was the Mann-Whitney U test, which according to Siegal (1956:116) was the most powerful of the nonparametric tests and a useful alternative to the parametric t-test. The present study was concerned with the assumption that the values for imported type diversity were on average larger for households with high social level than for households with a low social level.

The null hypothesis being tested was:

  Ho: imported type diversity was equal for households with low and high social status.

H1: imported type diversity was not equal for households with low and high social status.

Procedure:

(1) The values of the independent samples were determined. Sample one ($n1$) equalled the number of cases of low household social status ($n1=30$), while sample two ($n2$) equalled the number of cases of high household social status ($n2=23$).

(2) Scores (values) for both samples were ranked together (lowest rank=lowest score) with tied observations receiving the average of the tied scores. The sum of the ranks for each sample was computed. The rationale behind this procedure, according to Fox and Guire (1976:223), was that, if the distributions of the two populations differed in location, then the low ranks tended to fall in one sample, and the high ranks tended to fall in the other sample. If a rank sum for either sample was too high (or too low) the null hypothesis could be rejected.

(3) Since $n1>n2$, the value of U was determined by the formula:

$$U = Wn - (n2\,(n2+1))/2$$

where,

Wn= the sum of the ranks assigned to the sample with the smaller number of observations (in this case $n2$)

When $n1$ and $n2$ were large (>10) the distributions of the Mann-Whitney U statistic could be approximated by a normal distribution. The attained significance level was twice the area under a standard normal distribution to the right of the value (Fox and Guire 1976:223):

$$\frac{|U\text{-}mean(U)|}{\sqrt{var(u)}}$$

where the mean of the sample distribution,

$$Mean(U)= \frac{n1(n2)}{2} = \frac{37(16)}{2} = 296$$

and the variance of the sample distribution,

$$Var(U)= \frac{N1(N2)}{(n1+n2)(n1+n2-1)}[\frac{(n1+n2)^3-(n1+n2)}{12} - \sum_{i=1}^{k}Ti]$$

where k = the number of different sets of ties,

and $\sum_{i=1}^{k}$

directs one to sum over the number of different sets of ties,

and $Ti = (ti^3 - ti)/12$,

where ti= the number of tied observations in the ith tied set

(4) If the observed value of U had an associated probability equal to or less than the previously set significance level ($\alpha=.01$), H0 could be rejected.

(5) In the present trial, the computer value $U=238$ had a probability of occurrence under the null hypothesis of $p<.0506$, with an average rank $n1$ of 23.4 and for $n2$ of 31.7. Since the associated probability level for the computed value of U was larger than the previously set significance level ($\alpha =.01$), the null hypothesis could be accepted. *Imported type diversity was not significantly different for households with low versus high social status.* Further, the Kendall's tau point biserial correlation indicated a weak degree of association between the two variables ($t=.25$, $p< .038$). The relationship between these two variables might be somewhat obscured by the fact that household social status was not a true dichotomy. The combined effects of the constituent variables might be hiding what seems intuitively a stronger relationship.

Trial #4: Pottery and industrial equivalent type diversity

As in trail #3, only the single variable household social status was chosen by the SELECT command. Again the Mann-Whitney test was used. The assumption which was of interest in this trial was that the value for pottery and industrial type diversity were on average larger for households with high social level than for households with low social level.

The null hypothesis being tested was:

Ho: pottery and industrial type diversity was equal for households with low and high social status.

H1: pottery and industrial type diversity was not equal for households with low and high social status.

In the present test (where n1=30 and n2=23), the computed value U=160 had a probability of occurrence under the null hypothesis of p<.0009, with an average rank for n1 of 20.8 and for n2 of 35.0. Since the associated probability level for the computed value of U was considerably less than the previously set significance level (α =.01), the null hypothesis could be rejected. The evidence supported the alternate hypothesis, implying that the bulk of the values in sample two was higher than the bulk of values in sample one, or that *higher status households tended to have more pottery and industrial type diversity than households with lower status.* However, the Kendall's tau point-biserial correlation indicated only a moderate degree of association between the two variables (t=.38, p< .001). This result was interesting, in that many industrial equivalents (especially serving vessels) seemed to be used today as imported pottery vessels were being used prehistorically. If this was true, then this result might be a relatively accurate reflection of the prehistoric situation.

Trial #5: Food preparation and serving type diversity

This variable included all of Chanal domestic vessel types directly used in food preparation and consumption. Four independent variables were chosen by SELECT runs for the predictive model: (1) number of economic males, (2) annual income, (3) presence/absence of yearly festival, and (4) presence/absence religious *cargo* position. The former two were believed to be representative of

household accessibility, while the latter two (and to some extent the number of economic males) were representative of household need. The regression equation took the form of:

$$Y = 4.04 + .38 (X1) - .0009 (X2) + .83 (X3) + .53 (X4)$$

where,

Y = food preparation and serving vessel diversity
X1 = number of economic males
X2 = annual income
X3 = presence/absence yearly festivals
X4 = presence/absence religious *cargo* position

The coefficient of variation (CV) indicated an average error of 19%. In other words, the prediction of diversity of food preparation and serving vessels of a given household would be on the average 19% (or approximately one type) when predicted using the above equation. The predictive ability of the equation must be considered relatively high despite the fact that the average diversity for this variable was only 4.8 types per household. The negative association with household annual income might be, in part, reflective of the fact that diversity of domestic types tended to decrease in wealthier households which were more closely linked to the cash economy and more likely to replace domestic pottery with industrial forms (i.e., ritual types had fewer industrial equivalents). Also, the number of economic males in this case might be reflective of family size and therefore family pottery requirements. The relative strength of the predictor variables, according to beta weight values were:

(1) economic males = .36
(2) presence/absence yearly festival = .35
(3) presence/absence religious *cargo* position = .23
(4) annual income =.33

TABLE 6.4.

Socioeconomic Variables Chosen by SELECT RUNS for Six Dependent Variables
(+ = Positive Relationship, / = Negative Relationship).

SELECT RUNS for each trial:*	1	2	3	4	5	6
Need-related Variables:						
1. Number of children/household	—	—	—	—	—	—
2. Presence/absence lineage head	—	—	—	—	—	—
3. Presence/absence *Alferez*	+	+	—	—	—	+
4. Presence/absence yearly festival	—	—	—	—	+	—
5. Presence/absence civil *cargo*	—	—	—	—	—	—
6. Presence/absence religious *cargo*	—	+	—	—	+	—
7. Age of household head	—	—	—	—	—	—
8. Family type	—	—	—	—	—	—
9. Proportion produce of income	—	—	—	—	—	—
10. Social status	—	—	+	+	—	—
Accessibility-related Variables:						
11. Number of economic males	—	+	—	—	+	—
12. Number of economic females	—	—	—	—	—	—
13. Annual income	—	—	—	—	/	—
14. Presence/absence potter	+	—	—	—	—	—
15. Store owner	—	—	—	—	—	—
16. Number of trips	—	—	—	—	—	—

*Trial 1 = functional-morphological type diversity; Trial 2 = pottery ware diversity; Trial 3 = exotic type diversity; Trial 4 = pottery plus industrial equivalent type diversity; Trial 5= food preparation and serving type diversity; Trial 6 = ritual type diversity.

Trial #6: Ritual type diversity

As in cases #3 and #4 only a single dichotomous variable (presence/absence *Alferez*) was chosen for inclusion in the predictive formula. Similarly, a Mann-Whitney U statistic was calculated, using absence of a former *Alferez* as n1 and presence of *Alferez* as n2. The null hypothesis being tested was:

Ho: ritual type diversity was equal for households with a former *Alferez* (n2) and households without a former *Alferez* (n1).

H1: ritual type diversity was not equal for households with a former *Alferez* and households without a former *Alferez*.

Since both n1 and n2 were greater than 10 (n1=37; n2=16), the U statistic was derived by the same formula used in case #3. The computed value of U=68.5 had a probability of p<.0000, with average ranks for n1 of 20.9 and for n2 of 41.2. Since the associated probability level for the computed value of U was again considerably less than the previously set significance level (α =.01), the null hypothesis could be rejected. The evidence supported the alternate hypothesis, implying that the bulk of values in sample two (presence of *Alferez*) was higher than the bulk of values in sample one (absence of *Alferez*), or that *household's with a former Alferez tended to have more diversity of ritual types than those without an Alferez.* Further testing using Kendall's tau, indicated a moderate degree of association between the variables ritual type diversity and presence/absence of a former *Alferez* (t=.54, p< .001).

DISCUSSION

As with pottery type frequency, it seems that we can expect to find only weak to moderate relationships between socioeconomic conditions and pottery type diversity. Other factors besides those included in the tests must also influence type diversity. There are obviously no single factors which can account for all the variability in any of the pottery diversity variables tested above. However, there are some general conclusions that can be drawn concerning the variability of pottery diversity at the household level (see Table 6.4).

(1) Four of the pottery diversity measures showed some, and often strong, association with one or more religious, need-related variables (i.e., presence/absence *Alferez* in three cases, presence/absence religious *cargo* position in two cases and presence/absence yearly festivals in one case). This is consistent with the statement made above that higher type diversity scores for households seemed to be accounted for mostly by the presence of more ritual vessel types. The presence/absence of a former *Alferez* in particular seems to be related to pottery type diversity. In terms of archaeological interpretations, our Chanal sample suggests that a knowledge of type diversity (especially of ritual types) could be usefully included among other factors for inferring relative household religious involvement at some time during it's existence, that is, *high ritual type diversity or high overall type diversity seem to suggest high relative religious status.*

(2) Variables representing the accessibility of pottery seem to have an equally important role in determining overall household pottery diversity as variables related to household requirements.

(3) Variables related to household size and development (e.g., number of children, family type, and age of household head) seem to have surprisingly little affect on household pottery diversity in Chanal, except possibly to the extent that social status and *cargo* position also imply certain degrees of family development.

(4) It would also appear that high diversity in domestic pottery vessels tends to be associated with low income, more traditional households. This may to be due to the greater use of industrial equivalents in higher income households (see Chapter 4).

In general, household pottery diversity may be of some use, although not sufficient by itself, for inferring those socioeconomic conditions selected by the predictive models. There is no reason at present for recommending it's use for inferring any of the independent variables not chosen by the models. A surprisingly large amount of pottery diversity seems to be associated with religious or social status.

The measurement of type diversity has been discussed and presented as a useful alternative or supplementary method to measurement of type frequency in dealing with household assemblages. Present methods used to measure type frequency seem to be inadequate for making statistical inferences concerning relative household (or housesite) socioeconomic characteristics. In fact, recent studies of modern material culture suggest that material culture frequencies and socioeconomic and demographic conditions may not be as strongly correlated as is generally believed (e.g., Hayden and Cannon 1984b; Rathje 1979; Schiffer et al. 1981).

While the relationships between type diversity and household socioeconomic conditions appear to be nearly as complex in nature as type frequency and socioeconomic conditions, diversity measures have enough advantages over type frequency measures to recommend a wider archaeological application and cautious use in inferring household characteristics. Possibly more refined partitioning of pottery assemblages into subassemblages reflecting specific activities (i.e., activity set diversity) and relative availability of types (i.e., local versus imported diversity) will produce more accurate interpretations in a wider range of archaeological realms of inference.

There is also the possibility that even if socioeconomic inferences at the household level may prove to be too unreliable to use in archaeological interpretations, ceramic diversity measures of households from entire communities may be useful for characterizing socioeconomic inequality in those communities. Hayden and Cannon (1984b) have used household data in this fashion to describe economic inequality in Chanal, Aguacatenango, and San Mateo. Such approaches might equally be applied to ritual-specific assemblages to monitor ritual specialization in communities. Thus diversity measures may have considerable potential for inferring socioeconomic characteristics of communities.

7

Maya Pottery Ethnoarchaeology in Retrospect

Unless ceramic studies lead to a better understanding of the cultural context in which the objects were made and used, they form a sterile record of limited worth. (Matson 1965:202)

Controlled ethnoarchaeological approaches may be our best hope for discovering the range of modern pottery-related behavior, as well as suggesting reasonable expectations for the variability in past pottery-related behavior (*sensu* Gould 1990:13). Similarly, Sullivan (1995:185) suggests that the major contribution of behavioral approaches (including ethnoarchaeology) has been an "expansion of and appreciation for variability." This study has focussed on modern pottery variability in terms of vessel frequency and type diversity and the spatial organization and patterning of pottery-related behavior and materials in Maya households. In recent years, such pottery ethnoarchaeological studies have become an important aspect of household archaeological research (Arnold and Santley 1993). Further, the use of ethnoarchaeological models has become increasingly important in the interpretation of archaeological contexts (e.g., Metcalfe and Heath 1990; Oetelaar 1993; Simms and Heath 1990; Smyth 1993; Stahl and Zeidler 1990; Varien and Mills 1997; Zeidler 1983). This concluding chapter explores some the archaeologically relevant issues related to household pottery assemblages and suggests some future possibilities for pottery ethnoarchaeological and archaeological research in the Maya Highlands.

HOUSEHOLD AS PRODUCTION UNIT

Pottery production itself is seen as the initial source of pottery variability and patterning in Tzeltal households, not only between potting and nonpotting households, but between households representing different intensities of pottery production. Three levels of production are recognized, with each successive level representing an increase in (1) the number of production events per year, (2) the number of vessels produced per event, (3) the number of vessel forms produced by the potter, and (4) the size of the distribution sphere associated with the pottery products. The level of production of a given household is constrained by environmental factors (e.g., climate and resource availability) and the household learning environment, while the necessity of production appears to be related largely to the relative agricultural self-sufficiency of the household. Production of pottery for sale or trade is viewed as a means of supplementing household economies where agricultural production is inadequate.

Environmental conditions of a given area influence the level of production in terms of material availability and scheduling. The quality of local clays and tempering materials limit the quality and formal diversity of the pottery produced in the area. For instance, the production of narrow-mouth jars requires special materials. Knowledge of the resources available in a given area are useful to the archaeologist attempting to differentiate locally made from imported vessels and to understand the development of craft specialization. For example, pottery specialization is not likely to develop in an area with poor pottery making resources (clays, tempers, and fuels). Specialist communities may acquire some exotic materials (e.g., pigments, smoothing stones) through trade or kin connections, but nonspecialist communities tend to use only local resources. Seasonal variations in climate (wet versus dry seasons) tend to regulate the scheduling of nonspecialist production, and especially drying and firing, while specialists use alternative methods to allow year-round production.

Microtraditions at the individual, household, work group, lineage, or community levels are largely the archaeological manifestations of pottery-learning frameworks. Intracommunity microtraditions have a complex structure, in which technological, formal, and stylistic information is exchanged. In nonspecialist communities, pottery making seems to occur so infrequently that most individuals do not develop the skill or expertise to produce highly standardized stylistic forms. As a result, technological qualities of products are stressed over stylistic variation. Another result of infrequent production is that potters often learn to make pottery late in life, and therefore teaching models are as likely to occur through nonkin as through kin relationships. In specialist communities, learning pottery making is more likely to take place early in life and to be concentrated within the family of orientation, and especially mother-daughter relationships. Because of the greater control in the potting medium and the tendency to learn the craft within the family of orientation, significant stylistic variability between households or residential corporate groups is more likely to occur.

In nonspecialist communities like Chanal, where there was little product uniformity beyond a basic community form for commonly produced vessel forms (e.g., the wide-mouth jar), pupils often began experimenting and innovating while still leaning the craft. This generally took the form of variations in rim form and location of handles. Many functionally related and formal criteria, such as body shape and neck height, were found to be most useful for differentiating between individual potters and to a large extent reflected different individual potting activity. Sources of inspiration for variations in pottery characteristics came primarily from imported vessels, and especially vessels from peripheral communities, rather than through teaching connections. Furthermore, when production was only seasonal, rather than a year-round occupation, vessel forms produced by a given potter were more likely to reflect the changing idiosyncratic tastes of the potter.

In general, the relatively loose framework of pottery-making instruction and lack of cultural controls on innovation, such as that recorded in Chanal, results in an intracommunity mixing of pottery stylistic patterning which would seriously affect the inference of residence behavior in nonspecialist archaeological communities. However, in some Maya communities innovation is not welcome (Reina 1963). It might be more reasonable to restrict such inferences on residence behavior to interhousehold work groups, since Chanal teachers and pupils tended to live together, or in close proximity, and their pottery tended to serve a relatively restricted area within the community. This situation occasionally resulted in groups of households whose pottery inventories showed basic formal similarities in locally made plainwares because they purchased their pottery from a group of potters who generally worked together, and whose pottery shared some basic formal attributes (body shape, rim forms, handle placement, basal trimming, etc.). These households might have no lineage or other connections beyond buying from the same potter or potters.

In order to study intracommunity craft specialization, or in order to make inferences concerning residence behavior based on pottery data related to pottery production, it is necessary to be able to recognize archaeological potting households. The Tzeltal production model indicates a number of useful criteria for distinguishing between potting and nonpotting households. To begin with, pottery-making supplies, and especially clays and tempers, were usually kept on hand year-round and most often were stored in reused vessels. These vessels, as well as loose materials, were of relatively little value and would probably be left upon the abandonment of the site. Unless there was a local shortage of potting materials, these supplies would probably not be scavenged from the deserted houselot.

Pottery-making supplies and some tools (especially *metates*) were generally stored near the area of their use. In Chanal, this was usually the household patio, so that supplies were often stored near the edge of the patio (e.g., along the external walls of structures, or on the roofs of sweatbaths). Residues of calcite powder in activity and storage areas might also provide evidence of pottery making. Many pottery-making tools were very distinctive in terms of condition, wear-patterns and embedded residues (especially smoothing stones, reused *manos* and *metates*, and crude hammerstones). *Manos* and *metates* used for potting were generally reused, so that their poor condition made them less likely to be scavenged. In addition, potters tended to keep extra *manos* on hand, so that there was more likelihood that this tool form would be present in archaeological potting households than in nonpotting households. Furthermore, smoothing stones were small and often misplaced and lost, especially by nonspecialists, who did not use them on a regular basis, and were therefore likely to occur in archaeological deposits.

Besides having more *manos*, potting households in Chanal generally had more reused pottery (an average of 16 vessels per household versus eight vessels per household for nonpotters). Some of these were obviously used for storage of potting materials. Reused vessels might be recognized by location within compounds (e.g., provisional discard areas), use-wear patterns (e.g., evidence of repair or reworking for reuse), and residues related to secondary versus primary use.

Potting households might also be expected to contain a greater diversity of formal-functional types (see Chapter 6). One type in particular, the small unrestricted bowl *(sets')*, was generally found only in potting households, because they were made with clay left over from the production of other types.

Firing areas might be visible due to regular reuse of the same hearth(s) and the buildup of sherdage from numerous breakage events during firing. They were usually found away from structures and patio areas. Furthermore, firing equipment might be visible in the form of fire-cracked rocks used for propping up vessels and firewood, and pottery wasters used to separate pottery from firewood.

Ethnographic studies of the spatial organization of pottery production allow archaeologists to predict the locations of production facilities and activity areas in prehistoric contexts (e.g., Sullivan 1988). A cross-cultural comparison of Maya and traditional Cypriot pottery production highlights some of the ways different societies solve basic organizational problems that are shared by all potters, such as placement of kilns or open hearths, scheduling conflicts with other activities and disposal of production byproducts (Deal 1994b).

HOUSEHOLD AS CONSUMPTION UNIT
The model of household pottery use and reuse indicates the ways that pottery variability and patterning are affected by the specific requirements of the individual household, especially in terms of changing household socioeconomic and demographic conditions. Household inventories are characterized by groups of vessels (i.e., activity sets) which are seen to be used and generally stored together. Activity sets are seen as the manifestation of broad, regional, functional subcomplexes at the household level.

Basic Chanal and Aguacatenango activity sets were related to food preparation and serving (i.e., four bowl forms, three jar forms, one plate and one solid), watercarrying and storage (i.e., one jar form), and ritual (i.e., four bowl forms, four jar forms, and one cylinder) functions. These were supplemented by gourd containers (i.e., three bowl forms, one ladle, one bottle, and one cup) and a variety of industrial equivalents. Some vessel forms had been replaced, at least in wealthier households, by industrial forms, and especially pottery serving bowls by metal bowls and cups. In addition, some vessel forms made for the tourist market were found in Tzeltal household inventories, such as miniature vessels and figurines used as children's toys. Use and storage locations of activity sets generally did not overlap.

The relative stability of basic vessel forms over time in the Chiapas Highlands should make the activity set concept useful for archaeological interpretation. At the household level, the activity set concept may be useful for differentiating the function of various structures (i.e., domestic, sleeping, ritual or storage) and also for recognizing activity areas within structures (also see Flannery and Winter 1976:34).

Household vessel frequency and type diversity were seen to be sensitive to complex socioeconomic and demographic conditions of the household (see Chapter 4). In archaeological investigations, type diversity, where it can be applied, might be more useful as an indicator of household socioeconomic conditions than vessel frequency. In general, pottery diversity variables seemed to be most strongly related to social status, and especially the ritual position of the household head, while they did not seem to be closely linked to economic (wealth) status. However, when industrial equivalents were included with pottery types, pottery diversity became more sensitive to economic (wealth) ranking. Elsewhere, studies by Smith (1987) and Trostel (1994) found that pottery volume is better correlated with household wealth than is vessel frequency. Of the pottery variables considered here, ritual pottery diversity and imported type diversity were the most sensitive to the range of socioeconomic variables considered.

The affects of industrial vessels on modern household pottery inventories not only appears to vary between households of different wealth status, but also between communities with different degrees of involvement in the regional (Ladino) economy (also see Skibo 1994). In Chanal, industrial equivalents are most often additions to the household inventory, while in Aguacatenango they seem more likely to be replacements for pottery. If this is in fact the case, then the pottery inventories of Chanal households would be comparable to Precolumbian household inventories, while in Aguacatenango, pottery plus industrial replacements would be more comparable to Precolumbian pottery inventories. Furthermore, the most common industrial replacement vessels in modern households were serving bowls, which might be equated with the use of imported fine quality bowl forms in the past. It is quite likely that the presence of metalware containers, and especially serving bowls, in household inventories is a reflection of family wealth and status, as it is among the Bariba of Bénin (Sargent and Friedel 1986:192).

As long as the type diversity and vessel frequency of a given household are relatively stable (i.e., as long as breakage and replacement rates coincide), vessel uselife variation will have a strong influence on the amount of each type to be disposed of over time. The longevity of a vessel is conditioned by a number of factors, including (1) basic strength, in terms of wall hardness and thickness, and vessel size, (2) use and reuse frequency and variation, (3) drying and storage practices, (4) opportunity for breakage, especially due to children and animals, (5) the potential for vessel repair, (6) the number of vessels in the household inventory, and (7) the amount of industrial replacements in the household inventory. According to Orton and others (1993:167), when archaeologists are comparing the composition of different assemblages, a working assumption should be that the relative uselife of different types remain constant over time.

There seems to be a belief among archaeologists that once a pottery vessel is broken it is generally not reusable (Renfrew 1977:6). In the Maya region, at least, this was not the case. At the prehistoric Cerén site, Sheets

(1992:45) identified several cases of pottery reuse, including large sherds used as crude plates and water carrying jar handles used as doorbar holders. Both Chanal and Aguacatenango households averaged at least 21% reused vessels in their pottery inventories. In fact, any part of a broken vessel had potential for immediate reuse (for paving muddy areas, in wall or poultry nest construction, for planting seedlings, etc.), and many vessels were stored in provisional discard locations for possible future reuse. In addition, certain reuse functions, such as the planting of seedlings, might cause seasonal increases in the proportions of vessels in reuse. Furthermore, narrow-mouth, watercarrying jars were likely to represent a larger proportion of vessels being broken during the rainy season when pathways were slippery.

The reuse of vessels in Tzeltal households provides a number of other interesting insights related to the interpretation of archaeological pottery assemblages (see Deal and Hagstrum 1995). For example, use-wear and residues associated with reused vessels are likely to reflect secondary rather than primary use. However, the distinctiveness of many reused vessels (e.g., storing of potting materials), and their frequent location away from structures may help to differentiate them from primary-use vessels. Furthermore, reused vessels are generally of little value, so that they would be the most likely vessels to be left at the site upon abandonment and would have little potential value for scavengers.

HOUSEHOLD AS DEPOSITIONAL UNIT

In an ongoing household (i.e., the preabandonment stage), depositional activity is characterized by several intentional and unintentional modes of disposal. Intentional modes include one clustered and one dispersed strategy of provisional discard, maintenance disposal, and dumping (i.e., broadcast dumping, discrete dumping, and tossing). Unintentional modes include loss and pathway breakage. All of these depositional modes, except for vessel loss, result in the de-

position of relatively large, damaged or fragmented vessels. Under normal abandonment conditions, single vessels or fragmented vessels may be associated with the floors of structures due to provisional discard, the patio toft area due to broadcast and tossing behavior, or pathways due to pathway breakage. Clusters of vessels may be associated with the structure walls due to provisional discard, patio toft areas due to maintenance disposal, and discrete or broadcast dumping, drainage ditches or pit features due to maintenance disposal.

In archaeological compounds, vessel clustering due to such depositional behavior should represent the last configuration of structures on the site. There is some danger that such patterning may wrongly be interpreted as activity areas. Structural renovation and rebuilding, when it occurs, may result in the mixing of refuse patterns within the toft area, while not affecting refuse patterning which results from pathway breakage, maintenance and disposal or discrete dumping. The optimal archaeological context for examining pottery disposal is the short-term, single occupation, such as those found in semisedentary communities (see Deal 1985).

In contrast to the above patterns, the artifact patterning which results from maintenance disposal is almost exclusively composed of small fragments of pottery. The spatial distribution of these fragments, such as concentrations in drainage ditches and along patio edges, as well as trampling within structures or on patios or pathways, may indicate the limits of household patio and structure-related work areas. Relative sherd densities may be useful for identifying toft areas associated with structures and general activity areas, such as patios, which are usually devoid of refuse. Recent microdebitage studies indicate that microsherd and macrosherd distributions reveal different aspects of prehistoric pottery-related behavior and site formation (eg., Sherwood et al. 1995:452).

Modes of housesite abandonment are

more likely to affect vessel frequency and type diversity rather than the spatial patterning of pottery. For example, differential modes of abandonment are not likely to affect discarded vessels or vessel fragments. They will be left behind more or less in the same location under all conditions of abandonment. The number and diversity of whole or damaged vessels left upon abandonment are directly related to the speed of abandonment and whether or not return is anticipated. Whole vessels, especially those in storage or use locations, are only likely to be left under rapid abandonment conditions, or under gradual abandonment conditions where return is planned but not achieved. The fact that the frequency and diversity of whole or slightly damaged vessels is likely to increase with the rapidity of abandonment may be useful for identifying the conditions of abandonment, or for comparing abandonment conditions which can be monitored in other ways, such as the magnetic alterations of soil due to house burning.

Further variations in vessel frequency and diversity are likely to occur due to postabandonment activity. For example, scavenging causes decreases in both frequency and diversity by the removal of any vessels of potential reuse value, while the dumping of new refuse increases frequency and diversity. Fortunately, refuse dumping on abandoned housesites tends to leave predictable patterns. The short-term intensity of postabandonment alterations differs according to the open or closed nature of the housesite during the occupation of the community. The length of time a housesite remained closed prior to community abandonment should be inversely related to the intensity of postabandonment alterations.

Several recent studies have sought to develop methods for deriving information on formation processes from archaeological pottery assemblages. For example, conjoinability (also known as refitting or cross-mending) studies can provide useful inferences concerning cultural formation process (i.e., behavior that causes the reduction of whole items into pieces) and can help to distinguish among whole (or reconstructible) vessels, usable fragments, and discarded fragments (Lindauer 1992:210; also see Schiffer 1987:286). For example, Lindauer (1992:211) identifies two situations that suggest vessel reuse, (1) orphan sherds (i.e, sherds that do not conjoin to form whole or fragmented vessels) that are modified in ways that make them unconjoinable, and (2) conjoined, but incomplete, vessels with evidence of use-wear that is not consistent with original vessel use or changes in surface color due to heat exposure (also see Hally 1983b:171; Sullivan 1988:32). The distribution of conjoinable sherds within a site can also provide information on their original dispersal mechanisms (Bollong 1994). Inferences on pottery assemblage formation based on refitting studies can be valuable for the reinterpretation of ceramic collections (Skibo et al. 1989).

Orton and others (1993:178) use the measures of vessel "brokenness" and "completeness" to evaluate the effects of formation processes on a site assemblage. Brokenness is an estimate of the total number of sherds into which a vessel is broken. The brokenness of a given type for an entire assemblage is derived by dividing the number of sherds of the type by the number of vessel equivalents (e.g., based on rim sherds). Brokenness starts with a value of 1 and increases with consecutive breakage events, according to depositional context and breakage factors related to the vessel form (see Chapter 4). Completeness is an estimate of the proportion of a vessel present after recovery. The completeness for a given type for an entire assemblage is derived by dividing the vessel equivalents by the estimated number of vessels represented. Completeness also starts with a value of 1, but decreases according to depositional context. Completeness is considered to be the more valuable indicator of formation processes, but it is less reliable due to the difficulties of deriving the estimated number of vessels represented (Orton et al. 1993:179).

Schiffer (1987:282ff) recommends the use of weight to derive a Completeness Index (CI) for individual vessel batches and vessels of a given type within a deposit. The CI represents the recovered proportion of each vessel within a type and a total proportion for the type when the CI values for all vessels (i.e., vessel batches) of the type are added together. The CI of a given vessel equals the weight of the total sherdage (vessel batch) divided by the weight of a complete vessel of the same type. According to Schiffer (1987:283), high mean values for CI (i.e., approaching 1) may indicate grave goods, caches or certain types of de facto or secondary refuse, while low mean values are characteristic of residual primary refuse and extensively reworked deposits. A Fragmentation Index (FI) can also be used to monitor the variation in sherd counts for vessel batches. The FI range in value from 1 (i.e., a complete vessel) to values approaching zero (i.e., extremely fragmented vessels). FI for a single vessel equals $1/1+\log_{10}$ (P), where P is the number of sherds (or pieces) in a given batch (Schiffer 1987:283).

THE PREDICTION OF HOUSEHOLD SOCIOECONOMIC CONDITIONS

One of the most difficult problems of archaeological pottery studies is the establishment of reliable estimates of type frequency. However, this problem must be addressed if we are to use type frequency estimates for making inferences concerning the socioeconomic and demographic conditions represented by archaeological assemblages. Of the methods currently available, NIV (number of inferred vessels) measures are always preferable to NISP (raw sherd counts) measures for this purpose, especially when rim and basal arc or vessel equivalent methods are used for the NIV measures (Egloff 1973; Orton 1980, 1982). If analysis time and cost are not factors, and sherds are not too fragmentary, reconstructions using geometrical formulae (Ericson and DeAtley 1976; M. F. Smith 1985) may be a better alternative. Simulation experiments (e.g., Orton 1982), aided by data from controlled monitoring of breakage and deposition in the ethnographic context, may improve the archaeologist's understand-

ing of the interdependence among potsherds in archaeological assemblages. Further, new statistical methods are being developed to allow comparisons of pottery types between assemblages (Orton and Tyers 1992).

Statistical analyses presented here have indicated that type diversity is generally a more useful alternative than, or at least a good supplementary method to, type frequency for making socioeconomic inferences at the household level. Because it may reflect different socioeconomic or demographic conditions than vessel frequency, type diversity cannot be expected to replace measurements of type frequency for making socioeconomic and demographic inferences at the household level. However, type diversity has a number of advantages that justify its more extensive use with archaeological assemblages. Type diversity is easy to calculate, therefore time-efficient, and it is not affected (as are NIV and NISP) by differential breakage rates, reuse and disposal behavior, excavation techniques, or assumptions of sherd interdependence. In our Chanal sample, both graphic representations (Chapter 4) and regression analysis (Chapter 7) suggest that type diversity is closely associated with the social and religious status of the household head, and is a better predictor of these conditions than vessel frequency.

SOME SUGGESTIONS FOR FUTURE RESEARCH

One of the underlying goals of the Coxoh Ethnoarchaeological Project was to provide more extensive, better quality, and especially more archaeologically relevant ethnographic data than currently available to Mesoamericanists working in the Maya Highlands. Information was particularly lacking on variation in household requirements and pottery variability and patterning related to discard behavior. The present study rectifies this discrepancy to a certain extent, at least in terms of identifying areas of concern to future archaeological interpretation of pottery assemblages. The following discussion deals with a number of methodological problems associated with ethnoarchaeological fieldwork, some suggestions for improving the quality of data intended for use in making archaeological inferences, and an outline of the ideal conditions for evaluating the models presented here with archaeological data.

ETHNOARCHAEOLOGICAL CONSIDERATIONS
The Chanal and Aguacatenango statistical analyses would be more reliable if a random sample of households could have been obtained. Unfortunately, this is very difficult, and perhaps impossible, to attain in traditional communities such as Chanal and Cancuc. By contrast, the Kalinga Project had complete access to all households (J. Skibo, personal communication 1997). The Tzeltal situation could be improved by experimental sampling studies (e.g., Honigman and Honigman 1955, 1957) in communities which have had extensive and friendly contact with anthropologists (e.g., Zinacantan), in which comparisons could be made between samples of random and judgementally selected households. In this way, many of the biases involved with the use of judgemental samples of households might be predicted and possibly adjusted for in future studies.

Another advantage of selecting a community which has been previously studied, is that much of the initial groundwork involved with ethnographic fieldwork (e.g., mapping of the community and familiarity with internal sociopolitical organization) will have been completed. A restudy of Chanal or Aguacatenango, for example, would provide much useful data concerning the relationships between pottery production and household inventory change over time. Some of the practical and theoretical difficulties of the restudy method have been addressed elsewhere (Garbett 1967). One significant change noted from previous Maya studies is the decrease in the diversity of traditional vessel forms now being produced and an increase in vessels made for the tourist trade. This phenomenon has also been reported for the Peruvian Highlands (Hagstrum 1989). Arnold (1987) has reported significant changes in the organiza-

tion of pottery production among the Yucatecan Maya. Similarly, William Longacre (1991; Stark and Longacre 1993) indicates that the two major changes over the last two decades among the Kalinga have been the adoption of new decorative techniques due to restricted access to certain raw materials and the production of tourist vessels for cash. De-Boer's (1991) restudy of Chachi and Shipibo decorative styles demonstrates that change, in terms of design replacements and diminished or amplified elaboration, can be linked to decorative strategies across a variety of media (e.g., pottery, textiles, canoes, and tattoos). It is likely that future ethnoarchaeologists will even excavate housesites that were reported by previous researchers. This could provide a real test of the techniques we use to reassemble prehistoric ceramic assemblages for use in the interpretation of past social and economic conditions (Skibo et al. 1989).

Our method of household interviews, in which information was collected on a wide range of topics in a single visit, severely limited the kinds and amount of pottery data we could collect. While information on interhousehold variability in vessel use, reuse and disposal behavior could be observed in this manner, it is not conducive to collecting information on temporal variability and patterning. For example, if archaeologists are going to use simulation models to make predictions concerning vessel discard rates over time using ethnographic data, then they must monitor temporal changes in the lifespan of various pottery types, including duration of reuse of vessels, and replacement rates (e.g., in relation to changes in household wealth, social status, or family size).

Monitoring vessel use, breakage, storage, and disposal behavior has the disadvantage of requiring the investigator to remain in manageable proximity to the households participating in the experiment. However, such a study need not be time-consuming if records were updated periodically (e.g. once a week or biweekly) while the investigator is working on a separate project (such as a long term archaeological excavation). Records could be kept of relevant data such as date of vessel purchase, frequency of use, use and storage locations, date of breakage, condition after breakage, proportion of vessel, type of sherd (rim, body, etc.) saved for repair, reuse or discarded, location of discard, and any features associated with the discard location. Similar records could be kept for industrial replacements that will affect the uselives of specific vessel forms (e.g., see Sargent and Friedel 1986:193). Furthermore, careful records of mended vessels may provide useful information on ceramic value systems (Senior 1995). If vessels are too similar to be distinguished easily, then they can be tagged for individual recognition. Longacre's periodic returns to the Kalinga area have resulted in extensive records of the life histories of tagged pottery vessels and collections of pottery for future research (Longacre et al. 1991:10–11; Neupert and Longacre 1994).

Black and white photos of storage locations would be useful for monitoring changes in storage arrangements of vessels and relationships between pottery vessels and features. This can also be done by recording changes in vessel storage and use locations on transparent Mylar plastic used as overlays on scale maps of compounds. This latter method was found to be extremely effective for recording compound activity areas and refuse patterning in Chanal and Aguacatenango.

Another alternative is the use of portable video cameras. Beale and Healy (1975:985) consider ethnoarchaeological study and research films as an area of great untapped potential for archaeological film making. For example, films of actual pottery-related behavior in an ongoing community could be invaluable tools for ethnoarchaeological research. Such activities might include the collection and storage of raw materials, pottery production and the dispersal of production byproducts, the use and storage of different vessel types, the movement of vessels between production stages and between production and sale, and the actual abandonment of compounds. Recent research by the

author (Deal et al. 1993) involved the videotaping of traditional Cypriot potters, with the purpose of establishing a video archive to direct future ethnoarchaeological research.

In order to form a better understanding of the relationships between pottery frequency and type diversity and differential socioeconomic and demographic conditions, it would also be useful to experiment with different systems for ranking such conditions. For example, a combined ranking of social and economic factors (such as that used by Price and Price 1972; also see O. Lewis 1960:37) might be more sensitive to pottery variability in some communities.

If archaeologists are to use emic formal-functional typologies in their predictive models, then they must have a clear understanding of the range of variation in vessel size and formal attributes within their formal-functional types. The cognitive prototype method presented by Kempton (1981) would provide one way of addressing this problem. Kempton uses drawing sheets exhibiting line drawings of pottery vessels in which gradual changes in body form, attachments, and spouts were emphasized. Different sheets could be used to emphasize more abrupt changes. Using this method, informants could indicate which drawings they consider to represent a wide-mouth jar. A comparison of these sheets could then be used to establish clearer definitions of individual types. Also, variations between how producers and vessel users perceived different types could be monitored in this way. Categories established by the cognitive prototype method could also serve as a convenient checklist for recording frequencies of basic formal variants per household, since photographing all the pottery in each Tzeltal household would have been an expensive and time-consuming task.

ARCHAEOLOGICAL CONSIDERATIONS

An area of great potential for pottery ethnoarchaeology is experimental studies. Experimental approaches in archaeology are generally associated with controlled laboratory experiments, but many experiments have also been conducted in ethnographic contexts or have involved a combination of field and laboratory work. Recent research in the Philippines by William Longacre and other members of the Kalinga Ethnoarchaeological Project have relied heavily on experimental methods (Longacre et al. 1991; Longacre and Skibo 1994). According to Longacre (1992), the combination of experimental and ethnoarchaeological approaches is "the way of the future for developing important interpretative principles for archaeology," that is, principles that link material culture with human behavior. Two members of Longacre's team, James Skibo (1994) and Masashi Koybayashi (1994) monitored the use of new pottery vessels provided to selected Kalinga households. The vessels were later shipped back to the United States, where laboratory studies were conducted on vessel use-wear and residues. Their results are directly applicable to functional reconstructions of archaeological assemblages. A separate study involved experiments to test the performance of metal and pottery rice cooking pots. The results supported informant claims relating to why the Kalinga were slow to adopt metal pots for rice cooking. While metal pots heat up faster and are more durable, they are more likely to boil over and burn the rice. Laboratory analyses of clays also supported informant claims concerning which of two villages made stronger vessels.

Other experimental studies have been devised to test existing methodologies on ethnographic materials. For example, Dean Arnold and others (1991) have tested the Neutron Activation technique on modern pottery from the Valley of Guatemala. Their work supports the ongoing use of this technique on archaeological pottery. James Skibo (1992) has tested certain assumptions concerning the use of Gas Chromatography and Mass Spectrometry to analyze food residues on pottery vessels (also see Skibo and Deal 1995). This technique also held up when characterizing fatty acid biomarkers from single sources, such as rice, but had difficulty dealing with mixtures.

Clarifying the relationships between vessel form and function has great potential as a field of study in its own right (see Renfrew 1977:3). Indeed, it has received much needed attention in the archaeological literature in recent years (see Chapter 2). However, more experimentation is needed both with ethnographic and archaeological pottery assemblages, in order to delimit functional boundaries within formal classes. Besides formal attributes, more work is needed to relate functional variation in chemical (elemental) and petrographic content of pastes, and use-wear and use-residue characteristics. Furthermore, extensive use of ethnohistoric sources (e.g., the Maya Codices, the Motul dictionary, archival records) may provide additional insights into the functions of vessel forms no longer in use.

Experimental sampling of ethnographic households indicates some problems with standard archaeological practices. Archaeologists generally do not sample entire housesites, even if they can be effectively isolated within a larger site. Total areal samples of recently abandoned Aguacatenango housesites show that most of the material culture was actually deposited away from structures (Chapter 6). They indicate that former pottery-related activity areas will be difficult to identify, except under unusual conditions, such as rapid abandonment (Deal 1985). Nevertheless, recent work in Oaxaca, Mexico (Joyce and Johannessen 1993), suggests that under normal abandonment conditions, special-purpose structures, such as kitchens, have a higher likelihood of activity area survival. Furthermore, production locations that were used on a continual basis may be identifiable through the study of microrefuse in soil samples (Deal 1988b; also see Barba and Ortiz 1992; Manzanilla and Barba 1990). These studies can be used as controls for problem-oriented sampling strategies. Given limited time and resources, they suggest where to sample for activity areas related to ceramic production, use, and disposal, as well as the range of variability to expect in terms of vessel condition, type diversity, and postabandonment activities.

The emphasis in the present study has

been on model building. Yet, under what conditions can we evaluate these models for making archaeological interpretations? Ideally we would begin with sites located within the Tzeltal Highlands, then the remainder of the Maya Highlands. Ethnographic pottery assemblages can be compared with those of recently abandoned modern housesites followed by recent historic, colonial, and prehistoric sites. Beginning with recently abandoned sites is particularly useful in cases where previous occupants are available to allow an assessment of interpretations based on archaeological methods (e.g., Bonnichsen 1973; Lange and Rydberg 1972; Longacre and Ayres 1968; Stevenson 1982). Another useful condition would be household compounds or house clusters with clear boundaries, such as the late prehistoric site at Yerba Buena (Bryant 1988). Samples should be taken from as large an area as possible within each compound, preferably throughout the whole compound or a large random sample, and including areas away from structures, such as gardens (also see Tani 1995:249; Webster and Gronlin 1988). In this way refuse patterning is more likely to be recognized and postabandonment alterations assessed, and thus reducing or eliminating the effect of these biases on estimates of type frequency based on NIV or NISP measures. It would also be useful to begin by excavating isolated housesites, which would be less likely to be affected by postabandonment cultural alterations and overlapping of occupations (also see Bogucki and Grygiel 1981; Dillehay 1973; Mosely and MacKey 1972). In such situations preabandonment structural zones, patios, work areas, and other kinds of refuse areas are more likely to survive. This situation would also provide ideal conditions for differentiating refuse from activity patterning before excavation of larger

sites where more complex patterning would be expected. Criteria should be established for ruling out provisional discard before considering activity areas or activity sets. This can be addressed by paying special attention to the condition of all vessels and vessel fragments, especially those found in clusters in the vicinity or within structures.

The results of the present study exemplify the kinds of pottery-related information which can be obtained through a synchronic approach to ethnographic fieldwork. The study was exploratory in nature and clearly further work is needed to investigate relationships between the full range of pottery-related behavior, from production to discard, and resulting pottery variability and spatial patterning at the household level. Such work could be most efficiently achieved in association with a long-term archaeological research project. Any such project would benefit by conducting coincident ethnographic fieldwork directed toward specific problems related to the site or sites being excavated.

In many areas of the world, longstanding traditional technologies are rapidly disappearing. For example, in Cyprus, a single potter makes the traditional goat-milking vessel that can be traced back to a Bronze Age prototype (Deal et al. 1993). In her recent review of West African archaeology, S. K. McIntosh (1994:182) referred to attempts to record such technologies as "salvage ethnoarchaeology." The opportunity for doing ethnoarchaeological research in many parts of the Maya area may also be lost. Traditional Maya culture survives, but largely in areas in political turmoil. While the potential for ethnoarchaeological research in the Chiapas Highlands is enormous, the question is for how long? Maya pottery ethnoarchaeology itself may soon be reduced to a salvage operation.

Appendix A

Glossary

GENERAL VESSEL (AND NON-VESSEL) FORMS:

Bowl Vessel having a height no more than equal to but no less than one-third of its maximum diameter (R.E. Smith 1955:4).

Cup Small hemispherical vessel with a single vertical handle.

Jar Vessel with restricted orifice, whose height and width are approximately equal, and where greatest diameter lies at approximately half its height.

Pestle Hand-held bar (non-vessel pottery object).

Pitcher Jar or vase with a single vertical handle and occasionally a lip-spout.

Plate Vessel with height less than one-fifth its maximum diameter (R.E. Smith 1955:4).

Vase Vessel having a height obviously greater than its width (Lothrop 1927:109).

Whorl Perforated flywheel (non-vessel pottery object).

FORMAL AND DECORATIVE ATTRIBUTES:

Basal ridge Unpolished portion around the base of a vessel, where access clay has been removed after burnishing.

Base Bottom of a vessel to a point where change of angle or curve indicates the start of the vessel side (Sabloff 1975:24).

Body Vessel wall segment between the base and shoulder (or rim if there is no shoulder).

Burnishing Decorative surface polishing done with a smooth pebble (usually quartzite).

Cylindrical body Vessel body approximates the shape of a cylinder.

Direct rim Rim as direct continuation of body or neck wall (R. Thompson 1958: 33).

Elliptical body Vessel body approximates the shape of an ellipsoid or, in the case of a bowl, a segmented ellipsoid positioned on its vertical or horizontal axis.

Everted rim Rim turned sharply outward forming an angle with neck and vessel wall (R. Thompson 1958:33).

Flaring mouth Diameter of vessel opening is greater than the maximum diameter of the vessel body (characteristic rim form of bowl, dish, and plate forms which approximate the shape of a frustrum or segmented hyperboloid).

Flat bottom Nearly plane undersurface of a vessel which varies from very slightly convex to slightly concave (R. Thompson 1958:33).

Frustrum body Vessel body shape approximates the shape of a truncated cone.

Glaze Watery, colored or transparent lead coating with a grainy texture to the touch.

Hemispherical body Vessel body approximates one half of a sphere.

Horizontal handle Loop with opening on the vertical plane (thickest at juncture with vessel wall: see R. Thompson 1958:33).

Incurving (or restricted) orifice Vessel opening formed by the converging of the vessel walls, which is characteristic of hemispherical bowl forms and spherical, elliptical, and ovaloid jar forms.

Lip Edge or tip of rim.

Lip-spout Small, shallow, everted depression in the edge of a vessel lip (R. Thompson 1958:33).

Loop-handle Vertical handle crossing above the center of a vessel orifice and attached to the lip of the rim.

Neck Body segment of restricted vessel form between the shoulder and rim of a vessel.

Node Subconical projection on the exterior of a vessel.

Opposed lugs Subtriangular lumps or ridges on opposite sides of a vessel.

Oval body Vessel body approximates the shape of an ovaloid or segmented ovaloid standing on its long axis with the widest diameter above or below the center of the vessel.

Pedestal base Flaring, trumpet-like, hollow or solid foot with the line of cleavage between the pedestal and the vessel bottom being visible (R. Thompson 1958:31).

Piecrust rim	Finger-impressed fillet, encircling the rim of a vessel (resembles the ridge of a piecrust).
Plainware	Unslipped or otherwise undecorated vessels.
Pock marks	Circular depressions on vessel exterior produced by use-wear.
Red slip	Watery, red or red-orange clay employed as background color on Amatenango vessels.
Rim	Area between the change of direction of side or neck of vessel and lip , or the margin of vessel orifice ... only when the margin is thickened or displays change in wall direction or both is the rim set as a distinct part of the vessel (Sabloff 1975:24).
Rim thickness	Characterized by (1) location of maximum thickness of rim (at lip, low on rim, or medial on rim), (2) location of thickest portion of rim in relation to vessel wall (interior, exterior, or indeterminate), and (3) relative degree of thickening of rim in relation to vessel wall (or rim junction), which is either gradual or abrupt (Shepard 1976:246).
Shoulder	Point of maximum diameter of a restricted vessel (Shepard 1976:241).
Spherical body	Vessel body approximates a sphere (R. Thompson 1958:31).
Subhyperboloid body	Vessel body approximates the shape of a bisected hyperboloid.
Unrestricted orifice	Vessel opening (or mouth) from the neck, or upper body, if the vessel has no neck (characteristic of spheroid, ellipsoid, and ovaloid bowl forms).
Vertical handle	Loop with opening on the vertical plane, and thickest at juncture with wall (R. Thompson 1958:33).
White slip	Watery, white clay paint employed as background color on Amatenango vessels.

Appendix B

Classification of Chanal and Aguacatenango Pottery

INTRODUCTION

A pottery vessel is here defined as a container which serves for the temporary or long-term storage of liquids or dry goods. In a liberal interpretation of this definition, cooking and beer-mixing activities are said to require containers on a temporary storage basis. Tzeltal vessels are first divided into easily recognizable classes of general vessel form, including plate, dish, bowl, jar, vase, and cup. These terms are widely used in Maya archaeological and ethnographic reports (see glossary in Appendix A). Following Raymond Thompson's classification model (1958:27), vessel types are given a name that consists of a noun which refers to a defined general vessel form (such as bowl, jar, or vase, etc.) and one or more adjectives referring to the most distinctive formal attributes of the class (such as small bowl or small restricted bowl).

Descriptions of body shapes are modelled on simple geometrical forms similar to those proposed by Anna O. Shepard (1976) and more recently by Ericson and Stickel (1973).

The use of geometrical descriptions for body shape are more explicit than commonly used terms such as "globular, "egg-shaped" and "pear-shaped," which may have different meanings to different researchers. Further, Ericson and Stickel have found that by translating real body forms into abstract geometrical ones, they could estimate vessel capacity using formulae for deriving the volumes of the geometrical solids which approximate a vessel's shape. Their system is designed for functional considerations, in that the volume of various behavioral activities which utilize pottery vessels (assuming that vessel form can be used to derive vessel function), could be estimated for a given culture, past or present (1973:366). In our own research, since we had only one day to spend at each household surveyed, just three measurements (i.e., maximum height, width and rim diameter) could be made on each vessel. These measurement were augmented by photographs. The Ericson and Stickel method did prove useful, however, in establishing the size ranges of small and large unrestricted bowls.

APPENDIX B

DOMESTIC—FOOD PREPARATION AND SERVING—TYPES 1–9;
FIGURES B1–16

1 SMALL HEMISPHERICAL BOWL:

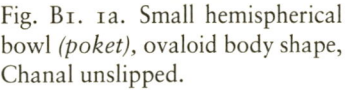

Fig. B1. 1a. Small hemispherical bowl *(poket)*, ovaloid body shape, Chanal unslipped.

Fig. B2. 1b. Small hemispherical bowl *(poket)*, spherical body shape, Chanal unslipped.

Fig. B3. 1c. Small hemispherical bowl *(poket)*, spherical body shape, Amatenango slipped.

Ware classes: Amatenango slipped, Yocnajab slipped, Chanal unslipped, San Fernando unslipped, San Pedro unslipped.

Emic terminology: *poket* or *apaxtle* (Spanish: *apastli*).

Sample size: Chanal 85 slipped, 124 unslipped; Aguacatenango 440 slipped.

Size: slipped forms, height 4–22 cm, rim diameter 10–31 cm, volume 103–7800 cubic cm; unslipped forms, height 3–30.5 cm, rim diameter 8.5–32 cm, and volume 297–7800 cubic cm.

Shape: body shape varies from spherical to ovaloid (with maximum width above center); orifice varies from slightly restricted to unrestricted; slightly concave or flat base; rim thickness interior, low, gradual for slipped forms (occasionally unslipped forms have exterior, medial, gradual rim thickness); unslipped forms have thick base relative to vessel wall, and basal ridges are common.

Primary function: general utility (hand-washing and serving). Occasionally larger ones are reserved for ritual hand-washing.

Comments: calcite temper; slipped vessels have red to red-orange or white slip; decorations on upper body and rim and interior body and rim; floral design common; unslipped forms seem to be locally made copies of the imported slipped forms.

2 SMALL RESTRICTED BOWL:

Ware classes: Amatenango slipped, Aguacatenango slipped.

Emic
terminology: *sets'* (Spanish *vasija*).
Sample size: Chanal 16; Aguacatenango 57.
Shape: restricted mouth, hemispherical body shape; rim indeterminate; flat base.
Size: height range 3–18 cm, rim diameter 14–19 cm.

Primary
function: utility bowl (serving, dry storage, etc.).
Comments: calcite temper; red to red-orange or white slip; exterior burnishing; one vessel had a white slip with geometrical designs on the interior body and rim and exterior rim.

Fig. B4. 2. Small restricted bowl *(sets')*, spherical body shape, Amatenango slipped.

3 SMALL ELLIPTICAL BOWL:

Fig. B5. 3. Small elliptical bowls *(chalten)*, ellipsoid body shape, San Ramon glazed.

Fig. B6. 3. Small elliptical bowl *(chalten)*, ellipsoid body shape, Chanal unslipped.

Ware classes: San Ramon glazed, Chanal unslipped, San Pedro unslipped; Amatenango unslipped, Aguacatenango unslipped.

Emic
terminology: *chalten* (Spanish *sarten*).
Sample size: Chanal 38 unslipped; Aguacatenango 45 glazed, 43 unslipped.
Shape: ellipsoid (horizontal axis) body shape; rim indeterminate; slightly concave or flat base; thick base relative to walls; basal ridge common; 5 vessels have 1 or 2 horizontal handles; unrestricted orifice.
Size: height range 3–35 cm, rim diameter 5.5–45 cm.

Primary
function: frying vegetables, and occasionally meat or fish.
Comments: San Ramon glazed vessels are modelled in Chamula and sold to San Ramon potters, who glaze the interiors and resell them (Rus 1969:42); all are calcite tempered; often crudely formed.

4 SMALL FRUSTRUM BOWL:

Ware classes: Chanal unslipped, Amatenango unslipped.

Emic terminology: *sets'* (Spanish *cazuela*).

Sample size: Chanal 44; Aguacatenango 8.

Shape: frustrum or occasionally elliptical (vertical axis) body shape; rim is indeterminate; slightly concave or flat base; thick base relative to walls, basal ridge common.

Fig. B7. 4. Small frustrum bowls *(sets')*, frustrum body shape, Chanal unslipped.

Size range: height range 3–15 cm, rim diameter 6–26 cm.

Primary function: frying vegetables or general utility.

Comments: calcite temper; generally crudely formed; size is often determined by amount of leftover clay from manufacture of other vessels.

5 UNRESTRICTED PLATE:

Ware classes: Amatenango unslipped, Aguacatenango unslipped, Chanal unslipped, San Pedro unslipped, San Fernando unslipped, Yocnajab unslipped.

Emic terminology: *samet* or *tzamet* (Spanish *comal*).

Sample size: Chanal 223; Aguacatenango 115.

Shape: frustrum body shape; rim thickness exterior, medial, abrupt; flat base; basal ridge common; one Amatenango vessel had a cylindrical body shape, a curving (lifter-like) horizontal handle and indeterminate rim thickness.

Fig. B8. 5. Unrestricted plate *(samet)*, frustrum body shape, Chanal unslipped.

Size: height range 1–5.5 cm, rim diameter range 9–65 cm.

Primary function: griddle for roasting tortillas and occasionally for roasting or drying seeds.

Comments: calcite temper (large grained inclusions); often crudely made.

6 FRUSTRUM SOLID:

Fig. B9. 6. Frustrum solid *(makil sti')*, frustrum solid, Chanal unslipped.

Ware classes: San Ramon glazed; Chanal unslipped.

Emic
terminology: *makil sti'* (Spanish *tapa*).

Sample size: Chanal 5 unslipped; Aguacatenango 1 glazed.

Shape: frustrum-shaped solid; flat base and truncation; 2 examples have a single loop handle.

Size: height approximately 1 cm, and rim diameter range 11.5–16 cm.

Primary
function: cover (potlid) for small wide-mouth jar.

Comments: unslipped forms have calcite temper; crude form; the 5 unslipped forms were made by 3 different potters.

7 SMALL WIDE-MOUTH JAR:

Fig. B10. 7a. Small wide-mouth jar *(oxom)*, ellipsoid body shape, Chanal unslipped.

Ware classes: San Ramon glazed, Amatenango unslipped, Aguacatenango unslipped, Chanal unslipped, Floresta unslipped, San Fernando unslipped, San Pedro unslipped, Siberia unslipped, Yola unslipped, Yocnajab unslipped, Onija unslipped, Pinola (Villa Las Rojas) unslipped, Frontera Tsjanish unslipped, Natilton unslipped, Tzajala unslipped, Palizada unslipped.

Emic
terminology: *oxom* in Chanal and *pin* in Aguacatenango (Spanish *olla*; glazed form is sometimes called *boca*).

Sample size: Chanal 3 glazed and 1435 unslipped; Aguacatenango 5 glazed and 521 unslipped.

Shape: unslipped and glazed vessels generally have an elliptical (vertical axis) body, while ovaloid shapes (with maximum width either above or below mid-height) are also very common; spherical and

Fig. B11. 7b. Small wide-mouth jar *(oxom)*, ovaloid body shape, Chanal unslipped.

horizontal elliptical body shapes occur rarely; divergent neck; rim thickness is most often indeterminate, but sometimes exterior, medial, abrupt; flat base; occasionally has 2 handles.

Size: unslipped and glazed wares have a height range of 2–42 cm, width range of 6–22 cm and a rim diameter range of 3–17 cm.

Primary
function: unslipped and glazed vessels are used for cooking vegetables and preparing corn gruels (*pozol* and *atole*); miniature forms are children's toys.

Comments: unslipped vessels have only calcite temper; thick base; rough uniform wall thickness; often crudely made with sagging or poorly shaped walls; vessels walls are usually at least partially burnished; occasionally coiling rings are visible on exterior.

Fig. B12. 7c. Small wide-mouth jar *(oxom)*, ovaloid body shape, Chanal unslipped.

8 SINGLE-HANDLED JAR:

Fig. B13. 8a. Single-handled jar *(chikpin)*, ovaloid body shape, Aguacatenango unslipped.

Fig. B14. 8b. Single-handled jar *(chikbin)*, ellipsoid body shape, San Ramon glazed.

Fig. B15. 8c. Single-handled jar *(chikbin)*, double frustrum body shape, Aguacatenango unslipped.

Ware classes: San Ramon glazed, Mexican glazed, Amatenango slipped, Amatenango unslipped, Marcos Becerra unslipped, Aguacatenango unslipped, Chanal unslipped, San Pedro unslipped, San Fernando unslipped, Pinola (Villa Las Rojas) unslipped, Yocnajab unslipped, San Jose unslipped.

Emic
terminology: Chanal term is *chikbin* and Aguacatenango terms are *chikpin* or *sharu* (Spanish *jarro*); when this form is used for mixing lime it is sometimes called *puk'-tan* (Spanish *olla por cal*) in Chanal. Chanal term for spout is *yosholye* (Spanish *pice* or *vertedera*).

Sample Size: Chanal 27 glazed (2 with spouts), 9 slipped, 151 unslipped (9 with spouts); Aguacatenango 49 glazed, 1657 unslipped (90 with spouts).

Shape: glazed vessels have an ovaloid body with the maximum width below the center of the vessel, while most unslipped vessels have an elliptical (vertical axis) or ovaloid (both forms) body shape; two Aguacatenango potters make a jar body that resembles 2 frustrum shapes with the bases joined to form an angular ridge at the center of the vessel height (ridge angle is approximately 130 degrees); divergent neck; rim thickness is indeterminate; wide (unrestricted or flaring) mouth; flat base; basal ridge is common; one vertical handle; restriction on rim to form spout on 104 vessels.

Size: height range 1–38 cm, width range 2–34 cm, and rim diameter range 2–28 cm, maximum width of spout 2–9 cm at rim.

Primary
function: heating water for coffee in Chanal and for heating water for coffee, corn gruels (*pozol* and *atole*) in Aguacatenango; occasionally used for boiling other vegetables or mixing lime water. Slipped vessels used to serve cold liquids.

Comments: glazed vessels are often decorated on the upper body and glazed on the exterior (except for the base and underside of handle); unslipped vessels have a calcite temper; often crudely formed body; normally partially burnished; occasionally coiling rings are visible on the exterior of the vessel. Slipped vessels have a white slip; sand and calcite temper; body and neck decoration; floral or geometrical designs.

9 LARGE PERFORATED JAR:

Ware classes: Amatenango slipped, Aguacatenango slipped, Chanal unslipped.

Emic
terminology: Chanal term is *chixnajab'il*; in Aguacatenango *chichina* (Spanish *pichacha*).

Sample size: Chanal 3 unslipped; Aguacatenango 96 slipped.

Shape: ovaloid (with maximum width above center) or elliptical (vertical axis) body shape; neck divergent; rim thickness indeterminate; flat, perforated base; perforated body.

Size: height range 20–33 cm, width range 25–29 cm, rim diameter range 18.5–22 cm.

Fig. B16. 9. Large perforated jar *(chixnajab'l)*, ovaloid body shape, Amatenango slipped.

Primary
function: straining corn kernels and limewater mixture.

Comments: calcite tempered; red to red-orange slip; burnished body; perforations with incised circle around each (made with a large U-shaped fence nail); plainware vessel perforations are made with a metal spike or twig; bodies are often crudely formed.

WATERCARRYING AND STORAGE: TYPE 10; FIGURE B17

10 NARROW-MOUTH JAR:

Fig. B17. 10. Narrow-mouth jar *(kib)*, ovaloid body shape, Amatenango slipped (left) and Yocnajab slipped (right), at Comitan pottery shop.

Ware classes: Amatenango slipped, Aguacatenango slipped.

Emic terminology: *kib* (Spanish *cantaro*), and *buruxi-kib* (jar without handles; Chanal term only)

Sample size: Chanal 343; Aguacatenango 389.

Shape: body shape ovaloid (with the maximum body width below the center of the vessel) or elliptical; divergent neck; rim thickness is exterior, medial, abrupt; generally three horizontal handles (five have two handles, two have one handle, and four have no handles).

Size: height range 3–54 cm, width range 7–43 cm, rim diameter range 3–14 cm.

Primary function: two three-handle vessels is a watercarrying and water storage jar; one handle and handless forms are storage vessels for dry goods; miniature forms are children's toys.

Comments: tempered with a fine-grained dolomite sand (Heyman 1960:1); thick base; uniform wall thickness, red to red-orange or white slip; upper body, handle, and neck decoration; occasionally embossed design; painted designs of flowers and occasionally roosters; burnished exterior.

RITUAL VESSELS: TYPES 11–19; FIGURES B18–29

11 LARGE HEMISPHERICAL BOWL:

Fig. B18. 11a. Large hemispherical bowl *(poket grande)*, ovaloid body shape, Chanal unslipped.

Fig. B19. 11b. Large hemispherical bowl *(poket grande)*, spherical body shape, Amatenango slipped.

Ware classes:	Amatenango slipped, Amatenango unslipped, Chanal unslipped, San Pedro unslipped.
Emic terminology:	*poket grande* (Spanish *apastli grande*).
Sample size:	Chanal 19 slipped, 30 unslipped; Aguacatenango 56 slipped, 54 unslipped.
Shape:	ovaloid (with maximum width above center of vessel) and occasionally spherical body shape; rim thickness, exterior, medial, abrupt for slipped vessels and indeterminate for unslipped vessels; flat base; thick base and vessel walls; basal trim common on unslipped vessels.
Size:	slipped vessels have a height range of 18–41 cm, rim diameter range of 29–47 cm, and a volume range of approximately 8000–41,494 cubic cm; unslipped vessels have a height range of 17–46 cm, rim diameter range of 22–49 cm, and a volume range of approximately 6653–48,556 cubic cm.
Primary function:	ritual beer *(chicha)* mixing bowl.
Comments:	calcite temper; red to red-orange slip and exterior and interior burnishing on Amatenango slipped vessels; unslipped vessels are often crudely formed.

12 SMALL UNRESTRICTED BOWL:

Ware classes:	Chiapa de Corzo glazed, Mexican glazed.
Emic terminology:	*borcelana* (Spanish *porcelana* or *cajete*).
Sample size:	Chanal 291, Aguacatenango 406.
Shape:	ovaloid (with maximum width above center) body shape; rim thickness indeterminate; flat or slightly ringed base, unrestricted orifice.

Fig. B20. 12. Small restricted bowl *(borcelana)*, ovaloid body shape, Mexican glazed.

Size: height 4–13.5 cm; rim diameter 7–23 cm.

Primary

function: ritual serving and general utility.

Comments: Chiapa de Corzo glazed bowls have interior and exterior (except for base) glaze; decoration on interior; floral designs. Mexican glazed bowls (probably representing various workshops in Central Mexico) are highly vitrified; interior (except base) glaze; undecorated.

13 SINGLE-HANDLE BOWL:

Ware classes: Chanal unslipped.

Emic

terminology: *neochab* (no Spanish term).

Sample size: Chanal 9; Aguacatenango none.

Shape: three have ovaloid (with maximum width above center of vessel) body shape; three have an elliptical (vertical axis) body shape; two have a frustrum body shape and one has a spherical body

Fig. B21. 13. Single-handled cup *(neochab)*, ovaloid body shape, Chanal unslipped.

shape; rim thickness indeterminate; flat base; single vertical handle.

Size: height range 8–17.5 cm, rim diameter range 12.5–19 cm.

Primary

function: making beeswax candles for a single festival.

Comments: calcite temper; some are crudely formed; made on order by Chanal potters for one specific occasion and kept by the family as an heirloom.

14 PEDESTAL-BASED BOWL:

Ware classes: Amatenango slipped, Aguacatenango slipped, Chanal unslipped, San Pedro unslipped, Tzajala unslipped and Yocnajab unslipped.

Fig. B22. 14. Pedestal-based bowl *(chik'pom)*, ovaloid bowl shape, Chanal unslipped.

Emic

terminology: Chanal term *chik'pom* and Aguacatenango term *akolbil* (Spanish *incensario*, and less frequently *bracero*).

Sample size: Chanal 7 slipped, 101 unslipped; Aguacatenango 57 slipped, 1 unslipped.

Shape: slipped vessels have an ovaloid (with maximum width below center) shaped bowl; hollow pedestal base; three nodes spaced equidistantly around rim; rim thickness indeterminate; unslipped vessels have an ovaloid (with maximum width below center) or spherical bowl shape; solid or partially hollow base; rim thickness indeterminate; orifice unrestricted.

Size: height range 6–22.5 cm, bowl diameter range 5.5–18 cm, basal diameter 3.5–17 cm.

Primary
function: receptacle for offering incense (see Deal 1982).

Comments: slipped vessels have sand temper; red to red-orange or white slip; decoration on bowl exterior and base; floral design; burnishing on bowl; one vessel had a frustrum shaped bowl and flat tipped nodes; unslipped vessels had calcite temper; interior fire-blackening; often crudely formed.

15 PEDESTAL CYLINDER:

Fig. B23. 15a. Pedestal cylinder *(somjebal cantela)*, small cylinder body and trumpet base, Chanal unslipped.

Fig. B24. 15b. Pedestal cylinder *(somjebal cantela)*, hyperboloid body shape, Chanal unslipped.

Ware classes: Amatenango slipped, Aguacatenango unslipped, Chanal unslipped.

Emic
terminology: *somjebal cantela* or *yahuil cantela* (Spanish *candelero*).

Sample size: Chanal 1 slipped, 20 unslipped; Aguacatenango 1 slipped, 2 unslipped.

Shape: small cylindrical body with trumpet-like base; sometimes resembles a hyperboloid; hollow body to base; slightly hollow or flat solid base; rim thickness indeterminate.

Size: height range 4.5–17.5 cm, rim diameter range 3–5.1 cm, and basal diameter 5.15 cm.

Primary
function: candleholder.

Comments: slipped forms have a white slip; sand and calcite temper; body decoration; floral and geometrical designs; unslipped forms have calcite temper; often crudely formed.

Fig. B25. 16a. Large wide-mouth jar *(oxom grande)*, ellipsoid body shape, Chanal unslipped.

Fig. B26. 16b. Large wide-mouth jar *(oxom grande)*, ovaloid body shape, Chanal unslipped.

Ware classes: Amatenango unslipped, Aguacatenango unslipped, Chanal unslipped, San Pedro unslipped, San Augustine unslipped, Siberia unslipped, Yola unslipped, San Antonio unslipped, San Fernando unslipped, San Jose unslipped.

Emic terminology: *oxom grande* in Chanal and *pin grande* in Aguacatenango (Spanish *olla grande*).

Sample size: Chanal 200; Aguacatenango 81.

Shape: elliptical (vertical axis) or ovaloid (with maximum width above the center of the body) body shape; divergent neck; rim thickness is indeterminate or exterior, medial, abrupt; flat base.

Size: height range of 43–81 cm, width range of 23–58 cm, and rim diameter range of 18–37 cm.

Primary function: cooking meals for large groups of people (generally ritual gatherings), and for storage of dry goods between gatherings.

Comments: tempered with relatively coarse-grained calcite; vessel walls and base are thick; often crudely formed body; normally partially burnished on exterior; occasionally coiling rings are visible on exterior.

17 LARGE COMPOSITE JAR:

Ware classes: Amatenango slipped, Aguacatenango slipped.

Emic terminology: *tenosha grande* in Chanal and *mucuc tencha* in Aguacate-nango (Spanish *tinaja grande*).

Sample size: Chanal 14; Aguacate-nango 64.

Shape: ovaloid (maximum width above the center) body shape; divergent neck; rim thickness exterior, medial, abrupt; 1 vessel has 3 handles; unrestricted orifice.

Size: height range 26–73 cm, width range 32–52 cm, and rim diameter range 20–50 cm.

Primary function: fermentation of corn beer *(chicha)* for festivals and the storage of dry goods between festivals.

Fig. B27. 17. Large composite jar *(tenosha grande)*, ovaloid body shape, Amatenango slipped.

Comments: temper consists of fine-grained sand and calcite; vessel walls and base are thick; red to red-orange or white slip; upper body and neck decoration; floral designs most common; occasionally embossed design; burnished on exterior.

18 SMALL PERFORATED JAR:

Fig. B28. 18a. Small perforated jar *(chixnajab'il)*, ellipsoid body shape, Chanal unslipped.

Fig. B29. 18b. Small perforated jar *(chixnajab'il)*, ovaloid body shape, Chanal unslipped.

Ware classes: Amatenango slipped, Chanal unslipped, Aguacatenango unslipped.

Emic terminology: Chanal term is *chixnajab'il*; Aguacatenango term is *chichina* (Spanish *pichacha*).

Sample size: Chanal 10 slipped, 31 unslipped; Aguacatenango 36 slipped and 1 unslipped.

Shape: slipped vessels have an ovaloid (with maximum width above the center of the

193

vessel) or spherical body shape; unslipped vessels are usually elliptical (vertical axis) in body shape; neck divergent; rim thickness is indeterminate; flat, perforated base, perforated body from base to neck; 4 have handles.

Size: height range 10–21 cm, width range 10.5–17 cm, and rim diameter range 8–16.5 cm.

Primary
function: straining corn gruel *(atole)* on ritual occasions.

Comments: calcite temper; red to red-orange slip; a U-shaped fence nail is used to make the perforations and an incised circle around each perforation (on slipped vessels only); perforations on unslipped vessels are made with a small straight nail or twig; slipped vessels are burnished on exterior; unslipped vessels are often crudely formed.

19 PEDESTAL JAR:

Ware classes: Amatenango slipped; Aguacatenango slipped and unslipped.

Emic
terminology: *yahuil nichim* (Spanish *florero*).

Sample size: Chanal 10; Aguacatenango 12.

Shape: ovaloid (with maximum width below center of vessel) body shape; divergent neck; rim thickness exterior, medial, abrupt; filleted (piecrust) rim common; hollow pedestal base; vertical opposed lugs common; one vessel had a single vertical handle.

Size: height range 5–23 cm, width range 4.5–19 cm, and rim diameter range 2.7–16.8 cm.

Primary
function: receptacle for ritual offering of flowers.

Comments: fine-grained sand and calcite temper; red to red-orange or white slip; burnishing on exterior neck and body; decorated on all of exterior; interior of bowl and pedestal base not slipped; floral and geometrical designs; opposed lugs have one or two perforations.

SPINNING; FIGURE B30

20 WHORL:

Ware classes: Chanal unslipped.

Emic
terminology: *pe'tet* (Spanish *malacate*).

Sample size: Chanal 62; Agua-catenango 3 (unknown origin).

Shape: segmented ovaloid (width below center) and frustrum solid, with base of frustrum joining the truncation of the ovaloid; perforation through the center of the object (from frustrum truncation to curvature of ovaloid); coils on frustrum exterior.

Fig. B30. 20. Whorl *(pe'tet)*, segmented ovaloid, Chanal unslipped.

Primary
function: flywheel for spindle (spindle-whorl).

Comments: calcite temper; perforation made with a nail or twig. Whorls sold in San Cristóbal de las Casas pottery shops were made in Oxchuc, so the three Agua-catenango whorls may have been made in that community.

TOURIST TRADE, TYPES 21–29; FIGURES B31–37

21 TRIPOD BOWLS:

Ware classes: San Ramon glazed.

Emic
terminology: use Spanish *molcajete* and *majador*.

Sample size: Chanal 1; Aguaca-tenango 1.

Shape: body shape; filleted (piecrust) rim; rim thickness exterior, medial, abrupt, interior coils;

Fig. B31. 21. Tripod bowl *(molcajete/majador)*, spherical body shape, San Ramon glazed.

round base; three equidistantly placed legs; rim thickness indeterminate; round base.

Size: height range 4.5–8.4 cm, and rim diameter range of 8–16 cm.

Primary
function: mortar and pestle for grinding chile peppers.
Comments: glazed vessels have an interior and exterior glaze; no decoration; a pestle con-
                   sisting of a solid bar with a disk at one end accompanies each bowl; the bar
                   section and upper part of disk are glazed, while the base of the neck is coiled,
                   flat, and unglazed.

22 EFFIGY VESSEL:

Ware classes: Amatenango slipped.
Emic
terminology: use Spanish *alcancia*.
Sample size: Chanal 4; Aguacatenango 5.
Shape: hollow elliptical (horizontal axis) body
                  shape; pig effigy; four legs; slot for inserting
                  money.
Size: height range 10–14 cm, width range
                  12–16 cm.

Primary   Fig. B32. 22. Effigy vessel *(alcan-*
function: child's money bank.   *cia)*, ellipsoid body shape, Amate-
Comments: calcite and sand temper; white slip;   nango slipped.
                  decorated on exterior with features of a pig;
                  burnished on exterior.

23 FIGURINE:

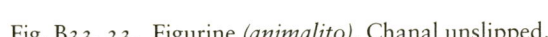

Ware classes: Mexican glazed,
                  Amatenango slipped,
                  Chanal unslipped.
Emic
terminology: use Spanish *animalito*
                  or *estatuilla*.
Sample size: Chanal 3 glazed,
                  2 unslipped; Aguaca-
                  tenango 6 glazed,
                  4 slipped.
Shape: anthropomorphic or
                  zoomorphic shaped;
                  both unslipped forms   Fig. B33. 23. Figurine *(animalito)*, Chanal unslipped.
                  have two shallow
                  depressions on back of zoomorphic figure.
Size: height range 10–21 cm.
Primary
function: glazed forms are Christian icons, slipped forms are children's toys and
                  unslipped forms are candleholders.
Comments: glazed forms are probably from various sources in Central Mexico; unslipped
                  figurines are calcite tempered and crudely formed; slipped forms have red to
                  red-orange or white slip and the features of animals are painted on.

24 SMALL COMPOSITE JAR:

Ware classes: Amatenango slipped, Aguacatenango slipped.

Emic
terminology: *tenosha* in Chanal and *tencha* in
Aguacatenango (Spanish *tinaja*).

Sample size: Chanal 10, Aguacatenango 10.

Shape: ovaloid (with maximum width
above the center) body shape; divergent neck; rim thickness is exterior,
medial, abrupt; one vessel has two
vertical handles.

Size: height range 9–25 cm, width range
7–31 cm, and rim diameter range
6.5–16.5 cm.

Primary
function: wet and dry storage.

Fig. B34. 24. Small composite jar *(tenosha)*, ovaloid body shape, Amate-nango slipped.

Comments: temper consists of sand and calcite;
bases are thick relative to vessel
walls; red to red-orange or white
slip; upper body and neck decoration; occasionally embossed; flower designs
predominate; burnished exterior.

25 FLARING-MOUTH DISH:

Ware classes: Amatenango slipped.

Emic
terminology: use Spanish *cenicero*.

Sample size: Chanal none; Aguacatenango 1.

Shape: elliptical (horizontal axis) body shape; slight ring base; burnished interior and
exterior; thick base; rim indeterminate.

Size: height 9 cm, rim diameter 16.5 cm.

Primary
function: serving vessel?

Comments: sand and calcite temper; red-orange slip.

26 SINGLE-HANDLE CUP:

Ware classes: San Ramon glazed, Mexican glazed, Amatenango slipped, Chanal unslipped.

Emic
terminology: *basso* (Spanish *vasso*).

Sample size: Chanal 4 glazed, 2 unslipped; Aguacatenango 12 glazed, 3 slipped.

Shape: ovaloid (with maximum width below center) body shape; rim indeterminate;
flat- or low-ring vase; single vertical handle.

Size: height range 2–9.5 cm, rim diameter range 6.5–9 cm.

Primary
function: serving hot liquids.

Comments: Mexican glazed vessels are highly vitrified and probably represent various
workshops in Central Mexico (one vessel had HECHO EN MEXICO on base);

thin transparent glaze with no decoration; San Ramon glazed vessels have an exterior glaze (except for base and under handle); upper body and neck decoration; floral designs; slipped vessels have sand temper, red to red-orange or white slip; burnished exterior; floral designs; unslipped vessels have calcite temper; often very crudely formed.

27 WIDE-MOUTH VASE:

Ware classes:	Amatenango slipped, Chanal unslipped, Aguacatenango unslipped.
Emic terminology:	use Spanish *maceta*.
Sample size:	Chanal 4; Aguacatenango 16.
Shape:	ovaloid (with maximum width below center) body shape; thick base; uniform wall thickness; rim thickness indeterminate; two have flat bases; 18 have round bases and three equidistant legs.
Size:	height range 6.5–30.5 cm, rim diameter 7.5–31 cm.
Primary function:	flowerpot (for young seedlings).
Comments:	calcite temper; crudely formed body; slipped form has sand and calcite temper; white slip; shoulder to rim decoration; floral designs.

Fig. B35. 27. Wide-mouth vase *(maceta)*, ovaloid body shape, Chanal unslipped.

28 LOOP-HANDLE BOWL:

Ware classes:	Amatenango slipped.
Emic terminology:	*mochelum* (Spanish *canasta*).
Sample size:	Chanal none; Aguacatenango 2.
Shape:	elliptical (horizontal axis) body shape; filleted (piecrust) rim; flat base; single loop handle.
Size:	height range 7–11 cm, width for both examples 16 cm, rim diameter for both 13 cm.
Primary function:	unknown.
Comments:	sand and calcite temper; red to red-orange slip; burnished interior; thick base; uniform wall thickness.

Fig. B36. 28. Loop-handled bowl *(mochelum)*, ellipsoid body shape, Amatenango slipped.

29 INCURVING RIM BOWL:

Ware classes: Aguacatenango slipped.
Emic terminology: *poket* (Spanish *batea*).
Sample size: Chanal none; Aguacatenango 1.
Shape: elliptical (horizontal axis) body shape; slightly incurving rim; rim thickness indeterminate; flat base.

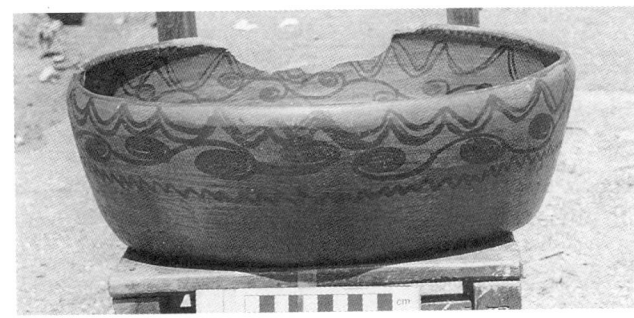

Fig. B37. 29. Incurving-rim bowl *(poket)*, ellipsoid body shape, Aquacatenango slipped.

Size: height 12 cm, maximum rim diameter 32 cm.
Primary function: general utility or washing clothes.
Comments: sand and calcite temper; decoration on interior rim and base, and exterior rim; red-orange slip; floral and geometrical designs.

OBSOLETE FORMS, TYPES 30–31; FIGURES B38–39

30 CYLINDRICAL JAR:

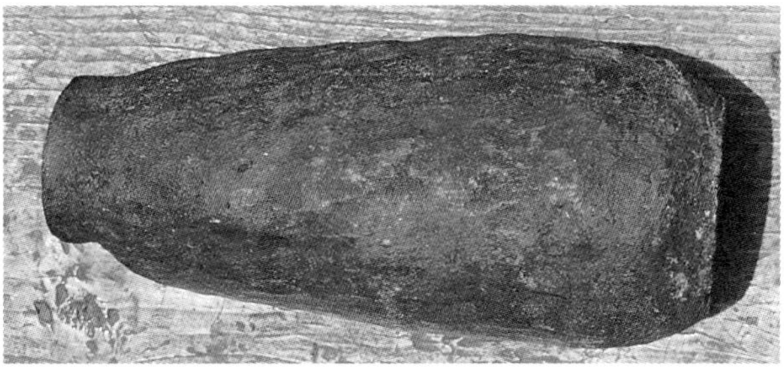

Ware classes: Chanal unslipped
Emic terminology: *balal oxom* (Spanish *olla* or *tecomate*).
Sample size: Chanal 3; Aguacatenango none.
Shape: cylindrical to ovaloid (with maximum width below center) body shape; narrow mouth; rim thickness indeterminate; flat vase; basal ridge.

Fig. B38. 30. Cylinder jar *(balal oxom)*, ovaloid body shape, Chanal unslipped.

Primary function: temporary storage of coffee, limes or tobacco-lime mixture *(peligo)*.
Comments: calcite temper; crudely formed body; no longer made. All examples recorded were heirlooms.

31 PEDESTAL VASE:

Ware classes: Amatenango slipped.

Emic
terminology: *chinpin* (Spanish *jarra*).

Sample size: Chanal none; Aguacatenango 5.

Shape: spherical body shape; rim thickness indeterminate; hollow pedestal base; one vertical handle.

Size: height range 6–18 cm, width range 13–15 cm, rim diameter range 9–11 cm, basal diameter 6–11 cm.

Primary
function: support for serving bowls and storage of dry goods.

Comments: calcite and sand temper; red to red-orange slip; decoration on body; floral and geometrical designs; burnished designs.

Fig. B39. 31. Pedestal vase *(chinpin)*, spherical body shape, Amatenango slipped.

Fig. B40. Long-necked jar, with orange slip, believed to be of Precolumbian origin.

Fig. B41. Large composite jar of unknown origin.

PRECOLUMBIAN FORMS

Three complete vessels and two slipped potsherds were recorded in Chanal and Aguacatenango that do not seem to have originated from any known pottery sources. The two potsherds were stored with fragments of human bone on a family altar in Chanal. They are probably of Precolumbian origin since the household head claimed to have found them in one of the sacred caves in the nearby hills. These caves are the homes of ancestral spirits, known as the *poco winic.*

Two other vessels of unknown origin (Figure B40–41) are a long neck jar form with an orange slip and elliptical (horizontal axis) body shape (height 23 cm, width 19 cm, and rim diameter 5.5 cm), and a large composite jar with reddish-brown slip, elliptical (vertical axis) body shape, straight neck, and exterior, medial, abrupt rim thickness (height 56 cm, width 42 cm, and rim diameter 24 cm). Our informants in Chanal claimed that both forms were made in the pottery center of Tenango (Tenam). The relative fine quality of both vessels suggests that this is unlikely. The former may be of Precolumbian origin.

A large orange slipped, tripod bowl with an elliptical (horizontal axis) body shape was recorded in an Aguacatenango household, and has since been acquired by the New World Archaeological Foundation, San Cristóbal de las Casas (Figure 5.7). Although the owners of the vessel claimed that they had purchased it in San Cristóbal de las Casas, it is obviously of Precolumbian origin. The modern community of Aguacatenango is situated on a Postclassic settlement, and this vessel may have been found within the community, or it may have been obtained from the nearby Classic-period site of Yerba Buena.

References

Adams, R. M.

1961 Changing Patterns of Territorial Organization in the Central Highlands of Chiapas, Mexico. *American Antiquity* 26(3):341–360.

Adams, W. R.

1988 Religious Practices of Southeastern Chiapas and Tzeltal-Tojolabal Interaction. In *The Linguistics of Southeast Chiapas,* by L. Campbell, pp. 183–198. Papers of the New World Archaeological Foundation, No. 50. Brigham Young University, Provo.

Albores Z., B. A.

1978 *El Funcionalismo en la Etnografía Tzeltal-Tzotzil: Un Analisis de Sus Implicaciones Teoricas y Politicas.* Universidad Autónoma de Chiapas, Tuxtla Gutierrez.

Arnold, D. E.

1971 Ethnomineralogy of Ticul: Yucatan Potters. *American Antiquity* 36(1): 20–40.

1976 Ecological Variables and Ceramic Production: Towards a General Model. In *Primitive Art and Technology,* edited by J. S. Raymond, B. Loveseth, C. Arnold, and G. Reardon, pp. 92–108. University of Calgary Archaeological Association.

1978a Ceramic Variability, Environment, and Culture History Among the Pokom in the Valley of Guatemala. In *Spatial Organization of Culture,* edited by I. Hodder, pp. 39–60. University of Pittsburgh Press.

1978b Ethnography of Pottery Making in the Valley of Guatemala. In *The Ceramics of Kaminaljuyu,* edited by R. K. Wetherington, pp. 327–400. Pennsylvania State University Press, University Park.

1980 Localized Exchange: An Ethnoarchaeological Perspective. In *Models and Methods in Regional Exchange,* edited by R. E. Fry, pp. 147–150. Society for American Archaeology, Papers, No. 1.

1984 The Ethnoarchaeology of Pottery Production. *Reviews in Anthropology* 11(1):12–19.

1985 *Ceramic Theory and Cultural Process.* Cambridge University Press.

1987 Maya Pottery after 20 Years: Archaeological Implications. In *Maya Ceramics: Papers from the 1985 Maya Ceramics Conference,* edited by P. M. Rice and R. J. Sharer, pp. 545–561. BAR International Series 345(i), Oxford.

1993 *Ecology and Ceramic Production in an Andean Community.* Cambridge University Press.

Arnold, D. E., H. Neff, and R. L. Bishop

1991 Compositional Analyses and "Sources" of Pottery: An Ethnoarchaeological Approach. *American Anthropologist* 93:70–90.

Arnold, D. E., and A. L. Nieves

1992 Factors Affecting Ceramic Standardization. In *Ceramic Production and Distribution: An Integrated*

Approach, edited by G. J. Bey III, and C. A. Pool, pp. 93–113. Westview Press, Boulder.

Arnold, P. J., III
1988   Household Ceramic Assemblage Attributes in the Sierra de los Tuxtlas, Veracruz, Mexico. *Journal of Anthropological Archaeology* 44(4): 357–383.
1990   The Organization of Refuse Disposal and Ceramic Production within Contemporary Mexican Households. *American Anthropologist* 92:915–932.
1991a *Domestic Ceramic Production and Spatial Organization: A Mexican Case Study in Ethnoarchaeology.* Cambridge University Press.
1991b Dimensional Standardization and Production Scale in Mesoamerican Ceramics. *Latin American Antiquity* 2(4):363–370.

Arnold, P. J., III, C. A. Pool, R. R. Kneebone, and R. S. Santley
1993   Intensive Ceramic Production and Classic-Period Political Economy in the Sierra de los Tuxtlas, Veracruz, Mexico. *Ancient Mesoamerica* 4:175–191.

Arnold, P. J., III, and R. S. Santley
1993   Household Ceramics Production at Middle Classic Period Matacapan. In *Prehispanic Domestic Units in Western Mesoamerica: Studies of the Household, Compound and Residence,* edited by R. S. Santley, and K. G. Hirth, pp. 227–248. CRC Press, Ann Arbor.

Ascher, R.
1977   Time's Arrow and the Archaeology of a Contemporary Community. In *Experimental Archaeology,* edited by D. Ingersoll, J. E. Yellen, and W. MacDonald, pp. 228–240. Columbia University Press, New York.

Baer, P., and M. Baer
1950   *Materials on Lacandon Culture of the Petha (Pelha) Region.* University of Chicago, Microfilm Collection, Manuscripts on Cultural Anthropology, Series 6, No. 34, Chicago.

Baer, P., and W. R. Merrifield
1971   *Two Studies on the Lacandones of Mexico.* Summer Institute of Linguistics of the University of Oklahoma, Norman.

Baerreis, D.
1961   The Ethnohistoric Approach and Archaeology. *Ethnohistory* 8:49–77.

Baker, C. M.
1975   Site Abandonment and the Archaeological Record: An Empirical Case for Anticipated Return. *Proceedings of the Arkansas Academy of Science* 29:10–11.

Balkansky, A. K., G. M. Feinman, and L. M. Nichols
1997   Pottery Kilns of Ancient Ejutla, Oaxaca, Mexico. *Journal of Field Archaeology* 24(2):139–160.

Balfet, H.
1965   Ethnological Observations in North Africa and Archaeological Interpretation: the Pottery of the Magreb. In *Ceramics and Man,* edited by F. R. Matson, pp. 161–177. Aldine, Chicago.

Ball, J. W.
1977   Review of *Prehistoric Pottery Analysis and Ceramics of Barton Ramie in the Belize Valley,* by J. E. Gifford. *American Antiquity* 42(4):661–664.

Barba, L., and A. Ortiz
1992   Analisis Quimico de Pisos de Ocupacion: un Caso Etnografico en Tlaxcala, Mexico. *Latin American Antiquity* 3(1):63–82.

Barker, P.
1977   *Techniques of Archaeological Excavation.* Universe Books, New York.

Basauri, C.
1931   *Tojolabales, Tzeltales y Mayas: Breves Apuntes Sobre Antropologica, Etnografia y Lingüistica.* Talleres Graficos de la Nacion, Mexico.

Baumhoff, M. A., and R. F. Heizer
1959   Some Unexploited Possibilities in Ceramic Analysis. *Southwestern Journal of Anthropology* 15(3): 308–316.

Bawden, G.
1982   Community Organization Reflected by the Household: A Study of Pre-Columbian Social Dynamics. *Journal of Field Archaeology* 9:165–182.

Beale, T. W., and P. F. Healy
1975   Archaeological Films: The Past as

Present. *American Anthropologist* 77:889–897.

Beaudry-Corbett, M.

1992 From Artifact Assemblage to House-hold Inventory: The Material Remains of the Cerén Site. Paper presented at the Annual Meeting of the Society for American Archaeology, Pittsburgh.

Becker, M. J.

1973 Archaeological Evidence for Occupational Specialization Among the Classic Maya at Tikal, Guatemala. *American Antiquity* 38(4):396–406.

Becquelin, P.

1973 Ethnologie et Archéologie dans l'Aire Maya: Analogies et Évolution Culturelle. *Journal de la Société des Américanistes* n.s. 62: 43–55.

Becquelin, P., and C. Baudez

1979 *Tonina, une Cité Maya du Chiapas (Mexique)*. Etudes Mesoamericaines, vol. 6, Tome 1. Mission Archeologique et ethnologique Française au Mexique, Mexico.

Bedaux, R.

1987 Aspects of Life-span on Dogon Pottery. In *A Knapsack Full of Pottery: Archaeo-ceramological Miscellanea Dedicated to H. H. Franken.* Newsletter of the Department of Pottery Technology 5:137–153. University of Leiden, The Netherlands.

Berlin, B., D. E.. Breedlowe, and P. H. Raven

1974 *Principles of Tzeltal Plant Classification*. Academic Press, New York.

Binford, L. R.

1962 Archaeology as Anthropology. *American Antiquity* 28(2):217–225.

1964 A Consideration of Archaeological Research Design. *American Antiquity* 29:425–441.

1965 Archaeological Systematics and the Study of Culture Process. *American Antiquity* 31:203–210.

1968 Methodological Considerations of the Archaeological Use of Ethnographic Data. In *Man the Hunter,* edited by R. B. Lee, and I. DeVore, pp. 268–273. Aldine, Chicago.

1977 General Introduction. In *For Theory Building in Archaeology,* edited by

L. R. Binford, pp. 1–13. Academic Press, New York.

1978 Dimensional Analysis of Behaviour and Site Structure: Learning from an Eskimo Hunting Stand. *American Antiquity* 43(3):330–361.

1983 *In Pursuit of the Past: Decoding the Archaeological Record*. Thames and Hudson, London.

Bishop, R. L.

1980 Aspects of Ceramic Compositional Modeling. In *Models and Methods in Regional Exchange,* edited by R. E. Fry, pp. 47–65. SAA Papers No. 1. Society for American Archaeology, Washington, D.C.

Bishop, R. L., R. L. Hands, and G. R. Holley

1982 Ceramic Compositional Analysis in Archaeological Perspective. In *Advances in Archaeological Method and Theory, Vol. 5,* edited by M. B. Schiffer, pp. 275–330. Academic Press, New York.

Blackman, M. J., G. J. Stein, and P. B. Vandiver

1993 The Standardization Hypothesis and Ceramic Mass Production: Technological, Compositional, and Metric Indexes of Craft Specialization at Tell Leillan, Syria. *American Antiquity* 58(1):60–80.

Blake, M.

1988 House Features and Social Processes in a Modern Maya Community. In *Ethnoarchaeology Among the Highland Maya of Chiapas, Mexico,* edited by T. A. Lee, and B. Hayden, pp. 45–60. Papers of the New World Archaeological Foundation, No. 56. Brigham Young University, Provo.

Blake, M., and S. Blake

1979 Coxoh Ethnoarchaeological Project 1978 – Community Assessment for Future Intensive Investigation. Ms on file, Department of Archaeology, Simon Fraser University, Burnaby, B.C.

Blake, S.

1988 House Materials, Environment and Ethnicity in Southeastern Chiapas, Mexico. In *Ethnoarchaeology Among the Highland Maya of Chiapas, Mexico,* edited by T. A. Lee, and B. Hayden, pp. 21–37. Papers of the New World Archaeological

Foundation, No. 56. Brigham Young University, Provo.

Blake, S., and M. Blake
1988 Regional Study of Household Features in Modern Maya Communities. In *Ethnoarchaeology Among the Highland Maya of Chiapas, Mexico,* edited by T. A. Lee, and B. Hayden, pp. 39–43. Papers of the New World Archaeological Foundation, No. 56. Brigham Young University, Provo.

Blalock, H. H.
1972 *Social Statistics.* 2nd ed. McGraw-Hill, New York.

Blom, F.
1954 Ossuaries, Cremation, and Secondary Burials Among the Maya of Chiapas, Mexico. *Journal de la Société des Américanists, n.s.* 43: 123–136. Paris.

Blom, F., and O. LaFarge
1927 *Tribes and Temples. A Record of the Expedition to Middle America Conducted by the Tulane University of Louisiana in 1925.* 2 vols. Tulane University, Middle American Research Series, Publication No. 1. New Orleans.

Bogucki, P. I., and R. Grygiel
1981 The Household Cluster at Brzesc Kujawski 3: Small-site Methodology in the Polish Lowlands. *World Archaeology* 13(1):59–72.

Bollong, C. A.
1994 Analysis of Site Stratigraphy and Formation Processes Using Patterns of Pottery Sherd Dispersion. *Journal of Field Archaeology* 21:15–28.

Bonnichsen, R.
1973 Mille's Camp: An Experiment in Archaeology. *World Archaeology* 4:277–291.

Bordez, J.
1964 *Pre-Columbian Ceramic Kilns at Penitas, a Post-Classic Site in Coastal Nayarit, Mexico.* Ph.D. dissertation, Columbia University, New York.

De Borhegyi, S. F.
1959 The Composite or Assemble-it-yourself Censer: a New Lowland Variety of Three-pronged Incense Burner. *American Antiquity* 25(1):51–58.

Bradley, R., and M. Fulford
1980 Sherd Size in the Analysis of Occupational Debris. *University of London, Institute of Archaeology, Bulletin* 17:85–94.

Braun, D. P.
1980 Experimental Interpretation of Ceramic Vessel Use on the Basis of Rim and Neck Formal Attributes. In *The Navajo Project,* by D. Fiero, R. W. Munson, M. T. McClach, S. M. Wislon, and A. H. Zier, pp. 171–223. Museum of Northern Arizona, Research Papers 11. Flagstaff.
1982 Radiographic Analysis of Temper in Ceramic Vessels: Goals and Initial Models. *Journal of Field Archaeology* 9:183–191.
1983 Pots as Tools. In *Archaeological Hammers and Theories,* edited by J. A. Moore, and A. S. Keene, pp. 107–134. Academic Press, New York.

Bray, A.
1982 Mimbres Black-on-white, Melamine or Wedgewood? A Ceramic Use-wear Analysis. *The Kiva* 47: 133–149.

Bray, W., and D. Trump
1970 *The Penguin Dictionary of Archaeology.* Penguin, Middlesex.

Breton, A.
1973 Groupes, Groupements et Structures de l'Habitat Chez les Indiens Tzeltal de Bachajón, Chiapas (Mexique). *Journal de la Société des Américanistes, n. s.* 62:57–87.

Brockington, D. L.
1967 *Santa Rosa Ceramic History.* Papers of the New World Archaeological Foundation 23. Brigham Young University, Provo.

Brose, D. S.
1970 *The Archaeology of Summer Island: Changing Settlement Systems in Northern Lake Michigan.* University of Michigan, Museum of Anthropology, Anthropological Papers, No. 41. Ann Arbor.

Brown, J. A.
1982 On the Structure of Artifact Typolo-

gies. In *Essays on Archaeological Typology*, edited by R. Whallon, and J. A. Brown, pp. 176–189. Center for American Archaeology Press. Evanston, Illinois.

Brulotte, R.
1979   Untitled Manuscript Concerning Two Recently Abandoned House-sites in Aguacatenango, Chiapas, Mexico. Ms. on file, Department of Archaeology, Simon Fraser University, Burnaby.

Bryant, D. D.
1988   *Excavations at House 1, Yerba Buena, Chiapas Central Highlands, Mexico.* Papers of the New World Archaeological Foundation, No. 54. Brigham Young University, Provo.

Bryant, D. D., and M. J. Brody
1986   Modern and Prehistoric Maya Pottery Manufacture. *Ceramica de Cultura Maya et al.* (14):73–86.

Bryant, D. D., and J. E. Clark
1979   The Late Classic Community of Guajilar. Paper presented at the 63rd International Congress of Americanists, Vancouver.

Burgh, R. F.
1959   Ceramic Profiles in the Western Mound at Awatovi, Northeastern Arizona. *American Antiquity* 25(2):184–202.

Butzer, K. W.
1982   *Archaeology as Human Ecology.* Cambridge University Press, New York.

Calder, A. M.
1972   *Cracked Pots and Rubbish Tips: An Ethnoarchaeological Investigation of Vessel and Sherd Distribution in a Thai-Lao Village.* M.A. thesis, Department of Anthropology, University of Otago, Dunedin, New Zealand.

Calnek, E. E.
1959   Chanal: a Summary. In *Report on the Man-in-Nature Project of the Department of Anthropology of the University of Chicago in the Tzeltal-Tzotzil Speaking Region of the State of Chiapas, Mexico,* edited by N. A. McQuown. University of Chicago, Microfilm Collection, Manuscripts

on American Indian Cultural Anthropology, Series 14, Pt. 2, No. 12.
1962   *Highland Chiapas Before the Spanish Conquest.* Unpublished Ph.D. dissertation, Department of Anthropology, University of Chicago.
1988   *Highland Chiapas Before the Spanish Conquest.* Papers of the New World Archaeological Foundation, No. 55. Brigham Young University, Provo.

Cameron, C. M.
1991   Structure Abandonment in Villages. *Archaeological Method and Theory* 3:155–194.
1993   Abandonment and Archaeological Interpretation. In *Abandonment of Settlements and Regions: Ethnoarchaeological and Archaeological Approaches,* edited by C. M. Cameron, and S. A. Tomka, pp. 3–7. Cambridge University Press.

Campbell, L.
1978   Coxoh and Southeastern Tzeltal. Paper presented at the Annual Meetings of the American Anthropological Association, Los Angeles.
1988   *The Linguistics of Southeast Chiapas.* Papers of the New World Archaeological Foundation, No. 50. Brigham Young University, Provo.

Cannon, A.
1983   The Quantification of Artifactual Assemblages: Some Implications for Behavioral Inferences. *American Antiquity* 48(4):785–792.

Cancian, F.
1965   *Economics and Prestige in a Maya Community: The Religious Cargo System in Zinacantan.* Stanford University Press, Stanford.
1967   Political and Religious Organization. In *Social Anthropology,* edited by M. Nash, pp. 283–298. Handbook of Middle American Indians, vol. 6, R. Wauchope, general editor. University of Texas Press, Austin.

Carr, C.
1984   The Nature of Organization of Intrasite Archaeological Records and Spatial Analytic Approaches to Their Investigation. In *Advances in Archaeological Method and Theory*

vol. 7, edited by M. B. Schiffer, pp. 103–222. Academic Press, New York.

Chance, J. K.
1990 Changes in Twentieth-century Mesoamerican *Cargo* Systems. In *Class, Politics, and Popular Religion in Mexico and Central America,* edited by L. Stephen, and J. Dow, pp. 27–42. Society for Latin American Anthropology Publication Series, vol. 10. American Anthropological Association, Washington.

Chance, J. K., and W. B. Taylor
1985 Cofradías and Cargos: A Historical Perspective on the Mesoamerican Civil-Religious Hierarchy. *American Ethnologist* 12(1):1–26.

Chang, K. C.
1972 *Settlement Patterns in Archaeology.* Anthropology Module 24. Addison-Wesley, Reading.

Charters, S., R. P. Evershed, P. W. Blinkhorn, and V. Denham
1995 Evidence for the Mixing of Fats and Waxes in Archaeological Ceramics. *Archaeometry* 37(1):113–127.

Chatterjee, S., and B. Price
1977 *Regression Analysis by Example.* Wiley and Son, New York.

Chernela, J.
1969 In Praise of the Scratch: The Importance of Aboriginal Abrasion on Museum Ceramic Ware. *Curator* 12(3):174–179.

Clark, J. E.
1979 Personal Communication Concerning Pottery Production in Amatenango, Chiapas.

Coe, M.
1973 *The Maya Scribe and His World.* Grolier Club, New York.

Collier, G. A.
1975 *Fields of the Tzotzil. The Ecological Bases of Tradition in Highland Chiapas.* University of Texas Press, Austin.

Colton, H. S.
1939 Primitive Pottery Firing Methods. *Museum Notes* 11(10):63–67. Museum of Northern Arizona, Flagstaff.

Cook, S. F.
1972 Can Pottery Residues Be Used as an Index to Population? *University of California, Contributions of the University of California Archaeological Research Facility, Miscellaneous Papers on Archaeology* (14):17–39. Berkeley.

Costin, C. L.
1991 Craft Specialization: Issues in Defining, Documenting, and Explaining the Organization of Production. *Archaeological Method and Theory,* Vol. 3, edited by M. B. Schiffer, pp. 1–56. University of Arizona Press, Tucson.

Costin, C. L., and M. B. Hagstrum
1995 Standardization, Labor Investment, Skill, and the Organization of Ceramic Production in Late Prehispanic Highland Peru. *American Antiquity* 60(4):619–639.

Culbert, P.
1959 Modern and Prehistoric Pottery Making in Chiapas, Mexico. Paper presented at the 5th Annual Meeting of the American Anthropological Association, Mexico.
1965 *The Ceramic History of the Central Highlands of Chiapas, Mexico.* Papers of the New World Archaeological Foundation 19, Publications, No. 14. Brigham Young University, Provo, Utah.
1967 Preliminary Report of the Conference on the Prehistoric Ceramics of the Maya Lowlands (1965). *Estudios de Cultura Maya* 6:81–109. U.N.A.M., Mexico.

Culebro, C. A.
1932 *Historia de Chiapas.* Huixtla, Chiapas.

Curet, A.
1993 Regional Studies and Ceramic Production Areas: An Example from La Mixtequilla, Veracruz, Mexico. *Journal of Field Archaeology* 20:427–440.

Daltabuit, M., and C. Alvarez
1977 La Ceramica de Yalmuz, Chiapas. *Estudios de Cultura Maya* 10:231–242. U.N.A.M., Mexico.

D'Altroy, T. N., and C. A. Hastorf
1984 The Distribution and Contents of Inca State Storehouses in the Xauxa Region of Peru. *American Antiquity* 49(2):334–349.

Dark, K. R.
  1995   *Theoretical Archaeology.* Cornell
          University Press, Ithaca.
David, N.
  1971   The Fulani Compound and the Ar-
          chaeologist. *World Archaeology*
          3(2):111–131.
  1972   On the Life Span of Pottery, Type
          Frequencies, and Archaeological
          Inference. *American Antiquity*
          37(1):141–142.
  1992   Integrating Ethnoarchaeology: A
          Subtle Realist Perspective. *Journal
          of Anthropological Archaeology*
          11:330–359.
David, N., and H. Hennig
  1972   *The Ethnography of Pottery: A Fu-
          lani Case Seen in Archaeological
          Perspective.* McCaleb Module in
          Anthropology 21. Addison-Wesley,
          Reading.
Deal, M.
  1982   Functional Variation of Maya
          Spiked Vessels: A Practical Guide.
          American Antiquity 47(3):614–633.
  1983   *Pottery Ethnoarchaeology Among
          the Tzeltal Maya.* Unpublished Ph.D
          dissertation, Department of Archae-
          ology, Simon Fraser University,
          Burnaby.
  1985   Household Pottery Disposal in the
          Maya Highlands: An Ethnoarchaeo-
          logical Interpretation. *Journal of
          Anthropological Archaeology*
          4:243–291.
  1987   Ritual Space and Architecture in the
          Highland Maya Household. In *Mir-
          ror and Metaphor: Material Con-
          struction of Reality,* edited by D. W.
          Ingersoll, Jr. and G. Bronitsky, pp.
          171–198. University Press of Amer-
          ica, Lanham, Maryland.
  1988a   Recognition of Ritual Pottery in
          Residential Units: an Ethnoarchaeo-
          logical Model of the Maya Family
          Altar Tradition. In *Ethnoarchaeol-
          ogy among the Highland Maya of
          Chiapas, Mexico,* edited by T. A. Lee
          and B. Hayden, pp. 61–89. Papers of
          the New World Archaeological
          Foundation, No. 56. Brigham
          Young University, Provo.
  1988b   An Ethnoarchaeological Approach
          to the Identification of Maya Do-
          mestic Pottery Production. In *Ce-
          ramic Ecology Revisited, 1987: the
          Technology, and Socioeconomics of
          Pottery,* edited by C. C. Kolb, pp.
          111–142. BAR International Series
          436(ii), Oxford.
  1994a   Foreword. In *Kalinga Ethnoarchae-
          ology: Expanding Archaeological
          Method and Theory,* edited by W. A.
          Longacre and J. M. Skibo, pp. vii-xi.
          Smithsonian Institution Press, Wash-
          ington, D.C.
  1994b   The Archaeological Visibility of Do-
          mestic Pottery Production: an Eth-
          noarchaeological Perspective. Paper
          presented at the Annual Meeting of
          the American Anthropological Asso-
          ciation, Atlanta.
Deal, M., and M. B. Hagstrum
  1995   Ceramic Reuse Behavior Among the
          Maya and Wanka: Implications for
          Archaeology. In *Expanding Archae-
          ology,* edited by J. M. Skibo, W. H.
          Walker, and A. E. Nielsen, pp.
          111–125. University of Utah Press,
          Salt Lake City.
Deal, M., and B. Hayden
  1987   The Persistence of Pre-Columbian
          Lithic Technology in the Form of
          Glassworking. In *Lithic Studies
          Among the Contemporary Highland
          Maya,* edited by B. Hayden, pp.
          235–331. University of Arizona
          Press, Tucson.
Deal, M., N. Serwint, and C. Sohn
  1993   *Traditional Potters of Cyprus, 1993.*
          Thirty-minute documentary film
          presented at the June 25th–26th
          workshop "Making pottery: a prac-
          tical approach to ceramic technol-
          ogy in the ancient world." Cyprus
          American Archaeological Research
          Institute (CAARI), Nicosia.
DeBoer, W. R.
  1974   Ceramic Longevity and Archaeolog-
          ical Interpretation: An Example
          from the Upper Ucayali, Peru.
          American Antiquity 39(2):335–343.
  1983   The Archaeological Record as
          Preserved Death Assemblage. In
          *Archaeological Hammers and Theo-
          ries,* edited by J. A. Moore, and A. S.
          Keene, pp. 19–36. Academic Press,
          New York.

1984 The Last Pottery Show: System and Sense in Ceramic Studies. In *The Many Dimensions of Pottery,* edited by S. van der Leeuw, and A. C. Pritchard, pp. 529–568. Amsterdam Institute for Pre- and Protohistory, Amsterdam.

1986 Where the Pots Are. Paper presented at the Annual Meeting of the Society for American Archaeology, New Orleans.

1991 The Decorative Burden: Design, Medium and Change. In *Ceramic Ethnoarchaeology,* edited by W. A. Longacre, pp. 144–161. University of Arizona Press, Tucson.

DeBoer, W. R., and D. W. Lathrap
1979 The Making and Breaking of Shipibo-Canibo Ceramics. In *Ethnoarchaeology: Implications of Ethnography for Archaeology,* edited by C. Kramer, pp. 102–138. Columbia University Press, New York.

Deetz, J.
1965 *The Dynamics of Stylistic Change in Arikara Ceramics.* University of Illinois Studies in Anthropology, No. 4. Urbana.

1968 Inferences of Residence and Descent Rules. In *New Perspectives in Archaeology,* edited by L. R. Binford, and S. R. Binford, pp. 41–48. Aldine, Chicago.

1977 *In Small Things Forgotten. The Archaeology of Early American Life.* Anchor-Doubleday, Garden City, New York.

DeWalt, B. R.
1975 Changes in the Cargo System of Mesoamerica. *Anthropological Quarterly* 48:87–105.

Dickens, R. S., Jr., and J. H. Chapman
1978 Ceramic Patterning and Social Structure at Two Late Historic Upper Creek Sites in Alabama. *American Antiquity* 43(3):390–398.

Dillehay, T. D.
1973 Small Archaeological Site Investigation for Interpretation of Site Activities. *Bulletin of Texas Archaeological Society* 44:169–177.

Dillon, B. D.

1984 Ethnoarchaeology in Middle America: An Introduction. *Journal of New World Archaeology* 6(2):1–3.

Doran, J.E., and F. R. Hodson
1975 *Mathematics and Computers in Archaeology.* Edinburgh University Press, Edinburgh.

Earle, D.
1990 Appropriating the Enemy: Highland Maya Religious Organization and Community Survival. In *Class, Politics, and Popular Religion in Mexico and Central America,* edited by L. Stephen, and J. Dow, pp. 115–139. Society for Latin American Anthropology Publication Series, vol. 10. American Anthropological Association, Washington, D.C.

Egloff, B.J.
1973 A Method for Counting Ceramic Rim Sherds. *American Antiquity* 38(3):351–353.

Ericson, J. E., and S. P. DeAtley
1976 Reconstruction of Ceramic Assemblages: An Experiment to Derive the Morphology and Capacity of Parent Vessels from Sherds. *American Antiquity* 41(4):484–489.

Ericson, J. E., D. W. Head, and C. Burke
1972 Research Design: The Relationships Between Primary Functions and Physical Properties of Ceramic Vessels and Their Implications for Distributions of an Archaeological Site. *Anthropology U.C.L.A.* 3(2):84–95.

Ericson, J. E., and E. G. Stickel
1973 A Proposed Classification System for Ceramics. *World Archaeology* 4:357–367.

Esponda J., V. M., and A. C. Guiteras Holmes
1986 Estructura y Nomenclatura de Parentesco de los Tzeltales de Chanal. *Anuario de Centro de Estudios Indígenas,* pp. 219–251. UNACH, San Cristóbal de las Casas, Chiapas.

Evans, J. D.
1973 Sherd Weights and Sherd Counts: A Contribution to the Problem of Quantifying Pottery Sherds. In *Archaeological Theory and Practice,* edited by D. E. Strong, pp. 131–149. Seminar Press, London.

Fehon, J. R., and S. C. Scholtz

1978 A Conceptual Framework for the Study of Artifact Loss. *American Antiquity* 43(2):271–273.

Feinman, G. M., S. Upham, and K. G. Lightfoot
1981 The Production Step Measure, an Ordinal Index of Labor Input in Ceramic Manufacture. *American Antiquity* 46(4):871–884.

Feldman, L. H.
1982 Paper Pots. *Journal de la Société des Américanistes* 68:41–47.

Finsten, L.
1995 *Jalieza, Oaxaca: Activity Specialization at a Hilltop Center.* Vanderbilt University Press, Nashville.

Fitch, J. M., and D. P. Branch
1960 Primitive Architecture and Climate. *Scientific American* 203:134–144.

Fladmark, K.
1982 Microdebitage Analysis: Initial Considerations. *Journal of Archaeological Science* 9(2):111–126.

Flannery, K. V., and M. C. Winter
1976 Analysing Household Activities. In *The Early Mesoamerican Village,* edited by K. V. Flannery, pp. 34–47. Academic Press, San Francisco.

Folan, W. J., S. Daoutis, and K. Kreklow
1979 Cerámica y Códices: Un Análisis de Cerámica Maya Desde el Punto de Vista del Observador Precolombino. *Boletín de la Escuela de Ciencias Antropológicas de la Universidad de Yucatán* 6(35):36–43.

Foley, R.
1981 Off-site Archaeology: An Alternative Approach for the Short-sited. In *Pattern of the Past,* edited by I. Hodder, G. Isaac, and N. Hammond, pp. 157–183. Cambridge University Press.

Ford, J. A.
1951 *Greenhouse: A Troyville–Coles Creek Period Site in Avooyelles Parish, Louisiana.* Anthropological Papers 44(1). American Museum of Natural History, New York.
1954 The Type Concept Revisited. *American Antiquity* 56(1):42–54.

Foster, G. M.
1960 Life-expectancy of Utilitarian Pottery in Tzintzuntzan, Michoacan, Mexico. *American Antiquity* 25(4):606–609.
1967 Contemporary Pottery and Basketry. In *Social Anthropology,* edited by M. Nash, pp. 103–124. Handbook of Middle American Indians, vol. 6, R. Wauchope, general editor. University of Texas Press, Austin.

Fox, D. J., and K. E. Guire
1976 *Documentation for MIDAS.* 3rd ed. Statistical Research Laboratory. University of Michigan, Ann Arbor.

Fraser, D.
1968 *Village Planning in the Primitive World.* George Braziller, New York.

Freide, H. M., and R. H. Steel
1980 Experimental Burning of Traditional Nguni Huts. *African Studies* 39(2):175–181.

Friedrich, M. H.
1970 Design Structure and Social Interaction: Archaeological Implications of an Ethnographic Analysis. *American Antiquity* 35(3):332–343.

Fry, R. E.
1970 *Ceramics and Settlement in the Periphery of Tikal, Guatemala.* Ph.D. dissertation, Department of Anthropology, University of Arizona. University Microfilms, Ann Arbor.
1979 The Economics of Pottery at Tikal, Guatemala: Models of Exchanges for Serving Bowls. *American Antiquity* 44(3):494–512.

Fry, R. E., and S. C. Cox
1974 The Structure of Ceramic Exchange at Tikal, Guatemala. *World Archaeology* 6:209–225.

Fulford, M. G.
1973 Excavation of Three Romano-British Pottery Kilns in Amberewood Enclosure, Near Fortham, New Forest. *Proceedings of the Hampshire Field Club Archaeological Association* 28:5–28.

Garbett, G. K.
1967 The Restudy as a Technique for Examination of Social Change. In *Anthropologists in the Field,* edited by D. G. Jongmans, and P. C. W. Gutkind, pp. 116–132. Royal Van Gorcum, Assen, Netherlands.

Gifford, E. W.
  1976 *Archaeological Excavations in Fiji.* University of California, Anthropological Records 13(3). Originally published 1951. Kraus, New York.

Gifford, E. W., and R. Shutler, Jr.
  1976 *Archaeological Excavations in New Caledonia.* University of California, Anthropological Records 18(1). Originally published 1956. Kraus, New York.

Gifford, J. C.
  1976 *Prehistoric Pottery Analysis and the Ceramics of Barton Ramie in the Belize Valley.* Peabody Museum of Archaeology and Ethnology, Memoirs, No. 18. Harvard University, Cambridge.

  1978 The Ancient Maya in Light of Their Ethnographic Present. In *Cultural Continuities in Mesoamerica,* edited by D. L. Browman, pp. 205–227. Aldine, Chicago.

Gossen, G. H.
  1974 *Chamulas in the World of the Sun.* Harvard University Press, Cambridge.

  1979 Temporal and Spatial Equivalents in Chamula Ritual Symbolism. In *Reader in Comparative Religion: An Anthropological Approach,* 4 ed., edited by W. A. Lessa, and E. Z. Vogt, pp. 116–129. Harper and Row, New York.

Gotthilf, V.
  1982 *Maize Storage Strategies: An Ethnoarchaeological Perspective.* Unpublished Master's thesis, Department of Archaeology, Simon Fraser University, Burnaby.

  1983 Personal Communication Concerning the Use of Pottery Vessels in the Burial of Afterbirths in Oaxaca and Guatemala Highlands.

Gould, R. A.
  1978 Beyond Analogy in Ethnoarchaeology. In *Explorations in Ethnoarchaeology,* edited by R.A. Gould, pp. 249–293. University of New Mexico Press, Albuquerque.

  1980 *Living Archaeology.* Cambridge University Press, New York.

  1990 *Recovering the Past.* University of New Mexico Press, Albuquerque.

Graves, M. W.
  1994 Kalinga Social and Material Culture Boundaries: A Case of Spatial Convergence. In *Kalinga Ethnoarchaeology: Expanding Archaeological Method and Theory,* edited by W. A. Longacre and J. M. Skibo, pp. 13–49. Smithsonian Institution Press, Washington, D.C.

Grayson, D. K.
  1980 On the Quantification of Vertebrate Archaeofaunas. In *Advances in Archaeological Method and Theory,* vol. 2, edited by M. B. Schiffer, pp. 199–237. Academic Press, New York.

Grebinger, P.
  1971 The Potrero Creek Site: Activity Structure. *Kiva* 37(1):30–52.

Green, E.
  1972 The Use of Analogy for Interpretation of Maya Prehistory. *Kroeber Anthropological Society, Papers* 45:18–39. Berkeley.

Green, H. J. M.
  1961a An Analysis of Archaeological Rubbish Deposits: Part Two. *Archaeological Newsletter* 7(4):91–93, 95. London.

  1961b An Analysis of Archaeological Rubbish Deposits. *Archaeological Newsletter* 7(3):51–54. London.

Griffiths, D. M.
  1978 Use-marks on Historic Ceramics: A Preliminary Study. *Historical Archaeology* 12:68–81.

Guillini, G.
  1969 Contributions to the Study of the Preservation of Mud Brick Structures. *Mesopotamia* 3/4:443–473.

Hagstrum, M. B.
  1985 Measuring Prehistoric Craft Specialization: A Test Case in the American Southwest. *Journal of Field Archaeology* 12(1):65–76.

  1989 *Technological Continuity and Change: Ceramic Ethnoarchaeology in the Peruvian Andes.* Unpublished Ph.D. dissertation, Department of Anthropology, University of California, Los Angeles.

Hally, D. J.
  1983a Use Alteration of Pottery Surfaces: An Important Source of Evidence

for the Identification of Vessel Function. *North American Archaeologist* 4(1):3–26.

1983b The Interpretive Potential of Pottery from Domestic Contexts. *Midcontinental Journal of Archaeology* 8(2):163–196.

Hammond, N.

1982 *Ancient Maya Civilization.* Rutgers University Press, New Brunswick.

Hammond, G., and N. Hammond

1981 Child's Play: A Distorting Factor in Archaeological Distribution. *American Antiquity* 46(3): 634–636.

Hammond, P. C.

1971 Ceramic Technology of South-west Asia, Syro-Palestine: Iron IIb, Hebron. *Science and Archaeology* (5):11–21.

Harris, M.

1980 *Cultural Materialism: The Struggle for a Science of Culture.* Vintage, New York.

Hartwig, F., and B. E. Dearing

1979 *Exploring Data Analysis.* Quantitative Applications in the Social Sciences, No. 16. Sage, Beverly Hills.

Harvey, B., III

1964 Is Pottery Making a Dying Art? *The Masterkey* 38:55–65.

Hayden, B.

1978 Snarks in Archaeology: Or, Inter-Assemblage Variability in Lithics. (a View from the Antipodes). In *Lithics and Subsistence. The Analysis of Stone Use in Prehistoric Economics,* edited by D. D. Davis, pp. 179–198. Vanderbilt University, Publications in Anthropology, No. 20, Nashville.

1979 Material Culture in the Mayan Highlands: A Preliminary Study. In *Settlement Pattern Excavations at Kaminaljuyu, Guatemala,* edited by J. W. Michels, pp. 183–222. Pennsylvania State University Press, University Park.

1984 Are Emic Types Relevant to Archaeology? *Ethnohistory* 31(2):79–92.

1987 Past to Present Uses of Stone Tools in the Maya Highlands. In *Lithic Studies Among the Contemporary Highland Maya,* edited by B. Hayden, pp. 160–234. University of Arizona Press, Tucson.

1988a Some Essential Considerations in Interaction Interpretation. In *Ethnoarchaeology among the Highland Maya of Chiapas, Mexico,* edited by T. A. Lee, and B. Hayden, pp. 91–98. Papers of the New World Archaeological Foundation, No. 56. Brigham Young University, Provo.

1988b The Coxoh Ethnoarchaeological Project. In *Ethnoarchaeology among the Highland Maya of Chiapas, Mexico,* edited by T. A. Lee, and B. Hayden, pp. 1–4. Papers of the New World Archaeological Foundation, No. 56. Brigham Young University, Provo.

Hayden, B., M. Blake, M. Deal, and G. Spurling

1977 The Coxoh Ethnoarchaeological Project: 1977, Preliminary Report. Report submitted to the Humanities and Social Sciences Division, Canada Council, Ottawa.

Hayden, B., and A. Cannon

1983 Where the Garbage Goes: Refuse Disposal in the Maya Highlands. *Journal of Anthropological Archaeology* 2:117–163.

1984a *The Structure of Material Systems: Ethnoarchaeology in the Maya Highlands.* Paper No. 3, Society for American Archaeology, Washington, D.C.

1984b Interaction Inferences in Archaeology and Learning Frameworks of the Maya. *Journal of Anthropological Archaeology* 3:325–367.

Hayden, B., and M. Deal

1989 Vitreous Materials Used by the Contemporary Maya. In *La Obsidiana en Mesoamerica,* edited by M. Gaxiola G., and J. E. Clark, pp. 435–441. Serie Arqueología, Instituto Nacional de Antropología e Historia, México.

Hayden, B., and R. Gargett

1990 Big Man, Big Heart? A Mesoamerican View of the Emergence of Complex Society. *Ancient Mesoamerica* 1:3–20.

Hayden, B., and M. Nelson.

1981 The Use of Chipped Lithic Material in the Contemporary Maya High-

lands. *American Antiquity* 46(4):
885–898.

Healan, D. M.
1979　Appendix II. Description of a Possible Ceramic Tube Kiln in House VIII, Canal Locality. In *Tula of the Toltecs, Excavations and Surveys,* edited by D. M. Healan, pp. 254–260. University of Iowa Press, Iowa City.

Heizer, R. F.
1962　Village Shifts and Tribal Spreads in California Prehistory. *The Masterkey* 36(2):60–67.

Hendry, J. C.
1992　*Atzompa: A Pottery Producing Village of Southern Mexico in the Mid-1950's.* Vanderbilt University Press, Nashville.

Henrickson, E. F., and M. M. A. McDonald
1983　Ceramic Form and Function: An Ethnographic Search and an Archaeological Application. *American Anthropologist* 85(3):630–643.

Henrickson, R. C.
1992　Analysis of Use Wear on Ceramic Potter's Tools. *Materials Issues in Art and Archaeology III,* edited by P. B. Vandiver, J. R. Druzik, G. S. Wheeler, and I. C. Freestone, pp. 475–493. Materials Research Society Symposium Proceedings, vol. 27. Materials Research Society, Pittsburgh.

Heron, C., and R. P. Evershed
1992　The Analysis of Organic Residues and the Study of Pottery Use. In *Advances in Archaeological Method and Theory,* vol. 5, edited by M. B. Schiffer, pp. 247–284. Academic Press, New York.

Heyman, A.
1960　Analysis of Amatenango Pottery. Ms. on file, New World Archaeological Foundation, Chiapas, Mexico.

Hildebrand, J. A.
1978　Pathways Revisited: A Quantitative Model of Discard. *American Antiquity* 43(2):274–279.

Hill, J. N., and R. K. Evans
1972　A Model for Classification and Typology. In *Models in Archaeology,* edited by D. L. Clarke, pp. 231–273. Methuen, London.

Hinton, D. A.
1977　"Rudely Made Earthen Vessels" of the Twelfth to Fifteenth Centuries A.D. In *Pottery and Early Commerce,* edited by D. P. S. Peacock, pp. 221–238. Academic Press, London.

Hodder, I.
1991　*Reading the Past: Current Approaches to Interpretation in Archaeology.* Second Edition. Cambridge University Press.

Hodges, H.
1964　*Artifacts: An Introduction to Early Materials and Technology.* John Baker, London.

Holland, W. R.
1964　Contemporary Tzotzil Cosmological Concepts as a Basis for Interpreting Prehistoric Maya Religion. *American Antiquity* 29(3):301–306.

Honigmann, J., and I. Honigmann
1955　Sampling Reliability in Ethnological Field Work. *Southwestern Journal of Anthropology* 11:282–287.
1957　Another Experiment in Sampling Reliability. *Southwestern Journal of Anthropology* 13:99–102.

Hosler, D.
1996　Technical Choices, Social Categories and Meaning among the Andean Potters of Las Animas. *Journal of Material Culture* 1(1):63–92.

Hotchkiss, J. C.
1959　Chanal, Teopisca and Venustiano Carranza. In *Report on the Man-in-Nature Project of the Department of Anthropology of the University of Chicago in the Tzeltal-Tzotzil Speaking Region of the State of Chiapas, Mexico,* edited by N. A. McQuown. Manuscripts on American Indian Cultural Anthropology Series 14, Vol. 3, Sec. 15. University of Chicago, Microfilm Collection.

Houston, S. D., D. Stuart, and K. A. Taube
1989　Folk Classification of Classic Maya Pottery. *American Anthropologist* 91:720–726.

Howry, J. C.
1973　Ethnographic Realities for Maya Prehistory. Paper presented at the 9th International Congress of Anthropological and Ethnological Sciences, Chicago.

1976 *Fires on the Mountain: Ceramic Traditions and Marketing in the Highlands of Chiapas, Mexico.* Unpublished Ph.D. dissertation, Department of Anthropology, Harvard University.

1978 Ethnographic Realities of Mayan Prehistory. In *Cultural Continuities in Mesoamerica,* edited by D. L. Bowman, pp. 239–257. Aldine, Chicago.

Hughs, P. J., and R. J. Lampert

1977 Occupational Disturbance and Types of Archaeological Deposit. *Journal of Archaeological Science* 4:135–140.

Hulthen, B.

1974 On Choice of Element for Determination of Quantity of Pottery. *Norwegian Archaeological Review* 7(2):1–5.

Hunter-Anderson, R. I.

1977 A Theoretical Approach to the Study of House Form. In *For Theory Building in Archaeology,* edited by L. R. Binford, pp. 287–315. Academic Press, New York.

Hunt, M. E.

1962 *The Dynamics of the Domestic Groups in Two Tzeltal Villages: A Contrastive Comparison.* Unpublished Ph.D. dissertation, Department of Anthropology, University of Chicago.

Hunt, M. E., and J. Nash

1967 Local and Territorial Units. In *Social Anthropology,* edited by M. Nash, pp. 253–282. Handbook of Middle American Indians, vol. 6, R. Wauchope, general editor. University of Texas Press, Austin.

Hurst, J. G.

1971 A Review of Archaeological Research (to 1968). In *Deserted Medieval Villages,* edited by M. Beresford, and J. G. Hurst, pp. 76–144. Lutterworth, London.

Jelinek, A. J.

1967 *A Prehistoric Sequence in the Middle Pecos Valley, New Mexico.* Anthropological Papers, No. 31, Museum of Anthropology, University of Michigan, Ann Arbor.

Joesink-Mandeville, L. R. V.

1973 The Importance of Gourd Prototypes in the Analysis of Mesoamerican Ceramics. *Katunob* 8(3):47–53.

1976 Ceramics from the Motul: Sixteenth Century Yucatec Maya Terms and Definitions. *Katunob* 9(2):42–51.

Joyce, A. A., and S. Johannessen

1993 Abandonment and the Production of Archaeological Visibility at Domestic Sites. In *Abandonment of Settlements and Regions: Ethnoarchaeological and Archaeological Approaches,* edited by C. M. Cameron, and S. A. Tomka, pp. 138–153. Cambridge University Press.

Keighley, J.

1973 Some Problems in the Quantitative Interpretation of Ceramic Data. In *The Explanation of Culture Change: Models in Prehistory,* edited by C. Renfrew, pp. 131–137. Duckworth, London.

Kelsall, R. K., and H. M. Kelsall

1974 *Stratification: An Essay on Class and Inequality.* Longman, New York.

Kempton, W.

1981 *The Folk Classification of Ceramics: A Study of Cognitive Prototypes.* Academic Press, New York.

Kent, S.

1984 *Analysing Activity Areas: An Ethnoarchaeological Study of Spatial Analysis* University of New Mexico Press, Albuquerque.

1987 Understanding the Use of Space: An Ethnoarchaeological Approach. In *Method and Theory for Activity Area Research: an Ethnoarchaeological Approach,* edited by S. Kent, pp. 1–62. Columbia University Press, New York.

Kidder, A. V.

1934 Report on Investigations of the Division of Historical Research. *Carnegie Institution of Washington, Yearbook* (33):81–120.

Killion, T.

1990 Cultivation Intensity and Residential Site Structure: An Ethnoarchaeological Examination of Peasant Agriculture in the Sierra de los Tuxtlas, Veracruz, Mexico. *Latin American Antiquity* 1(3):191–215.

Kobayashi, M.
1994 Use Alteration Analysis of Kalinga Pottery: Interior Carbon Deposits and Cooking Pots. In *Kalinga Ethnoarchaeology: Expanding Archaeological Method and Theory,* edited by W. A. Longacre and J. M. Skibo, pp. 127–168. Smithsonian Institution Press, Washington, D.C.

Kramer, C.
1982 *Village Ethnoarchaeology: Rural Iran in Archaeological Perspective.* Academic Press, New York.
1985 Ceramic Ethnoarchaeology. *Annual Review of Anthropology* 14:77–102.

Kramer, C., and J. E. Douglas
1992 Ceramics, Caste, and Kin: Spatial Relations in Rajastan, India. *Journal of Anthropological Archaeology* 11:187–201.

Krotser, P. H.
1980 Potters in the Land of the Olmec. In *In the Land of the Olmec, vol. 2,* edited by M. D. Coe, and R. A. Diehl, pp. 125–138. University of Texas Press, Austin.

Kvamme, K., M. Stark, and W. A. Longacre
1996 Alternative Procedures for Assessing Standardization in Archaeological and Ethnoarchaeological Assemblages. *American Antiquity* 61(1):116–126.

Lange, F. W., and C. R. Rydberg
1972 Abandonment and Post-abandonment Behavior at a Rural Central American House Site. *American Antiquity* 37(3):419–432.

Lathrap, D. W.
1977 Our Father the Caymen, Our Mother the Gourd: Spinden Revisited, or a Unitary Model for the Emergence of Agriculture in the New World. In *Agricultural Origins,* edited by C. Reed, pp. 713–751. Moulon, The Hague.

Lee, T. A., Jr.
1972 *Jmetic Lubton. Some Modern and Pre-hispanic Maya Ceremonial Customs in the Highlands of Chiapas, Mexico.* Papers of the New World Archaeological Foundation, No. 29. Brigham Young University, Provo.
1977 Coapa, Chiapas: A Sixteenth Century Coxoh Maya Village on the Camino Real. In *The Upper Grijalva Basin Maya Project, Reports on Fieldwork of 1975–1976,* pp. 173–202. New World Archaeological Foundation, Brigham Young University, Provo.
1979a Early Colonial Coxoh Maya Syncretism in Chiapas, Mexico. *Estudios de Cultura Maya* 12:93–109.
1979b Coxoh Colonial Domestic Patterns. Paper presented at the 43rd Session, International Congress of Americanists, Vancouver.
1980 The Long Path to Extinction: Colonial Coxoh Maya of Chiapas, Mexico. *Mexicon* 2(2):21–24.

Lee, T. A., Jr., and D. D. Bryant
1988 The Colonial Coxoh Maya. In *Ethnoarchaeology Among the Highland Maya of Chiapas, Mexico,* edited by T. A. Lee, and B. Hayden, pp. 5–20. Papers of the New World Archaeological Foundation, No. 56. Brigham Young University, Provo.

Lee, T. A., Jr., and S. D. Markman
1977a The Coxoh Colonial Project and Coneta, Chiapas, Mexico. A Provincial Maya Village Under the Spanish Conquest. *Historical Archaeology* 11:56–66.
1977b Coxoh Maya Acculturation in Colonial Chiapas: A Necrotic Archaeological-ethnohistorical Model. In *The Upper Grijalva Basin Maya Project: Reports on the Fieldwork of 1975–1976,* pp. 203–219. New World Archaeological Foundation, Provo.

Leone, M.
1968 Neolithic Autonomy and Social Distance. *Science* 162:1150–1151.

Lewis, K.
1976 *Camden: A Frontier Town.* Anthropological Series, No. 2, Institute of Archaeology and Anthropology, University of South Carolina, Columbia.

Lewis, O.
1960 *Tepoztlan: Village in Mexico.* Holt, Rinehart and Winston, New York.

Lind, M.
1979 *Postclassic and Early Colonial Mix-*

tec Houses in the Nochixtlan Valley, Oaxaca. Publications in Anthropology, No. 23. Vanderbilt University. Nashville, Tennessee.

Lindahl, A., and E. Matenga
1995   Present and Past: Ceramics and Homesteads. An Ethnoarchaeological Project in the Buhera District, Zimbabwe. Studies in African Archaeology 11, Department of Archaeology, Uppsala University.

Lindauer, O.
1992   Ceramic Conjoinability: Orphan Sherds and Reconstructing Time. In Piecing Together the Past: Applications of Refitting Studies in Archaeology, edited by J. L. Hofman, and J. G. Enloe, pp. 210–216. BAR International Series, No. 578. Oxford.

Lischka, J. J.
1975   Broken K Revisited: A Short Discussion of Factor Analysis. American Antiquity 40(2):220–227.
1978   A Functional Analysis of Middle Classic Ceramics at Kaminaljuyu. In The Ceramics of Kaminaljuyu, edited by R. K. Wetherington, pp. 224–278. Pennsylvania State University Press, University Park.

London, G. A.
1987   Cypriote Potters: Past and Present. Report of the Department of Antiquities of Cyprus pp. 319–322.
1991   Standardization and Variation in the Work of Craft Specialists. In Ceramic Ethnoarchaeology, edited by W. A. Longacre, pp. 182–204. University of Arizona Press, Tucson.

Longacre, W. A.
1964   Sociological Implications of the Ceramic Analysis. In Chapters in the Prehistory of Eastern Arizona, vol. 2, edited by P. S. Martin, pp. 155–170. Field Museum of Natural History, Chicago.
1974   Kalinga Pottery-making: The Evolution of a Research Design. In Frontiers of Anthropology, edited by M. J. Leaf, pp. 51–67. Van Nostrand, New York.
1981   Kalinga Pottery: An Ethnoarchaeological Study. In Pattern of the Past,

edited by I. Hodder, G. Isaac, and N. Hammond, pp. 49–66. Cambridge University Press.
1992   The Perfect Marriage: The Essential Joining of Ethnoarchaeology and Experimental Archaeology. In 12e Rencontres International d'Archéologie et d'Histoire d'Antibes. Actes des Rencontres, Octobre 1990, pp. 15–24. Centre de Recherches Archéologiques du C. R. A., Paris.

Longacre, W. A., and J. E. Ayres
1968   Archaeological Lessons from an Apache Wickiup. In New Perspectives in Archaeology, edited by S. R. Binford, and L. R. Binford, pp. 151–159. Aldine, Chicago.

Longacre, W. A., K. L. Kvamme, and M. Kobayashi
1988   Southwestern Pottery Standardization: An Ethnoarchaeological View from the Philippines. The Kiva 53(2):101–112.

Longacre, W. A., and J. M. Skibo
1994   Kalinga Ethnoarchaeology: Expanding Archaeological Method and Theory. Smithsonian Institution Press, Washington, D. C.

Longacre, W. A., J. M. Skibo, and M. T. Stark
1991   Ethnoarchaeology at the Top of the World. New Ceramic Studies Among the Kalinga of Luzon. Expedition 33(1):4–15.

Longacre, W. A., and M. T. Stark
1992   Ceramics, Kinship, and Space: A Kalinga Example. Journal of Anthropological Archaeology 11:125–136.

Lopez, A. G.
1977   Oxchuc. K'op Tik 2(5):8.

Lothrop, S. K.
1927   The Potters of Guatajiagua, Salvador. Heye Foundation, Museum of the American Indian. Indian Notes 4(1):109–118.

Lowe, G. W.
1971   The Civilizational Consequences of Varying Degrees of Agricultural and Ceramic Dependency Within the Basic Ecosystems in Mesoamerica. In Observations on the Emergence of Civilization in Mesoamerica, edited by R. F. Heizer, J.A. Graham, and

C.W. Clewlow, pp. 212–248. Contributions of the University of California Archaeological Research Facility, No. 11. University of California, Berkeley.

McBryde, F. W.
1947 *Cultural and Historical Geography of Southwestern Guatemala.* Institute of Social Anthropology, Publication, No. 4. Smithsonian Institute, Washington, D.C.

McIntosh, R. J.
1974 Archaeology and Mud Wall Decay in a West African Village. *World Archaeology* 6(2):154–171.

1977 The Excavation of Mud Structures: An Experiment from West Africa. *World Archaeology* 9(2):185–199.

McIntosh, S. K.
1994 Changing Perceptions in West Africa's Past: Archaeological Research since 1988. *Journal of Archaeological Research* 2(2): 165–198.

McNemar, Q.
1962 *Psychological Statistics.* John Wiley and Sons, New York.

McPherron, A.
1967 *The Juntenen Site and the Late Woodlands Prehistory of the Upper Great Lakes Area.* Anthropological Papers 30, University of Michigan, Museum of Anthropology, Ann Arbor.

McQuown, N. A. (editor)
1959 *Report on the Man-in-Nature Project of the Department of Anthropology of the University of Chicago in the Tzeltal-Tzotzil Speaking Region of the State of Chiapas, Mexico.* Microfilm Collection of Manuscripts on American Indian cultural Anthropology, Series 14. University of Chicago.

Majewski, T.
1974 Ethnohistoric and Ethnographic Inference for Determining Precolumbian Social Structure. *41st Session, International Congress of Americanists* 2:156–163.

Manzanilla, L., and L. Barba
1990 The Study of Activities in Classic Households: Two Case Studies from Coba And Teotihuacan. *Ancient Mesoamerica* 1:41–49.

Marascuilo, L. A., and M. McSweeney
1977 *Nonparametric and Distribution-free Methods for the Social Sciences.* Brooks/Coles, Monterey.

Markman, S. D.
1972 Pueblos de Españoles and Pueblos de Indios in Colonial Central America. *International Congress of Americanists, Stuttgart-Munchen, 1968* 4:189–199.

Matheny, R. T.
1970 *The Ceramics of Aguacatal, Campeche, Mexico.* Papers of the New World Archaeological Foundation, No. 27. Brigham Young University, Provo.

Matson, F. R.
1965 Ceramic Ecology: An Approach to the Study of the Early Cultures of the Near East. In *Ceramics and Man,* edited by F. R. Matson, pp. 202–217. Viking Fund Publications in Anthropology, No. 41. Wenner-Gren Foundation, New York.

1969 Some Aspects of Ceramic Technology. In *Science in Archaeology,* edited by D. Brothwell, and E. Higgs, pp. 592–602. Praeger, New York.

Matthews, J. M.
1965 Stratigraphic Disturbance: The Human Element. *Antiquity* 39(156):295–298.

Meggers, B. J., and C. Evans
1957 *Archaeology Investigations at the Mouth of the Amazon.* Bureau of American Ethnology, Bulletin, No. 167. Washington, D. C.

Mehrer, M. W.
1995 *Cahokia's Countryside: Household Archaeology, Settlement Patterns and Social Power.* Northern Illinois University Press, DeKalb.

Menget, P.
1968 Death in Chamula. *Natural History* 78(1):48–57.

Metcalfe, D., and K. M. Heath
1990 Microrefuse and Site Structure: The Hearths and Floors of the Heartbreak Hotel. *American Antiquity* 55(4):781–796.

Michels, J. W.

1979 *The Kaminaljuyu Chiefdom.* Pennsylvania State University Press, University Park.

Miles, S. W.

1957 Maya Settlement Patterns: A Problem for Ethnology and Archaeology. *Southwestern Journal of Anthropology* 13(1):239–248.

1965 Summary of Preconquest Ethnology of the Guatemala-Chiapas Highlands and Pacific Slopes. In *Archaeology of Southern Mesoamerica, Part 1,* edited by G. R. Willey, pp. 276–287. Handbook of Middle American Indians, Vol. 2, R. Wauchope, general editor. University of Texas Press, Austin.

Millett, M.

1979 How Much Pottery? In *Pottery and the Archaeologist,* edited by M. Millett, pp. 77–80. Institute of Archaeology, Occasional Publication, No. 4. University of London.

Mills, B. J.

1989 Integrating Functional Analysis of Vessels and Sherds Through Models of Ceramic Assemblage Formation. *World Archaeology* 21(1):133–147.

Montagu, R.

1958 Preliminary Summary of a Survey in the Tojolabal Region, Chiapas, Mexico. Ms. on file, Nabalom Library, San Cristóbal de las Casas, Chiapas.

Moore, H.

1982 The Interpretation of Spatial Patterning in Settlement Residues. In *Symbolic and Structural Archaeology,* edited by I. Hodder, pp. 74–79. Cambridge University Press.

Morris, C.

1974a Reconstructing Patterns of Nonagricultural Production in the Inca Economy: Archaeology and Documents in Institutional Analysis. In *Reconstructing Complex Societies,* edited by C. D. Moore, pp. 49–68. Bulletin of the American School of Oriental Research, No. 20, Supplement. Chicago.

1974b The Identification of Function in Inca Architecture and Ceramics.

Revista, El Museo Nacional 37:135–144. Lima.

Moseley, M., and C. Mackey

1972 Peruvian Settlement Pattern Studies and Small Site Methodology. *American Antiquity* 37(1):67–81.

Murray, P.

1980 Discard Locations: The Ethnographic Data. *American Antiquity* 45(3):490–502.

Nash, J.

1959 Amatenango del Valle. *Report on the Man-in-Nature Project,* edited by N. A. McQuown. Manuscripts on American Indian Cultural Anthropology, Series 14, Pt. 2, Sec. 10.University of Chicago.

1970 *The Eyes of the Ancestors: Belief and Behavior in a Mayan Community.* Yale University Press, New Haven.

1985 Epilogue. In *The Eyes of the Ancestors: Belief and Behavior in a Mayan Community,* pp. 333–337. Reprint of 1970 edition.Waveland Press, Prospect Heights, Illinois.

Nash, M.

1959 The Small Scale Economy: The Context of Economic Choice. *Report on the Man-in-Nature Project,* edited by N. A. McQuown. Manuscripts on American Indian Cultural Anthropology, Series 14, Pt. 3, Sec. 22. University of Chicago.

1960 Witchcraft as Social Process in a Tzeltal Community. *America Indigena* 20:121–126.

1961 The Social Context of Economic Choice in a Small Society. *Man* 61:186–191.

1966 *Primitive and Peasant Economic Systems.* Chandler, San Francisco.

1967 Indian Economies. In *Social Anthropology,* edited by M. Nash, pp. 87–102. Handbook of Middle American Indians, vol. 6, R. Wauchope, general editor. University of Texas Press, Austin.

Nelson, B.

1981 Ethnoarchaeology and Paleodemography: A Test of Turner and Lofgren's Hypothesis. *Journal of Anthropological Research* 37(2):107–129.

1985 Reconstructing Ceramic Vessels and Their Systemic Contexts. In *Decoding Prehistoric Ceramics,* edited by B. Nelson, pp. 310–329. Southern Illinois University Press, Carbondale.

1991 Ceramic Frequency and Use-life: a Highland Mayan Case in Cross-cultural Perspective. In *Ceramic Ethnoarchaeology,* edited by W. A. Longacre, pp. 162–181. University of Arizona Press, Tucson.

Neupert, M. A., and W. A. Longacre
1994 Informant Accuracy in Pottery Use-life Studies: A Kalinga Example. In *Kalinga Ethnoarchaeology: Expanding Archaeological Method and Theory,* edited by W. A. Longacre, and J. M. Skibo, pp. 71–82. Smithsonian Institution Press, Washington, D.C.

Newell, H. P., and A. D. Krieger
1949 *The George C. Davis Site, Cherokee County, Texas.* Memoirs No. 5. Society for American Archaeology, Washington, D.C.

Nicklin, K.
1971 Stability and Innovation in Pottery Manufacture. *World Archaeology* 3:13–48.

1979 The Location of Pottery Manufacture. *Man* n.s.14(3):436–458.

Nielsen, A. E.
1991 Trampling the Archaeological Record: An Experimental Study. *American Antiquity* 56(3):483–503.

Nissen, H. J.
1968 Survey of an Abandoned Modern Village in Southern Iraq. *Sumer* 24(1/2):107–117.

Oetelaar, G. A.
1993 Identifying Site Structure in the Archaeological Record: An Illinois Mississippian Example. *American Antiquity* 58(4):662–687.

O'Neale, L. M.
1977 Notes on Pottery Making in Highland Peru. *Ñawpa Pacha* (14): 41–60.

Orton, C. R.
1975 Quantitative Pottery Studies; Some Progress, Problems and Prospects. *Science and Archaeology* 16:30–35.

1980 *Mathematics in Archaeology.* Collins, London.

1982 Computer Simulation Experiments to Assess the Performance of Measurements of Quantity of Pottery. *World Archaeology* 14(1):1–20.

1993 How Many Pots Make Five? An Historical Review of Pottery Quantification. *Archaeometry* 35(2):169–184.

Orton, C., and P. A. Tyers
1992 Counting Broken Objects: The Statistics of Ceramic Assemblages. *Proceedings of the British Academy* 77:163–184.

Orton, C., P. Tyers, and A. Vince
1993 *Pottery in Archaeology.* University of Cambridge Press, Cambridge.

Palerm, A.
1967 Agricultural Systems and Food Patterns. In *Social Anthropology,* edited by M. Nash, pp. 26–52. Handbook of Middle American Indians, vol. 6, R. Wauchope, general editor. University of Texas Press, Austin.

Papousek, D. A.
1974 Manufactura de Alfareria: En Temascalcingo, Mexico, 1967. *America Indigena* 34:1009–1045.

Parsons, E.W.
1966 *Mitla: Town of the Souls: And Other Zapoteco-speaking Pueblos of Oaxaca, Mexico.* Originally published 1936. University of Chicago Press, Chicago.

Pastron, A. G.
1974 Preliminary Ethnoarchaeological Investigations among the Tarahumara. In *Ethnoarchaeology,* edited by C. B. Donnan, and C. W. Clewlow, pp. 93–114. Institute of Archaeology, Monograph, No. 4. University of California, Los Angeles.

Peacock, D. P. S.
1981 Archaeology, Ethnology and Ceramic Production. In *Production and Distribution: A Ceramic Viewpoint,* edited by H. Howard, and E. Morris, pp. 187–194. BAR International Series 120. Oxford.

Pearce, R. J.
1978 *A Preliminary Report on Draper Site Rim Sherds.* Research Report, No. 1. University of Western Ontario, Museum of Indian Archaeology.

Pielou, E. C.
1977   *Mathematical Ecology.* John Wiley & Sons, New York.

Plog, S.
1980   *Stylistic Variation in Prehistoric Ceramics.* Cambridge University Press, Cambridge.

Pollock, H. E. D., R. L. Roys, T., Proskouriakoff, and A. L. Smith
1962   *Mayapan, Yucatan, Mexico.* Publications 619. Carnegie Institution, Washington, D.C.

Popper, V. S.
1988   Selecting Quantitative Measurements in Paleoethnobotany. In *Current Paleoethnobotany: Analytical and Cultural Interpretations of Archaeological Plant Remains,* edited by C. A. Hastorf, and V. S. Popper, 53–71. University of Chicago Press.

Pozas, R.
1977   *Chamula: Un Pueblo Indio en los Altos de Chiapas.* Instituto Nacional Indígenista, Coleccion I-I. Originally published 1959. Editorial Libros de Mexico.

Price, B. J.
1974   The Burden of the Cargo: Ethnographical Models and Archaeological Inference. In *Mesoamerican Archaeology: New Approaches,* edited by N. Hammond, pp. 444–465. University of Texas Press, Austin.

Price, S., and R. Price
1972   Aspects of Social Organization in a Maya Hamlet. *Estudios de Cultura Maya* 8:297–318.

Ralph, D. M., and D. E. Arnold
1988   Socioeconomic Status, Kinship, and Innovation: The Adoption of the Tornete in Ticul, Yucatán. In *Ceramic Ecology Revisited, 1987: The Technology and Socioeconomics of Pottery,* edited by C. C. Kolb, pp. 145–164. BAR International Series 436(ii), Part I. Oxford.

Rands, R.
1964   Ceramic Patterns and Traditions of the Highland and Lowland Maya. *35th Session, International Congress of Americanists, Mexico,* pp. 263–277.
1967   Ceramic Technology and Trade in the Palenque Region, Mexico. In *American Historical Anthropology, Essays in honour of Leslie Spier,* edited by C. L. Riley, and W. V. Taylor, pp. 137–152. Southern Illinois University Press, Carbondale.
1988   Least-cost and Function-optimising Interpretations of Ceramic Production: An Archaeological Perspective. In *Ceramic Ecology Revisited, 1987: The Technology and Socioeconomics of Pottery,* edited by C. C. Kolb, pp. 165–198. BAR International Series 436(i). Oxford.

Rands, R., P. H. Benson, R. L. Bishop, P. Chen, G. Harbottle, B. C. Rands, and E. V. Sayre
1975   Western Maya Fine Paste Pottery: Chemical and Petrographic Correlations. *41st Session, International Congress of Americanists, Mexico* pp. 534–541.

Rands, R. L., and R. L. Bishop
1980   Resource Procurement Zones and Patterns of Ceramic Exchange in the Palenque Region, Mexico. In *Models and Methods in Regional Exchange,* edited by R. E. Fry, pp. 19–46. Papers No. 1. Society for American Archaeology, Washington, D.C.

Rathje, W. L.
1979   Modern Material Culture Studies. In *Advances in Archaeological Method and Theory, vol. 3,* edited by M. B. Schiffer, pp. 1–37. Academic Press, New York.

Read, D. W.
1982   Toward a Theory of Archaeological Classification. In *Essays on Archaeological Typology,* edited by R. Whallon, and J. A. Brown, pp. 56–92. Center for American Archaeology Press, Evanston, Illinois.

Redfield, R., and A. Villa Rojas
1939   *Notes on the Ethnography of Tzeltal Communities of Chiapas.* Contributions to American Anthropology and History 5(25):107–119. Carnegie Institution, Washington, D.C.

Redman, C. L.
1979   Description and Inference with

Late Medieval Pottery from Qsar es-seghir, Morocco. *Medieval Ceramics* 3:63–79.

Reents-Budet, D., R. L. Bishop, and B. MacLeod
1994 Painting Styles, Workshop Locations and Pottery Production. In *Painting the Maya Universe: Royal Ceramics of the Classic Period,* edited by D. Reents-Budet, pp. 164–233. Duke University Press, Durham.

Reina, R. E.
1963 The Potter and the Farmer: The Fate of Two Innovators in a Maya Village. *Expedition* 5(4):18–30.

Reina, R. E., and R. M. Hill, II
1978 *The Traditional Pottery of Guatemala.* University of Texas Press, Austin.

Renfrew, C.
1977 Introduction: Production and Exchange in Early State Societies: The Evidence of Pottery. In *Pottery and Early Commerce,* edited by D. P. S. Peacock, pp. 1–20. Academic Press, London.

Rey, R.
1976 Amatenango and Tenango Pottery Catalogues. Ms. on file, New World Archaeological Foundation, Chiapas.

Rice, P. M.
1976 Rethinking the Ware Concept. *American Antiquity* 41(4):538–543.
1977 Whiteware Pottery Production in the Valley of Guatemala: Specialization and Resource Utilization. *Journal of Field Archaeology* 4(2):221–233.
1981 Evolution of Specialized Pottery Production: A Trial Model. *Current Anthropology* 22(3):219–240.
1984 Change and Conservatism in Pottery-producing Systems. In *Many Dimensions of Pottery: Ceramics in Archaeology and Anthropology,* edited by S. E. van der Leeuw, and A. C. Prichard, pp. 231–288. University of Amsterdam.
1987 *Pottery Analysis: A Sourcebook.* University of Chicago Press.
1989 Ceramic Diversity, Production, and Use. In *Quantifying Diversity in Archaeology,* edited by R. D. Leonard,

and G. T. Jones, pp. 109–117. Cambridge University Press.
1996a Recent Ceramic Analysis: 1. Function, Style, and Origins. *Journal of Archaeological Research* 4(2): 133–163.
1996b Recent Ceramic Analysis: 2. Composition, Production, and Theory. *Journal of Archaeological Research* 4(3):165–202.

Ricketson, O. G., and E. B. Ricketson
1937 *Uaxactun, Guatemala. Group E 1926–1931.* Publication No. 403, Contributions No. 1. Carnegie Institution, Washington, D.C.

Robbins, L. H.
1973 Turkana Material Culture Viewed from an Archaeological Perspective. *World Archaeology* 5:209–214.

Robles U., C.
1966 *La Dialectología Tzeltal y el Diccionario Compacto.* Instituto Nacional de Antropología e Historia, México.

Rock, J. T.
1974 The Use of Social Models in Archaeological Interpretation. *The Kiva* 40(1/2):81–91.

Romney, A. K.
1967 Kinship and family. In *Social Anthropology,* edited by M. Nash, pp. 207–237. Handbook of Middle American Indians, vol. 6, R. Wauchope, general editor. University of Texas Press, Austin.

Rus, J.
1969 *Pottery Making in Chamula.* B.A. Honor's thesis, Department of Anthropology, Harvard University, Cambridge.

Rus, J., and R. Wasserstrom
1980 Civil-religious Hierarchies in Central Chiapas: A Critical Perspective. *American Ethnology* 7(3):462–478.

Rye, O. S.
1976 Keeping Your Temper Under Control: Materials and the Manufacture of Papuan Pottery. In *Archaeology and Physical Anthropology in Oceania* 11(2):106–137.
1981 *Pottery Technology: Principles and Reconstruction.* Manuals on

Archaeology Series, No. 4. Tarax-
acum, Washington, D.C.

Sabloff, J. A.
1975 *Excavations at Seibal, Department
of the Peten, Guatemala: the Ceramics.* Peabody Museum of Archaeology and Ethnology, 13(2). Harvard
University, Cambridge.

Sabloff, J. A., and R. E. Smith
1969 The Importance of Both Analytic
and Taxonomic Classification in the
Type-variety System. *American Antiquity* 34(3):278–285.

Salmon, M. H.
1981 Ascribing Functions to Archaeological Objects. *Philosophy of Social
Science* 11:19–26.

Sanders, W. T.
1961 *Ceramic Stratigraphy at Santa Cruz,
Mexico.* Papers of the New World
Archaeological Foundation, No. 13,
Publication, No. 9. Brigham Young
University, Provo.

Santley, S. S., P. J. Arnold, and C. A. Pool
1989 The Ceramics Production System
at Matacapan, Veracruz, Mexico.
Journal of Field Archaeology
16(1):107–132.

Santley, R. S., and K. G. Hirth (editors)
1993 *Prehistoric Domestic Units in Western Mesoamerica: Studies of the
Household, Compound and Residence.* CRC Press, Ann Arbor.

Sargent, C. F., and D. A. Friedel
1986 From Clay to Metal: Culture
Change and Container Usage
Among the Bariba of Northern
Bénin, West Africa. *African Archae-
ological Review* 4:177–195.

Scheufler, V.
1968 Classification System of Pottery
Making Tools. *Proceedings of the
8th International Congress of Anthropological and Ethnological Sciences* 3(Sec. B-10):1–3. Science
Council of Japan, Tokyo.

Schiffer, M. B.
1972 Archaeological Context and Systemic Context. *American Antiquity*
37(2):156–165
1976 *Behavioral Archaeology.* Academic
Press, New York.
1978 Methodological Issues in Ethno-

archaeology. In *Explorations in Ethnoarchaeology,* edited by R. A.
Gould, pp. 229–247. University of
New Mexico Press, Albuquerque.
1983a Review of *Cultural Materialism: The
Struggle for a Science of Culture,* by
M. Harris. *American Antiquity*
48(1):190–194.
1983b Toward the Identification of Formation Processes. *American Antiquity*
48(4):675–706.
1987 *Formation Processes of the Archaeological Record.* University of New
Mexico Press, Albuquerque.
1989 A Research Design for Ceramic Use-
wear Analysis at Grasshopper
Pueblo. In *Pottery Technology:
Ideas and Approaches,* edited by
G. Bronitsky, pp. 183–205. Westview Press, Boulder.

Schiffer, M. B., T. E. Downing, and
M. McCarthy
1981 Waste Not, Want Not: An Ethnoarchaeological Study of Reuse in Tucson, Arizona. In *Modern Material
Culture: the Archaeology of Us,*
edited by R. A. Gould and M. B.
Schiffer, pp. 67–86. Academic Press,
New York.

Schortman, E., and P. Urban (editors)
1992 *Sociopolitical Hierarchy and Craft
Production: The Economic Bases of
Elite Power in a Southeast Meso-
american Polity. Part III - The 1992
Season of the Naco Valley Archaeo-
logical Project.* Kenyon College,
Kenyon, Ohio.

Senior, L. M.
1995 The Estimation of Prehistoric Values: Cracked Pot Ideas in Archaeology. In *Expanding Archaeology,*
edited by J. M. Skibo, W. H. Walker,
and A. E. Nielsen, pp. 92–110. University of Utah Press, Salt Lake City.

Shafer, H. J.
1985 A Mimbres Potter's Grave: An Example of Mimbres Craft-specializa-
tion? *Bulletin of the Texas
Archaeological Society* 56:185–200.

Shaughnessy, R., and P. Luciw
1979 Untitled Preliminary Report on a
Regional Survey of Maya Communities in Western Guatemala, 1979.

Ms. on file, Department of Archaeology, Simon Fraser University, Burnaby.

Sheets, P. D.

1979 Maya Recovery from Volcanic Disasters Llopango and Ceren. *Archaeology* 32(3):32–42.

1992 *The Ceren Site: A Prehistoric Village Buried by Volcanic Ash in Central America.* Harcourt Brace Jovanovich, New York.

Shepard, A. O.

1964a Ceramic Development of the Lowland and Highland Maya. *35th Session, International Congress of Americanists, Mexico,* pp. 249–262.

1964b Temper Identification: "Technological Sherd Splitting" or an Unanswered Challenge. *American Antiquity* 29(4):518–520.

1976 *Ceramics for the Archaeologist.* Originally published in 1956. Publication 609. Carnegie Institution, Washington, D.C.

Sherwood, S. C., J. F. Simek, and R. R. Polhemus

1995 Arifact Size and Spatial Process: Macro- and Microartifacts in a Mississippian House. *Geoarchaeology* 10(6):429–455.

Shott, M. J.

1996 Mortal Pots: On Use Life and Vessel Size in the Formation of Ceramic Assemblages. *American Antiquity* 61(3):463–482.

Siegel, S.

1956 *Nonparametric Statistics for the Behavioral Sciences.* McGraw Hill, New York.

Simms, S. R., and K. M. Heath

1990 Site Structure of the Orbit Inn: An Application of Ethnoarchaeology. *American Antiquity* 55(4):797–813.

Sinopoli, C. M.

1988 The Organization of Craft Production at Vijayanagara, South India. *American Anthropologist* 90(3):580–597.

1991 *Approaches to Archaeological Ceramics.* Plenum Press, New York.

Skibo, J. M.

1992 *Pottery Function: A Use-alteration Perspective.* Plenum Press, New York.

1994 The Kalinga Cooking Pot: An Ethnoarchaeological and Experimental Study of Technological Change. In *Kalinga Ethnoarchaeology: Expanding Archaeological Method and Theory,* edited by W. A. Longacre, and J. M. Skibo, pp. 113–126. Smithsonian Institution Press, Washington, D.C.

Skibo, J. M., and M. Deal

1995 Pottery Function and Organic Residue: An Appraisal. In *Conference Papers on Archaeology in Southeast Asia,* edited by C. Yeung, and B. Li Wai-ling, pp. 319–330. University Museum and Art Gallery, University of Hong Kong.

Skibo, J. M., M. B. Schiffer, and N. Kowalski

1989 Ceramic Style Analysis in Archaeology and Ethnoarchaeology: Bridging the Analytical Gap. *Journal of Anthropological Archaeology* 8(4):388–409.

Slocum, M. C., and F. L. Gerdel

1976 *Vocabulario Tzeltal de Bachajon.* 3rd ed. Serie de Vocabularios Indigenas, Mariano Silva y Aceves, Núm. 13, Instituto Lingüístico de Verano, México, D.F.

Smith, A. L.

1929 Report of A. Ledyard Smith on the Map of Environs of Uaxactun. *Carnegie Institution of Washington, Yearbook* (28):325–327.

Smith, M. E.

1987 Household Possessions and Wealth in Agrarian States: Implications for Archaeology. *Journal of Anthropological Archaeology* 6:297–335.

Smith, M. F.

1985 Toward an Economic Interpretation of Ceramics: Relating Vessel Size and Shape to Use. In *Decoding Prehistoric Ceramics,* edited by B. Nelson, pp. 254–309. Southern Illinois University Press, Carbondale.

1988 Function from Whole Vessel Shape: A Method and an Application to Anasazi Black Mesa, Arizona. *American Anthropologist* 90:912–922.

Smith, R.E.

1955 *Ceramic Sequence of Uaxactun, Guatemala.* Tulane University,

Middle American Research Institute, Publication No. 20. New Orleans.

1971 *The Pottery of Mayapan. Including Studies of Ceramic Materials from Uxmal, Kabah, and Chichen Itza.* Papers No. 66. Harvard University, Peabody Museum, Cambridge.

Smith R. E., and J. C. Gifford

1965 Pottery of the Maya Lowlands. In *Archaeology of Southern Mesoamerica, part 1,* edited by G. R. Willey, pp. 498–534. Handbook of Middle American Indians, vol. 2, R. Wauchope, general editor. University of Texas Press, Austin.

Smyth, M. P.

1989 Domestic Storage Behaviour in Mesoamerica: An Ethnoarchaeological Approach. In *Archaeological Theory and Method, vol. 1,* edited by M. B. Schiffer, pp. 89–138. University of Arizona Press, Tucson.

Solheim, W. G., III

1960 The Use of Sherd Weights and Counts in the Handling of Archaeological Data. *Current Anthropology* 1(4):325–329.

South, S.

1979 Historic Site Content, Structure, and Function. *American Antiquity* 44(2): 213–237.

Sommer, U.

1990 Dirt Theory, or Archaeological Sites seen as Rubbish Heaps. *Journal of Theoretical Archaeology* 1:47–60.

Spier, R. F. G.

1976 Skill as a Component of Technological Complexity. In *Primitive Art and Technology,* edited by J. S. Raymond, B. Loveseth, C. Arnold, and G. Reardon, pp. 162–166. University of Calgary Archaeological Association.

Stahl, P. W., and J. A. Zeidler

1990 Differential Bone-refuse Accumulation in Food-preparation and Traffic Areas on an Early Ecuadorian House Floor. *Latin American Antiquity* 1(2):150–169.

Stanislawski, M. B.

1969 What Good Is a Broken Pot? An Experiment in Hopi-Tewa Ethnoarchaeology. *Southwestern Lore* 35:11–18.

1973 Ethnoarchaeology and Settlement Archaeology. *Ethnohistory* 20(4): 275–393.

1977 Hopi and Hopi-Tewa Pottery Making Styles of Learning. In *Experimental Archaeology,* edited by Y. E. Yellen, pp. 379–409. Columbia University Press, New York.

1978 If Pots Were Mortal. In *Explorations in Ethnoarchaeology,* edited by R. A. Gould, pp. 201–227. University of New Mexico Press, Albuquerque.

1980 Review of *Ethnoarchaeology: Implications of Ethnography for Archaeology,* edited by C. Kramer. *American Antiquity* 45(3):647–649.

Stanislawski, M. B., and B. B. Stanislawski

1978 Hopi and Hopi-Tewa Ceramic Tradition Networks. In *The Spatial Organization of Culture,* edited by I. Hodder, pp. 61–76. Duckworth, London.

Stark, B.

1985 Archaeological Identification of Pottery-production in Mesoamerica. In *Decoding Prehistoric Ceramics,* edited by B. A. Nelson, pp. 158–194. Southern Illinois University Press, Carbondale.

Stark, M. T.

1992 From Sibling to Suki: Social Relations and Spatial Proximity in Kalinga Pottery Exchange. *Journal of Anthropological Archaeology* 11:137–151.

1994 Pottery Exchange and the Regional System: A Dalupa Case Study. In *Kalinga Ethnoarchaeology: Expanding Archaeological Method and Theory,* edited by W. A. Longacre, and J. M. Skibo, pp. 169–197. Smithsonian Institution Press, Washington, D.C.

Stark, M. T., and W. A. Longacre

1993 Kalinga Ceramics and New Technologies: Social and Cultural Contexts of Ceramic Change. In *The Social and Cultural Contexts of New Ceramic Technologies,* edited by W. D. Kingery, pp. 1–32. Ceramics and Civilization, vol. 6, American Ceramic Society, Westerville, Ohio.

Steponaitis, V. P.
1983 *Ceramics, Chronology, and Community Patterns: An Archaeological Study at Moundville*. Academic Press, New York.

Stevenson, M. G.
1979 *Looking for Gold. Historic Sites Survey of Kluane National Park, Southwest Yukon*. Unpublished Master's thesis, Department of Archaeology, Simon Fraser University, Burnaby.
1982 Toward an Understanding of Site Abandonment Behaviour: Evidence from Historical Mining Camps in the Southwest Yukon. *Journal of Anthropological Archaeology* 1(3):237–265.

Stiles, D.
1977 Ethnoarchaeology: a Discussion of Methods and Applications. *Man* 12:87–103.

Stockton, E. D.
1973 Shaw's Creek Shelter: Human Displacement of Artifacts and Its Significance. *Mankind* 9:112–117.

Sullivan, A. P., III
1978 Inference and Evidence in Archaeology: A Discussion of the Conceptual Problems. In *Advances in Archaeological Method and Theory, vol. 1*, edited by M. B. Schiffer, pp. 183–222. Academic Press, New York.
1983 Storage, Nonedible Resource Processing, and the Interpretation of Sherd and Lithic Scatters in the Sonoran Desert Lowlands. *Journal of Field Archaeology* 10(3): 309–323.
1988 Prehistoric Southwestern Ceramic Manufacture: The Limitations of Current Evidence. *American Antiquity* 53(1):23–35.
1989 The Technology of Ceramic Reuse: Formation Processes and Archaeological Evidence. *World Archaeology* 21(1):101–114.
1995 Behavioral Archaeology and the Interpretation of Archaeological Variability. In *Expanding Archaeology*, edited by J. M. Skibo, W. H. Walker, and A. E. Nielsen, pp. 178–186. University of Utah Press, Salt Lake City.

Swezey, W. R.
1973 Mound 91, Lambityeco, a Description of an Ancient Kiln. *Mesa Redonda* 12:179–184. Sociedad Mexicana de Antropologia, Mexico.

Tani, M. K.
1994 Why Should More Pots Break in Larger Households? Mechanisms Underlying Population Estimates for Ceramics. In *Kalinga Ethnoarchaeology: Expanding Archaeological Method and Theory*, edited by W. A. Longacre, and J. M. Skibo, 51–70. Smithsonian Institution Press, Washington, D.C.
1995 Beyond the Identification of Formation Processes: Behavioral Inference Based on Traces Left by Cultural Formation Processes. *Journal of Archaeological Method and Theory* 2(3): 231–252. University of Arizona Press, Tucson.

Taylor, W. W.
1948 *A Study of Archaeology*. Memoir No. 69. American Anthropological Association. Washington, D. C.

Thompson, D. E.
1954 *Maya Paganism and Christianity: A History of the Fusion of Two Religions*. Middle American Research Institute, Publication 19:1–36. Tulane University, New Orleans.

Thompson, J. E. S.
1963 *Maya Archaeologist*. University of Oklahoma Press, Norman.
1970 *Maya History and Religion*. University of Oklahoma Press, Norman.

Thompson, R. H.
1974 *Modern Yucatecan Maya Pottery Making*. Memoirs No. 15, Society for American Archaeology. Orginally printed in 1956. Kraus, New York.
1991 The Archaeological Purpose of Ethnoarchaeology. In *Ceramic Ethnoarchaeology*, edited by W. A. Longacre, pp. 231–245. University of Arizona Press, Tucson.

Tozzer, A. M.
1966 *Landa's Relation de las Cosas de Yucatan. A Translation*. Papers No. 43, Peabody Museum, Harvard University. Originally published in 1941. Kraus, New York.

Trens, M. B.
 1942 *Historia de Chiapas, Desde los Tiempos Más Remotos Hasta el Gobierno del General Carlos A. Vidal* (? . . . 1927). La Impresora, México.

Trigger, B. G.
 1995 Expanding Middle-Range Theory. *Antiquity* 69:449–458.

Trostel, B.
 1994 Household Pots and Possessions: An Ethnoarchaeological Study of Material Goods and Wealth. In *Kalinga Ethnoarchaeology: Expanding Archaeological Method and Theory*, edited by W. A. Longacre, and J. M. Skibo, pp. 209–224. Smithsonian Institution Press, Washington, D.C.

Tschauner, H.
 1996 Middle-Range Theory, Behavioral Archaeology, and Postempiricist Philosophy of Science in Archaeology. *Journal of Archaeological Method and Theory* 3(1):1–30.

Turner, C. G., and L. Lofgren
 1966 Household Size of Prehistoric Western Pueblo Indians. *Southwestern Journal of Anthropology* 22:117–132.

Upham, S., K. G. Lightfoot, and G. M. Feinman
 1981 Explaining Socially Determined Ceramic Distributions in the Prehistoric Plateau Southwest. *American Antiquity* 46(4):822–833.

van der Leeuw, S. E.
 1991 Variation, Variability and Explanation in Pottery Studies. In *Ceramic Ethnoarchaeology*, edited by W. A. Longacre, pp. 11–39. University of Arizona Press, Tucson.

Varien, M. D., and J. M. Potter
 1997 Unpacking the Discard Equation: Simulating the Accumulation of Artifacts in the Archaeological Record. *American Antiquity* 62(2):194–213.

Varian, M. D., and B. J. Mills
 1997 Accumulations Research: Problems and Prospects for Estimating Site Occupation Span. *Journal of Archaeological Method and Theory* 4(2):141–191.

Verbitsky, M. E.
 1959a Aguacatenango. In *Report on the Man-in-Nature Project*, edited by N. A. McQuown. Microfilm Collection of Manuscripts on American Indian Cultural Anthropology, Series 14, Pt. 2, Sec. 11. University of Chicago.
 1959b Residence Patterns. In *Report on the Man-in-Nature Project*, edited by N. A. McQuown. Microfilm Collection of Manuscripts on American Indian Cultural Anthropology, Series 14, Pt. 3, Sec. 28. University of Chicago

Vogt, E. Z.
 1962 Review of *Perils of the Soul: The World View of a Tzotzil Indian*, by C. Guiteras-Holmes. *American Anthropologist* 64:649–651.
 1964 Some Implications of Zinacantan Social Structure for the Study of the Ancient Maya. *International Congress of Americanists* 35:307–317. Mexico.
 1969 *Zinacantan*. Harvard University Press, Cambridge.

Wagner, P. L.
 1959 Physiographic Sketch of the Transect. In *Report on the Man-in-Nature Project*, edited by N. A. McQuown. Microfilm Collection of Manuscripts on American Indian Cultural Anthropology, Series 14(1):Figure 5. University of Chicago.

Wagner, P. L., and J. C. Hotchkiss
 1959 Habitat and Human Activity. In *Report on the Man-in-Nature Project*, edited by N. A. McQuown. Microfilm Collection of Manuscripts on American Indian Cultural Anthropology, Series 14(1). University of Chicago.

Walker, W. H., J. M. Skibo, and A. E. Nielsen
 1995 Introduction: Expanding Archaeology. In *Expanding Archaeology*, edited by J. M. Skibo, W. H.Walker, and A. E. Nielsen, pp. 1–12. University of Utah Press, Salt Lake City.

Wasserstrom, R.
 1983 *Class and Society in Central Chiapas*. University of California Press, Los Angeles.

Watson, P. J.
 1973 The Future of Archaeology in Anthropology: Culture History and So-

cial Science. In *Research and Theory in Current Archaeology*, edited by C. L. Redman, pp. 113–124. John Wiley and Sons, New York.

1977   Design Analysis of Painted Pottery. *American Antiquity* 42(3):381–393.

1979   *Archaeological Ethnography in Western Iran*. Viking Fund Publications in Anthropology, No. 57. University of Arizona Press, Tucson.

Wauchope, R.

1934   House Mounds of Uaxactun, Guatemala. *Contributions to American Archaeology* (7):107–171. Publication No. 436. Carnegie Institution, Washington, D.C.

1938   *Modern Maya Houses: a Study of Their Archaeological Significance*. Publication No. 502. Carnegie Institution, Washington, D.C.

1970   *Protohistoric Pottery of the Guatemala Highlands*. Peabody Museum Papers 61:89–244. Harvard University, Cambridge.

Webster, D., and N. Gonlin

1988   Household Remains of the Humblest Maya. *Journal of Field Archaeology* 15(2):169–190.

Weigand, P. C.

1969   *Modern Huichol Ceramics*. University Museum Mesoamerican Studies, Southern Illinois University, Carbondale.

Whallon, R.

1968   Investigations of Late Prehistoric Social Organization in New York State. In *New Perspectives in Archaeology*, edited by S. R. Binford, and L. R. Binford, pp. 223–244. Aldine, Chicago.

1969   Rim Diameter, Vessel Volume, and Economic Prehistory. *Michigan Academician* 2(2):89–98.

Whitaker, T. W., and H. C. Cutler

1967   Pottery and Curcurbita Species. *American Antiquity* 32(2):225–226.

Whittlesey, S. M.

1974   Identification of Imported Ceramics Through Functional Analysis of Attributes. *The Kiva* 40:101–112.

Wilk, R. R., and W. Ashmore (editors)

1988   *Household and Community in the Mesoamerican Past*. University of New Mexico Press, Albuquerque.

Wilk, R. R., and M. B. Schiffer

1979   The Archaeology of Vacant Lots in Tuscon, Arizona. *American Antiquity* 44(3):530–536.

Willey, G.

1961   Volume in Pottery and the Selection of Samples. *American Antiquity* 27(2):230–231.

Willey, G. R., W. R. Bullard, J. B. Glass, and J. C. Gifford

1965   *Prehistoric Maya Settlements in the Belize Valley*. Papers No. 54, Peabody Museum of Archaeology and Ethnology. Harvard University, Cambridge.

Willey, G. R., T. P. Culbert, and R. E. W. Adams

1967   Maya Lowland Ceramics: A Report from the 1965 Guatemala City Conference. *American Antiquity* 32(3): 289–315.

Winter, M. C., and W. O. Payne

1976   Hornos para Cerámica Hallados en Monte Albán. *Boletín, Instituto Nacional de Antropología e Historia*. 2(16):37–40.

Wilson, D. C.

1994   Identification and Assessment of Secondary Refuse Aggregates. *Journal of Archaeological Method and Theory* 1(1):41–68.

Wisdom, C.

1940   *The Chorti Indians of Guatemala*. University of Chicago Press.

Wolf, E.

1957   Closed Corporate Peasant Communities in Mesoamerica and Central Java. *Southwestern Journal of Anthropology* 13:1–18.

Wood, W. R., and D. L. Johnson

1978   A Survey of Disturbance Processes in Archaeological Site Formation. In *Advances in Archaeological Method and Theory, vol. 1*, edited by M. B. Schiffer, pp. 315–381. Academic Press, New York.

Woods, A.

1984   Methods of Pottery Manufacture in the Kavango Region of Nambia: Two Case Studies. In *Earthenware in Asia and Africa*. Colloquies on Art and Archaeology in Asia (12):303–325. Percival David Foundation of Chinese Art, London.

1985   Form, Fabric, and Function: Some Observations on the Cooking Pot in Antiquity. In *Ceramics and Civilization, Vol. II, Technology and Style, vol. 1, Ancient Technology to Modern Science*, edited by W. D. Kingery, and E. Lense, pp. 156–172. American Ceramic Society, Columbus, Ohio.

Wright, J.V.
1974   *The Nodwell Site.* Paper No. 22, Archaeological Survey of Canada, Mercury Series. National Museums of Canada, Ottawa.

Younger, M. S.
1979   *A Handbook for Linear Regression.* Duxbury, North Scituate, Massachusetts.

Zeidler, J. A.
1983   La Etnoarqueologia de una Vivienda Achuar y sus Implicaciones Arqueologicas. *Miscelánea Antropológica Ecuatorian, Boletin de los Museos del Banco Central del Ecuador* 3:155–193.

Zier, C. J.
1979   The Ceren Site: A Classic Period Maya Residence and Agricultural Field in the Zapotitan Valley. In *Archeology and Volcanism in Central America: The Zapotitan Valley of El Salvador*, edited by P. D. Sheets, pp. 119–143. University of Texas Press, Austin.

About the Author

Michael Deal is an associate professor of anthropology at the Memorial University of New-foundland. He has participated in archaeological projects in Mexico, Cyprus, and four Canadian provinces. The majority of his publications concern ceramic studies (ethnoarchaeology and residue analysis) and eastern Canadian archaeology. He coedited (with S. Blair) the 1991 volume *Prehistoric Archaeology in the Maritime Provinces: Past and Present Research*.

Index